Celebrating the Family

Celebrating the Family

ETHNICITY, CONSUMER CULTURE,
AND FAMILY RITUALS

ELIZABETH H. PLECK

HARVARD UNIVERSITY PRESS
Cambridge, Massachusetts, and London, England   2000

For Joe and Dan

Library of Congress Cataloging-in-Publication Data

Pleck, Elizabeth Hafkin.
  Celebrating the family : ethnicity, consumer culture, and family rituals /
Elizabeth H. Pleck.
    p. cm.
  Includes bibliographical references and index.
  ISBN 0-674-00230-X (cloth : alk. paper)—ISBN 0-674-00279-2 (paper : alk. paper)
  1. Holidays—Economic aspects—United States.
  2. Special events—Economic aspects—United States.
  3. Family—United States.
  4. Rites and ceremonies—United States.
  5. Consumption (Economics)—United States.
  6. United States—Economic conditions.
  7. United States—Social life and customs. I. Title.
GT4986.A1 P54 2000
394.26973—dc21   99-045200

Contents

Acknowledgments *vii*

1 Festivals, Rites, and Presents *1*

2 Family, Feast, and Football *21*

3 Holiday Blues and Pfeffernusse *43*

4 Easter Breads and Bunnies *73*

5 Festival of Freedom *95*

6 Eating and Explosives *117*

7 Cakes and Candles *141*

8 Rites of Passage *162*

9 Please Omit Flowers *184*

10 The Bride Once Wore Black *207*

11 Rituals, Families, and Identities *233*

Notes *251*

Index *325*

Illustrations follow page 140.

Acknowledgments

I began this book shortly after my father's funeral. He lived his last twelve years in a nursing home, the last five not recognizing any of his family. My mother had died two years before. I had finished a book about the history of family violence and could not bear to write about another unhappy subject. I was also seeking some academic way to continue thinking about what the death of my parents meant to me. Many times in my writing about family ritual, I found myself drifting off into memories of a simpler past. I would have to pull myself back from my reveries, reminding myself of the tricks that ritual can play with memory.

Many librarians and archivists have offered their assistance in my work. I want to thank the staff at the University of Illinois, Urbana/Champaign Library, especially the interlibrary loan and special collections departments and the Illinois Historical Survey. I am also indebted to the staffs at the Sophia Smith Collection of the Smith College Library, the Minnesota Historical Society, the Immigrant History Research collection, the Marriott Library at the University of Utah, the Fife Folklore Collection of Utah State University, the Arizona Historical Society, the Chicago Historical Society, the Jewish Historical Society at Brandeis University, Widener Library of Harvard University, the University of California at Berkeley, the Balch Institute for Ethnic Studies, the Philadelphia Public Library, and the La Salle University library. For help in finding illustrations and photographs I am grateful to Alma Rosa Aguirre of the University of Texas at Browns-ville and the staffs at the American Antiquarian Society, Winterthur Library, the Prints and Photographs Division of the Library of Con-gress, the Notre Dame Archives, the Frankenmuth Historical Associa-tion, the Florida State Archives, the Archives Center of the Smith-sonian, the National Museum of American Jewish History, and the Minnesota Historical Society.

John Gillis pointed me in the right direction with his comments on a draft of the first chapter I wrote, about Thanksgiving. For sugges-tions on specific chapters I want to thank Jacqueline Jones, Melanie Kimball, Nicole Ranganath, Leslie Reagan, Caroline Waldron, and Chiou-ling Yeh. I learned about the history of churching, a ritual for Catholic new mothers, from Paula Rieder's dissertation on this sub-ject and from conversations with her. I have learned a great deal from discussions about ritual with Micaela di Leonardo, Ramona Oswald, Cele Otnes, and Ellen Rothman. For specific leads in research and an-swers to my queries about history or folklore I am grateful to H. Ar-nold Barton, Joan Jacobs Brumberg, Matt Garcia, Nancy J. Hafkin, Robert Johannsen, Daniel Littlefield, Colleen McDannell, June Namias, Andrew Nolan, Vicki Ruiz, Michelle Salcedo, and Judy Yung. Barbara Tenenbaum of the Library of Congress gave me many good leads to track down in finding more about the history of the quinceañera. Johanna Jacobsen did research for this book in the Folk-lore Archives of the University of California at Berkeley. Drafts of var-ious chapters were delivered at the Center for Research on Women at Wellesley College, the History Workshop of the University of Illinois, the third annual Family History conference at Carleton University, the Institute for the Study of Values and Ethics at the University of Illinois, and the history faculty at Michigan State University. A por-tion of Chapter 2 was published, in somewhat altered form, as "The Making of the Domestic Occasion: The History of Thanksgiving in the United States," *Journal of Social History* 32 (Summer 1999), pp. 773–789.

For their valuable suggestions in reading the entire manuscript I owe special thanks to Howard Chudacoff, Estelle Freedman, Donna Gabaccia, Fred Jaher, Leslie Moch, and Louise Tilly. A mentor and friend for several decades, Louise helped sharpen my argument and encouraged me to cut unnecessary detail. An Illinois Research Board Grant in 1995 made it possible for me to travel to several archives.

I wrote several chapters of this book while enjoying a fellowship from the University of Illinois's Institute for the Study of Values and Ethics in 1997. At Harvard University Press I have benefited from the advice of Aida Donald and from Donna Bouvier's careful pruning of my sentences.

The latest thinking about ritual describes it as a process, rather than as a distinct and separate activity. My own process has been aided at every step by my husband, Joseph Pleck, and my son, Daniel Pleck. Joe has been the finest critic of my writing. Some of my best sources have come from articles he clipped from magazines. When I was searching for a phrase to describe the changes in twentieth-century ritual, he suggested "postsentimental." Dan has asked me who the Pilgrims were, what the origins of the goody bag were, and many other questions about ritual. I was proud to be able to answer most of his questions. I am also grateful to have been able to share both ordinary and special times with the two of them.

CHAPTER ONE

Festivals, Rites, and Presents

Why should we not, as families, make more account of commemorative occasions?

—MRS. C. A. HALBERT, 1871

At certain times of year or moments in life it is important "to have family" and difficult to be without one.[1] Sociologist Theodore Caplow, in studying a Midwestern city, which he dubbed Middletown, in the 1970s, argued that American holidays had become celebrations of the family, their main purpose being to pay homage to an ideal of the privatized, affectionate family, with a mother nurturing her children at its center. He wrote, "Every widely observed festival in Middletown now celebrates the family and the related ideas of home, mother and child, and feminine roles."[2] Caplow did not look closely enough at the holiday atmosphere of the 1970s, however, because a basic shift had already occurred.

This book traces three phases in the development of family ritual. The first, which began in colonial America and derived from the Protestant Reformation, was characterized by either a carnivalesque, outdoor form of celebration or a lack of attention to ritual. The second phase, dating from the early nineteenth century, saw the rise of the sentimental occasion, a family ritual either inside or outside the home that centered around consumerism and a display of status and wealth to celebrate home and family. After World War I and especially in the 1970s and later, what I shall call a postsentimental attitude toward family celebration began to appear. Framed often as a reaction to what was perceived as the excesses of sentimentality, the postsentimental approach to holiday celebration recognizes, if not celebrates, family diversity as well as ethnic and racial pluralism. These transformations in how the family is celebrated and how the family celebrates holidays and special events were the result of changes on many fronts—in the family, in women's roles, in ethnic group consciousness, and in nationalism, consumer culture, and popular entertainment.

An easy way to understand the significance of American family rituals is to demonstrate their economic importance to the modern American economy. Every October the sale of Halloween supplies such as Ross Perot masks, Count Dracula fangs, and miniature peanut butter cups contributes $400 million to the gross domestic product. In 1996, weddings generated revenues of $31 billion a year; funerals brought in about $11 billion; and the greeting card industry earned $6.3 billion. Christmas, which I call a "family ritual" (or "domestic occasion") but is also considered a holiday, accounted for about $149 billion in gift and card purchases in November and December 1996.³ Nearly one fourth of all yearly retail sales in the United States in 1992 came from Christmas purchases. That year even supermarkets generated 20 percent of their receipts and made 30 percent of their profits between Thanksgiving and New Year's.⁴ If it is true, as Joyce Hall, the founder of Hallmark, claimed, that "sentiment sells," then even these partial sales figures suggest that sentiment, expressed in family rituals, adds up to almost $200 billion a year.

The commercialism of so many family rituals causes great unease. The din of the cash register during the Christmas season, the "jingle of gilded trinkets," it is said, drowns out the religious meaning of the holiday. Almost everyone complains that Christmas is too commercialized. The public castigates merchants, advertisers, manufacturers, and even guileless consumers taken in by Muzak and colored lights. Many cultural critics argue that consumer culture has not only cheapened the meaning of Christmas and other holidays but has created ersatz ones as well. Greeting card manufacturers, confectioners, and florists sugar-coated Mother's Day, transforming what had been a day to contemplate world peace into a holiday to send flowers to mother. Advertisers and neckwear manufacturers made Father's Day, a holiday that many men considered silly, into a fixture on the American calendar. Kodak and Hallmark, AT&T and Macy's, Coca-Cola and Montgomery Ward have shaped American celebrations, creating new representations of Santa, new folkloric figures (such as Rudolph the

Red Nosed Reindeer), new rituals (such as parades), and new visual
images of ritual, all in the service of encouraging consumers to buy
their products and services.

Such complaints are neither of recent origin nor unique to late-
twentieth-century America. But celebrants often designed the postsentimental occasion as an active critique of the values of home,
family, and woman's place honored in the sentimental occasion, in
addition to complaining about excessive commercialism. Because the
postsentimental approach depends on parody or critique of American
sentimentality, it requires the continued existence of sentimentalism.
In the postsentimental era of celebration, sentimentality has not disappeared, but instead has become a subject of debate.

Just as the sentimental occasion was the ideal form of festivity for
the affectionate family, so too the postsentimental occasion fit the reality of postmodern family life.[5] According to anthropologist Judith
Stacey, who coined the term "postmodern family," the American family since the 1970s has no longer had a single dominant form; there
has been a great deal of public debate about what the family should
be; and family life has become highly fluid and flexible. The male
breadwinner–female homemaker family is no longer the universal
standard for the family, nor is it even the most frequent household
type. These changes were caused by a series of overlapping revolutions in attitudes toward sex, contraception, and abortion; intermarriage across religious, ethnic, and racial lines; women's roles; race; homosexuality; and divorce. Family residential arrangements changed.
Many people, especially the elderly, lived in single-person households.
Cohabitation became an alternative to marriage as well as a stage
prior to it, and became more acceptable among the privileged classes,
rather than a way of life found mainly among the poor. Such vast,
sweeping changes led to acceptance of new styles of living as well as to
backlash against the changes. A political and cultural shouting match
began in the late 1970s, which invoked the much-disputed term "family values." One side advocated a single standard of family life and
sexual morality; the other held that Americans had to accept cultural
pluralism and diversity of sexual mores and family forms.

Of the wrenching changes that affected the American family between the 1960s and the 1980s the most important, from the point of
view of family ritual, was the growth in married women's employment. From temporary work before marriage and after their children

were of school age, women moved to a more or less permanent commitment to paid work. This single dramatic change reverberated in almost every facet of the marital relationship. Pursuing an education and having a job, in some cases a career, women were beginning to put their own happiness and independence first, and even postponed marrying.

As part of the postsentimental era, magazines and newspapers began to print articles on how to combat "holiday blues." Families began to use celebrations as a special time to assert a waning ethnic identity. Women put in less time organizing and preparing postsentimental occasions and as a result experienced less affirmation of their central role in the family. People brought new values to understanding such rituals: they saw them through the prism of their search for privacy, personal fulfillment, happiness, and individuality. Sociologist Robert Bellah nicely summarized the postsentimental desire for family privacy combined with the quest for self-realization. In the nineteenth century, he argued, writers often described the family as the refuge from individualism. In the last third of the twentieth century, he added, "individualism is in the family as well as outside it."[6]

Most students of U.S. history date the emergence of postsentimental values to the 1890s or even earlier, because so much of postsentimentalism partakes of consumerism and individualism, traces of which can be found in America as early as the eighteenth century.[7] One characteristic of individualism—noted even in the earliest novels—was the wish to marry for love. Another was the desire for personal fulfillment through marriage. The United States has always had the highest divorce rate in the industrialized world because more U.S. couples than elsewhere try to realize their expectations for personal happiness through marriage—and end up disappointed.

As for consumerism, the desire to seek personal fulfillment, and even identity, through purchases had for centuries been an element of celebrations among the elite. Mass production and mass consumption made luxury items available to the average American. In addition, as early as around 1900 American advertising and movies appealed to the emotions and reinforced values already present: that one should seek pleasure, gain satisfaction, realize one's fantasies, find the man or woman of one's dreams. Films, magazines, and advertisements conveyed the view that the American consumer—often seen as a woman—could take on a new, improved identity (as a fairy princess or queen for a day, for example). What changed was less the desire for personal satisfaction and happiness than the means available to the average person to realize that desire. Thus, the precise dating of the holiday consumer economy varies by holiday and commodity. Most Americans did not buy candy bars as an everyday treat until the 1920s; the average working-class family did not own a radio (to listen to a football game on Thanksgiving) until the 1930s. Overall, by the 1950s the white working class, and in the 1960s the emerging black middle class, began to live in an economy of abundance rather than scarcity. They may have wanted to buy and spend before that, but could not afford to, except for an occasional splurge.

This view of the decline of the carnivalesque and the rise of the sentimental and then the postsentimental is quite different from Caplow's and from popular understanding. Most people believe the contemporary family is in a state of moral decline. To them the past is the place where virtue resides. The transformation of some rituals and the disappearance of others furnishes evidence of the demise of the family and its moral lapse. There are two forms of discourse about family decline, one for the American mainstream, and another for ethnic groups perceived as being outsiders to the mainstream.

Commentators on mainstream culture invariably bemoan one symptom of family decline, the disappearance of the family meal. Families, they claim, lack any fixed time when they converse and eat a leisurely meal together. With the decline in a set meal time, critics argue, a sense of common family purpose and a feeling of togetherness have been lost. When employed mothers are not blamed, the problem is said to arise from divorce, the decline in religious belief and practice, the effects of a narcissistic, individualistic culture, the overly scheduled life children lead, and the omnipresent television set.

In the ethnic discourse about family decline, the main target is not consumer culture, but the demise of a sense of kinship, family solidarity, and community within the ethnic group. Many "ethnic" films express this theme, among them Francis Ford Coppola's *The Godfather* (1970). The movie portrays a close-knit Sicilian-American family, presided over by a Mafia chieftain, who, although a criminal, is deeply committed to family solidarity and his own code of ethics. After the godfather dies, so does the sense of community and family solidarity he stands for. Many social critics, such as Stephen Steinberg, agree with Coppola's point of view. Steinberg argues that ethnicity in modern America consists "mainly of vestiges of decaying cultures that have been so tailored to middle-class patterns that they have all but lost their distinctive qualities."[8] Unlike in the mainstream jeremiad, in this one ritual persists, but has lost its authenticity with the decline in community.

Research has shown, however, that many so-called traditions practiced in America are little more than a century and a half old. Historians Eric Hobsbawm and Terence Ranger coined the term "invented tradition" to describe a ritual that implies continuity with the past, even though that continuity is largely fictitious.[9] Hobsbawm and Ranger traced the history of public, not private, rituals, especially in the late nineteenth century, although their concept is elastic enough to pertain to both. Invented traditions, they note, are a social construction, created by people in the present out of a need for a sense of connection with the past, and from a desire to stop the clock in order to keep at least one small part of life always the same.[10] In their view invented traditions are indications of change, not stability. Hobsbawm and Ranger noted that Bastille Day, kilt-wearing, the Olympics, and the pledge of allegiance are all "traditions" that originated since the eighteenth century, the last three being created in the late nineteenth century. These were entirely new ceremonies, they argued, intended to create the fiction of shared national identity and national unity during times when national unity appeared fragile.

Kwanzaa, devised by Ron (Maulana) Karenga in 1966, conforms most closely to Hosbawm and Ranger's concept of an invented tradition. Kwanzaa was a nationalist—specifically, black nationalist—holiday and had a specific creator, who designed it as a celebration of the African harvest, with the intention that American blacks, in exile from their African homeland, would continue tradition and celebrate their African heritage. Fifty-eight years earlier Anna Jarvis had invented another American family ritual, Mother's Day. A church organist and Sunday school teacher, Jarvis, mourning the loss of her mother, helped organize Mother's Day services in her hometown of Grafton, Virginia, and in Philadelphia. A few years later Sonora Dodd of Arizona suggested a day for fathers to honor men like her own father, who raised her and her siblings after her mother's death. Kwanzaa, Mother's Day, and Father's Day, created by specific individuals for specific purposes, fall at one end of the scale. At the other are family rituals such as graduation parties, wedding anniversaries, and family reunions that have no explicit creator and no single date of origin.[11]

Four centuries ago the annual cycle of holidays and feasts was either simple and sparse or raucous and communal. As a result of the Reformation, many Protestants turned away from the pagan rituals of recognizing life and death at the winter solstice and celebrating the rebirth of spring to make the Sabbath their major weekly ritual, indeed their most important one. Among American Puritans, for example, family rituals were few and modest. They opposed celebrating Christmas and Easter, since they viewed these holidays as "papist," and observed only one occasion—the Sabbath—regularly. Even their funerals and weddings were relatively simple affairs, at which kin were not expected to gather. The Puritans are significant both for the nature of their ritual—its lack of seasonality and its simplicity—and for their attitude toward celebration. Religious leaders in the Protestant Reformation defined ritual as a legitimate subject of controversy. By singling out Catholic practices they did not approve of, Protestant reformers developed the idea of ritual as a distinct form of rote, often liturgical, action. From them we also derive some of our condemnation of false or hollow celebration as "mere" ritual.[12]

At the same time, holidays for the popular classes, at least for non-Puritans, varied from today's in a quite different respect. These people celebrated some of their festivals as community events or as carnivals, times for begging and ritualized aggression, cross-dressing and masquerading, gluttony and sexual license. Wearing costumes and masks, revelers had a great deal of freedom to misbehave. The celebrants often inverted class or racial hierarchy and lampooned the ruling elite, violating rules governing ordinary behavior with seeming impunity.[13] In this way the elite, by permitting some social conflict to be expressed, defused it and rendered it harmless. The day after the carnival, the world returned to normal, unchanged. In both premodern Europe and America carnival was a time of disorder, but only in Europe did rowdies turn into rebels, causing riots and murders, resulting in celebrants occasionally being forbidden to wear masks.[14] American masking and mumming could be disorderly, but it was less political. Carnival processions and dances usually took place out-of-doors. Men pulled down their pants and joked; women watched and laughed. People also celebrated much more as communities rather than as nuclear families. Thus, for example, in many rural areas and especially among slaves and ex-slaves, corn shucking was a special time—an outdoor gathering that combined work, food, drinking, singing, and conviviality.[15]

Because the growing middle class saw carnivalesque celebrations as lawless and debauched, they tried and mainly succeeded in stamping them out. They regarded the carnival style as an improper way to celebrate Christmas, Thanksgiving, and many other holidays. As a result, a sentimental and commercial style of celebration, the form preferred by the more powerful and respectable bourgeoisie, became dominant, just as the urban middle class itself triumphed in short stories and sentimental novels. In the nineteenth century this stratum of society had the means to purchase both metal caskets for funerals and rocking horses as Christmas gifts. The Victorians (whose era I roughly define as the decades from 1820 to 1890) virtually created the child-centered, sentimentalized occasion. Wealthy and middle-class Victorians wanted to make their family events displays of new standards of etiquette, respectability, beauty, and wealth.

They invented a long list of new holidays and made their rites of passage into beautiful pageants. During these seven decades Santa Claus and the Christmas tree entered the parlor. Family, friends, and sweethearts began to send lace paper greetings on St. Valentine's Day. The white wedding—a bride in white, a wedding cake in white—departed dramatically from the plain, informal services that had been the norm. Couples married for decades began to hold formal gatherings to commemorate the anniversary of the date of their wedding. Parents took note of the date of a child's birth by hosting a special party. After a death, the wake went on for several days; the funeral service took place in a church, and hundreds of men and women might walk or ride in carriages from there to the grave. In wearing mourning clothes grieving relatives were a living symbol of how death sundered family ties. As for happier occasions, middle-class families sought a pastoral setting away from the home for a family vacation. The Protestant Sabbath became child-oriented and mother-directed.

The Victorians dressed up some of the grandest rituals of the modern calendar—Thanksgiving, Christmas, and Easter—and added glamour to celebrations of the major transitions of life. It is at first easy to conclude, as Caplow did, that people in the contemporary United States are simply drawing on Victorian style, using little embellishments (such as "Jingle Bell Rock" or *The Grinch Who Stole*

Christmas for that holiday, for example) as modern additions. Moreover, some of the key meanings of these festivals have also been
passed down—Thanksgiving as a holiday of the family and of a nation blessed with liberty and bounty, Christmas and Easter as special
times for children. By these standards, the twentieth century may appear to be culturally impoverished. However, some highly popular
traditions were invented then, such as baby showers, Mother's Day,
Father's Day, Kwanzaa, and Superbowl Sunday.

Though it is true that the time pressures of modern life have generally caused family rituals to be shortened and simplified, and many
traditions to be cast aside entirely, at the same time, weddings have
become more elaborate, expensive, and time consuming. By making
the lavish wedding the grandest occasion of all, Americans, who define the wedding as the essence of family, are actually rejecting Victorian beliefs about the sentimental occasion. Part of the essence
of sentimentalism was that the sad event was more significant than
the happy one, and that families needed to gather for all the special
times in the life cycle. Thus, Victorians gave about equal attention to
christenings as to weddings, and made funerals the grandest occasion
of all.

Postsentimentalism gives less attention to the sad occasion, in part
because of the desire to deny death, in part because of an optimistic
consumer and popular culture that defines spending as a means to
achieve happiness. Family parties after christenings, first commu-
nions, and confirmations have become optional. But since the 1960s,
the church wedding followed by a large reception has become very
grand. Bar and bat mitzvahs and quinceañeras (a girl's fifteenth birthday celebration among Hispanics) have also grown fancier, taking on
all the trappings of a lavish wedding.

In this book I examine how a variety of life cycle rituals (birth,
coming of age, marriage, death), major holidays (Christmas, Easter,
Thanksgiving, Chinese New Year, Passover), and children's birthday
parties were invented and reinvented. The five holidays just mentioned involve significant family feasts that combine the sacred and
the secular.[16] Three of them are the main domestic occasions of the
dominant culture; the other two, Chinese New Year and Passover, are
the major family feasts of two American ethnic groups. In my discussion of life cycle rituals, I consider the main rituals of the dominant
culture as well as some ethnic variations.

What Is a Family Ritual?

I define family ritual as a highly stylized cultural performance involving several family members that is repeated, has a formal structure, and involves symbolic behavior (gestures; highly scripted or repeated words, such as "I do" in a wedding and "Dayenu" in the Passover seder; or actions). The formal structure usually has a fixed order, with a distinct beginning, middle, and end.[17] When rituals recur, participants usually repeat the sequence of routines in exactly the same order.

Although rituals have a distinct and recognizable structure and sequence, families often personalize them, adding some idiosyncratic elements. Thus, a family can refer to "our Christmas tradition," meaning a unique custom or practice not found throughout the entire culture. Family rituals may be small events or gatherings of several hundred, bedtime stories for children or a Thanksgiving feast for three generations of the family and assorted strangers. In this book I concentrate on the highly elaborate, relatively rare rituals of the family. These usually involve feasts, where the guests gorge themselves on food and overindulge in drink. At many of these feasts there are also special ritual objects and purchased goods from party hats to Christmas presents.[18] Mary Douglas and Baron Isherwood refer to these kind of family rituals as "low frequency, high rank" ones precisely because special foods are served, ceremonial objects are brought out, and gifts are often given. In part such occasions are high in rank precisely because they occur infrequently.[19]

Family rituals are also distinctive because of the highly stylized behavior of the celebrants. Participants are consciously aware of themselves as acting a part, behaving as if reading from a script. (Passover uses a printed prayer book; the script at the wedding can be read from a printed text, such as the Book of Common Prayer, or improvised.) Participants come to rituals expecting that certain rules will be followed, and they notice deviations. In addition, family rituals occur at special places and at a set time. As in plays, some actors have larger parts than others. But those who might be considered the audience are still bit players in the drama.

Not every ritual succeeds, but when it does, it is said to express and convey emotion. Ritual often is said to fail precisely because the audience does not "feel something" from participating in it (thus, the hollow or empty ritual). Because ritual is a form of symbolic communication, a nest of symbols, interpreters have tried to determine what the symbols mean. Some historians and anthropologists have concluded that symbols are inherently ambiguous or have multiple meanings; for them meaning lies in the emotions the symbols generate. Others find meaning in the verbal statements and the ordering of activities in a ritual (processions, blessings, kneeling, bowing). I straddle these positions, explaining the meanings participants assign to the rituals as well as giving my own suggestions about symbolic meanings.

Ritual properly performed can address any number of anxieties and unresolved issues in a culture. However, too often rituals fail to achieve these lofty goals; they do not work as planned. Except for funerals, family rituals are supposed to be happy occasions, and they often are. Yet many participants experience disharmony, conflict, and anguish at family gatherings. In the postsentimental era magazines and newspapers carry unending complaints about failed domestic occasions, describing them as racist, sexist, homophobic, monocultural, materialist, or simply unhappy.

The study of American ritual tells us not only about the history of festivity in the United States, but also about the social and cultural life of the American people in the last two centuries. Americans have always celebrated the family with the values and resources of abundance and some luxury. Most have been drawn to goods and services to display family status, even as critics have continually regarded love of luxury as a sign of weakness and moral failing. Because the American bounty was unequally distributed, the "haves" were the first to celebrate the domestic occasion. As goods flooded the consumer market and income for the masses rose, the ordinary child, not just the rich one, came to expect bounteous holiday gifts and birthday presents; most families can now mark special occasions with a splurge of spending.

Nationalism, consumerism, religiosity, and popular culture have not been separate forces shaping family ritual and the calendar of special days, but instead are braided strains of mutual influence. All of these forces have helped to disseminate a homogenized, standardized, but ever-changing ritual. The American urge to celebrate has certainly been stimulated by merchants and advertisers. But the desire for family celebration has not simply been market driven. Family events are also affirmations of the national mission and celebrations of ethnic group identity and consciousness. To trace the rise and decline of the sentimental occasion is to reveal the multiple processes that help to generate ethnic identity, the conservative drag of ritual on changing gender roles, and the role of consumer culture and popular entertainment in remaking family traditions. The same forces of ethnicity, gender, and consumer and popular culture have also helped to renew and perpetuate family ritual.

Ethnicity and Ritual

Several recent books have investigated the rise of the domestic occasion among the Protestant middle class in the nineteenth century. Many rituals, from Christmas to the birthday party, have such origins. Yet historians have told only half of the story. What makes the United States so distinctive a nation is that it is comprised of people from so many areas of the globe. Certain rituals, such as Christmas, Easter, the fancy church wedding, the elegant christening, and the children's birthday party, express the cultural and religious hegemony of the white Protestant majority. This group once held the power to decide what holidays would be celebrated in the public schools. The Protestant version of the Christian calendar became the national one, with other calendars (the Muslim, the Jewish, the Chinese, the Japanese, the eastern Orthodox) clearly subordinated. While the Protestant majority imposed its culture on others, the subordinated groups fought back and have edged their way onto the official or semiofficial calendar. Columbus Day, St. Patrick's Day, and Martin Luther King's birthday are now recognized; individual states honor regional or ethnic heroes with special days. My main concern here is not to chart this ebb and flow between mainstream and side channels but to understand how and why certain rituals provide opportunities for cultural imposition as well as cultural creativity.

Outsiders have sometimes wanted to join the mainstream; other times they have wanted to shut it out. In the conventional interpretation of immigrant history each group of newcomers arrived in America with a distinctive set of traditions. They clung to these as a means of adjusting to American life, but gradually abandoned their heritage as they moved into the middle class. In entering the middle class, they adopted the rituals of the mainstream culture. Sociologists usually look at family ritual as evidence of acculturation. If a group still celebrates its own holidays, it is believed to be maintaining its culture. If, instead, the group has abandoned all of its own rituals and has adopted the mainstream ones, it is said to have lost its culture and become "assimilated."[20]

I believe this view is wrong-headed, because everything is changing: the group's ritual, its sense of self-definition, its interaction with others, and the relationship of the ritual to the group. There is not one single process of change in ritual but many. In the earliest stages of immigration, ritual was one means of (selectively) preserving a tradition, which could help the newcomers adjust to a new life. For the descendants of U.S. immigrants, ritual was one of the few vestiges of ethnic identity to persist for a group living a mostly middle-class American life. In both earlier and later phases of adjustment, ethnic entrepreneurs and community leaders saw advantage in promoting ethnic public festivals, or in inventing new ethnic rituals to promote group solidarity and pride. The process of adjusting to life in the United States usually involved accommodating to a different gender division of labor, with the responsibility for making or maintaining ritual, preserving a foreign language or dialect, or transmitting a religious heritage given over to women.

To compensate for the stress in previous research on the history of white Protestants, I emphasize the history of Catholics, nonwhites, and non-Christians. In analyzing mainstream holidays and rites of passage, I begin with the creation of the dominant form among white Protestants of substantial means and then analyze later ethnic adaptations. These adaptations ranged from direct imitation, to syncretization, to the creation of new rituals masquerading as ancient ones, which occasionally carried a critique of the dominant culture.

An ethnic group can be defined as a group of people who see themselves, and are seen by others, as having a shared history and culture. An ethnic group is rarely simply a "community of descent." Newly arrived immigrants created group identity out of the circumstances they faced—their concentration in distinct regions and areas of settlement, and their shared occupational or entrepreneurial niches. An ethnic group has often derived its identity from defining and maintaining a boundary between itself and others. This was not difficult for immigrants to do initially; lines were drawn by the newcomers' forms of religious worship and by strictures on not marrying outside one's own kind as much as from customs brought over from their homeland.[21] In American history, however, the boundary line between one group and the rest is never firmly drawn, but is instead constantly shifting.

Ethnic group is the larger category here; race is a subset. Race, often thought of as a biological or genetic inheritance made visible in skin color, hair texture, or eye shape, is rather a malleable construct. Jews, Irish, Slavs, and Italians, for example, were once considered "darker" races, even though they are now perceived as "white." Latinos, generally considered "white" around 1900, are now often seen as "brown." Under the pressure of anti-immigrant attitudes in the 1920s, Asian Indians were reclassified from Caucasian to nonwhite. People often determine someone's race by looking at visible forms of classification, but these determinations are highly inaccurate. Some African Americans, for example, are lighter in skin shade than many Caucasians. Many people thought of as white today have some African ancestry. Some of these whites are the descendants of black people who passed as white, or of Hispanics who became "Spanish" and then eventually white. In general, ethnic groups wanted to be seen as white because it gave them superior status.[22]

The sentimentalized family rituals of the dominant culture were created in a seventy-year period of invention, from around 1820 to 1890. There is no comparable period of cultural creativity when American ethnic groups developed rituals, in part because so many of their rituals were transformations of customs brought to America at various times. Even so, the period since the 1960s has been an unusually significant one for the assertion of group identity and the reinvention of tradition. In Chapter 3 I show how black nationalism in the 1960s and "the search for roots" by many, not just African Americans, in the subsequent decade led to the rediscovery of many ethnic traditions.

The 1960s were noteworthy for another enduring social change. The United States in 1965 eliminated immigration quotas based on national origin; subsequently, immigration from around the world, but especially from Asia, Mexico, the Caribbean, and Latin America, soared. Although the majority of the new immigrants were Christians, they also included Muslims, Hindus, Jews, Buddhists, Taoists, Bahais, and Sikhs. The influx of these newcomers from abroad has served to refresh ethnic traditions in America. Just as Poles and Italians once selected some rituals to preserve from their cultural fabric,

Dominicans and Ethiopians in the United States are doing the same. The children of these immigrants, like earlier immigrants, are learning from their friends at school about birthdays and sweet sixteen parties. They are also continuing to celebrate their families' ethnic traditions. American-born youngsters of Indian parentage who do not understand Sanskrit are returning to India for an initiation rite, and Muslims are adapting Eid-al-Fitr to American conditions. While I occasionally note these developments among the "new immigrants," I leave more detailed study of such changes to anthropologists, students of contemporary religion, and other historians.

Gender

To think about the gender roles invoked and reinforced in family ritual requires widening the focus from the event itself to the longer process of preparation for it, which can sometimes last many months. Women organized the sentimentalized domestic occasion; their planning and execution of it demonstrated how certain general principles of gender operated at both a practical and a symbolic level.

Families have usually divided household tasks by age and gender; in this respect, domestic occasions were simply part of women's everyday work of cooking and cleaning and of their responsibility for creating the family's social life. This valuable but invisible work both reflected and contributed to the unequal relations between men and women. Women were supposed to provide food and solace at home; they did not feel entitled to receive it. Men sat at the head of the table and were waited on by women. Because women believed their work was never done, they endlessly sacrificed their sense of self—and time for themselves—in favor of service to others.

At the same time rituals showcased gender ideals, a play within a play, with scripted lines and actions for men and women. These events were a more stereotypic performance of gender roles than in everyday life, which had to accommodate demands, crises, and emergencies on a more gender neutral basis. Erving Goffman's concept of "gender display" is a useful way of understanding the parts people play at rituals: they are scripted (even if not written in text), highly differentiated, and seen by both participants and audience as affirmations of the innate differences between men and women.[23] At these performances participants pay homage to the cultural ideals of proper relations between men and women—to the ideas that women are nurturant, and that men, the ceremonial heads of the family who deliver a family blessing, are to be waited upon.

The sentimentalized domestic occasion reflected the sway of a nineteenth-century ideal of the family, often called the "ideology of domesticity," a belief system of the middle class, indeed a definer of what it meant to be a member of the middle class. This ideology divided the world into two separate spheres, public and private, with the sphere of the home becoming "the empire of the woman," a quasi-sacred space over which the middle-class mother as homemaker presided. Here she did the symbolic work of maintaining family feeling along with celebrating certain holidays. The mother, as chief liturgist of domestic ritual, taught her children their catechism and their etiquette, especially table manners and rules for greeting and saying thank you. Antebellum writers described housework as a labor of love, a selfless act that benefited the family.[24] This ideology of domesticity created new roles for women as organizers of family ritual and keepers of kin connections.

The middle-class mother was at the center of the sentimental ritual, symbolizing tradition and cultural identity, whereas men were free to adopt or reject group identity as they saw fit. In the developing middle class the woman (or mother and child) stood for Christmas, Thanksgiving, and Easter at the family hearth, and the cultural identity of the respectable middle class. In short stories and novels, writers portrayed the mother as the preserver of the values of a simpler, rural world.

Many sentimentalized occasions arose to validate the central role of the middle-class mother in the home and, implicitly, her absence from the paid labor force. Certainly one of the main reasons for the rise of postsentimentalism has been the growth in employment of married women and mothers. This trend increased throughout the twentieth century, with the curve turning steeply upward after the 1960s. Once female work roles changed, preparation for domestic occasions came at the expense of women's leisure. As a result of rising feminist consciousness in the 1970s, women began to voice greater unhappiness with the burden of preparing holidays, complaining that the sentimentalized holiday was unfair to them.

Among various ethnic groups, middle-class women were also the greatest updaters of ethnic traditions, seeking to combine tradition with beauty, elegance, and luxury. Meanwhile, most immigrant women, who were poor or working class, were not setting out displays of wedding gifts or purchasing dozens of wagons and dolls for their children at Christmastime. Children from poorer households recall palm fronds the Sunday before Easter and an orange on Christmas—certain foods, family stories, and religious customs figure largely in their holiday celebrations. Autobiographies as various as those of poor Jewish mothers at the turn of the century and Mexican-American women in a barrio in the 1980s describe immigrant and second generation women as guardians of tradition, who made the home into a refuge from the forces of assimilation.[25]

Immigrant women might be guardians of tradition, but they occasionally embraced sentimentalized occasions, especially weddings. Immigrants from abroad and migrants from poor rural areas to American cities in the early twentieth century moved from a world of scarcity to an urban world with more goods to purchase. The poor Catholic immigrant mother saved her pennies in Christmas club accounts and took her children for first communion photographs; her Jewish counterpart bought bronze mezuzahs for the front door. Such women were active consumers as well as culture bearers. For their daughters, the scales tipped in favor of consumption, especially for the kind of the wedding such girls preferred. They dreamed of marrying in a white satin wedding dress, following the ceremony with a lavish banquet for dozens of guests.

Consumer Culture

Purchased objects and services are central to the sentimentalized occasion, and are just as important in the postsentimental one. The role of consumer culture in the sentimental and the postsentimental occasion is similar. It is difficult to conceive of Christmas without store-bought presents or birthdays without manufactured candles on a cake. In a consumer society the desire for new goods and services, and the status and novelty they bring, gradually become a central feature of social life. The distinguishing feature of family ritual is that it especially partakes of luxury goods, or what were once thought of as luxury goods. What we buy helps define who we are and how we can achieve happiness. The differences between the sentimental and the postsentimental occasion in this respect are that, for the latter, families often rely on third-party services instead of women's unpaid work, and more ritual is taking place outside the home, often in an establishment where the family pays to gather.

Americans' increasing use of goods in celebration is neither a form of freedom nor a conspiracy foisted on unwitting consumers. Advertisers, industry trade groups, and the popular media did not simply trick American consumers into celebrating the family. Rather, families used goods and services to shape individual and group identity, provide status, and even bestow a sense of the sacred.[26] To be sure, commerce and advertising stimulate demand, and in so doing may indeed corrupt, even trivialize, the sacred. There is much truth in the criticism that advertising sells image and perception, not reality—indeed, that it transforms perception into the major form of reality. But just as families remade rituals, they also removed the standard packaging from commodities and made them their own.[27]

In both sentimental and postsentimental times it was most often women who combined tradition with the purchase of certain manufactured items. They saw commodities as artifacts to prompt their memories and connect past events with personal relationships.[28] In so doing, women redefined wedding rings and candlesticks, menorahs, and mourning brooches as sacred objects. The family photo and its container, the family album, became a domestic memento, which revived fading memories and helped cement kin connections. Others used framed photos as domestic decoration, key elements in making a house a home. And what about the men? Even in the mid-nineteenth century, when keepsakes and family photographs began to proliferate, intellectuals such as Ralph Waldo Emerson tended to see gifts as bribes, blackmail, a symptom of "degrading dependence," whereas middle-class women writers and editors more often spoke of bibelots as symbols of friendship and connection.[29]

Several family rituals were gift-giving occasions, and a present, often bought in a store rather than handmade, added excitement to the event. Women became the major purchasers of gifts. In joining ritual with consumer culture, women shoppers used the goods they bought as a means of strengthening family solidarity.[30] Gift-giving transformed a commodity into an object of sentiment. It represented an expression of feeling, a way of establishing an intimate connection between two people and of maintaining social relations with friends and kin. Women sometimes sent packages by mail, but they more often paid a visit to deliver their present, embedding the presentation of a gift within social life.[31]

Judging Family Rituals

The subject of the domestic occasion often provokes moral assessments, wholly positive or negative. Are American domestic occasions harmful or wholesome? In both the nineteenth and the twentieth centuries one could find a similar list of positive claims for rituals. In linking the present with the past, rituals are said to make people less fearful about the future. They are believed to contribute to maintaining an orderly society based on respect for rules and tradition, to promote social cohesion by engendering emotional bonds in participants, to regulate social conflict, to socialize children in a culture and teach them to be respectful and get along with other people, to promote a sense of group identity and solidarity, and to reveal the magic and meaning of religious belief. Anthropologists even claim that rituals can create a sense of group solidarity where before there had been conflict and dissent. Individual initiation rites are thought to aid individuals as they move from one stage of life to the next. Each ritual has its own set of positive outcomes, but those for a funeral differ from the rest, because it is a sad occasion. The funeral, it is claimed, can help people come to accept the reality of death and find an appropriate way of expressing grief.[32]

The list of the harm that rituals are said to cause is just as long, although the complaints have grown more shrill and more frequent in the postsentimental era. Rituals may generate stress rather than relieve it, create as much conflict as they reduce, provoke bad feelings as well as good. Alongside those who feel included by rituals are those who feel excluded by them. There are those who feel let down either during or after special occasions. At a broader level, history-teaching family rituals convey a "mythic" view of history that reduces complexity and can even foster xenophobia. The postsentimental critique borrows from feminism, gay liberation, and the swelling of racial and ethnic consciousness. Critics point out that rituals are associated with patriarchy, and with assumptions that heterosexuality is the norm and the desired state and that homosexuality is marginal and invisible.[33] Feminists assert that women have carried the burden of having to make an occasion perfect. Newspaper columnists often note the hypocrisy of trying to create family solidarity when kin have already grown apart. Closeted gay people feel uncomfortable returning home for Thanksgiving and Christmas and having to pretend to be heterosexual. Jews find themselves profoundly ambivalent at Christmastime, in deciding whether to embrace this children's festival as a secular event or avoid it as a Christian one. The white-skinned Santas and dolls for sale in stores at Christmas make many African Americans feel like outsiders.

Tradition and ritual are seen as links to the past even as they are created and shaped by people in the present. The practice of tradition and ritual reassures people about the continuity of their family, their group, and their religion as they cope with a changing world. People have always found ways to inject new meaning into old rituals and to create new forms that satisfy the longing to combine modernity and tradition.[34] At the same time, the domestic occasion has evolved out of carnival times and communal festivity, moving into the family home, and from there to the funeral parlor, the caterer's hall, and the restaurant. In *A World of Their Own Making* John Gillis argues that contemporary families are victims of an unchanging form of celebration inherited from the Victorians.[35] Our rituals, he suggests, have changed very little. As this book demonstrates, however, Americans have invented and reinvented their family rituals several times since the Victorians. They have usually found a way to modify what were relatively rigid forms, to change the scripts and alter the meanings of these rituals. They have shortened and lengthened, simplified and elaborated, and created some entirely new celebrations. Most Americans have not isolated and removed themselves from modern culture, but instead have become enmeshed in it, using consumer and popular culture both as symbols to rail against and as tools to enhance their celebrations. Ultimately a history of the rise and decline of the sentimental occasion is the story of change in both the form and the meaning of American family celebrations or, more accurately, the acceptance of varying forms and new sets of meanings.

CHAPTER TWO

Family, Feast, and Football

> Savoury smells were in the air; on the crane hung steaming kettles, and
> down among the red embers copper sauce-pans simmered, all suggestive
> of some approaching feast . . . Two small boys sat on the wooden settle
> shelling corn for popping, and picking out the biggest nuts from the
> goodly store their own hands had gathered in October. Four young girls
> stood at the long dresser, busily chopping meat, pounding spice, and
> slicing apples.
>
> —LOUISA MAY ALCOTT, *AUNT JO'S SCRAP-BAG*, 1872

Thanksgiving, a uniquely North American celebration that commemorates the harvest feast of the Pilgrims in 1621, is the major travel holiday in the contemporary United States. Canadians have their own
day of thanksgiving, about a month before the American one. Nine
out of ten people in the United States, when queried in 1981, said that
getting together on Thanksgiving was a tradition in their family. As a
result, more Americans travel just before and after Thanksgiving than
at any other time of the year.[1]

The story of Thanksgiving as a sentimental occasion begins not
with the Pilgrims but in the middle of the nineteenth century. The editor of a woman's magazine, Sarah Josepha Hale, proposed the idea of
a national holiday, and Abraham Lincoln responded favorably to her
suggestion in 1863.[2] They gave Thanksgiving some of its modern
meaning, as a commemorative ritual at which Americans symbolically return to a founding event of their nation and reaffirm their basic national, familial, and religious values.

Thanksgiving in the mid-nineteenth century fused two fundamental
attitudes. The first was that this occasion should be a homecoming, a
family feast preferably at the home of the older generation, reuniting
far-flung kin. The second was that the national holiday of Thanksgiving should affirm the "civil religion," the spiritual but nonsectarian
faith in the special purpose and destiny of the United States.[3] These
two ideas arose from the cultural needs and concerns of people living

through the commercial, social, and cultural transformations of the early nineteenth century and the victories and defeats of the Civil War.

In the late nineteenth and early twentieth centuries the celebration of Thanksgiving continued to change. Schoolteachers made Thanksgiving into a ritual of Americanization, a festival that welcomed immigrants as potential citizens and patriots. In the 1870s football games for the first time were played on Thanksgiving day. Football on Thanksgiving was initially a spectator sport that took place outside the home. With the introduction of radio, listening to the game became a form of entertainment at home. Even as Thanksgiving acquired these two new elements, it shed an old one: carnival-like drunken parades, accompanied by beggars. By the 1940s these kinds of parades had disappeared.

The sentimental Thanksgiving, so long in the making, and so rich in evocation, eventually became a victim of the cultural changes of the 1960s. During that decade, Thanksgiving served as a symbol of family hypocrisy, cultural dominance of a Protestant elite, and theft of Indian land.[4] Even in the sentimental era, there was controversy as to whether Thanksgiving was to be a day of football or family, of carnival or family gathering. In the postsentimental era, the contest of meaning became a defining feature of the way the holiday came to be understood.

The Invention of Thanksgiving

Through the efforts of Sarah Josepha Hale, and later Abraham Lincoln, Thanksgiving by the end of the Civil War had become a holiday both legal and cherished, at least in the North. Best known as the author of the nursery rhyme "Mary's Lamb," Hale was also the editor of *Godey's Magazine and Lady's Book,* a monthly journal widely read among middle-class women in cities and in prosperous farming areas. Beginning in 1846 Hale published yearly editorials in her magazine encouraging national celebration of Thanksgiving. She also sent letters to state governors urging them to proclaim Thanksgiving a state holiday. Hale believed that all Americans celebrating one special day could bolster national unity as well as restore the religious morality of an earlier generation. In printing recipes for the feast and publishing stories of prodigals returning home for the holiday, Hale showed *Godey's* readers how to celebrate Thanksgiving and explained its cultural meaning. She believed that the celebration of Thanksgiving established the importance of "the gratified hospitality, the obliging civility and unaffected happiness" of the American family.[5] Hale found an ally in Abraham Lincoln, who, during the Civil War, saw a day of thanksgiving as a time to praise God for the nation's blessings. Responding to Hale and to a wartime country's need for prayer, Lincoln issued a proclamation in October 1863, establishing the last Thursday in November as an annual national day of Thanksgiving.

As a holiday of family homecoming, Thanksgiving soothed the social dislocations of the industrial and commercial revolutions. The ritual of returning home at Thanksgiving, "when the fledged birds once more flew back to the mother nest," made it possible to reconcile individualism and obligation to family.[6] An American man could be both self-made and an obedient son, so long as he reunited with family for this special feast. The homecoming also affirmed the importance of the extended family at a time when large-scale migration from New England had weakened kin ties. Thanksgiving was also supposed to uphold a variety of ideals the public believed to be threatened, from the family itself to charitableness and patriotism. Two anthropologists, Sally Moore and Barbara Myerhoff, recognized the value of ritual for this purpose. They wrote, "Since ritual is a good form for conveying a message as if it were unquestionable, it is often used to communicate those things which are most in doubt."[7]

The family and the nation, it was believed, had lost a sense of spiritual mission as the elite in the generation after the American Revolution became wealthier, more urban, and less civic-minded. The growth of commerce, railroads, immigration, and city life created moral doubts as well as a gulf between past and present, a gulf that could be bridged through the creation of an "old-fashioned holiday." Nostalgia at Thanksgiving was a yearning for a simpler, more virtuous, more public-spirited and wholesome past, located in the New England countryside, not the city. At the same time, antebellum Americans imagined an optimistic future even as they longed for the old homestead and its blazing fireplace.

By having Lincoln as its midwife, Thanksgiving celebrated the blessings of American nationhood as well as its domestic ideals. This holiday of civil religion proclaimed that the United States had the unique obligation of carrying out God's will on earth. Lincoln intuitively recognized that a national commemoration of historical origins (added to the one on July Fourth) would help build consensus about the worthiness and longevity of the Union. To Lincoln, Thanksgiving was the time for a grateful nation to praise God for blessings bestowed, for the many years of "peace and prosperity," for the growth in national wealth, power, and population, "as no other nation has ever grown." Lincoln (or, more accurately, Secretary of State William Seward, who actually wrote the proclamation) saw Thanksgiving as a holiday when the "whole American people," presumably even those at war with one another, invoked God. In response to Lincoln's proclamation, Northern women baked pot pies to donate to soldiers' families and others sent turkeys to soldiers in the field. Abolitionist Sojourner Truth went door to door in Battle Creek, Michigan, to collect food for the Thanksgiving dinners of black troops stationed in Detroit.[8] These contributions toward Thanksgiving meals for the battle-weary expressed the belief of Northern families in twinned ideas: the affectionate family and the Union cause.

Gender Roles

The sentimentalized occasion Hale proposed upheld the role of the nurturing mother in the home even as it robbed her of her leisure. In households with servants, it was common to give the hired girl a day off on Thanksgiving, although apparently not the black cook.[9] Thanksgiving was a day of intensified patriarchy, when the difference between male and female responsibilities was pronounced. Men picked up their relatives at the train station while women tended the oven; boys chopped wood while girls helped their mother pound the spices.

The unequal labor in preparing for Thanksgiving was freely chosen. Women willingly took on extra work because they believed in the ideal of the home as a refuge from the world. Their roasting and baking proved the goodness of their mothering. As Jeanne Boydston pointed out, antebellum writers (male and female) often shifted their portrayal of housework from the simple performance of multiple duties and responsibilities to a labor of love, a selfless act designed for the benefit of the family. It was crucial to the ideology of domesticity that women not think of themselves as workers, for if they did so, the home would become simply another artisan's shop rather than a haven against a hostile, even corrupt, world.[10]

As organizers of family rituals and keepers of kin connections, women derived domestic power from "being needed."[11] They were aware that their cooking and cleaning produced a sense of family solidarity, sociability, and feelings of pleasure through surfeit of food. Women counted on fond memories of a future generation as the dividend for their investment of time. A woman dreaded the day when she grew too old to baste the turkey and stir the gravy, and had to turn to daughters and other female kin to host the feast.

Thus the satisfactions of Thanksgiving were several, beginning with the aesthetic. The crowning achievement of the nineteenth-century Thanksgiving feast was the pies, often baked the day before. The dessert pies—apple, mince, pumpkin, and cranberry—were prepared in advance and stored in "butteries and dressers and shelves and pantries." Women baked mince pie as much as ten days in advance to allow it time to ripen. On the morning of the event, many cooks put the chicken pot pie in the oven with the turkey—two main dishes for the feast. The artistry of piemaking lay in the decoration of the top crust, "fanciful fluting and architectural strips laid across and around."[12] A New England woman might shape the crust to make intertwined initials of an engaged couple, leafy ferns, or a replica of the *Mayflower*. In addition, because they cooked together on Thanksgiving day, and in the days of preparation before that, women enjoyed female companionship in the kitchen and could display their mastery of womanly skills to each other.[13] One basted the turkey while another made the gravy. One held the bird while the other stuffed it. While working in the kitchen women talked about the hard luck of relatives, a neighbor's choice of a bride, and the (sexual) reputation of friends and neighbors. In gathering information as well as disseminating it, women exercised their power to shape reputations and draw lines between the violators of community norms and the insiders.[14]

At the meal's end women were rewarded for their skill in baking, appreciated more than they might be after an ordinary meal.[15] Grateful aunts asked for a hostess's recipes; stuffed diners called out their compliments. In the recipes they chose, women remembered and honored a dead mother or other female relative. The act of using a mother's or grandmother's recipes was a way for women to make a powerful, loving connection with the dead.[16]

The telling of the family story was another commemorative act that linked the younger generation with their forebears. Families who felt that kin ties were being sundered were more keenly aware of the need to pass on the family past, through daguerreotypes, heirlooms, family Bibles, and stories. At the dinner table or in the evening after the feast, the elder generation regaled the young ones with tales of long ago. Elderly women, it seems, were the main raconteurs.[17] Women were more knowledgeable not only about their own lives but also about those of the men in the family. One New England girl recalled that she and her cousins gathered around Grandma Pratt after dinner and clamored for her "stories of their fathers and grandfathers, and of her own youth."[18]

John Gillis argues that whereas the idea of family once meant sharing a common space, by the mid-nineteenth century it stood for sharing a common past.[19] Storytelling had of course been done since humans first gathered around a campfire.[20] About the table talk of colonial times or the Revolutionary era little is known, although the subjects were likely to be religion or the harvest. Nineteenth-century families, Gillis suggests, added to these topics discussions of family history. Folklorists have discovered general patterns to the kinds of stories families usually tell: a description of a colorful relative or the family saga, in particular some turning point for the family, such as migration. According to Amy Kotkin and Steven Zeitlin, most family stories to this day fall into these patterns. Thanksgiving gave families a special opportunity to instruct the younger members in family genealogy, to impart to children a sense of the kind of family they belonged to.[21]

It was in New England and the mid-Atlantic states, where the dislocations of industrialism were greatest, that the holiday of Thanksgiving was most needed and hence most widely celebrated in the nineteenth century. Across the rest of the nation Thanksgiving was observed in other ways. The Pennsylvania Dutch and the Lutherans had their own harvest celebrations (though not at the end of November) and were reluctant to adopt the national holiday. Around 1900 African Americans often went to church services at Thanksgiving but rarely had feasts at home.[22] Men and boys in the west often hunted on the holiday.[23] In the rest of the country at this time Thanksgiving often passed unobserved. To Southerners and Germans in Iowa, Thanksgiving was a Yankee holiday; to Catholics, it was a Protestant one.[24] Some, but certainly not the majority, of employers handed out free turkeys to their employees. Political bosses who sought to curry favor with new voters would send their minions to hand out turkeys to poor families in immigrant neighborhoods. Many urban families could not afford to buy a turkey. Unless they were willing to accept a mission's charitable Thanksgiving meal, they had to go without.[25]

Assimilating the Immigrants

American nationalism shaped the celebration of Thanksgiving even before Lincoln's election. At the beginning of the twentieth century, reformers saw in Thanksgiving the means to enlist recent immigrants in the national enterprise. Their attempts to Americanize the new-comers were both a gesture of welcome and an exercise in cultural power of the English-ancestry Protestant elite. Between 1890 and 1920 the tableaux of the friendly Pilgrims making peace with their Indian neighbors became a prominent part of Thanksgiving newspaper advertisements and school pageants. Even in antebellum America, the chronicle of the Pilgrims' early years of settlement had comprised the first chapter in American history. The lyrics of the song "America," written in 1846, made clear that the "sweet land of liberty" had been the "land of the Pilgrims' pride."[26] But antebellum stories and popular paintings had tended to emphasize the landing at Plymouth Rock and the Pilgrims' first encounters with Indians. In the 1890s the Pilgrims attracted the attention of the educated elite as they sought examples of "intense faith, imagination, and courage," respectable ancestors, founders of their country who "could not be accused of religious intolerance or intellectual arrogance."[27]

Initially the Progressive era interest in the Pilgrims seemed to partake more of prejudice than of inclusion. Beleaguered by the onslaught of so many former peasants, many of them Catholics or Jews, Anglo-Protestants looked to American history as a form of cultural superiority. Genealogical fervor, snobbery, and the desire to differentiate themselves from the great wave of new immigrants standing on the national doorstep led to the founding of the Daughters of the American Revolution, the Colonial Dames of America, the Society of Mayflower Descendants, and dozens of other patriotic societies. Between 1895 and 1912 William Bradford's *Of Plimouth Plantation* went through three printings. William DeLoss Love, a Congregationalist minister and member of the Sons of the American Revolution, chronicled the history of Thanksgiving. He published *The Fast and*

Thanksgiving Days of New England in 1895. Love argued that Plymouth was the birthplace of the nation and that the New England family of the past was "one of the grandest conceptions of family life known in history."[28]

While the Pilgrims functioned for the Progressive-era elite as respectable ancestors (even as "our Pilgrim parents" in one chromolithograph), for newcomers to America they were the first immigrants, refugees from religious persecution uprooted from their homeland. In the classroom and, to a much lesser extent, the settlement house, immigrants became American, learning about their new nation's history and holidays. Teachers taught their students that America had borrowed the best of Greek democracy and Roman republicanism. Immigrant children could take pride in becoming part of a great nation. Textbooks claimed that the Pilgrims believed in the democratic ideal, and cited as evidence the fact that they had drawn up the Mayflower Compact, the first democratic constitution in the New World. By the 1920s, Thanksgiving was the most celebrated holiday in the schools, edging out Christmas by a single percentage point, according to one survey of elementary school principals.[29] One Jewish student at a Flatbush, New York, high school later recalled that the reason he liked the Pilgrims so much was that "they were a means of reconciliation between us offspring of Jewish immigrants—our own exiled fathers who had crossed the seas—and the traditions of Protestant America."[30]

Portraying Thanksgiving as a day to be thankful for the blessings of American freedom, of "home and community," teachers staged elaborate tableaux with girls dressed in white caps and cuffs made out of paper and boys in round collars and cuffs. In their classrooms and in school assemblies students recited poems, acted out parts in short plays, cut out paper pumpkins, and drew log cabins. Teachers sat at the piano and taught their students to sing "We gather together and ask the Lord's blessing."[31] All Americans were either immigrants or descendants of immigrants, teachers told their students; some had simply arrived in America earlier than others. One Italian immigrant student noted that "the Pilgrim fathers had come in pursuit of religious freedom; we had come in pursuit of more and better bread."[32] His teacher then confided that her grandparents were Pilgrims, too, since they had emigrated from Scotland. The American nation was unique, she explained, because it was a congregation of many peoples.

Schoolteachers recognized that they had to develop an emotional bond between the immigrant and the nation, a love of country. Immigrant children could be taught American history and learn about the holidays, but the home was where the deepest feelings of patriotism were conveyed. The love of country needed to be reinforced there. A feast around a common table represented an acceptance of American customs and history by the newcomers and their recognition that they would do their part in encouraging their child's budding patriotism. Schoolchildren acted as cultural conduits, bringing home ideas about celebration, national history, and cultural symbols learned at school. One boy even cut out paper pumpkins and turkeys and pasted them on the windowpanes of the family's apartment.[33] Children implored their mothers to buy a turkey and roast it.

How were the teachers' efforts received? It might be thought that because Thanksgiving celebrated the family, immigrants would be especially eager to embrace it.[34] Here was an opportunity for good food and socializing, a chance to tell the saga of the family's migration to the new world and to praise God for the blessings of life in the new country.[35] Yet immigrants to the United States, except for those from Canada, had never before celebrated Thanksgiving. As a result, and because it was an expression of the culture of the American nation, its cuisine, and its style of entertaining, some immigrants perceived Thanksgiving as entirely alien. The reasons why Pearl Kazin's mother said no to her daughter's request to celebrate Thanksgiving were overtly religious and covertly cultural. Kazin was a short story writer who published her recollection of growing up in Brooklyn in the *New Yorker* in the 1950s. One November when she was about ten years old she asked her mother, "But Mama, *why* can't we have turkey for Thanksgiving like everybody else?" Her mother replied, characteristically answering a question with a question, "Who's everybody? . . . The Feins eat turkey Thanksgiving? . . . We don't have enough *our* holidays for you[?]"[36] The distinction between Jewish and school holidays revealed the distance between Mrs. Kazin's concept of festivity and the middle-class (Christian) one taught in the schools. A Chinese mother in California, also not a Christian, did prepare the feast. She saw Thanksgiving as a means of extending Chinese hospitality to the host society. But her reasons were more complicated; as she explained, "We share the holiday of our American neighbors . . . because we wish to live in peace and harmony with them and because I do not wish you children to grow wicked with envy of others."[37]

Even at a national holiday, which presumed a unity of citizens, ethnic groups sought to articulate their vision of American identity as a balanced fusion of their group culture with dominant American elements. Food was the symbolic medium for making the mixture. To be sure, there were a few families who adopted the entire American menu, including the chestnut stuffing and sweet potatoes.[38] For most, the turkey became the symbol of the dominant culture, and the stuffing, side dishes, and desserts were the immigrants' contribution. The son of an Irish immigrant explained that his mother served rutabaga and parsnip at Thanksgiving because she ate these root vegetables her first November in the United States. Others added spices distinctive to their homeland to the stuffing. Greek families sprinkled pine nuts in the stuffing; an American-born wife of an Armenian husband used pomegranate. A Chinese-American mother steamed the turkey first, then stuffed it with the glutinous rice mixture she usually used with chicken.[39] Desserts could also add an ethnic touch. Most groups were, consciously or unconsciously, trying to assimilate by combining a few elements of their culture with America's holiday and its cuisine. Only a few cooks discarded the traditional American meal entirely.[40] In some cases these culinary fusions persisted for many generations.

The Carnival of the Fantastics

William Dean Howells noted in 1907, "The poor recognize the day largely as a sort of carnival," as men escaped from the family, broke rules, and engaged in spontaneous mirth.[41] Some form of the older, carnival-like celebration of Thanksgiving lasted until the late nineteenth century in eastern Pennsylvania.

Thanksgiving, as a harvest feast, originated in the raucous English celebrations in the fields, whereas Thanksgiving's carnival-like activities began at about the time of the American Revolution. The Fantastics, or Fantasticals, masqueraded on Thanksgiving day beginning in the 1780s. Originally they were revolutionary war veterans who paraded in the rags of Continental soldiers. The name Fantastic was English, and the practice seems to have been borrowed from the English custom of door-to-door masquerading for treats. The Fantastics copied many elements of English mumming—ridiculing authority, masquerading and cross-dressing, begging for treats, and getting drunk. In the 1830s many Fantastics were militia regulars who dressed as women and poked fun at their superiors. Costumed boys ran after them, begging for coins. The Fantastics paraded not only on Thanksgiving, but also on New Year's Eve and Day, Battalion Day, Washington's birthday, and the Fourth of July.[42] In rural areas of eastern and central Pennsylvania Fantastics rode on horseback from house to house, demanding food and drink, their faces blackened or masked.

In New York City and Philadelphia the Fantastics held elaborate parades, enlisting other groups and marching bands. In the late nineteenth century in lower Manhattan the event began at the call of a horn. Costumed men staggered out of saloons, where they had been given free drinks. They mounted horses and carts for their parade. Along the way they would stop briefly to blow a horn into the ears of women spectators crowded along the sidewalks. At the end of the parade they feasted on turkey and drink at an afternoon picnic, where fistfights often broke out. The evening ball that followed went on until the early morning.[43] Most New York City Fantastics were Irish and working class; many were fish sellers at Fulton Fish market; some were politicians and prison guards. As a boy, Al Smith, the Democratic governor of New York and failed presidential candidate, who grew up on Manhattan's Lower East Side and worked at the market himself, liked to watch the parade.[44]

By 1900 adult male revelers seem to have disappeared from Thanksgiving parades. The major reason for their demise was changing public attitudes. As late as 1885, the *New York Times* had considered the Fantastics "hilarious" and "quaint." Ten years later they found them "intolerable" and a "public nuisance," although conceding that children might think them funny.[45] A devastating economic depression and fear of strikers, anarchists, and unruly mobs seem to have contributed to the change of opinion. Parts of the masquerade and carnival were siphoned off in two directions. The ball was celebrated in the 1910s and 1920s by gay men in Greenwich Village, many of whom came in drag. The masquerade persisted, but among children, who went begging dressed in old trousers, women's dresses, or clown costumes.[46] On Thanksgiving eve and morning children frequented the subway and the elevated tracks, knocked on doors, and rang the doorbells of Park and Fifth Avenue townhouses, asking, "Anything for Thanksgiving, Mister?"[47] Although many of these children were poor, more privileged children, with a mother's permission, also donned costumes and went from one neighbor to the next demanding treats and coins.[48]

Progressive era reformers disliked the idea of children begging on a day that was meant to celebrate national moral purpose and the sanctity of the family. Teachers lectured against begging in their classrooms and at assemblies, and police tried to enforce an outright ban. The *New York Times* in November 1930 worried that demanding coins would teach children to become professional beggars and blackmailers, adding that the young mendicants were annoying the public.[49] The clergy and school superintendents also tried to eliminate the custom. To discourage begging, boys' clubs and other child welfare agencies organized parades and costume contests. As a result of all these efforts, by the 1940s child begging had disappeared.[50]

Children's begging could not be eliminated entirely; in fact, it reemerged at Halloween in the late 1930s. Before then trick-or-treating was virtually unknown. Middle-class mothers had held Halloween parties in their homes, and young vandals took to the streets, sometimes causing damage to neighbors' property and local businesses. Police and the heads of social agencies saw trick-or-treating as a way to tame the anarchy of destructive youth. Originally, neighbors treated the costumed children as guests, inviting them into their homes. By the 1950s most children simply stopped at the door and demanded their candy; some also soaped windows and defaced property.[51] We have no satisfactory explanation as to why child begging was permitted at Halloween but not at Thanksgiving. Perhaps trick-or-treating was seen as preferable to hooliganism on Halloween, whereas child begging on Thanksgiving was seen as a violation of the sacred and sentimental character of the holiday.

Cultural critics, such as literary theorist Mikhail Bakhtin, have not only relished the antics of masqueraders like the Fantastics but also treasured their challenge to the subdued piety and sentimentality of the domestic occasion. Bakhtin suggested that carnival, "a world free from cast and cant," threatened the established order because it marked "the suspension of all hierarchical rank, privileges, norms, and prohibitions."[52] Bakhtin further argued that there was a special quality of laughter at carnival—ribald, hearty, spontaneous—that made the event almost by definition an affront to serious and solemn public events. The Fantastics mocked gender conventions, played with race by wearing blackface, and made fun of the elite. Cross-dressing blurred the line between male and female, and blackface erased that between black and white. Marjorie Garber argued that changing one's identity from male to female or from white to black by cross-dressing or masking is a sign of cultural anxiety among people who want the lines between both races and genders clearly drawn.[53] In the contest between the sentimental and the carnival at Thanksgiving, the sentimental clearly triumphed in the end.

Commercialization and the Thanksgiving Football Game

The Macy's Thanksgiving Day parade, begun in 1924, was a symbol of the commercialization of a holiday the general public regarded as noncommercial. In truth, Thanksgiving had some commercial elements as early as the beginning of the nineteenth century, when a man might give his brother a Bible as a Thanksgiving present.[54] By the early twentieth century newspapers and magazines had begun to carry Thanksgiving advertisements. A Crisco ad from 1916, for example, showed a grey-haired granny with wire-rimmed glasses holding her mince pie made with its product. In the Thanksgiving issue of the *Saturday Evening Post* for 1931, an advertisement for Camels touted the cigarettes as "something to be thankful for."[55] Macy's parade was the most significant commercial addition to Thanksgiving, although its purpose was to encourage Christmas shopping on the day after Thanksgiving and the weeks thereafter. Appearing at the end of the parade, Santa, riding in his sleigh, signaled to child and parent alike that the time had arrived to make their Christmas lists. So clear was the connection between the two holidays that Macy's at first called its November spectacle a "Christmas parade."[56]

The organizers of Macy's parade, even in the 1920s, found themselves engaged in a schedule conflict with the afternoon football game, a conflict they lost. Football was clearly the more significant of the two forms of out-of-home entertainment even then. Initially Macy's parade, held in the morning, offended patriotic groups, who decried a spectacle on "a national and essentially religious holiday."[57] Macy's then hired a public relations expert, who decided that the critics could be placated if the parade was postponed until at least after church services had ended. By moving the time the parade began, however, Macy's event started at the same time as the kickoff for most football games. Customers and football fans complained. By the 1920s, Macy's had decided on a morning parade after all, presumably so as not to offend football fans.

The Thanksgiving Day football game began in the 1870s as the culminating contest in the Ivy League football season. By the 1920s football had become a form of home entertainment, mainly for the urban middle class. In 1930, 40 percent of American homes had a radio; a decade later, 90 percent of American households owned one.[58] By listening to a radio broadcast, a family could combine feast and football without leaving the home. By 1956 football games were televised. Listening to the football game in the living room represented a distinct stage in the reinvention of Thanksgiving, as a highly feminized occasion became more appealing to men. Families came to regard the game as traditional, part of what made Thanksgiving authentic and meaningful. Football even helped to overcome the lingering Southern prejudice against the Yankee holiday of Thanksgiving. Because college football was beloved in the South, some of its glow rubbed off on the holiday.

What does the popularity of football on such a sacred national day as Thanksgiving signify? There is not one interpretation, but several, as the meaning of football to Americans has changed as the prevailing intellectual climate has become more jingoist, secular, modern, or pro-business. Opponents of the game since the early twentieth century have thought football too aggressive, violent, and dangerous. To its proponents football is seen as a training ground for war (a common World War I theme) or an antidote to it (a post–World War I theme). In the 1890s the game was seen as a symbol of imperialism and social Darwinism (proof of the "dominance of the white race" and the success of the fittest). Proponents in the same era argued that football expressed Christian manliness or served as an excellent introduction to the concepts of bureaucracy, teamwork, and management. Many late-nineteenth-century writers argued that football demonstrated the success of Victorian virtues, such as regularity, self-restraint, and fair play. Some writers also noticed that the Thanksgiving Day game generated loyalty among college students and alumnae and that attendance at the Thanksgiving Day game provided an opportunity for a fur-coated elite to arrive at the athletic grounds in decorated carriages.[59]

What was lost on the mostly male defenders of the game was the irony that a family event was being punctuated by (mostly) men experiencing a game noted for its aggressive body contact, warlike language, male bonding, and the ability of the players to withstand pain. There had always been gender segregation at the Thanksgiving meal, with men talking to other men and women conversing with women both before and after the meal. Apparently uninterested in the game, women would wash dishes in the kitchen, mixing gossip and housework in an activity that provided pleasure. The spheres were physically separate, and permeable, but only in one direction. It was easier for a woman to enter the living room where men were listening to the game than for a man to don an apron and help in the kitchen.[60]

This physical separation of male and female appeared to reflect men's need to escape into an all-male group after having stuffed themselves and participated in an event so female in ambience. One function of Thanksgiving Day football, even when the men enjoyed the game only as spectators, was to reaffirm their bonds with other men and their own masculinity, to inject some manliness into the sentimentality. Sons would learn from their fathers the rules of male sociability as they were being weaned from their mothers. The football game gave the Thanksgiving holiday an additional symbol of manhood: man the gladiator side by side with man the hunter.[61]

Celebration and Its Unraveling

The portrait of a happy family seated around a Thanksgiving dinner table in Norman Rockwell's *Freedom from Want* symbolized for the World War II generation the unity of family and nation. Rockwell provided a visual explanation of why Americans at home and on the battleground had to sacrifice during World War II. Before the United States entered the war, President Roosevelt sought to justify his policy of Lend Lease and the aims of American neutrality. He listed four American freedoms the United States hoped to secure in the world: freedom of speech, freedom from fear, freedom of worship, and freedom from want. After the Japanese bombed Pearl Harbor, FDR explained that the aims of the world war were to secure the Four Freedoms for Americans and the entire world. Inspired by Roosevelt's speech, Norman Rockwell in 1942 set out to show ordinary Americans enjoying these freedoms. The war loan drive used Rockwell's illustrations, published as covers of the *Saturday Evening Post,* in selling war bonds. Millions of copies of Rockwell's drawings were published and the originals were part of a highly successful traveling exhibition by the war bond board. Rockwell's illustration, and Roosevelt's formulation of freedom as "freedom from want," underscored the New Deal belief that economic security was necessary to undergird human freedom.

As preparation, Rockwell had taken photographs of his own family Thanksgiving dinner in Vermont, and he included his mother in the finished painting, though the family cook was the model for the grandmother.[62] Like Sarah Josepha Hale or Currier and Ives, Rockwell found the family in small-town New England a source of moral strength and evocative imagery. Rockwell portrayed the happy multigenerational family gathered around the Thanksgiving dinner table, and implied the naturalness of the gender division of labor.[63] In Rockwell's portrait an apron-clad, short, plump grandmother leans over the table, holding a large serving platter that displays a well-roasted turkey. Behind her stands her grey-haired husband, tall and gaunt, his carving knife on the table.[64] Despite the domestication of the holiday and the civilizing of modern man, man was still the hunter and provider, the "priestly authority," woman his servant and the family's nurturer. The large roasted bird on the platter symbolized the abundance of the feast, and American plenty. In the act of carving, the whole would be broken into many pieces and served to all.[65] Although Rockwell's painting had its origins in World War II, it became the major postwar iconic representation of Thanksgiving and of the ideal American family. The family in the Rockwell illustration was white and presumably Protestant, and the grandparents were portrayed as old-fashioned elders of modest means. Rockwell also depicted the proper style of consumption during wartime—abundant (no rationing evident) but not showy or wasteful.

In less than two decades, Rockwell's work became an object of ridicule, a symbol of the dominant culture and white Americans' ignorance of other cultures. Artists and writers mocked and parodied Norman Rockwell's portrait of the family gathered around the dinner table. In the 1980s Frank Moore, intending to dramatize the plight of AIDS victims, made significant alterations to the Rockwell illustration. Grandpa and the grandchildren became black. An aunt appears to be Hispanic. Grandma, although still Caucasian, was shown serving a platter of medications and syringes.[66]

The postsentimental Thanksgiving emerged in the 1960s because American families and the nation were undergoing disruptive changes. The Vietnam war, race riots, assassinations of the Kennedys, Martin Luther King, and Malcolm X, and unrest on college campuses undermined the respect for authority and belief in a single cultural ideal of the family. The faith of the American people in the moral standing of their nation was shaken. Whether protesting against the war or against university bureaucracies, American young people were questioning national morality and the values of tradition. The national origin myth, that the United States was a country descended from Pilgrims, no longer served to unify the nation or provide a compelling national identity. Whereas immigrants at the turn of the century saw a resemblance between themselves and the Pilgrims, the atmosphere of the 1960s changed the image of the Pilgrims from that of brave pioneers to that of land-hungry whites. The national story could no longer begin with them. Thanksgiving was attacked as a symbol of national unity achieved at the expense of the Indians. Schoolteachers in the 1960s began to describe the Indians at Thanksgiving as the first settlers. Just before the holiday they taught the children Indian customs, not Pilgrim ones. The Pilgrims fell out of favor. A cartoonist in the 1970s even portrayed a Pilgrim family seated around a dinner table, ready to eat an American Indian![67] Indian activist Vine Deloria related the story of how he began to sing the lines in "America" about how this country was "the land of the Pilgrims' pride," only to realize "that our fathers undoubtedly died trying to keep those Pilgrims from stealing our land."[68]

Some writers in a postsentimental vein described feeling stifled or smothered by the obligatory family gathering at Thanksgiving. As a graduate student at the University of Chicago in the 1970s, Brent Staples, an African American student at a largely white university, usually turned down invitations to friends' homes for the holidays. It was not simply that he resented being the object of charity, although he may have felt that. "The few that I accepted gave me the same sense of imprisonment that I felt with my family," he wrote. "Holidays were a form of tyranny; it was best to face and fight them alone."[69] To the metaphor of the family as a prison Francine duPlessix Gray added that of the devouring beast. She wrote that "Thanksgiving was the day of guilt and grace, when the family hangs over you like an ax over the sacrificial victim. What a perfect day to go loony."[70] Family stories of Thanksgiving before the 1960s had described eating competitions between cousins and contests as to who got the drumstick, or relied on the stock themes of family folklore—the freakish accident, the eccentric personality, the lost fortune, the parent's courtship. Most had presented a portrait of family harmony; writers in postsentimental times, by contrast, described at length quarreling and unhappiness. Humor columnist Dave Barry prided himself on his honesty when he wrote, "Thanksgiving is a time to have over relatives who live a half hour away whom we rarely see otherwise because we really hate them."[71] Instead of representing the ideal of family harmony, some writers described family conflict, even violence, on this hallowed day. In her autobiography *Coal Miner's Daughter*, for example, country music singer Loretta Lynn recalled one Thanksgiving when her father had grown so angry because one of her siblings had eaten before her father was served that he picked up the table and dumped the whole Thanksgiving meal out the window.[72] For others, Thanksgiving became an occasion for self-disclosure. The traditional practice of bringing a fiancé to the meal persisted, but now adult gay children also chose the family homecoming as the time to come out.[73] Not going home for Thanksgiving became an accepted feature of gay life in major cities. Having one's partner invited and warmly welcomed to the dinner symbolized family social acceptance.

To be sure, films before the 1960s showed family fights breaking out over the turkey, but American films portrayed more family conflict in the years following 1963, when President Kennedy was assassinated. In *Avalon* (1990), filmmaker Barry Levinson portrayed his Jewish childhood in 1950s Baltimore. The movie presents three scenes of family Thanksgivings: the first depicts a happy multigenerational gathering of several Jewish brothers in Baltimore and their families, while the second and third show the decline and then disintegration of that kin group in the years around 1960. In the second, the family is divided into two warring camps at the Thanksgiving dinner table where twenty-six people have gathered, because one brother feels the other has rejected him by starting the meal before he and his wife arrived. After that, the two brothers rarely see each other. Prior to the third Thanksgiving scene, one brother's wife is seen dying in the hospital, so the brother and his wife are unable to take part in the gathering. Instead, the adult son, his wife, and their children sit down to their meal on tray tables while silently watching television.[74]

In the postsentimental era women put less time into preparing for the Thanksgiving feast. As more mothers came to hold paying jobs, the burdens of cooking and cleaning for Thanksgiving loomed larger. The gender division of labor at Thanksgiving began to reflect the reality that American men since the 1970s were doing more housework and cooking. At the same time, women seemed to want to prove that they still knew how to cook—and how to nurture properly—even if the regular meals they served were makeshift affairs. Women who were employed at full-time jobs still wanted to put a home-cooked meal on the table, which could serve as a symbol of their love and nurturance.

They also retained their control over organizing and shopping for the event, although children and men were expected to be willing to assist. Men still carved the turkey, but increasingly in the kitchen rather than at the table. Since so few fathers taught their sons to carve, men had to learn from reading instructions in a cookbook.[75] Magazines of the 1980s from *Sunset* to *Esquire* described men making turkey dressing and gravy, simmering giblets, peeling and mashing potatoes, and taking instruction from svelte grandmothers as to how to trim the edges of pie pastry. Fieldnotes of University of Arizona students who observed their own family Thanksgivings in 1988 reported that men were not doing much of the cooking, but they were helping with the clean-up.[76]

Male involvement in housework was only one of several solutions to the burden women faced at Thanksgiving. Some organized a pot-luck meal, with each guest bringing a dish. Eating out in restaurants, which began to take place on Thanksgiving in the 1890s after the football game, was another. A consumer survey in 1995 found that 10 percent of American households ate Thanksgiving at a restaurant.[77] Being the guest of someone who made the meal was a solution, as was cooking with convenience foods. By the late 1980s restaurants, gourmet food shops, and supermarkets sold complete pumpkin pies or even entire meals to take home, refuting the notion of consumer researchers that women were willing to buy the fixings but wanted to roast the turkey themselves.[78] As an ironic touch, Hallmark, one of the purveyors of sentimentality, joined in the new trend. In 1995 the company cafeteria offered pumpkin pies and corn bread dressing to take home for Thanksgiving.[79]

American women seemed to want to find a way to display their competence as cooks while cutting back on the labor it took to do so. Since the Thanksgiving ideal had been one of the simple countryside, the meal was supposed to be made from home-grown ingredients. The modern reality was that the dinner was being assembled from canned, packaged, and frozen foods. Libby introduced canned pumpkin in 1929, which removed the necessity of scooping out the inside of a pumpkin and removing the seeds.[80] Many people considered canned cranberry sauce traditional since they had eaten it as children.[81] Cooking skills declined in the general population. Callers to Swift's Butterball turkey hot line, inaugurated in 1980, were asking increasingly basic questions. Many wanted to know what basting (the practice of pouring natural juices over the bird) was. They needed to be told to put the bird in a roasting pan before putting it into the oven. The company was amazed to find how many callers had to be told to turn on the oven.[82]

Although the use of packaged foods made meal preparation less time consuming, there were a few ingredients that had to be "real." Women who regularly used margarine would switch to butter for Thanksgiving. One mother taught her daughter how to roll out a frozen pie crust and place it in a pie pan, so as to be able to serve a pie that looked homemade.[83] Whatever actually went on in the kitchen, the food brought to the table was supposed to have taken considerable time and effort to prepare. The Arizona students photographed women basting Butterball turkeys, opening a package of Pepperidge Farm bread cubes to make stuffing, stirring cans of Swanson chicken broth into turkey drippings to make gravy, squeezing Ocean Spray cranberry sauce from the can, pouring boiling water into a bowl of Jell-o powder and then adding ice cubes to speed the jelling and stirring in Dole canned pineapple chunks, and filling Pet-Ritz frozen pie crusts with Libby canned pumpkin mixed with evaporated milk for a pie to be topped later with Cool Whip.[84]

The Arizona students' photographs also revealed class and ethnic differences in the celebration of Thanksgiving, even in a single state in the American Southwest. Groups where the kin lived nearby, which was often the case with Mexican-Americans, might assemble in large family groups. Others with more dispersed kin (a common pattern in the upper middle class) tended to break bread with friends. Even within the upper middle class one could discern differences: some households displayed floral decorations, Bavarian china, Waterford crystal, and monogrammed silver; others used nonmatching sets of plates and cutlery. Those from the working class were often at the lower end of the decorative scale, putting plastic tubs of margarine and soda cans on the table and using paper plates.

Far from being an American tradition that went back to the Pilgrims, the ideal of Thanksgiving as a family homecoming emerged in tandem with the cult of domesticity and by the Civil War had become a celebration of American civil religion. To be sure, the ideals of neighborliness as well as family, community as well as kin, were upheld. But the main values Thanksgiving affirmed were the gathering of the family and the celebration of the national mission. Nonetheless, Thanksgiving had a distinctly regional and class appeal until the early twentieth century. Some mothers did not roast a turkey because they could not afford one; others considered Thanksgiving an alien holiday. It took a long time before Thanksgiving became beloved in all classes and regions, and among most homemakers. The main agents of change were children, who learned about the holiday at school and asked their parents if they could have turkey on the holiday.

While the man of the house, with carving knife in hand, affirmed the father's role as provider and head of household, the apron-clad mother created and organized Thanksgiving. As moral guardians of the home, women had special responsibility for tempering, but not eliminating, male pursuit of self-interest.[85] The Thanksgiving holiday was a woman's crowning achievement, designed to cement and affirm her skills as a cook and kinkeeper. From all the effort came a form of recognition, applause, and domestic power. Thanksgiving furthered the reordering of the family as the distinctive sphere of women. For men, the holiday symbolically presented them as the family's hunter and provider, and offered spiritual renewal, before their return the next day to worldly matters. Once the football game was broadcast on the radio and later on television, Thanksgiving offered men a separate, gender-affirming activity, just as the well-cooked meal did for women.

Thanksgiving as a sentimental occasion initially coexisted with and eventually triumphed over the Fantastics. Through the efforts of teachers, police, and social agencies, the element of misrule was gradually subtracted from the celebration of Thanksgiving. The begging child did not fit into the picture of domestic felicity and national religious gratitude the holiday had come to represent. Children laugh and relatives stuff themselves at Thanksgiving; in the newspaper columns and at the dining table Americans understand the holiday as an affirmation of, rather than a challenge to, the basic values of society. More precisely, values in the United States consist of various binary oppositions, and the celebration of Thanksgiving weighs in on the side of the family against individualism. In addition, Thanksgiving serves the cause of a unified nation, bridging differences between regions, religions, classes, races, and ethnicities through the combination of the mainstream cuisine served with distinctive side dishes.

The heyday of Thanksgiving lies in the postsentimental present rather than the sentimental past, when many families did not celebrate the holiday because of bad roads, lack of interest, religious or cultural objections, or low income. Most families nowadays, whether American-born or recent immigrants, celebrate Thanksgiving. In the years of increased immigration since 1965, newspapers have featured the theme of the Progressive era, Thanksgiving as a secular day for national inclusion of newcomers, be they refugees from Somalia or Bosnia or recent immigrants from Asia, Latin America, Ireland, or Italy. Alongside this earlier way of understanding Thanksgiving, newspapers slip in a few postsentimental elements: Indian groups protesting the holiday, accounts of children of divorce shuttling from the mother's feast to the father's, and restaurants touting their prix fixe holiday meal.

CHAPTER THREE

Holiday Blues and Pfeffernusse

I often pity men for being men, and never more than during the happy
Christmas time . . . when so much depends upon the ruling spirit of the
household, and when the wife and mother enjoys the divine privilege of
conferring happiness, flooding the house with interior sunshine, and
unlocking such golden stores of enjoyment as were hardly known to exist.

—JENNY JUNE, "TALKS WITH WOMEN," 1865

Santa Claus, the exchange of presents, a decorated evergreen tree, and
Christmas cards—all were major new elements added to Christmas
by the Victorians. Christmas was supposed to be a special time for
youngsters, when parents took pleasure from the delighted squeals of
children as they opened presents and gazed wide-eyed at a tree lit with
candles. Over time, Christmas moved from the home to the church,
the school, the town square, the movie theater, and the shopping
plaza. Cartoons and songs, movies and television shows, short stories and advertising helped to popularize a homogenized version of
Christmas, replete with the major folk figure of the nineteenth century, Santa, and the new one of the twentieth century, Rudolph the
Red-Nosed Reindeer.[1]

Historians and sociologists who have studied the holiday have generally focused on how Christmas was celebrated by the dominant culture, rather than by various ethnic groups. They have also often mis-
takenly assumed that the holiday the Victorians created remains with
us, unchanged in form and meaning. Observing Christmas in Muncie,
Indiana in the 1970s, for example, Theodore Caplow found an occasion thick with sentiment. Families were shopping, wrapping presents, hanging ornaments on a tree, visiting kin, and making phone
calls to distant relatives. He failed to note the holiday crisis hotlines,
Kwanzaa celebrations, giant menorahs in the public square, and divorce agreements specifying where the children would spend the holi-

day. Almost unseen, two discordant systems of meaning, the sentimental and the postsentimental approaches to the Christmas season, have snuggled uneasily together since the 1960s.

The wrapping of a sacred season within a consumer festival is a perennial source of discomfort and criticism, and has periodically led to efforts—sometimes even led by merchants—to "put Christ back into Christmas." One of the oldest complaints about Christmas celebrations was that the folk, in making merry, were profaning the religious character of the Savior's birthday. As early as the fourth century St. Gregory Nazianzen, the bishop of Constantinople and a theologian, urged Christians to commemorate the birth of Jesus in "a heavenly and not after an earthly manner."[2] Postsentimental critics added new complaints, which reflected the pressing social cleavages in the post-1960s United States. The holiday, they charged, was sexist and anti-gay, violated the separation of church and state, and could even cause mental illness.

The Christmas of the dominant culture, even in the nineteenth century, was a hybrid of German, English, and Northern European customs and folklore. At the same time some customs remained separate and distinct, unique to specific groups of Catholics or Protestants. The overall style of celebration might be communal and/or carnivalesque, and could take place in homes, churches, or on the streets. Nonetheless, in most immigrant homes it was not sentimental. Even in home celebrations, youngsters were given small treats, but only on condition of good behavior. Initially Catholic and Protestant immigrants to America celebrated Christmas in their own manner. Later they created a hybrid Christmas, retaining some of the Christmas customs of their homeland while accepting the bountiful, toy-filled U.S. version, with Santa and a floor-to-ceiling tree. Over the course of one or several generations, quite a few distinctive Christmas customs disappeared. But with the resurgence of ethnic identification in the 1970s many groups sought to rediscover the Christmas customs they had lost.

Christmas is a Christian holiday. Nonetheless, a surprising number of Christians, if black or gay, have felt excluded at this season of supposed goodwill to all. This feeling of alienation was especially strong among American Jews. Since the 1840s American Jews have found that the red and green lights and the wreaths and boughs that decorated houses, offices, shops, and streets were hard to ignore, and they have responded to Christmas in several ways. They transformed what had been a minor holiday, Chanukah, into the Jewish alternative to Christmas. And just as many Catholic and Protestant immigrants accepted the abundant American Christmas, so too did some American Jews, despite the great symbolic weight that the celebration of Christmas had for Jews. For all Jews, celebrating Christmas on the one hand might help them become more like other Americans through their enjoyment of the innocent pleasures of a children's and consumer festival but on the other hand might lead to excessive assimilation and a lack of respect for one's own religious heritage.

Colonial Carnivals and Lack of Celebration

In colonial America Christmas was often celebrated as a drunken festival of carousing, begging, overeating, and masquerading.[3] "Christmas without holiday," Southerners used to say, was "like a candle without a wick."[4] Wherever the Anglicans dominated in the seventeenth century, Christmas was a season of drunken and unruly merrymaking. It was also a time when normal values were flouted and reversed. In short, Christmas was a masculine, outdoor holiday rather than a feminine, domestic one. The carnivalesque antics of the Fantastics paled in comparison with door-to-door masquerading that went on at Christmastime, as costumed young men banged on the doors of the wealthy and demanded the best food and drink in the house.

Anthropologists and historians have interpreted this kind of merriment among the common folk as a social safety valve, a way of letting off steam that might otherwise threaten the social order. Young men from the lower ranks were allowed to express resentment of the elite, since it was understood by all that they never intended to overthrow the government or permanently challenge their social betters. Slave owners, shopkeepers, and craftsmen permitted the revels to go on unchecked because they regarded Christmas treats as harmless offerings to placate laborers, servants, or apprentices.[5] Life returned to normal when Christmas ended, except perhaps that a few unmarried girls had been made pregnant and many of the mischiefmakers had had too much to drink.

In part because of such drunken carousing on Christmas, Puritans, Presbyterians, Quakers, Methodists, and Congregationalists in the northern colonies opposed taking any notice of Christmas. The Quakers indicated their disapproval, referring to "the Day called Christmas." Ironically, many Protestant ministers and lay leaders objected to Christmas on religious grounds: they regarded it as a pagan festival, a holiday not mentioned in the New Testament. Particularly damning was the fact that the New Testament contains no references to the day of Jesus' birth or to any Christmas customs. Protestant reformers pointed out that the Church had settled on the date of December 25 in the fourth century, not because of any solid evidence about when Jesus was born but because the date roughly coincided with the winter solstice, when non-Christians held bacchanalian revels. John Calvin's disapproval of Christmas colored the views of Puritans in both England and America. Shops in colonial New England remained open on Christmas Day, as they did in England. The Massachusetts General Court in 1659 fined anyone found feasting or not working on Christmas.[6]

The New England Puritans considered Christmas a day like any other. There were no special church services; only the Sabbath was holy. Aware of the absence of Biblical authority for such a holiday, the Puritan colonists branded Christmas as "Popish" and the merrymaking of the season a "wanton Bacchanalian feast."[7] In the new nation, Congress remained in session on December 25, because the legislators regarded the holiday as a vestige of English custom. Even in early nineteenth century New England and Philadelphia, December 25 was not a special day. Shops and offices stayed open, children were required to attend school, courts convened, legislatures met and voted. Anglicans and the Dutch set the tone in New York City. Christmas there was a gay time for shoppers, who crowded the streets, weighted down with presents.[8] In the rural South, it was a time to shoot off firecrackers and rifles.

The Creation of the Sentimental Christmas

American and British authors and illustrators in the first sixty years of the nineteenth century invented Christmas, weaving together disparate elements from many cultures: the German Christmas tree, the Dutch Christmas cookie, the American Santa (the name Sinter Class was borrowed from the Dutch), the hanging of Christmas stockings (also Dutch), and the British Christmas card. These elements were quickly defined as tradition—in England, a celebration of "Merrie Old England" and in the United States old-fashioned Christmas on the family farm.[9] To writers Washington Irving, Clement Moore, and Charles Dickens, and to cartoonist Thomas Nast goes much of the credit for cobbling together these European cultural remnants and making them into an entirely new whole.[10] The imaginary characters of Tiny Tim, Ebenezer Scrooge, and Nast's jolly, plump Saint Nicholas became symbols of a special time for children, of abundance and festivity, generosity and goodwill.

Of the various foreign borrowings, the most important was the decorated evergreen or fir tree, which was originally a bough rather than a whole tree, placed on a table and decorated with nuts and bonbons. Initially only German immigrants had one. Beginning in the 1830s German families began to invite their neighbors to see the tree. These visitors enjoyed the ritual of opening the parlor doors on Christmas Eve to reveal to children a fir branch in a holder on top of a table and a room ablaze with light from the flames of small lit tapers. Other Americans learned about this custom from reading about it or seeing an illustration in a book or magazine. To the American middle class the decorated Christmas tree was a means of helping achieve the ideal of "a genial family life" and religious piety, living proof that parents cared about their children.[11]

The idea of family holidays being for children fit with the Victorians' belief in the innocence of the child. Middle-class families could view the birth of the Christ child and the loving family scene in the manger as the story of the first affectionate couple, taking delight in welcoming the birth of their firstborn.[12] Such families in the mid-nineteenth century were having on average four or five children rather than seven or eight. With the decline in the birth rate, parents of means could lavish more attention and spending on each child. The mother-child dyad became the symbol of domestic felicity. Children, it was believed, should be safeguarded from rushing into adulthood. The child was viewed less as an economic asset or insurance policy against destitution in old age and more as a repository of the virtues adults had to abandon as they took on a heavy load of responsibilities and worries. There was no better way to reward precious children than to given them special treats at Christmas.

Christmas also commemorated a historical and religious event, the birth of Jesus. American Protestants had taken little note of this anniversary of Christ's birth, because they associated this commemoration with Catholicism. The domestication of Christmas actually increased Protestant religious celebration: churches were gaily decorated with holly and berries and Santa appeared at Sunday school parties bearing gifts. Protestant ministers even came to favor the idea of giving gifts on Christmas rather than New Year's, in order to enhance the religious holiday of Christmas rather than the secular New Year's. As Santa entered consumer culture, he lost his robe and miter and became a secular saint of consumption. But many people gave as gifts Bibles, crosses as jewelry, models of Noah's ark, and illustrations of Jesus, thus warding off the dangers of rampant secularism. Despite Jesus' seeming war against the moneychangers and the rich, Protestant religious writers in the mid-nineteenth century insisted that consumers need not deny themselves the celebration of Christmas. Protestantism also consecrated the family home as a shrine; after all, the family gathered in the parlor to read from the Bible.

Wealthy Americans coupled the desire to buy presents, decorate a tree, and generally celebrate Christmas as a joyous family and religious festival with the impulse to quash the carnivalesque antics of those disturbing the peace. As Stephen Nissenbaum points out in *The Battle for Christmas,* the well-to-do urban elite in antebellum cities feared Christmastime youth gangs and rioters. Violent young men attacked the night watch, beat up local blacks, disrupted black church services, and harassed German immigrants. Shop owners, frightened enough to close early during the Christmas season, demanded police protection; rich families hired private guards to watch their homes. The New Year's parade grew so rowdy that New York City decided to ban it. Threatened and fearful, the urban elite, influenced by temperance agitation, disliked public drunkenness and excessive noise-making and resented intrusions on their privacy.[13] As we have noted, Christmas had been for centuries a time for masculine revels, but the costumed youths going door to door had once been neighbors of the people on whom they called. Now they were strangers, violent and menacing.

Nissenbaum further notes that in antebellum America marauding youths did not confine their revels to poor neighborhoods, but were invading wealthy ones. At Christmas—and at many other times of the year as well—youth gangs, called "Callithumpian bands," disturbed the public peace. The bands played instruments, blowing on penny-trumpets and long tin horns, beating on kettles, setting off firecrackers, and firing off missiles.[14] (They seem to have been more musical and noisy than the Fantastics, and had no connections to the militia.) The growth of urban capitalism increased the disparities of wealth and made the homes of the wealthy one of the targets for resentful and unruly urban mobs. Susan G. Davis views the Callithumpians as a "bridge between the traditional misrule of the English" tradition and a more direct challenge to the political and social order. Precisely because the old watch could not control Callithumpian bands, New York City organized a professional police force in 1828. The urban middle class, worried about the infringement that a police force would impose on their liberty, decided in the end that such paid law enforcers were the only means to control drunken louts. The same Christmas that a New York City newspaper complained about the danger these young men posed, Nissenbaum notes, Clement Moore wrote his poem "A Visit from St. Nicholas," suggesting a cozy way of celebrating Christmas at home, with children tucked snugly in their beds. New York City police may have been able to put an end to carnivalesque celebrations of Christmas, but they persisted much longer in rural areas of the United States and among many ethnic and racial groups, where there was no decisive effort made to stamp them out. Thus, in Polish-American neighborhoods residents went caroling door to door during an approximately two-week Christmas season. Swedes in rural Minnesota had a tradition of masquerading and going house to house on several nights around Christmastime (despite the cold weather). Urban blacks in many cities held open house parties with late night drinking and dancing for many nights during the Christmas holiday.

Women's Role

The sentimental Christmas involved a longer period of holiday preparations for middle-class women than Christmas celebrations in earlier times. Even in the eighteenth and early nineteenth centuries, women at Christmastime spent many hours in the kitchen, making Christmas dinner and baking cookies, fruitcakes, bread, and candy. Gradually, middle-class women also began to decorate the house—and the church—for Christmas, and they acquired a significantly new role, that of Christmas shopper. Whereas men were likely to buy presents at the last minute, women began to plan in advance. Desirous of being able to select an appropriate gift for each person, they tried to calculate the quality of a relationship in monetary terms, and fulfill the secret wishes of the recipient.

The department store, developed first in the 1850s, made Christmas buying a more pleasurable experience for the woman shopper. As William Leach points out, the design of many department stores featured balconied floors opening onto an indoor space, in which attractive staircases were built. Middle-class women could spend hours browsing (and pricing comparable goods), with no expectation that they would buy something, as had been true at dry goods stores. They did not have to bargain for a good price, either. In the older rituals of the season men strolled from house to house or shot off guns and firecrackers out-of-doors. Women had had no comparable recreational outlet. As Christmas shoppers, middle-class women took to the streets, with children in hand, even though they were often jostled in a crowd and eyed by pickpockets. They felt safer inside department stores and could enjoy looking at the merchandise, and being waited on courteously by clerks. Middle-class women became the main buyers of gifts because they were perceived to be caring, concerned with relationships, and had the time to do it. An urban mother was supposed to select durable Christmas gifts for her children and take them downtown to visit Santa or see the performance of clowns in a store.[15]

The number of days women devoted to shopping increased as they spent more time selecting appropriate gifts and pricing goods—and the gift lists grew longer. This was especially true beginning around 1880 as lists expanded because of the craze for "gimcracks," ugly, small, and relatively cheap items given to friends or relatives. Gimcracks were also used as stocking stuffers, but were not ordinarily given as presents to a spouse or a child, who received more expensive presents. Women spent long hours pushing and shoving, standing in line to buy souvenir spoons, glass hat pin holders, or cheap figurines. The craze seemed to end by the 1910 as women, instead of giving gimcracks, began to send cards to casual acquaintances and buy more expensive gifts for relatives and close friends.[16] The amount of time devoted to shopping probably remained the same, however, since the hours saved from buying gimcracks probably went into ordering and mailing Christmas cards.

Almost as soon as it became clear that Christmas would become a festival of store-bought goods, women began to complain about the difficulties in choosing gifts and the waste of money in buying toys that fell apart a few days after they were purchased. By the late nineteenth century middle-class women confessed in their diaries to being "dead tired but ready for Christmas" and noted the crush of crowds in shops.[17] Margaret Deland, a freelance journalist, wrote in *Harper's Bazaar* in 1912 of the trials of the middle-aged mother who sighed at the approach of Christmas and lay awake at night, planning and worrying.[18] She and other magazine writers in the early twentieth century offered a number of solutions to women's overwork: rediscover the spiritual meaning of the holiday; cut back on shopping by buying fewer gifts; give presents only to children. In keeping with the prevailing emphasis of the time on scientific housekeeping and the importance of women's adopting industrial management techniques in homemaking, other writers urged housewives to make lists, organize their kitchens, and plan their chores. Advisors also told women to shop early and mail presents before the crush.

In his editorials in the *Ladies' Home Journal,* Edward Bok made it a yearly Christmas tradition to complain about the unnecessary extravagance and undue stress of Christmas shopping. Bok sympathized with the women who, exhausted from the holiday, became sick the day after Christmas. Although Bok did not support women's suffrage, he believed that homemakers needed to be educated and respected for their role as consumers. Women's problems could be solved by helping the sick, the lonely, and the poor at Christmas, Bok thought. He and the writers for his magazine assumed that a woman did not need to earn wages if her husband was a good provider. Nonetheless, she might need to accept seasonal employment to earn holiday spending money. The *Ladies' Home Journal* even encouraged women to sell subscriptions to the magazine at Christmas for that purpose. In so doing, it recognized that one of women's problems at Christmas was not just exhaustion, but the need for money.[19] Bok was suggesting that women had a right to spend money, and it was this right to consume at Christmas that many women came to believe was a form of highly desirable freedom.

Gifts and Gift-Giving

Which came first, the Christmas gift or the sentimental occasion? The gift came first, but its meaning changed as the holiday became a home and children's festival. As historians Stephen Nissenbaum and Penne

Restad point out, the term "Christmas gift" appeared about 1780, followed soon after by the terms "holiday present" and "Christmas present." There were no terms for such exchanges before, which suggests that the concept did not exist. Treats rather than gifts were the elements of exchange in the community festival or carnival. Many families bestowed food, drink, or some coins out of a sense of obligation, hospitality, or the desire to placate a threatening visitor. They saw themselves compensating for a year's worth of injustices, small and great. Apprentices in seventeenth-century London devised a notion close to what we now call Christmas tipping. Masters placed coins in an earthenware box, which was broken open around Christmas, with the coins divided up among the apprentices.[20]

In the eighteenth century the term "Christmas box" came to refer not just to the box itself but to the act of giving out the coins. By 1810, the term "Christmas box" also meant "present." That year Parson Weems, seeking to boost sales of his biography of George Washington, offered a discount to buyers who bought multiple copies of his book, pointing out that it made a "good Christmas Box" for "young relations." Adults gave Christmas boxes to apprentices, servants, and children—that is, to the social inferiors living in their household. Because the gift-giving suggested a certain noblesse oblige, recipients were not expected to reciprocate.[21]

The first Christmas ads did not specify the identity of either the giver or the recipient, although it was assumed that relatives were buying presents for their kin. Advertising at the holiday season seems to have begun as early as 1738, with a published appeal to buy a book of religious catechism suitable as a New Year's gift. Magazines and newspapers carried advertisements for New Year's gifts, holiday gifts, or Christmas and New Year's gifts up to the 1820s. After that, advertisements for New Year's gifts disappeared almost entirely.

The availability of cheap labor contributed to the growth of new industries such as textile factories, and a mercantile economy. American aristocrats in the eighteenth century on plantations or in cities imported luxury goods from Europe. By the early nineteenth century a broader range of consumers, not just the elite, were beginning to purchase both luxury and consumer goods (textiles, boots, and shoes) that were American, not foreign, made. But the major shopping splurges had been at New Year's, rather than at Christmas. Christmas-only ads began to appear in newspapers in New England and New York in the 1830s. Leigh Eric Schmidt, analyzing the decline of the New Year's gift, notes that merchants and employers wanted to shorten the holiday season that began much before Christmas and lasted past Twelfth Night. They preferred a "Christmas season," one condensed into an evening plus a day, so less time would be lost from work. New Year's Eve also symbolized the rowdiness of drunken youths and the home visiting ritual of gentlemen on New Year's Day (known as calling), whereas Christmas evoked the image of the happy family warming themselves in front of the fire. Moreover, Christmas also had a deeper religious as well as secular resonance than New Year's.[22]

Why did parents, aunts, and uncles give books and small presents to children on Christmas (or on New Year's) when such gifts were clearly indulgent? Why spoil children when most of these presents served no religious purpose?[23] Middle-class people certainly wanted to indulge their whims and prove evidence of their good taste in buying luxury items. More important, as Nissenbaum points out, the gift helped flesh out the meaning of Christmas as a sentimental occasion. The glue that held the family together was sentiment, bonds of affection between husbands and wives, parents and children. People spoke of a gift as "a little token of my affections"; recipients were expected to experience gratitude and love. Horace Greeley in an 1846 *New York Tribune* made clear that giving a present merely to honor an obligation was simply charity, but that a "gift of affection should not so much satisfy a want as express a sentiment, speaking a language which if unmeaning to the general ear, is yet eloquent to the heart of the receiver."[24] The gift was also supposed to be something the recipient would like.[25]

Nonetheless, even the present resembled a treat because of the hierarchical nature of family relations. The imbalance of the gifts (husbands gave wives more expensive gifts than the ones wives gave them, children usually received more than they gave) reflected the fact that the husband was the main breadwinner and his wife and children economic dependents.[26] In the 1810s and 1820s, wives did not give gifts of any kind to their husbands, presumably because so few of them had their own spending allowance. In their kindly and generous beneficence husbands displayed their control of the family's funds.[27]

Christmas in the Twentieth Century

In the twentieth century consumer and popular culture, as well as civic boosterism, reinforced Christmas as a sentimental occasion, but also helped it develop as a community and national festival. One of the most significant developments in that century was the growth in celebrations of Christmas outside the home and church. These were not the raucous carnivals of old, but civic pageants designed to encourage the Dickensian ideal of the Christmas spirit. The first community Christmas tree was set up in Madison Square Park in New York City in 1912. Other towns and villages followed suit. Civic leaders, bands, and adult and school choirs participated in the ceremonial lighting of the community tree. The Christmas pageant, accompanied by carol singing, became popular during World War I as a means of building community spirit.[28] Its main promoters were the local chambers of commerce, the Rotary Club, and women's clubs. The lighting of the White House Christmas tree, first described on radio in 1923, became a national ritual, binding individual families to the nation's celebration. The Christmas tree at the White House was seen as belonging both to "the First Family" and to the entire country, and was originally designed to encourage other outdoor tree ceremonies.[29]

Instead of a folkloric figure eventually becoming a commercial symbol, in the 1930s commerce itself could create popular folklore in the form of a commercial product made to appear as if it were part of authentic oral tradition.[30] During the Christmas season of 1939 Robert May, a copywriter in the advertising department at Montgomery Ward's, wrote a child's fable, which the store handed out as a souvenir booklet. It was the story of an outcast animal, the butt of jokes, who used his ugly red nose as a way of aiding Santa in delivering gifts to children. As had been true of many families during the Great Depression, a childlike figure came to the aid of an adult in a crisis. Winning acceptance on his merit, Rudolph the Red-Nosed Reindeer proved that the worthy individual could turn a liability (a red nose) into an asset (a light that could guide Santa's sleigh).[31] The increasing commercialization of folklore was evident in the contrast between the creative contributions of Clement Moore and Robert May. Clement Moore wrote his poem "A Visit from St. Nicholas" to read to his children. Robert May drafted his children's story to encourage Christmas sales at Montgomery Ward's. As a rival folk figure to Santa,

Rudolph's distinctive image was easily affixed to jewelry, plates, toys, pajamas, and storybooks.[32]

Christmas films, songs, radio, and later television helped to make the holiday a national pageant by giving the impression that the audience was joining others across the country in celebrating Christmas as one big family.[33] The initial function of the Christmas movie was as a visual and action display of the ritual and the consumer objects needed (presents for children handed to them by Mother or Santa Claus). The consumer market at Christmas led to the creation of the Christmas movie, rather than the other way around. Early silent films targeted an audience of children and urban working-class adults. American Mutoscope and Biography Company, founded in 1896, realized that mothers might take their children to see a silent film showing a family receiving Christmas presents, just as they accompanied children on their visit to Santa. Thus, AM&B produced four short films about Christmas, aimed at the children's audience. Thomas Edison's *Christmas Carol* (1910) was more traditional: he adapted a favored Christmas story to the new visual medium. Films such as *Christmas Carol* were morality tales about Christmas in which decency and goodness triumphed.[34] To be sure, the theme of many Christmas movies, such as *Holiday Inn* (1942) and *White Christmas* (1954), was romantic love. Many others, however, elaborated Dickens's view of Christmas, namely that a confused and troubled world needed to embrace charity, peace, hope, and goodwill, abandoning the false attractions of luxury and avarice. The modern world, the movies claimed, had also lost its ability to enjoy magic, myth, fantasy, and belief based solely on faith.

Twentieth-century Christmas songs tended to emphasize longing for home and nostalgia for the Christmas of one's childhood. Bing Crosby first sang the Irving Berlin song "White Christmas" in the 1942 film *Holiday Inn*. The song quickly became a favorite among homesick American troops in World War II. Television Christmas specials in the 1950s and 1960s usually portrayed a return to a hometown, to ancestral roots in England or Scotland, to the national symbolic home of the White House, to the Christian religious home of Bethlehem or the Vatican, or to the living room of a fictional television family. Hallmark and the American Greeting card company often sponsored Christmas television programs in order to direct nostalgia for an old-fashioned Christmas into purchase of their cards.[35]

Deprived Children, Alienated Adults

The sentimentalized Christmas was an indulgent festival for wealthy and middle-class children, who quickly became sated from eating sweets and opening gift after gift. Jane Addams told the story of the impecunious employed older brother living in the tenements near Hull House, who, in responding to the appeals of his younger sisters, stole from a department store a manicure set for one and beads for the other.[36] Shoplifting at Christmas was a consumer strategy of the poor, but so was saving. By the early twentieth century, working-class families, especially working-class mothers, were putting aside small sums to buy children Christmas presents. Their budgets as early as 1907 included the category "gifts." Some immigrants regarded it as a "sacred duty" to send home "Christmas remittances" so that elderly parents in the homeland could "keep the Christmas . . . in a fitting manner."[37] People who had to scrimp to get by, usually wives and children in working-class families, were opening "Christmas club" savings accounts. A shoe factory owner in Carlisle, Pennsylvania, in 1905 first devised the idea of this special seasonal savings account for his workers as a means to encourage thrift. During the year savers deposited their money in the non-interest-bearing account and received a lump sum two weeks before Christmas. In the 1920s the average weekly deposit in a Christmas club account was about $1, but sometimes only pennies a week were added.[38]

Because there was less money to spend, shoppers of modest means had to take considerable time looking for and pricing goods, even though only a few items were actually purchased. In the 1990s low-income families spent a somewhat higher percentage of their income on Christmas gifts than the better off, but the differences were not striking.[39] We may assume that the same pattern existed for families at the beginning of the century. In 1890 the average industrial worker made $486 a year. The cheapest manufactured doll, imported from France, cost $3, or six tenths of one percent of family income. For a family earning $40,000 today, the equivalent purchase would be a doll costing $240. With their Christmas club savings, working-class mothers might buy one or two manufactured toys, perhaps a bright red fire truck for a boy and a doll for a girl. Others presented children with practical gifts—new shoes or a pair of shoes or several pairs of stockings. Parents also gave homemade gifts (socks, a wooden cradle) or handed out an orange or an apple, delicacies unavailable the rest of the year.

The effect of creating a child-oriented holiday, with gift-giving as its central feature, was to make class distinctions visible, if not painful. There was a clear line between the protection and privilege enjoyed by children of the middle class and the scavenging, stealing, and doing without of poor children. Charities and kindly individuals, who gave poor children warm coats and toys for Christmas, tried to bridge the gap in wealth, assuage their guilty feelings, and discharge some of the responsibility they felt for poor children during a festive season of conspicuous abundance.

Between 1900 and 1940, poverty in the United States was most highly concentrated in rural areas of the South and Southwest, where public assistance systems were less developed, and where such assistance often favored whites over people of color. In these regions charitable giving remained personal and paternalist; employers and ministers brought gifts to the family's shack or handed them out in their homes or at churches. Tenants and sharecroppers lived in cabins or shacks without screens, plumbing, electricity, phone service, running water, or sanitary wells. Though the rural poor were of all races, the impoverished in the rural South and the Southwest were disproportionately Mexican-American, black, and Indian. In 1940, two thirds of American households lacked running water; in rural areas the proportion was 60 percent among whites, 95 percent among blacks, and presumably the rates were equally high among Mexican-Americans and Indians. In rural areas there were no outdoor Christmas lights decorating homes because there was no electricity. Girls from such families never owned a store-bought doll; they made their own out of rags.[40]

Some Depression-era adults, reflecting on the impoverished circumstances of their own childhood, would remember happy occasions: an orange in the stocking, a tree decorated with homemade popcorn and strung with cranberries, kindly neighbors handing out treats and toys to all the children who lived nearby. Others looked back on pain, deprivation, stigma, and broken toys distributed by charity workers. African American journalist Carl Rowan, in phrasing that resembled Dickens, wrote, "Christmas usually is the best of time of childhood, but it so often was the worst time of mine." He never forgot his mother's angry reproach to his father: "You can't even provide thirty-five cents for me to buy our son a goddammed cap gun for Christmas!"[41] Rowan's mother blamed her husband for his failure, but her son, like most poor children at Christmastime, did not. As a child growing up during the Great Depression, he sensed that his family did not have the money for toys. As an adult he understood that his father "had been denied formal education and had no way to become 'a good provider.'"[42] His mother's diatribe, however, revealed that, at least for her, the Christmas gift was not only a symbol of parental affection for the child but of a father's breadwinning ability.

By the 1940s Christmas for urban blacks was a consumer festival, to which they brought racial resentments and bitterness. Black Americans often were alienated from the Irving Berlin songs and the Bing Crosby Christmas movies. For them, "white Christmas" meant the desire of whites to live in a world in which black people had no part. Even in the 1930s African Americans had turned to jazz artists, blues singers, and black actors to create their own version of a consumerist but sentimentalized Christmas. In Charles Brown's late 1940s song "Merry Christmas, Baby," an expensive holiday gift symbolized love ("You gave me a diamond ring for Christmas, / Now I'm living in paradise"). By the late 1940s black entertainers were also crossover artists, who may have recorded on a black label that was purchased and heard by whites. Nat King Cole's "The Christmas Song" (1946), famous for his smooth styling of "Chestnuts roasting on an open fire," appealed to both black and white audiences. The same was true of the few black entertainers on television. In the 1950s the *Amos 'n' Andy* Christmas episode on television was as sentimental as other Christmas specials, and showed the audience that goodness and decency triumphed in black as well as white homes. On Christmas Eve Amos read the Lord's Prayer to his daughter as she lay tucked in her bed, while Andy placed a doll for her under the Christmas tree. Still, it is possible that white and black audiences responded differently, with the white audience getting the message that goodness and decency can triumph in black as well as white homes and the black audience noting how the main characters shopped for black dolls in Harlem stores.[43]

Postsentimental Complaints about Christmas

In the 1960s Timothy Leary advised *Cosmopolitan* readers to consult a psychiatrist for Christmas. *Esquire* went so far as to wish readers "a very, very alienated Christmas" and "a disenchanted New Year."[44] In Kurt Vonnegut's *Mother Knight* (1961) the protagonist on death row hopes that at his execution he will not have to listen to a recording of Bing Crosby singing "White Christmas." Attitudes toward Christmas in the 1960s had become cynical, even harsh. Folklorist Sue Samuelson paged through issues of *Seventeen, House Beautiful, Parent's Magazine,* and forty-one other journals from the 1920s to the 1960s. She found a dramatic increase in what she called "festival malaise" in such magazines beginning in the 1950s, although the complaints became more vociferous in the 1960s.[45] Loathing of Christmas became chic; Elvis Presley's "Blue Christmas" was very popular. Songs, movies, and magazine articles reflected this new attitude and helped further it. The postsentimental Christmas was the result of cultural, social, and economic changes, including increases in married women's employment and divorce, the emergence of modern feminism, the resurgence of black nationalism, and a heightened consciousness of ethnicity. Youthful rebels of the 1960s included Christmas as well as Thanksgiving on their list of traditions and established institutions to be ridiculed.

In response to the women's movement, articles in women's magazines in the 1960s and the 1970s featured women at Christmas, tears filling their eyes, complaining of tight schedules and dirty dishes. These articles identified the home as well as the marketplace as the sources of woman's stress. The employed wife and mother no longer had the time to devote to choosing the right gifts, baking gingerbread men, decorating the house, and planning a festive party. She was buying Christmas cookies at the bakery and serving guests platters prepared at the grocery store. Psychiatrists writing in popular magazines claimed that women came down with headaches at Christmas because they were angry at being at the "giving rather than receiving end of things." Women should streamline their holiday efforts to avoid becoming Super-Celebrants, magazine writers and psychiatrists advised. (There were no suggestions, however, that men should share holiday responsibilities, or that children should pitch in.) Much as the working mother should not feel guilty for being employed, so, too, the woman holiday maker, writers explained, should not blame herself for failing to measure up to an ideal of an earlier age.[46]

In the postsentimental period women cut back on their Thanksgiving preparations. Whether they devoted fewer hours to baking Christmas cookies is hard to tell. Certainly sales at bakery counters and purchases of prepared mixes, packages, and platters were brisk. It was difficult to detect any diminution in women's shopping. One suspects that consumers bought from catalogs as well as driving to the mall, rather than the former being a substitute for the latter. Christmas sales increased each year—except for periodic cutbacks during recessions. Some affluent families went skiing on Christmas Day or took a cruise, but most remained closer to home. The postsentimental pattern was more evident in the frenetic arrangements required of blended families and in conflicts among the divorced as to where the children would spend the holiday.

By the 1960s newspapers and television programs were filled with stories of "holiday blues." Psychiatrists had been diagnosing this syndrome since the 1940s, but their research had largely been confined to psychiatric journals. Some of the articles were playful exercises, Freudian analyses of the sexual imagery in Christmas (Santa coming down the chimney was seen by at least one writer as a woman giving birth).[47] Others repeated stereotypical views of lesbians, career women, and single heterosexual women. Writing in this vein, one psychiatrist claimed that two women patients suffered "negative reactions to Christmas." He had learned that these patients dreamed of having a penis that Santa would supply.[48]

Edwin Diamond, a journalist, published an article in 1967 in the *New York Times Magazine* that popularized psychiatric opinion on the question of "holiday blues." For his article Diamond had interviewed psychiatrists, mainly in New York City, and summarized a study done by psychiatrists in Salt Lake City in the 1950s who reported that their patients suffered an emotional reaction to the pressures of Christmas. The psychiatrists claimed that they received more referrals at Christmastime than at other times of the year and that their patients exhibited more symptoms then, too. To Diamond "the holiday blues" were characterized by family quarrels, overeating, excessive drinking, loneliness, and despair.[49] He noted (and subsequent studies bore him out) that suicide was infrequent before and during the holidays, but spiked up just after New Year's Day.[50] The authors of such studies could never determine whether the January increase in suicide was due to the delayed effect of holiday depression or the bleakness of having to endure several more months of winter. Diamond's article also mentioned the unhappiness of divorced or separated parents at Christmas who did not have their children with them or who had to compete for the child's affections with the celebration organized by the other parent.

Diamond's article provided the substance and list of experts for subsequent articles in newspapers and magazines that appeared from the 1970s through the 1990s. Magazine and newspaper writers doled out advice on how to beat the blues, and churches and mental health clinics sponsored workshops.[51] In the 1980s San Francisco gay community organizations established special hotlines for gay people who felt lonely or depressed at Christmas. Some Christmas blues turned out to be simple loneliness, which had been a theme in writing about Christmas as far back as Dickens, and sadness about the death of relatives who had once been present at holiday celebrations, another common theme in Victorian literature about Christmas. What was new was the reliance on the diagnoses and solutions of psychiatric experts and the discussion of the problems of Christmas in terms of psychological depression and even suicide.

While the list of complaints included "family quarrels," the prevalence of family violence, which was found to be common around Christmas and New Year's, was not mentioned.[52] Except for the occasional reference to giddiness at holiday parties or driving while drunk, the articles also did not allude to the impact of holiday drunkenness on families, or the relationship between drinking and family violence. Nor was there any reference to the difficulties homosexuals faced in deciding whether to go home for the holidays. Up to around 1970, articles about "holiday blues" were only a selective inventory of problems recognized by psychologists and psychiatrists. Diamond's article did reflect the dawning recognition that divorce was wreaking havoc with Christmas arrangements. Nonetheless, as the articles about holiday blues became a yearly Christmas tradition, writers expanded the repertoire of complaints to include the suffering of time-squeezed employed mothers, depressed gay people, and interfaith couples.

Symbolic Ethnicity

Born out of a critique of Christmas and the desire to forge group identity, Kwanzaa is the major invented tradition of the postsentimental Christmas period. Black cultural nationalism in the 1960s led to its creation, and inspired a general quest to discover black roots and "tradition." Kwanzaa was not an African cultural legacy, but an entirely new holiday created by American blacks intent on fashioning an African tradition. Maulana Karenga, an advocate of black power and founder of a black nationalist organization called US (as opposed to Them), devised the event in 1966 as a positive cultural response to the Watts riot in a black neighborhood of Los Angeles the previous year, in which 34 people had been killed and at least 900 people injured. Karenga's intention was to use a mythical African past as a tool to develop black unity and cultural pride. In so doing, he put forward the view that American blacks, despite their having spent more than three hundred years on the North American continent and losing direct contact with their African ancestry, were not so much Americans as African people in exile. The word "Kwanzaa" (minus the second *a*) means "first" in Swahili, and was intended to refer to the first fruits of the year. Karenga proposed that Kwanzaa should be celebrated in the home by lighting a candle on each of its seven nights; later on, families gradually added feasts at which they served Southern black cooking. Members of US traveled around the country promoting the holiday, aided by black nationalist leaders in Chicago, Newark, and New Orleans.

The holiday also reflected another longstanding black holiday tradition: alienation from the "white Christmas." In West Africa there were several growing seasons and thus several harvest festivals interspersed throughout the year. There was certainly no African tradition of holding a festival between December 26 and January 1. Karenga had to admit that he chose the post-Christmas season because many American blacks had time off from work and could also buy modest Kwanzaa presents at post-Christmas sales. Karenga claimed that the holiday represented a black nationalist alternative and rejection of Christmas, with its "European cultural accretions of Santa Claus, reindeer, mistletoe, frantic shopping, [and] alienated gift giving."[53]

Initially the appeal of Kwanzaa was limited precisely because it was not a commercial holiday and implied that blacks should not celebrate Christmas. In the early 1980s black entrepreneurs, sponsoring holiday expos, encouraged the commercialization of the holiday. Stores began to sell Kwanzaa greeting cards, wrapping paper, teddy bears, cookbooks, and how-to manuals. Karenga began to worry that Kwanzaa was becoming too commercialized. As Kwanzaa became more popular, public, and consumerist, it increasingly appealed to middle-class blacks. Child care and community centers and public schools began to celebrate the holiday. As Kwanzaa entered the mainstream, it came to be understood as less as an alternative to Christmas than as a necessary supplement to it. Black churches began to hold Kwanzaa celebrations. For the burgeoning black middle class the celebration of Kwanzaa was not only a positive assertion of racial identity, but a response to middle-class unhappiness with the sleights they suffered in racially integrated neighborhoods and workplaces.

Writers in black mainstream (rather than nationalist) publications redefined Kwanzaa as a celebration of the black family, following the national trend toward family togetherness as a response to public fears about the high rate of divorce and worries that the family was "falling apart." An article in *Essence* in the 1980s touted the holiday as an expression of "family values." The writer explained that Kwanzaa was "an opportunity to reinforce the cooperative and family values that they're [a black couple] trying to communicate to their children."[54]

Many racial groups in the United States other than blacks followed the model developed by black nationalists. They, too, looked to ritual as a means of defining their identity and drawing together members of their own group (and excluding others). Taking their cue from black militants, activists in other racial groups demanded Red, Yellow, or Brown Power. Emulating the rhetoric of black nationalism, many white ethnic groups in the 1970s also began to speak about "community," group "strength," "survival," and "cultural richness." Alex Haley's fictional family history, *Roots,* first a book, and then a widely viewed thirteen-part television series in 1977, chronicled the history of one West African and his descendants, traced from capture in Africa to enslavement in America and ultimate freedom. Haley's saga provoked a renewed interest in genealogy and family history in heroic form.

By the 1970s many white Americans had grown dissatisfied with the idea of assimilating into an American society increasingly under attack. The nation began to celebrate pluralism. Americans of various backgrounds were finding the idea of an ethnic Christmas a pleasing alternative to the traditional one, especially as ethnic food became increasingly popular. Nor did the heritage celebrated have to be one's own: anyone could bake Austrian or Swedish Christmas cookies or even stage a *posada.*[55]

A domestic feast at Easter, Thanksgiving, and Christmas at which "ethnic foods" were served became one of few ways otherwise acculturated Americans proved that they belonged to a particular ethnic group. Food and other holiday customs became increasingly flexible, could be done in the home, and did not require isolation from American life. Women took on the work of holding the family together and passing on a "tradition." If the goal was to retain one's ethnic identity—or assert it occasionally—then food and calendric rituals were seen as the best elements to cling to. Many Americans defined ethnicity in terms of family origins, hardships faced, obstacles overcome— and food. The ethnic revival taught that to be an American was to take pride in one's heritage, not conceal it or be ashamed of it. At the same time people wanted to select from the storehouse of customs a few family traditions, and they often confused a tradition unique to their family with one from their group.[56]

The Christmas feast or Christmas cookies, made with recipes from the homeland, served to display "symbolic ethnicity," to maintain some connection with an ethnic identity even when most of the customs once commonly practiced had been lost. In its purest form, symbolic ethnicity is a self-conscious attempt to "feel ethnic" without living an ethnic life—that is, without endogamy, without residing in an ethnic neighborhood, without belonging to an ethnic association, without perceiving oneself as discriminated against on the basis of one's ancestry. Because grandchildren and great-grandchildren of immigrants had lost other bases for ethnic solidarity, they turned to food and holiday celebration as a means of asserting it.

At Christmastime women often made the feast and desserts of their ethnic group, cooking main dishes from scratch. According to a study of the 1980s, Catholic ethnic families in Albany, New York, were more likely to prepare special ethnic foods for holidays, funerals, weddings, and christenings than they were for everyday meals. Only 10 percent of Polish-Americans interviewed ate Polish food regularly. Those who did frequently came from an "undivided background" (both parents from the same group) and attached importance to their ethnic identity. Intermarried couples made culinary compromises. Among the ethnic dishes, breads and desserts were most likely to find their way to the modern table. These took a lot of effort to cook or bake and thus symbolized a way of life that had been lost with the manufacture of so many foodstuffs.[57]

Robb Walsh, the writer of a food column for the *Austin Chronicle* in the 1990s, explained his interest in Ruthenian food in precisely these terms. His mother never cooked a special feast on Christmas Eve, as had his grandmother. Walsh had married a Jew, and his wife and their children lit Chanukah candles for eight nights. After his children were born, Walsh "felt the urge to rediscover my lost culture. I wanted to give my kids their own sense of ethnic identity—especially at Christmastime." He checked out books at the library and visited the parish priest at his grandmother's Catholic church in western Pennsylvania, but he could not find enough information.

He eventually located a professor in Chicago who was able to explain Walsh's grandmother's Christmas customs. The professor took his visitor to the dining room of the Ukrainian Culture Center, where costumed elderly women volunteers served a Christmas Eve dinner (in October) as a demonstration of the cuisine. (After the breakup of the Soviet Union, Ruthenia was absorbed into the Ukraine.) The writer brushed away tears as the women gave him cabbage rolls, dumplings filled with potatoes, and homemade bread. He copied their recipes and began to serve them at home on Christmas Eve. He wrote that "it's the sitting down together at a feast commemorating the holiday in the manner of our ancestors that's important to me." Although he admitted that his children did not enjoy the sour taste of much of the food, he believed he was supplying them with precious memories. "I'm willing to bet," he wrote, "that when I'm a grandpa, they'll ask me for recipes."[58]

Rarely did people go to as much trouble as Robb Walsh, and most of those who did were women. But, like Walsh, only a few were producing recipes remembered from childhood. Sometimes they came across a recipe book or jotted down ingredients while visiting the Old Country. Or they learned how to prepare a dish from friends or from church. Food customs usually persisted because women wanted a sense of connection with their family's past and sought to carry on a heritage, even if it was not one they learned firsthand.[59]

Some historians and social critics claimed that the resurgence of interest in white ethnicity had an unattractive side. They suggested that the nostalgia behind the desire to recover one's roots encouraged the unrealistic belief that adopting a few simple measures would restore long-lost "family values." They also charged that the new ethnicity discouraged marrying an outsider, and stigmatized those who had intermarried. After all, the laments at dinner about Pole no longer marrying Pole could easily spill over into refusing to permit a child to intermarry, or not accepting such a marriage when it occurred. Probably the most serious criticism was that symbolic ethnicity among white ethnics encouraged racism. Sociologists and social commentators often attributed the rise of "white ethnicity" in the 1970s to a backlash against black power, which President Nixon tried to exploit in fashioning a new constituency of "the silent majority." Some in this new constituency of whites argued that many African Americans were poor because they lacked the strong families and work ethic that white immigrant grandparents and parents had.

Robb Walsh's voyage of ethnic self-discovery does not support these condemnations of symbolic ethnicity. Walsh was himself intermarried, and he accepted the fact that his children had dual ethnic identities. There is no evidence that he made any analogy between the economic mobility of Ruthenians and the qualities blacks needed to become successful. In cooking his Christmas meal, he was expressing his love for his children and his desire to give them a culinary ethnicity of equal importance to the ritual of lighting Chanukah candles.

The Postsentimental Christmas Festival

The public Christmas festival was another postsentimental assertion of ethnicity, but one in which the commercialization of Christmas played a more significant role. Main Street merchants, often in small towns, sponsored local Christmas festivals as a means of promoting Christmas shopping. In Lindsborg, Kansas, beginning in the 1960s the Swedish-American celebration of St. Lucia Day in December went hand in hand with the need to promote business in downtown Lindsborg shops. Making the private occasion public was a more common means of preserving ethnic group identity and building community associations; but the celebration of St. Lucia Day among Swedish-Americans spread from the public to the private sphere, and eventually more Swedish-Americans were moved to celebrate St. Lucia Day at home.

The story of the growth of St. Lucia Day celebrations also shows that immigrants did not just preserve old customs, but also gradually discarded many of them as they Americanized. Swedish immigrants to the United States did not commemorate St. Lucia Day when they first arrived in the mid-nineteenth century. But beginning in the 1890s in Sweden, a national romantic movement saw in St. Lucia Day a colorful folk custom to be rediscovered and encouraged. Journalists, doctors, and community leaders, some of them recent immigrants from Sweden, sought to introduce these ideas to Swedish America. The largest Swedish-American organization, the Vasa Order, was begun in 1896 to transmit Swedish cultural heritage in the United States. Gradually the Lucia Fest became an important part of the celebrations of local Vasa Orders throughout the United States. St. Lucia Day provided a pre-Christmas ritual that helped to cement group identity and foster a sense of connection between Swedish-American ethnicity and the newly developing Swedish national identity.[60]

In Lindsborg, Kansas, a town that was two thirds Swedish-American in the 1980s, St. Lucia Day was not widely celebrated until the 1960s. The Vasa Order did not make inroads in the pietistic settlements of the midwest. Swedish immigrants there associated peasant heritage—local dialect, folk songs and tales, superstitions and proverbs—with social inferiority and were eager to abandon their customs when they settled in Kansas. They found on the American Plains abundant land and plenty of room to establish their own churches and schools. For these immigrants their "culture" was not so much their national customs as their religion (usually Lutheran but other Protestant sects as well) and their ethics. These deeply religious immigrants, influenced by Swedish pietism, wanted to replace the revelry and drunkenness so often a part of folk holidays with drinking coffee and hymn singing.

The first public celebration of St. Lucia Day began in Lindsborg in 1962, a decade before the revival of interest in ethnicity. It was initiated by the Lindsborg Chamber of Commerce, which wanted to stimulate downtown shopping. They organized a special program on December 13, which included a visit by Santa, a pantomime of "The Night before Christmas," and the appearance of St. Lucia and two attendants. A couple of hundred shoppers witnessed this first celebration; by 1981, the crowd numbered about two thousand and the event received extensive newspaper and television coverage.[61] Residents saw the festival as a means of "bolstering community pride" in their small town, which was bypassed by a superhighway. One resident in the 1970s explained that "young people desperately need [roots] today," a sense of belonging that the festival and the revived sense of Swedish-American heritage provided. Roots could even strengthen family life by creating a sense of continuity. The celebration led the local newspaper to proclaim that the town was a "special place to live," one that "maintained a reputation of doing distinctive things in a tasteful way."[62] Ethnic display thus became the means for a small town to assert its uniqueness and advantages. In addition, a desire to escape the commercialism and homogeneity of the American shopping mall led tourists to Lindsborg on St. Lucia Day; and the festival also seems to have encouraged some local Swedish-American families unfamiliar with the custom to celebrate the day in their home.

The revival of St. Lucia Day across the country served several functions. In Bishop Hill, Illinois, no longer an entirely Swedish-American settlement as it had been in the 1860s, St. Lucia Day also reinvigorated community pride and business profits from tourism. In Andersonville, a Chicago neighborhood once Swedish-American that was becoming Asian and gay, the celebration helped to anchor the few surviving Swedish-American businesses and define a (long-fading) Swedish identity. In the suburbs of Minneapolis, the event served mainly as an added Christmastime program for the local Swedish-American church and an exercise in nostalgia for women who had been born in Sweden. Swedish-American museums in Minneapolis and Philadelphia looked to the day as a means of generating interest in their organizations.

Jewish Responses to Christmas

How to come to terms with the Christian world's most enticing sentimentalized occasion was a dilemma for American Jews from the first recorded American Jewish home celebration of Christmas in 1848 to the present day.[63] Jews in the United States gradually came to accept the Victorian ideal of the affectionate family, and remade many Jewish holidays into sentimentalized occasions. Many Jews also celebrated Christmas, and in doing so, entered both American society and American Christian life simultaneously. Because of this dual meaning of Christmas, the American Jewish adoption or rejection of the holiday is a more complicated story than it is for Christian ethnic groups. American Jews have responded to Christmas by rejection and resistance, acceptance and accommodation.[64]

The most significant Jewish response has been to imitate Christmas by transforming what had been a festival of limited religious import into a major children's holiday. Before the Civil War American Jews did not observe Chanukah. The Sunday schools of German Jews began to take note of it in the 1870s, probably to provide Jewish children with a celebration comparable to the December festivity in Christian Sunday schools. After World War I, pressures from the marketplace, the child-centeredness of Jewish culture, and the desire to provide a Jewish alternative to Christmas encouraged East European Jews to remake Chanukah into a family gathering, a festive week of games, songs, and music and, most of all, a time to give gifts to children. The Jewish rediscovery of Chanukah was not a protest or critique of Christian culture so much as an effort to fashion an alternative to it.[65]

German Jews in the late nineteenth century disliked mandatory hymn singing and Bible reading in the public schools and mounted many court challenges to such practices. They seem not to have objected to Christmas celebrations in the schools since many of them celebrated it at home. Immigrant Jews from Eastern Europe began to protest public celebration of Christmas in the schools in the early twentieth century. Jewish parents tended to object to Christmas pageants in public schools when Jewish children were the majority of the students; otherwise, they usually kept silent, or their children made individual protests (such as not singing Christmas carols). As Jews became more self-conscious about their identity in the 1960s, they brought lawsuits against the display of Nativity scenes in public squares and stepped up their complaints about the religious content of school Christmas pageants.

The Jewish response to Christmas included acceptance and accommodation as well as protest and imitation. The Christmas tree in the home (sometimes called "a Chanukah bush") stood at the symbolic center of the Jewish debate about celebrating Christmas. Since the late nineteenth century, putting up a Christmas tree has been seen as an index of assimilation, even of Jewish self-hatred. As early as 1888, a "Close Observer" sketched out how putting a Christmas tree in the parlor led the wayward Jew down the road to assimilation, to an "increase of intermarriages . . . disrespect of parents . . . disregard for religion."[66]

Like German Jews, the much larger group of Jewish immigrants from Russia and Poland at the turn of the century were both attracted to Christmas and opposed to the Jewish celebration of the birth of Jesus. But because they were mainly poor and recent immigrants, the holiday for them symbolized not only a Christian ritual but also a festival of American abundance and their desire to participate in a world of plenty. The American Yiddish press in the early twentieth century might report with awe and approval about "Christmas presents" at one moment and complain about the unfair fight between the "quiet, little Chanukah lights and the brightly illuminated, dressed-up and decorated Christmas tree" the next.[67] Having spent very little on holidays in the shtetl, many immigrants found the luxury and beauty of the American Christmas exhilarating. Quite a few newcomers eagerly selected new clothes from pushcarts on Christmas Eve, gaily decorated their tenements with evergreen boughs and holly, attended Christmas parties, and went uptown to gaze admiringly at department store windows. Presenting the settlement worker with a small Christmas gift was a token of respect. Husbands gave Christmas gifts to wives, wives to husbands, the gifts often purchased on the installment plan. How better to show one was not a greenhorn than to purchase Christmas gifts?[68]

In more recent times, the decision to have a Christmas tree depended on the religiosity and family background of a particular Jewish family. About 12 percent of Jews had a tree, according to two surveys, one in 1962 of Kansas City Jews and another a national sample of Jewish households in 1984. A 1990 study, however, noted that the overwhelming majority of intermarried and secular Jews had a Christmas tree.[69] As intermarriage rose, one assumes that the number of Jewish homes having Christmas trees rose as well. Before the 1970s the relatively small proportion of Jews who put up a tree were embarrassed about it. Only this keen sense of shame can explain the emblematic story of the temple president who had to hide his family's Christmas tree from the rabbi or older relatives who came to visit. In one version the wife of the temple president enlists her maid to haul the tree into another room before she lets the rabbi into the house. In other versions, the family hides the tree in a closet so that observant grandparents would not see it.[70]

As Jews became more accepted in American society—and as mainstream publications became more pluralist—Jewish writers adopted the popular confessional tone about their longing for the Gentiles' favorite holiday. In *Redbook* and *Ladies' Home Journal* Jewish writers explained that they had decided to put up a tree because they had been deprived of one as a child or had intermarried. Of these confessions, those of Anne Roiphe, a Jew who had a Jewish husband, made the biggest splash because they appeared in the *New York Times* (in

1978).[71] In "Christmas Comes to a Jewish Home" she admitted that despite a few guilt pangs, she enjoyed enormously hosting an annual holiday party, decorating her tree, and reading to her children from Dylan Thomas's "A Child's Christmas in Wales." Whereas in earlier decades Jews debated the merits of celebrating Christmas in general terms, Roiphe and others in the 1970s broke new ground by owning up to actual practice. In response to her article Roiphe received dozens of threatening phone calls. The *Times* printed a large number of responses, mainly from other Jews, who pitied her or considered her a traitor to her religion.[72] More common, and more accepted, were the anguished confessions of the intermarried, especially those who had young children.

Christmas past and Christmas present are both religious and secular holidays, a season as well as a day, a series of public and private occasions. Nonetheless, both the style of celebration and the meanings attached to Christmas have undergone a dramatic shift. Historians have emphasized the first phase of the transformation, the decline of the carnivalesque or the unnoticed Christmas and the rise of the sentimental and commercial one. The sentimental Christmas, which persisted for almost two centuries, itself underwent a number of reinventions: it became a public festival, an Americanizing one, a standardized national, and then global, holiday. The sentimental Christmas revealed divisions along class lines, between parlors loaded with presents and those containing few or none at all. These fissures persisted, even though Christmas charities tried to bridge them.

To be sure, Christmas was more religious and less nationalist than Thanksgiving. It emerged as a domestic occasion a couple of decades before Thanksgiving, because advertisers and merchants, not simply a single publicist like Sarah Josepha Hale, recognized its potential. Mass production, mass consumption, and later mass marketing were important in the development of the sentimental Christmas and continue to provide the holiday with its vitality. Because Christmas is a major gift-giving occasion, it is also the most exciting. The most exhausting for the middle-class mother, the most anticipated for children, the most difficult to ignore for indigent families, Christmas is also the holiday most criticized for its materialist excess.

The immigrants' contribution to Thanksgiving was mainly a side channel or supplement, whereas Northern Europeans, especially Germans, were central to the multiple customs of Christmas. Although the pull of ethnicity at Thanksgiving mainly fostered inclusion, Christmas allowed for many ethnic variations. Different religions, family needs, and local practices contributed to the retention of many ethnic Christmas customs over several generations.

At least since the early nineteenth century, the question of whether to celebrate Christmas has carried heavy symbolic weight among American Jews. They have perceived the glitter and tokenism of the dominant culture in the celebration of Christmas, even if Jewish songwriter Irving Berlin helped to create it. The options as to how and what to celebrate remained the same, even as the holiday become more ubiquitous. The response of Jews varied by national origin and the degree to which they felt emboldened to assert their rights as Jews. By the 1960s, Jews protested against public displays as confidence grew and fears of anti-Semitic attacks subsided. In the postsentimental era, possible responses included the assertion of group rights (lawsuits against public Nativity scenes) and the mixing of traditions among interfaith couples, as they lit Chanukah candles and placed wrapped gifts under the tree.

The most significant invented tradition of the postsentimental era was Kwanzaa. It fused the search for an African identity with the black critique of the white Christmas. Along with black and Jewish consciousness, the postsentimental Christmas also brought to the surface fault lines created by divorce and intermarriage, feminism, and gay liberation, just as American Indians had challenged the national myth of inclusion of Thanksgiving. In the 1960s and later blacks, gay people, and Jews began to ask how they fit into the nation's celebration of Christmas.

The holiday that was a special time of year for children had by then also come to be seen as a special time of year to be ethnic. In the last thirty years of the twentieth century Americans could take pride in combining ethnic and national identity. Ethnicity came to be seen as the source of family holiday traditions. What some perceived as shallow others accepted as the only kind of identification that was possible for people who did not wish to lead lives entirely tied to ethnic community. Christmas ethnicity made no particular demands on individuals. Families selected customs from diverse sources rather than from a single one, fragmenting and rearranging customs to create a truly postsentimental form of Christmas celebration.

CHAPTER FOUR

Easter Breads and Bunnies

Jes' a little bit o' feller—I remember still—
Ust to almost cry fer Christmas, like a youngster will.
Fourth o' July's nothin' to it! New Year's ain't a smell!
Easter Sunday—Circus Day—jes' all dead in the shell!

—JAMES WHITCOMB RILEY, 1890

On a par with Circus Day, even in the 1890s Easter lacked the magnetism of Christmas, or even the charming simplicity of Thanksgiving. A little less than a century later Easter placed as the third most important holiday for taking photographs, after Christmas and Thanksgiving.[1] For the sending of flowers, Easter also ranked third, behind Christmas and Mother's Day. In terms of greeting cards sold in the 1980s, Easter came in fifth, behind Christmas, birthdays, St. Valentine's Day, and Mother's Day. Easter was also the third major holiday for the purchase of chocolates, after Christmas and Halloween. Nor was the holiday a time for the exchange of family greetings. The average American did not call home on Easter. Long distance telephoning increased by only about 10 percent over regular Sunday calls on Easter in the 1980s, in comparison with a doubling of normal telephone usage on Christmas.[2]

The lack of American Jewish envy of Easter provides additional evidence of the holiday's failure to captivate. Many a Jewish novelist or short story writer could hardly suppress longing for the "house festivities" at Christmas.[3] Few Jewish parents commented on the dilemma of providing a Jewish child with an Easter basket or some colored eggs.[4] Sporadic Jewish protests against Easter celebrations in the public schools pale in comparison with Jewish complaints about Christmas pageants. The reason for the difference is that American Jews have never perceived Easter to be as seductive a holiday as Christmas.[5] Passover falls at the same time of year as Easter, yet the main influence of Easter on Passover is the chocolate-covered matzoh.

One reason Easter has not found its way into American hearts is that it is held on a Sunday and therefore does not offer a holiday from work. Because of this, Easter has been somewhat more difficult to commercialize. Merchants could easily prepare for Christmas because it fell on a predictable date, whereas Easter was a "movable feast" whose date of celebration varied each year. In fact, George Eastman, the founder of Kodak, recognized that the "wandering" date of Easter made advance planning more difficult for the apparel and tourist industries (and thus for the sale of cameras and film). Along with other businessmen, Eastman campaigned in 1927 for a fixed date for Easter in the middle of April, but his effort failed.[6]

The evolution of Easter as a sentimental occasion follows the outlines already described for Thanksgiving and Christmas. It became a sentimental occasion in the 1870s, several decades later than these two other holidays, for several reasons. Easter was more difficult to commercialize, and American Protestants still considered it a popish holiday. Although Easter was eventually redefined as a children's festival, there was no need for a third holiday of family homecoming. The custom of purchasing new clothes at Easter made the holiday first into a fashion show, and then a parade of the wealthy. Public school pageants, advertising, popular songs, and movies enhanced these new definitions of Easter. Even so, Easter stood so much in the shadow of Christmas that it provoked very little of the kind of anguish and alienation that lead to a postsentimental holiday.

Easter remains a religious holiday and a sentimental occasion that falls on a Sunday. For centuries the word also referred to a much longer season, culminating in processions and special services on Easter Sunday. This longer season included carnivals before the Easter season began and in the days and weeks after Easter Sunday. The sharp division between a few rowdy days before Easter and a couple of sacred ones has persisted, even though the celebration of pre-Easter carnival has dwindled: Mardi Gras is celebrated only in New Orleans and Cajun country, and April Fool's Day, though more widely acknowledged, is a decidedly minor event.

One of the few postsentimental features of Easter in the late twentieth century was the importance of the holiday in defining modern religious and ethnic identity. For many Catholics, Lutherans, and Eastern

Orthodox Christians Easter has retained a dual meaning as both a religious day and a time for family gathering. The feast often followed—or perhaps was preceded the night before—by Easter mass. Among Catholics Palm Sunday, Holy Week, and Easter Sunday were more religiously significant than among many Protestant denominations. Many Catholic and Eastern Orthodox immigrants celebrated the Easter season with distinctive customs, some of which were retained in subsequent generations. Parents often photographed children wearing their new clothes at Easter, but they also attended church and served traditional foods at a family feast. Many ethnic groups fused the American consumer holiday with the traditional one. Yet these groups also changed their ranking of holidays to the American one, in assigning Easter less importance than Christmas.[7]

Carnival Days

In the contemporary United States Easter is still a season as well as a special day. The season begins on Ash Wednesday, the first day of Lent, and ends on Easter Sunday. Church services and processions punctuate the entire week preceding Easter (called Holy Week), beginning with Palm Sunday. Good Friday, which commemorates the crucifixion of Christ, is a holiday from work in many places and a legal holiday in several states. The Easter season used to be longer. It began with Epiphany, the sixth of January, and extended fifty days past Easter to Whitsuntide (also called Pentecost). During the lengthier season there were pre- and post-Lenten festivities, and Lent itself, forty days of fasting, repentance, and sexual abstinence. Lent dragged on so long that some groups (Italian Americans, blacks in Louisiana) held celebrations at about the halfway point.

As with Christmas, the Puritans did not approve of observing a holiday so deeply associated with Catholicism. When Oliver Cromwell assumed power in England, the Parliament he controlled banned outright the celebration of Easter, Lent, and Whitsuntide as well as Christmas. Puritans in the American colonies followed suit.[8] Colonial Quakers, Methodists, and Presbyterians also found Easter too Catholic to be worthy of note. Quakers and other Protestants in colonial Pennsylvania forbade their German servants from attending services on Good Friday.[9] But the popular customs of the Easter season could not be suppressed so easily.[10] Like most other European festive traditions transplanted to America, carnival was compressed into a few days of revelry: Shrove Tuesday (the day before Lent), Easter Monday and Tuesday (the two days following Easter Sunday), and Whitsuntide, fifty days after Easter.

Shrove Tuesday was distinguished by a number of food customs as well as by masquerading and sports competitions involving the torture of animals. The name for the day derived from the practice of shriving, or purifying oneself of sins; the English translation of Mardi Gras, or Fat Tuesday, referred to the practice of eating fats and other rich foods still in the larder before discarding them for Lent. These prohibited foods included meat, butter, cheese, milk, eggs, lard (because it was made from animal fat), and bacon. During the days immediately prior to Lent families increased their consumption of rich foods and pastries. English women used up fats, milk, and eggs in making pancakes and fritters; German hausfraus fried donuts and baked yeastless cakes.[11]

Carnival was a style of pre-Easter celebration not confined to Mardi Gras in New Orleans. In colonial times, there were carnivals throughout the Spanish, Dutch, French, and English colonies.[12] The two days after Easter were also popular days for revelry and heavy drinking in much of colonial America and in the new republic. On Southern plantations Christmas was the main holiday for slaves, although some planters permitted slaves to celebrate Easter as a day off from work and a time for drunkenness and sexual license—if planting was on schedule.[13] A few antebellum masters granted an extra holiday on Easter Monday when, as one ex-slave recalled, "we frolicked an' danced all day long."[14]

Until the end of the nineteenth century men, sometimes farmers' servants and hired hands, held sporting contests on Shrove Tuesday and Easter Monday. One of these contests was gander pulling, or "riding the goose," which involved tearing at the bird's flesh before finally killing it. Young men, egged on by a shouting crowd of inebriated men and women "of the lower sort," engaged in this sport not just for its excitement but also to prove they were "real men," physically strong, brave, competitive, and willing to take risks.[15]

To set up the game an old gander was swabbed with grease and soft soap and hung by its heels from a rope attached to the branch of a tree. Mounted on a horse, the contestant rode past the goose at full speed, trying to break its neck, and rip off its head with his bare hands. Many riders fell off their horses while attempting this deed, some the worse for whiskey. Others could not get hold of the gander's neck because it had been so well greased. Gander pulling was not completely one-sided: the gander sometimes snapped off the finger or thumb of its assailant. In their brief lunges, some of the men on horseback would stretch or rip the gander's skin and cause hemorrhaging while the goose yelped in pain. To the man who killed the gander were awarded the gander and some of the pot from the betting pool.[16]

Among Pennsylvania Germans Easter Monday was the secular and frivolous second day of the holiday, equivalent to the day after Christmas, which they also celebrated as a secular holiday.[17] A letter in 1782 indicates that the Pennsylvania Germans kept Easter Monday as a "time for frolicking among them."[18] It was also a day for church dedications and shooting matches. Hucksters congregated to sell whiskey to the marksmen. The militia also often paraded on Easter Monday, and the Fantastics tagged along.[19] Lancaster, Pennsylvania, the center of Pennsylvania German settlement, closed its schools on Easter Monday as late as 1882.[20]

The post-Easter holiday of Whitsuntide—often also called Pentecost—was also a day (in some places, up to a week) when "restraints are flung off." Whitsuntide celebrated the reception of the holy spirit by Jesus' disciples; Anglican, Lutheran, and Huguenot churches held special services. The Dutch name for it, Pfingsten, easily became "Pinkster" in the American colonies. As the Dutch assimilated into Anglo culture around the time of the American Revolution, they no longer observed the holiday. But African Americans in New Jersey and New York, who learned about Pinkster from Dutch slave owners, did. In New Jersey and New York City, Pinkster became a syncretic combination of Dutch, English, German, French, and African cultures. The main West African contribution was the drumming and stringed instruments, and the songs. With their emphasis on role reversal, the songs resembled West African songs of derision.[21]

Because of the fun and the syncretic character of the holiday, Pinkster attracted Indian, German, Dutch, and French revelers to encampments on Capitol Hill in Albany, New York, between 1790 and 1811. The celebration included drumming, processions, and Guinea dancing (lengthy and wild dancing by men and women to the beat of an African drum, which ended in the embrace of couples in feigned—or actual—sexual intercourse). Sexually explicit Guinea dancing shocked the burghers of Albany. So did the easy association in "sin and folly" of blacks and "a certain class of whites" at the encampment. The Albany city council in 1811 passed an ordinance, banning music, the selling of liquor and food, gambling, dancing, and parading on Pinkster.[22] While this ordinance ended Pinkster in Albany, celebrations persisted on Long Island until the late nineteenth century.[23] In addition, middle-class and civic-minded blacks, emancipated from slavery in New York, favored parades as a demonstration of their sobriety, good citizenship, and racial pride.[24] Carnival customs have persisted in rural and urban areas of Alabama, Louisiana, and Texas. In the urban areas, carnival was taken up by the local elites and was perceived as good for business.

Eliminating distinctive regional and ethnic customs of carnival was unrelated to the emergence of Easter (or for that matter Thanksgiving) as a sentimental occasion. Boisterousness occurred during the days before Lent or the days following Easter, not during Holy Week. More important, the reformers' attempts to eliminate raucous Easter celebrations began decades before the domestication of Easter in the 1870s. The two developments had nothing to do with each other.

The Reinvention of Easter

German immigrants showed their fellow Americans how to make Easter more sentimental and festive, just as they had done for Christmas. They knew how to make the egg into a festive object by dying it, making chocolate in its shape, hanging it from a tree, and hunting for it in a children's game. But their major contribution was the Easter Bunny, which they called the Easter hare. The hare was a secular symbol; it never appeared in Christian symbolism. There are various stories about how the hare came to be a German springtime and then Easter symbol. One was that since the hare is born with its eyes open, it resembles the full moon, the time for the celebration of Easter. Another was that the female hare, which can give birth to several litters in a year, has a well-deserved reputation as an emblem of fertility, an appropriate symbol for a spring festival.

The idea of an Easter hare who laid eggs was not an ancient Frankish tradition, but one that arose around the time of the Protestant reformation. The first reference to the mammal who brings eggs dates from a German book published in 1572.[25] The German custom of children hunting for eggs did not appear before 1662.[26] (This was about the same time as the first record of a German Christmas tree, in Alsace.) Because the egg hunt was a localized German custom, the early German immigrants to William Penn's colony in the 1680s, who were mainly from the Rhineland, did not practice it. Newly arriving German immigrants in the late eighteenth and early nineteenth centuries did. They brought to America egg hunts and egg coloring, but their American neighbors did not adopt these customs until after the Civil War.[27] This lack of interest in the German customs is somewhat puzzling, since we know Americans in the 1830s adopted the German Christmas custom of lighting candles on a table-top tree branch.

After the Civil War non-German parents began to notice that children loved to hunt for colored eggs. Anthropologist Cindy Dell Clark explains why children so enjoy this game. They like to search and find, thrusting their hands into the inner recesses of couches or the thickest part of bushes, just as they enjoy the game of hide-and-seek. The game is not too challenging: most children can find colored eggs without much frustration. The egg hunt, she concludes, provides "the optimal state of involvement, without boring children or making them anxious."[28] In addition, although the child has to make an effort to find randomly hidden eggs and must often compete with siblings in the contest, he or she is relatively free from parental control.[29]

Well-to-do non-Germans not only took up the egg hunt but also changed the name of the German hare to the Easter Bunny. Children's and women's magazines and newspapers in the late nineteenth century explained how to color eggs and conveyed the story of the Easter rabbit or bunny. Candy makers (who also dyed eggs for women who did not want to color them) used the same term for their seasonal confections, perhaps because the hare was relatively uncommon in North America, whereas rabbits were ubiquitous.[30] Another factor may be that greeting card makers preferred the terms "bunny" and "rabbit" to "hare"; most Easter greeting cards, however, were decorated with crosses or lilies.

The Easter Bunny was to Easter what Santa Claus was to Christmas, a symbol of festivity and abundance, which encouraged adults to buy toys and candy for children. Both figures transported magical objects to children, whether toys made at the North Pole or colored eggs. Both characters became kinder as they Americanized and took on middle-class attitudes toward the innocence of children. Santa and the rabbit once punished disobedient children; during most of the nineteenth century Santa put coal in their stockings, and the rabbit placed pellets of manure in Easter baskets. By the late nineteenth century these folk figures were bestowing gifts on all children, regardless of their child's behavior. Also, merchants began to hire impersonators of both mythical characters to entice shoppers into stores.[31]

As a domestic occasion, Easter, like Christmas, is a holiday of the sweet tooth. As late as the nineteenth century most people had to satisfy a craving for sweets by using molasses, honey, or syrup made from tree sap. Refined sugar was still a luxury, used mainly by wealthy people. The delightful combination of chocolate and refined sugar was central to the creation of an Easter consumer market, just as the gift book spurred the growth of the commercialization of Christmas. Two major developments in the manufacture of chocolate made possible the chocolate bunny: the invention in Holland of a process for separating cocoa butter from the cocoa bean; and the mixing of cocoa butter with sugar to make a thin paste that could be molded into shapes. As a result of these two developments, cocoa was no longer consumed simply as a beverage, but could be eaten as a sweet.

In Europe the making of chocolate candy was a craft, its product a luxury available for people of means. French, German, and English confectioners produced handmade chocolate candy molded into pleasing shapes. The French and Germans were making chocolate Easter eggs in the early nineteenth century; English confectioners were offering hollow chocolate eggs for sale in the 1870s. German-American candy makers first made chocolate bunnies two decades later. Skeptics claimed that no one would want to buy a chocolate pig, bunny, or egg. But these candy objects of art proved wildly successful.[32]

The mechanization of candy manufacture lowered the cost of making candy and led to the creation other consumer products, including the chocolate creamed egg.[33] By World War I, troops received a manufactured chocolate bar as a quick source of energy. As a result of mechanization, the growth of candy manufacturing companies, and wartime uses of chocolate candy, candy became an everyday indulgence for the masses, rather than one enjoyed mainly by the more privileged at Christmas or Easter. Even so, Easter candy was special, since it was often shaped like a bunny or decorated with elaborate piping.[34]

The Easter Parade and Easter Finery

Protestant America discovered Easter as a "pastel wonderland" in the 1870s, even before the day was a holiday for chocolate candy. Magazines and newspapers began to publish Easter poems and stories. Ministers from various Protestant denominations delivered Easter sermons in churches draped with lilies, tulips, and crocuses. Sunday schools created special Easter programs, as they did at Christmas, and began to give Easter eggs to children.[35] President Rutherford B. Hayes held the first Easter egg roll on the White House lawn in 1879, although Dolley Madison had begun the practice of rolling eggs on the Capitol lawn more than half a century earlier.[36] The Easter parade in New York City emerged in the 1870s and quickly became the "great fashion show of the year." It began when curious and well-dressed churchgoers trooped from St. Patrick's to other churches on Fifth Avenue to observe each church's floral decorations. It eventually became a fashion procession along Fifth Avenue after church services had ended. The idea of the Easter parade quickly spread from New York City to the Atlantic City boardwalk, and from there to many other cities and towns.

Leigh Eric Schmidt argues that the New York City fashion parade helped make Easter a highly feminine as well as sentimental holiday. The parade was also a display of the beauty and style of the well-to-do. Not an interracial gathering like Pinkster, it was nonetheless interethnic, since the wealthy churchgoers were both Catholic, perhaps Irish, and Protestant, presumably Irish, Scottish, and English. Instead of the parade's being a rowdy street carnival or public parade dominated by men from fire companies marching in units, it was a more genteel affair, with wealthy women outfitted in lace, linen, and bows strolling down Fifth Avenue on the arm of their male escorts. The Easter parade "was preeminently about women in public procession," Schmidt notes. In purchasing and wearing hats made out of straw and ribbons and topped with feathers, women were shedding the image of themselves as meek and modest and asserting a colorful and dominating public presence.[37]

Those who claimed that Easter could never compete with Christmas because it was the story of death and resurrection rather than birth and childhood were proven wrong. Theologian Harvey Cox noted that the problem for Easter is that "it is easier for people to celebrate a holiday about a mother and child than it is to celebrate it about someone coming back from the dead."[38] True, Easter never approached the popularity of Christmas; but after the unprecedented slaughter of the Civil War, the public wanted to believe one could find redemption through death. Many wealthy Victorians decorated their parlors and hallways at Easter and created floral tributes to their beloved dead. In thinking about everlasting life, grieving families could demonstrate the eternity of "domestic affections."[39] The Civil War generated a number of rituals for the commemoration of death, by no means limited to Easter. Women, visiting the graves of the fallen, inspired the development of Memorial Day in the post–Civil War South and of its Northern version, Decoration Day. The cult of Lincoln reinforced the imagery of death and resurrection at Easter. The "powerful western fallen star," as Walt Whitman referred to the slain president, had been murdered on Good Friday. The Sunday before, Palm Sunday, Lee had surrendered at Appomattox. Moreover, the making of Easter into a more recognized holiday was part of a general crowding of the calendar that occurred between the Civil War and World War I. Along with Memorial Day and Decoration Day, the Civil War also led to commemorations of the birthdays of Robert E. Lee, Jefferson Davis, and of course Abraham Lincoln, and the celebration of many new holidays, from Labor Day to Arbor Day.[40] Although Easter might have a morose character on a rainy Sunday, when the sun was shining it was a springtime festival, a time to celebrate the chirping of birds and the appearance of the first blades of green grass.

As previously noted, Easter, occurring on a movable date, proved difficult to commercialize. In fact, the domestication of Easter preceded its commercialization, whereas at Christmas, the domestic and the commercial arose simultaneously. Businesses were slow to recognize the commercial possibilities of Easter. While milliners and clothing manufacturers advertised spring fashions beginning in the 1850s, they did not mention Easter. After wealthy New Yorkers began their fashion promenade on Easter Sunday, merchants saw the benefits in advertising spring finery specifically for Easter. In 1878 Macy's started to do so, and other New York City department stores followed three or four years later. By the 1890s merchants identified the fashion-conscious shop girl and the stylish matron as their chief market for Easter clothes.[41]

Women's Role

In the last third of the nineteenth century middle-class women's preparations for Easter were as extensive as those for Christmas, since they involved cooking, housecleaning, decorating the church, purchasing and sending cards, helping children to color eggs, and shopping. The one element that was more time-consuming at Easter than at Christmas was the housecleaning. Mothers and daughters washed the floors and windows, laundered and ironed the curtains, and scrubbed the floors. Men rarely had any housework responsibilities, but boys might be put to work in the yard.[42] The most significant difference between the two holidays was the importance of shopping for clothes, especially for women's and children's apparel.[43] A man did not feel compelled to buy a new suit for Easter. (The major touch of springtime in male dress might be a sprig of green pinned to a suit lapel.)[44] The purchase of matching outfits and straw bonnets for mother and daughter expressed a mother's desire to make her daughter in her own image, and to show the world that the two of them formed a single unit.

Fancy Easter outfits for mother and children were a departure from the typical family spending pattern on clothes of the late nineteenth century. In the working class, the father, as the main provider, required work clothes, and his clothing needs came first. The middle class reversed this pattern, and gradually the working class followed. Among the middle class an equal amount of money was spent on men's and women's clothes (one historian asserts that this change in spending pattern had occurred by the 1920s) and, later, more money went for women's than men's clothes. Spending on a new suit for a boy was more discretionary and seemed to depend on the family's prosperity. At the Easter fashion show women and children of the middle-class family demonstrated they could meet a certain standard of "appearance and style." The main familial role of a middle-class husband was as a good provider. A husband's generous allowance to his wife to purchase Easter finery proved his financial success.[45]

Thus the Easter outfit, like the large pile of Christmas presents and the Thanksgiving turkey, were symbolic markers of the privileges of wealth and the distinctions between social classes. The working class accepted the notion that children needed new clothes at Easter, but regarded women's display as optional. The good working-class mother sacrificed her leisure on behalf of her children. Careful planning and scrimping by the working-class mother of the late nineteenth and first half of the twentieth century was required to buy purses, hats, gloves, shoes, and stockings. She often purchased new outfits for her children while she did without.[46] Similarly, many mothers or sisters sewed new clothes for the children for Easter and made Easter baskets rather than buying them. Grown daughters recalled mothers who spent weeks staying up evenings or even all night to sew dresses for Easter.[47] The homemade Easter dress symbolized maternal sacrifice and denoted family penury.

Being a child deprived of new Easter clothes was as great a stigma as not receiving skates for Christmas. By the hundreds of thousands Depression-era children wrote to Eleanor Roosevelt because they had read in the newspapers of how she cared about the poor. Children most often requested new clothes or money to buy them. The children of the downwardly mobile seem to have been the most ashamed of their clothing, since they had a standard of affluence against which to measure their reduced circumstances. Thus, a New Jersey girl of fifteen told the First Lady, "We were once the richest people in our town but now we are the lowest, considered the worst people of Port Morris. For Easter some friends of mine are thinking of getting new outfits and I just have to listen to them. How I wish I could have at least a coat."[48]

If deprivation could produce shame, display in excess could lead to guilt. Of all the domestic occasions, Easter, because of its strong association with fashion, became the most woman-blaming holiday, at which middle-class and wealthy women became the prime target. The symbol of the commercialism of the holiday, of its unholy mixture of sacred and profane, was the woman in her Easter bonnet and pastel dress. The fashion show, the writer of an etiquette book from the 1870s claimed, made clear that "the gewgawed devotees" attended church on Easter to see what other women were wearing and to show off their finery. What made it worse, according to one etiquette book from 1873, was that women wearing their hats with fine feathers discouraged the impoverished from attending church on Easter Sunday because the poor were "so awed by the pretension of superior dress."[49] Women in the New York City Easter parade were the initial objects of scorn, since they were showing off their wealth for all to see. Muckrakers broadened their attack to include all women who purchased artificial flowers for their hats. These fashion plates, they charged, were concerned only with show and cared nothing about the sweatshop conditions and the exploitation of child labor where their bonnets were made.[50]

By the end of the 1920s ministers took on the role of social scolds, delivering sermons from the pulpit or writing in Christian magazines. One clergyman in the *Christian Century* in 1932 contrasted the suffering of Christ carrying his heavy wooden cross with the "fanfaronade of women in silks and furs" on Easter Sunday.[51] The informality of post-1960s America tended to silence much of this criticism. Instead ministers and priests complained about parishioners in blue jeans and dirty ski jackets, who no longer showed respect for Easter Sunday by wearing formal dress.[52]

The Development of the Sentimental Occasion

Like Christmas, Easter was a gift-giving holiday among family, female friends, or sweethearts, although the range of items given was narrower. A beau might give his sweetheart a jewel box in the shape of an egg; a woman might give her female friend stationery with crosses or lilies on it.[53] The most common purchases for Easter were clothes, cards, plants and flowers, stationery, and candy. An article in the *New York Times* in 1885 suggested that the Easter trade in greeting cards was second to Christmas, in contrast to modern times, where Easter ranks fifth.[54]

As Leigh Eric Schmidt notes, flowers, given as a gift, expressed a symbolic language of sorrow, hope, or the arrival of spring. One of the most common Easter gifts was a plant or bouquet of flowers. In 1882 a florist imported a simple white lily from Japan, which quickly was dubbed the Easter lily. Florists gradually recognized the sales potential of this flower. Initially, they sold lilies formed into floral crosses, suitable for church decoration. Then they began to offer pots of lilies to be taken home or given as a gift.[55]

One might think that Easter would have been incompatible with gift-giving and consumer culture because its central themes were the Christian ones of self-sacrifice and self-abnegation. Two explanations for gift-giving at Easter may be suggested. First, Easter was not simply a holiday of death, but of springtime, and gift-givers were symbolically taking note of the arrival of the growing season. Second, even the drama of crucifixion and resurrection had commercial appeal. Schmidt wrote that the cross was just as easily inserted as the Easter Bunny into department and jewelry store windows. Indeed, some jewelry stores even festooned a cross with diamonds and gold trinkets as a fetching window display. L. Frank Baum, a store window designer before he wrote *The Wizard of Oz*, professed as much. "The cross," he wrote, "is the principal emblem of Easter and is used in connection with many displays, being suitable for any line of merchandise. To be most effective it should be a floral cross."[56] When adorned with lilies, the larger-than-life cross on the main floor of a department store lost its association with pain, suffering, and death, and was transformed into a symbol of "legitimate luxury, elegance, and indulgence."[57] Although merchants may have decorated their store to show their piety, the cross was more often used to promote the sale of gloves, hats, and jewelry. To be sure, Baum also designed other window displays during the Easter season, such as a gigantic moving Easter egg and a huge collection of Easter flowers circulating on a conveyor belt.[58]

Families in the sentimental era celebrated Easter by going to church, having a large breakfast afterward, and hiding colored eggs for children to find. Middle-class mothers hosted parties for children on Easter weekend, perhaps on the day before Easter. The higher up the social scale, the more Easter festivity displayed status and prestige. The family celebration had several elements, in which the decorative elements of floral and pastel colors served as symbols of springtime. At Easter parties the mother who followed advice in the women's magazines adorned her table with floral arrangements of irises, tulips, anemones, pastel napkins, dishes of colored eggs or pastel candies, and served a color-coded menu, including, in one case, pistachio ice cream in the shape of a lily.[59]

The Bunny was the main symbol of Easter, but there was no single dish that was as important to Easter as the turkey was to Thanksgiving. Perhaps for this reason the Easter feast was not as important as Thanksgiving. The main dish could be lamb, ham, or turkey. The turkey, the American bird, was already identified with the family feast at Thanksgiving, but was suitable for Easter as well. The pig, thought to be a lucky animal as long ago as pagan Europe, was fattened for slaughter in the spring. Since Jesus was often seen as the sacrificial lamb of God, roasted lamb was a common meat for the feast.[60]

Easter was a national as well as a religious and secular holiday. Thanksgiving taught immigrant schoolchildren the ideas of citizenship. Easter became a national secular day when Dolley Madison organized the Capitol Hill egg roll. By the late nineteenth century, public schools, not just parochial ones, began to celebrate Easter, often in a religious as well as secular fashion. Teachers staged passion plays and read their students poems about the Easter rabbit. Although schools tended to make more of other holidays, teachers still set children to work making Easter gifts for their families.[61]

By the turn of the century, American popular culture took over.[62] Just as the first Christmas movie was a silent film, the first Easter movie was silent film footage of New York's Easter parade. Tin Pan Alley songs were bright and cheery, not gloomy or tragic. George M. Cohan wrote a song about the Easter parade in 1927, although his tune was eclipsed by Irving Berlin's far more memorable one five years later (and eventually by the movie of the same name in 1948). But there was also a great religious story to be told. Audiences flocked to Cecil B. DeMille's Biblical epics at Eastertime in the 1920s. In the 1950s, too, Hollywood turned to Biblical themes shown on a wide screen. *King of Kings, The Robe, The Ten Commandments, Ben-Hur,* and *The Silver Chalice* all attracted a large Eastertime audience. Later, movies with Biblical themes were broadcast on television during Easter week, and in the 1980s video stores reported brisk rentals of these titles during the holiday week.[63]

Despite complaints of ministers about informal dress at Easter, parishioners in many churches still showed off new clothes, although by the late 1960s women of fashion rarely wore hats to church. The huge brimmed hat with ostrich feathers and fake parrots became a thing of the past. Despite periodic attempts to revive hat wearing, it was only when Jacqueline Kennedy or Princess Diana wore one that the woman's hat became a renewed object of interest. Even so, Easter was still a time to buy new clothes. Purchases of outfits for women and children at Easter (but not for men's clothing) continued to account for surging retail sales in April.

From the 1950s to the 1990s going to church on Easter Sunday rose and fell in relationship to overall social conservatism. In the 1950s church attendance at Easter was almost as popular as *I Love Lucy.* Churchgoing on Easter Sunday fit with the prevailing emphasis on raising children and attaining family fulfillment through togetherness.

Regular church attendance was high in the 1950s, and higher still on Easter Sunday. After that decade, churchgoing on Easter plummeted. The decline in the 1960s may be seen as part of the general reaction against establishment institutions and "traditional" values. By 1994, however, 68 percent of American Christians said they attended church at Easter, a figure that surpassed the level of 1959. Some of the renewed interest in Easter seemed to derive from the desire of baby boomers to impart to their children ethics and values, even though many of them had rebelled against religious teaching in their youth.[64] The pollsters did not ask whether families were holding a feast after attending church services. But if part of the reason for going to church was to encourage family unity, we may assume that sitting down at a family meal after church belonged among the day's events.

Like the postsentimental Christmas, which grew out of the social turmoil of the 1960s and reflected the social problems of that decade, Easter saw some changes in the 1960s and beyond: protestors against the Vietnam War carried signs in Easter parades; in the 1970s, openly gay marchers joined in. The major criticism of Easter, that colored eggs and marshmallow Peeps profaned a sacred Christian day, persisted. But the range of complaints against the holiday never expanded to include Jewish protests against Easter celebrations in the schools, black nationalist alternatives, or gay hotlines. Because Easter had never been a holiday of family homecoming—because it failed to fill the heart with yearning—there was no such thing as Easter holiday blues.

Eliminating the feast at home and replacing it with a restaurant meal was a solution to the burden women faced at Easter, as at other holidays. We do not know when going to a restaurant for Easter first became popular, although we can assume that wealthy families in the late nineteenth century, having finished their promenade, took a meal at a fashionable restaurant. Today, having a restaurant meal at Easter has become more common than at Thanksgiving.[65] Fancy home luncheons during Easter weekend have also disappeared, as most women have reduced the effort they put into celebrating Easter.

Easter among the Immigrants

Easter among Catholics, Lutherans, and the Eastern Orthodox was a religious and ethnic holiday, which immigrants transplanted from the old world to the new. It was also a family feast, following six weeks of

Lenten fasting, penitence, and special church services. Catholics were obligated to take communion at Eastertime (performing one's "Easter duty"). In the modern American calendar the Christmas season has been squeezed into just an evening and a day; it has been more difficult to compress Easter, because it consists of a series of religious events, beginning with Ash Wednesday. Nonetheless, after Vatican II, the church shrunk the number of fast days to two, Ash Wednesday and Good Friday. As a result, the long cycle of fasting followed by feasting was truncated, diminishing the symbolic significance of the Easter feast on Sunday as the end to a lengthy period of food taboos.

As at Christmas, at Easter immigrants gradually combined the symbols of the sentimental holiday, its egg hunts, chocolate candy, and flowers, with their own culture's feast and Holy Week customs. From what we know about Christmas, we may assume that these changes occurred for most groups between 1900 and 1940. Christmas clubs among the working class emerged around the turn of the century. By the 1940s Polish immigrants, for example, were buying Christmas cards and tree ornaments.[66] During the same years, at Eastertime immigrants from many cultures were no doubt also purchasing chocolate eggs and stuffed animals, buying new clothes for children, and taking photographs of the children, or mother and daughter, in their Easter best.

Some Old World customs were transplanted, relatively unchanged, to the United States. One such custom was the craft of egg decorating. Ukrainian women scratched elaborate designs on waxed eggs, and Greek women dyed eggs red and made them the centerpiece of the dinner table.[67] However, not all immigrant groups colored and decorated eggs in their homeland; the Irish, for example, did not. The Easter feast, rather than egg dyeing, was the universal immigrant custom brought over from the old country. It changed when husbands left behind their wives in the Old Country. Thus, single Greek men at the turn of the century often ate their post-midnight feast of roasted lamb at a Greek restaurant.[68]

Many Easter customs disappeared as immigrant groups acculturated; they hung on the longest among groups living in isolated farming settlements or in ethnic neighborhoods of large cities. Some of the special days, and the customs associated with the longer Easter season, vanished among the children and grandchildren of immigrants. Fasting was not as strictly observed. The practice of the Easter walk in the fields, once common among German-American and French-Canadian families, no longer exists.[69] In addition, there are no remaining traces of superstitions associated with the holiday (for example, the Swedish belief in Easter hags, who took to their brooms on the Thursday before Easter to consort with the devil). The celebrations of Easter Monday persisted among Poles and Italians until around the 1940s because it was often a holiday from work. Polish-American workers in the 1930s insisted on a one-day Easter Monday sabbatical—even when their employers did not want to grant it. When Polish millworkers failed to show up on Easter Monday, the bosses at a brass mill in Connecticut decided it was best to give in.[70] As late as the 1940s clothing stores and tailor shops owned by Italians often closed on Easter Monday, and Italians often were married on the day (perhaps to benefit from the holiday and the still-fresh flowers decorating the church).[71]

Immigrants' moving to the suburbs and increasingly associating with people from other groups hastened the demise of certain customs. In northern and central Europe, Easter Monday and Tuesday were celebrated by switching and dousing, which were probably descended from pre-Christian fertility rites.[72] Among American Poles and Hungarians Easter Monday was called Dinkus, or Switching Day. Boys doused girls with water, sprinkled their girlfriends with water, or hit little girls lightly about the ankles with switches bundled together with colored ribbons. In Chicago and Newark boys sometimes squirted perfume rather than water. The next day girls did the same to the boys and kissed them. Some immigrants abandoned the traditional Easter Monday practices in favor of a dance on that day. Easter Monday traditions disappeared entirely by the 1950s. One historian argues that switching did not survive in America because it was too "barbaric."[73] More likely, Dinkus disappeared because it did not resemble U.S. courtship customs. One second-generation college student explained to an interviewer that his family abandoned Dinkus because "there weren't any other Lithuanian kids around and the kids would not understand it if you just started pouring water on them . . . We just forgot about it."[74] By 1984, only 18 percent of undergraduates at a college supported by the Polish National Alliance could explain what Dinkus was.[75]

Still, Dinkus had the potential to become the Polish-American St. Patrick's Day, a public celebration, perhaps with a parade, that could be used to advance Polish-American interests in the United States. In modern-day South Bend, Indiana, and Buffalo, New York, Dinkus is still celebrated in local bars, on Polish language radio stations, and at the Polish-American clubs. Elsewhere in Polonia Dinkus was forgotten, although American Poles had ethnic pride, promoted special heroes, and had enduring concerns about Poland.

With the exception of Dinkus Day in South Bend or Buffalo, most of the customs of Easter Monday have disappeared. Ethnic families retained the Easter Sunday feast, along with other special food customs. The feast on Easter survived because it occurred at the same time as the holiday for other Americans; and food customs, as noted earlier, were more likely to persist than costumes, dancing, superstitions, or other forms of folklore.

The most common food to be retained at Easter was a distinctive type of bread, since it was simultaneously a female craft, a religious symbol, and a gift to kin and neighbors. In baking loaves of Easter bread a woman showed her religious devotion. Women often sprinkled the bread with holy water, making their own form of benediction over their home. Baking bread linked home and faith, since for Catholics bread symbolized the communion wafer, which, once consecrated, was the body of Christ. Assembling Easter baskets and sending daughters to distribute them to friends and neighbors, mothers demonstrated their charity and neighborliness.[76] The baking of Easter bread also marked the boundary between assimilation and ethnic identity. The Protestant middle-class woman bought her bread at the bakery, while the "ethnic" woman supposedly made her own.[77]

Baking Easter bread was common among many groups of immigrant Catholic or Eastern Orthodox women. Italian-Americans had the *Columba* (Dove) and other regional breads; the Ukrainians had *kaska,* the Portuguese *folar de pascos,* the Czechs *berdnek,* the Slovenians *potica,* the Russian Orthodox *kulich,* the Finns *pulla.*[78] Baking Easter bread provides the strongest evidence of a female immigrant tradition lovingly passed down from one generation to the next. Daughters, in learning how to bake Easter bread from their mothers, were being instructed in their ethnic identity, their faith, and their female craft.[79] A Greek girl asked her grandmother, "How will I know if I have kneaded the bread long enough?" Her grandmother replied, "If you have sweat all over your body, the bread is kneaded enough."[80] One of the tests of a new wife was being able to make Easter bread. How difficult it was depended on how many loaves had to be baked; some women made only four or five, others dozens.

Many Catholic and Eastern Orthodox groups still host special fam-

ily feasts at Easter, at which three generations of a family may gather.
These multigenerational dinners depart from the norm of Protestant
middle-class America, where the gathering of kin at Easter is optional.
Such feasts showcase women's cooking skill. Still, an occasional immigrant father might take on the task, such as one Italian-American
who made the entire Palm Sunday meal, including his own egg noo-
dles.[81] In general, however, over time cooks streamlined and simplified
at Easter, as at other domestic occasions. The special Easter service in
the Greek Orthodox church is still held at midnight as Easter begins.
But after it, families used to return to drink lemon soup and consume
an Easter feast of roast lamb. Greek Orthodox families still might nap
during the day so that they could be awake for the midnight service.[82]
But they are likely to go to bed after returning from it and delay the
feast until Easter Sunday.

Similarly, Italian feasting changed between 1900 and 1970 because
of the Americanization of dietary habits, the replacement of the outdoor bake ovens (once common among Italian-Americans in Delaware, New Jersey, and Pennsylvania) with indoor stoves, and the
growth in women's education and employment prospects. Italian-
American women at the turn of the century might have devoted a
week to Easter preparations. The most difficult work was baking the
bread in the outside bake oven. The granddaughters of such women
cut back the hours of preparation and cooked in the kitchen. Because
of the impact of American dietary habits and health consciousness,
some of the high-cholesterol, high-sodium dishes were eliminated. In
addition, the family was no longer as patriarchal; women stopped
serving the father first. The Sicilian family practice of the father dip-
ping celery in holy water and then blessing each family member also
disappeared. Many families, however, continued to define certain
dishes—the rich ricotta pie and the Easter bread, *pan dolce*—as the
ceremonial core of the Easter tradition.[83]

Polish-American women modernized the Easter traditions of their
homeland in the twentieth century. Changes in the ritual of blessing
the Easter basket marked the emergence of a more child-centered Catholicism, in which the mother's role was less to participate in ritual
herself than to socialize her children in their faith. Catholics throughout Central Europe took food baskets to the priest to be blessed, or he
came to their home to do so. With each successive generation, the
blessing of the Easter basket on Holy Saturday became less common.

Still, in Polish areas around Pittsburgh in the 1960s, two out of three granddaughters of immigrants still brought baskets to the local parish to be blessed. In Poland the entire family took the basket to the priest; the pattern in America was for children to carry it. As early as the 1930s or 1940s mothers inserted a chocolate Easter egg in the basket, thus conflating the ethnic culture and the dominant one.[84] The cloth that immigrant women embroidered to cover the Easter basket was replaced by a crocheted cover and eventually by aluminum foil.[85]

There were several reasons why the ritual of blessing the Easter basket persisted. The custom became child-oriented, occurred only once a year, and was encouraged by the church in ethnic parishes. Some Poles drove to the urban parish from the suburbs to have the basket blessed because they wanted to maintain their social relationships with neighbors and friends still living in the old neighborhood. In addition, in some multinationality parishes other Catholics enjoyed the tradition and incorporated it into their religious practice.[86] Still, blessing the basket was probably less common in such parishes than in specifically Polish churches. Did the addition of the chocolate bunny or the decline of embroidered cloth change the meaning of the ritual? It seems likely that mothers saw themselves preserving tradition, even as they Americanized it. Yet a woman's definition of herself as the preserver of tradition itself resulted from American life. Maria Anna Knothe observes, "In the old country, the size and contents of the basket were a matter of womanly pride; in America, they were a tribute to tradition."[87]

By the end of the nineteenth century, an earlier way of celebrating the Easter season as raucous, communal, and public had disappeared. Some of the older rituals of Easter were rites of inversion, where the low were made high, and the high low. While gander pulling was a contest of manliness, the Easter parade was a demonstration of a wealthy woman's fashion sense. In gander pulling the male took the role of physical combatant; at the domestic Easter his task was to provide for his family's clothing purchases. Domestic occasions were not intended to reverse the roles of the classes or races, but to enshrine a middle-class concept of the separation between public and private, and celebrate the intimacy of the family, the maternal bond with children, the idea of childhood as a special time for innocent youngsters, and the view of the home as a sanctified space. Nonetheless, in this domestic occasion, as in many others, these kinds of displays occurred in public as well as in private, on the street or at the church as well as at home.

Easter had always symbolized springtime and fertility as well as the death and resurrection of Jesus. Consumer and popular culture enhanced both these meanings. The desire of wealthy New Yorkers to show off their fashions, as well as changing attitudes toward death after the Civil War, contributed to the sentimentalization of Easter. As was true of Christmas, Americans freely borrowed German customs, to which they added fashion, flowers, and a parade. The domestic Easter supplemented, some might say overwhelmed, the religious occasion. The display of crosses decorated with flowers reinforced the association of Easter with death and resurrection. But eventually, the bunny triumphed over the crucifix. At the same time, consumer and popular culture helped to make the holiday more joyous; flowers, plants, small toys, candy, and Irving Berlin's "Easter Parade" became symbols of love and hope, spring and redemption.

The multiple processes of ethnic acculturation evident at Christmas could be found at Easter as well. Many customs, such as Easter Monday, disappeared as ethnics moved out of single-nationality neighborhoods to multiethnic suburbs. Others, such as the baking of Easter bread, persisted. In general, Easter customs were streamlined, simplified, and became more child-centered. Certainly the Catholic church, especially in Polish parishes, was important in preserving the custom of blessing the Easter basket. Working-class immigrants combined the fashion, family photography, and chocolate candy of the holiday of the dominant culture with the customs of their own group. Even in the suburbs middle-class families could do likewise, if they returned to their nationality's church in an urban neighborhood. Kwanzaa, a significant invented tradition of the Christmas season, has no counterpart during the Easter season. A less important holiday, Easter did not provoke as much criticism or appear to be in need of as much renovation. Since the 1970s the persistence of ethnic feasts at Easter, as at Christmas, occurred among the few remaining elements of ethnic identity. The Catholic, Lutheran, and eastern Orthodox churches played a significant role in preserving and defining a specific identity to the holiday, simultaneously ethnic, familial, and religious.

CHAPTER FIVE

Festival of Freedom

And then there was the great classic, *matzo brei,* pieces of matzo soaked
in milk, squeezed into a delectable mess, and fried to gold curls and
flakes—one of the dishes that evokes piercing darts of nostalgia in every
Jewish breast and stories of childhood Passovers complete with slightly
drunken uncles.

—KATE SIMON, *BRONX PRIMITIVE,* 1982

Any reader of Philip Roth or Bernard Malamud knows that American
Jews fear their religious life and group identity is in peril. Sociologist
Marshall Sklare sarcastically titled an essay "American Jewry: The
Ever-Dying People."[1] Predictions about the demise of Jewry are in-
variably proven wrong. Nonetheless, statistics about Jewish religious
observance suggest that in comparison with Christian neighbors,
American Jews take spiritual matters rather lightly. American Jews
are less likely than Gentiles to join a religious congregation or attend
worship services. In a Gallup survey from 1986 Jews more often than
Gentiles agreed with the statement that religion was not very important in their lives.[2] As Deborah Dash Moore notes, contemporary
American Jews "present an extraordinary profile of an exceptionally
affluent and well-educated group with a distinctive brand of liberal
politics and weak ties to any version of religious faith."[3]

Having shredded the traditional religious calendar, most American
Jews in contemporary America celebrate important life cycle events
(birth, coming of age, marriage, death), the High Holidays of Rosh
Hashonah and Yom Kippur, Chanukah, and Passover. Despite the
steady upward movement of American Jews from the ghetto to the
suburbs, and the equally unimpeded decline in daily or weekly prayer,
Sabbath observance, and adherence to the Jewish dietary laws of
kashrut, the Passover seder remains a central American Jewish ritual.
One suburban Jew in the 1950s explained, "We gave up keeping a ko-

sher home [but] we *always* have a big seder."[4] Passover and Chanukah are the two most widely observed Jewish family holidays today. In 1990, 62 percent of American Jews attended a seder.[5]

Although Passover has remained a central Jewish ritual, it became a sentimental occasion with the emergence of the Jewish middle class and later acquired some postsentimental elements because of the rising rate of Jewish intermarriage and the growth of Jewish feminism since the 1970s. Since the beginning of the twentieth century American Jews have shortened and simplified Passover and redefined it in modern, secular terms. German Jews in the United States in the nineteenth century had already begun the process of making Passover a sentimental occasion. East European Jewish immigrants in the early twentieth century appeared to reverse course: they took the religious aspects of the ritual more seriously and turned the familial aspects of Passover into a celebration of the patriarchal household. Within a few decades, however, middle-class East European immigrants were refashioning the seder as a domestic occasion and a display the family's status and prestige. By the 1950s suburban middle-class Jews remade Passover again, this time into an instructional tool for the child.

Most Jews in twentieth-century America celebrated Passover not to fulfill religious obligations and the requirements of Jewish law but to express their sense of Jewish identity and family solidarity. Just as Thanksgiving was intended to resolve the tension between individualism and the family, Passover was meant to smooth over the conflict between living in a liberal, modern society and wanting to remain Jewish. By redefining Passover as a celebration of freedom, hope, and "family joy," Passover helped American Jews bridge these presumed opposites.[6] Amidst increasing assimilation of Jews into American life, the seder became one of the main ways Jews continued to assert their uniqueness.

The Decline in Religious Observance

Between 1882 and 1924 2.3 million Jews migrated to the United States. The bulk of them came from small towns in Eastern Europe and Russia. Immigration quotas, enacted into law in 1921 and 1924, cut off the flow of newcomers. The men most likely to move to America were laborers and craftsmen, not the scholarly elite. Many quickly abandoned daily prayer. Most of the immigrants rarely attended synagogue, except at the High Holidays or the anniversary of a parent's death. Keeping the Sabbath was a holy commandment, but many Jews found it difficult to make a living without working on the Holy Day. Jewish shops remained open on the Sabbath in the early twentieth century. As soon as just a few months after their arrival many men had cut off their *peyes* (sidelocks) and stopped wearing yarmulkes, except at synagogue.

By the 1920s Jewish women in America were also paring down rituals they observed. There were three special commandments for Jewish women: lighting Sabbath candles, burning a piece of dough used in making challah while saying a blessing at Sabbath, and observing the laws of family purity. These laws prescribed use of the ritual bath (the *mikveh*) after a regularly observed monthly period of sexual abstinence during and following menstruation.[7] American immigrant women continued to light Sabbath candles but often disregarded the other two commandments. Rare was the woman who took her monthly "dip" in the *mikveh* (usually rusty iron tanks located in the basements of tenements). Most no longer wore wigs or covered their hair with a kerchief, as required of Orthodox women. Still, many adult daughters of immigrant parents, after lighting the Sabbath candles, put a special dinner on the table Friday night, and kept a kosher house. In fact, women's participation in the synagogue increased with Americanization. Prior to emigration it was rare for women to worship at the synagogue, except for during the High Holidays or at a Yizkor service (commemorating the anniversary of a death). In America synagogue sisterhoods helped encourage women to attend services regularly.[8]

A holiday that required observance only once a year had more chance of surviving. Still, how many Jews observed Shavuot, Sukkoth, or Purim, even if these festivals occurred only once a year? Sukkoth, a harvest and originally a pilgrimage festival, had the misfortune of falling soon after the High Holidays, and thus deterred those who had had their surfeit of religious ritual. Purim, with its dress-up events and *hamantaschen* (fruit-filled pastries), appealed to children and brought back pleasant childhood memories to adults; but, like Shavuot, Purim did not coincide on the calendar with any Christian observance. Seven yearly calendric holidays, including Yom Kippur and Rosh Hashonah, are mentioned in the Bible.[9] Chanukah is not. Yet in three social surveys, conducted in 1957–1958, 1962, and

1981, where the frequency of attending synagogue on the High Holidays, attending a Passover seder, and lighting Chanukah candles was tabulated, Chanukah, which offers a Jewish alternative to Christmas, was ranked first in two of the studies. Passover finished second in two of the studies, and came in first in the third.[10]

The reason for the first-place ranking of Chanukah is obvious: it was seen as the Jewish alternative to Christmas. Passover fell at the same time as Easter, and offered a Jewish alternative to it. (To be fair, of course, the early Christian Easter borrowed heavily from Passover.) But the coincidence of the calendar was only one of several reasons for the popularity of Passover. Sociologists Marshall Sklare and Joseph Greenbaum understood that the process of preserving tradition is one of selecting "from the vast storehouse of the past what is not only objectively possible . . . to practice but subjectively possible . . . to 'identify' with." Sklare and Greenbaum found that the rate of ritual retention was highest when a ritual "(1) is capable of effective redefinition in modern terms, (2) does not demand social isolation or the adoption of a unique life style, (3) accords with the religious culture of the larger community and provides a 'Jewish' alternative which is felt to be needed, (4) is centered on the child, and (5) is performed annually or infrequently."[11] To this list the historian Jenna Weissman Joselit has added that a ritual survives when it can be combined with feasting, dressing up, home beautifying, and visiting relatives.[12] It was true that the blessing of the Easter basket was retained in part because it was encouraged at Polish churches. But the demand for Passover did not simply come from rabbis. While rabbis certainly encouraged members of their congregation to celebrate Passover, the event was common even among nonaffiliated Jews, who saw the seder as a celebration of the family and of freedom.

New Elements Added to the Seder

Although an ancient festival, Passover was an ever-changing one, which relatively early on unified two separate traditions, a spring festival and a historical commemoration. Nomadic Jews marked the coming of spring by sacrificing a newly born lamb or kid from their flock. They sprinkled the blood of the sacrificed lamb on tent posts to ward off evil and illness in the coming year. Later Jewish agriculturalists created a harvest festival, which they called the Feast of the Unleavened Bread. The priest cut and offered the first new sheaf of grain, the "omer," as a sacrifice to God in sight of the entire community. Jews fused elements from two separate festivals into a new one, a commemoration of Moses' deliverance of the Hebrew slaves from Pharoah's Egypt, which many date to around 2000 B.C.E. The Hebrew word Pesach, whose original meaning was unclear, was reinterpreted to mean "pass over," that the angel of death had passed over the homes of the Hebrew slaves while visiting death upon firstborn Egyptian sons. The matzoh, previously eaten during the Feast of the Unleavened, came to symbolize the bread the Hebrews hastily baked on their journey in the desert.

The ancient Hebrews in Israel celebrated Passover as a feast in the home and as a pilgrimage to a holy city. Priests at the Temple in Jerusalem celebrated Passover with animal sacrifice and encouraged believers to hold a feast at home and journey to Jerusalem for special worship. The home festival became a symbol of Jewish survival after the Romans destroyed the second temple in Jerusalem (ca. 70 C.E.). Later, the home ritual began to reflect influences of the Roman and Greek conquerors. Wine began to be served, men reclined on cushions during the meal, and food was dipped into water or wine.

In exile Jews in Spain, Portugal, Morocco, Ethiopia, and the Caucasus adapted the ritual and added distinctive customs that reflected local influences.[13] By the tenth century in Europe Passover, which had been a celebration of freedom from persecution, had become a time of fear. Some Christians spread the rumor that Jews used the blood of murdered Christian children to smear on their doorposts or to bake matzohs. The "blood libel" became an excuse for the persecution of Jews in Germany, Eastern Europe, and Russia. Fear of arson, pillage, and torture often outweighed the happy anticipation of feasting and family reunion.[14] Out of this fear Jews in medieval and early modern Europe at their seders began to open their doors only briefly so as to permit the prophet Elijah to enter. Previously Jews had left their door open during the entire seder to invite strangers and the needy to their table.[15]

Unlike other family feasts, which have an oral tradition for the order of events, the seder has a written script that celebrants are supposed to follow, although there are several unscripted parts. Each participant was given his or her printed, often illustrated, pamphlet, called a Haggadah (Hebrew for "telling the tale"), that contained

Biblical verses, blessings, psalms, prayers, and songs. The Haggadah, which may have originated during the Babylonian exile around 500 B.C.E., was once part of a book of common prayer. A rabbi in the ninth century issued the first separate text. Since the first Haggadah was printed in Spain in 1482, there have been more than two thousand editions published.

Initial Reinventions in the United States

Even among acculturated German Jews in the United States in the late nineteenth century, the celebration of Passover was a domestic occasion that mixed bourgeois aesthetics, sentimental attachment to family, and Jewish cuisine. Some German Jews attended a seder, while others simply ate matzoh during the eight days of the holiday. Out of respect for Jewish dietary laws, German Jews in late-nineteenth-century Minneapolis stayed away from nonkosher restaurants during Passover, although most did not observe the dietary laws, either at Passover or during the rest of the year.[16] German Jewish cookbooks at the turn of the century paid more notice to the ritual of Passover than did cookbooks in Yiddish, since German Jews needed more instruction. Many women consulted *Aunt Babette's Cookbook,* with the recipes of Mrs. Bertha F. Kramer. Her volume, which went through eleven editions and remained in print until 1914, provided instructions as to how to prepare gefilte fish and tsimmes (cooked carrots, apricots, and prunes in a thick sauce sweetened with honey) for Passover, although the recipes assumed that the cook did not keep kosher.[17]

Jewish women authors around the turn of the century offered three reasons why nonobservant Jews should celebrate Passover: Jews could earn the respect of Gentiles, honor the memory of their observant parents, and make their home happy and Jewish.[18] They sought to illustrate these benefits for an audience of Jews who had lost their faith. Esther Ruskay, an Orthodox Jew, poet, and author of a series of essays addressed to prodigal (German) Jews, lamented the lack of Jewish religious knowledge, a growing agnosticism, and a drift toward the humanistic religion of Ethical Culture among Jews in the Northeast. Her readers, she supposed, had servants and dined at fine restaurants, but lacked even a rudimentary knowledge of Jewish history and considered Passover "an antiquated ceremonial." Some of the unknowing, growing slightly nostalgic, would attempt to hold a seder but, ignorant of the laws of *kashrut* (rules about what foods Jews were allowed to eat), nibbled on decidedly *treyfe* (not kosher) lobster and oysters at the meal. The untutored had to invite a friend to conduct the ritual, because they did not know the blessings or the order of the service. Ruskay also described couples who, failing to find a kosher restaurant open on Passover, settled for Delmonico's.[19] Like the story of the wayward family member who was reformed at Thanksgiving, Ruskay recounted tales of errant Jews who rediscovered family ties while attending their first seder in years. One man was so overcome with memories of his long-lost widowed sister and her large family that he promised to bring them East for the next Passover.[20]

By German Jewish standards, East European immigrant Jews were decidedly observant. They did not eat *hametz* (any mixture of flour and water that was leavened) during Passover and rid their homes of it, putting it in a bag or wrapping it in a discarded cloth before burning it in a bonfire outside their tenements. In addition, observant Jews did not eat from any vessels or utensils that had absorbed *hametz*.[21] The "Jewish matrons' week of trial," although shorter than the month or more of preparation common in the shtetl, still entailed an intense period of housecleaning prior to the equally demanding preparations for family seders.[22] A housewife cleaned, scrubbed, scoured, and washed the walls, lamps, floors, and furniture. By holding utensils over a fire, she burned off the hametz. She washed wooden spoons, scraped and immersed them in boiling water, and then cleaned them with a hot iron or stone. Glasses were soaked in boiling water for three days, the water being changed each day.

Around the time of World War I, the wives of prosperous Jewish men began to seek escape from the chores of preparing Passover. They were a vanguard of sorts, abandoning their kitchens long before restaurants saw major increases in their clientele on Easter Sunday or Thanksgiving. Their desires were understandable since their burden was a heavy one. Moreover, hotel and resort owners beckoned to Jews at Passover, again before a tourist trade developed around Easter week vacation or between Christmas and New Year's. The owners of Stone's cottage on Long Island encouraged women to "avoid household cares, spend Passover at Arverne." Eisenberg's Wave Crest Hotel, near Arverne in Far Rockaway, offered a countryside setting by the sea, as well as the avoidance of "ritual household preparation."[23] These places as well as other resorts in the Adirondacks boasted of kosher kitchens and cantors available to conduct seders.[24]

Many middle-class families also celebrated the seder at a banquet hall in addition to, or instead of, at home. One rabbi in the 1930s explained (or rationalized) that because of the small size of the Jewish family and the inability of many Jews to conduct the ceremony, it was easier to host a seder in a public hall sponsored by a Jewish organization.[25] Secular Jewish activists reconciled their Jewish heritage with their commitment to socialism at the "third seder," a public banquet. Since this seder was held on the third evening of Passover, it did not conflict with family feasts on the first two nights. Yet for many the third seder was the only one they attended. A Zionist group in Philadelphia organized a third seder in 1919. The Workmen's Circle, a mutual aid society and center for Yiddish socialism, held their first seder in Clinton Hall, New York, in 1922.[26] Soon they had to move what had been a small affair for children attending their afternoon school to the Grand Ballroom of the Waldorf Astoria hotel. The Workmen's Circle developed its own Haggadah, which included Yiddish poetry, singing, and dancing as a means of planting their version of socialism in American Jewish soil. Both the Workmen's Circle and Histadrut (labor Zionist organizations) seders were largely catered events that celebrated Jewish socialism, although the Workmen's Circle was anti-Zionist, while the Histadrut favored the establishment of a Jewish state.

Passover, always the spring cleaning holiday, became a home-furnishing one as well not just among prosperous Jews but also among Jews of more modest means. Most immigrants could afford to buy new pots, tinware, and plates for Passover, which could be used only for the holiday. Airing the furniture, the custom of the shtetl, underwent considerable alteration. Many families simply dumped an old mattress, chair, plates, or lamp on the street and bought new items for the holiday. Street cleaners groaned under the load of having to remove discarded bedding and furniture from the Lower East Side at Passover.[27] Yiddish newspapers and downtown department stores encouraged Jewish consumerism. The newspapers urged young adults to buy presents for their parents on the holiday and to bring gifts to the homemaker hosting the meal. At the same time, American department stores enticed wealthier Jews to buy patterned tablecloths, doilies, glassware, silver, seder plates, and goblets to make the "Passover table most attractive."[28]

Because of the Passover buying rush, Andrew Heinze believes that immigrant Jews' celebration of the festival allowed American Jews to assert their religious and ethnic identity while embracing American consumerism.[29] To the immigrants, new purchases symbolized American abundance and prosperity, and relief for women tired of scrubbing, polishing, and cleaning. American abundance, however, proved the benefits of capitalism to some, but certainly not all, American Jews. Many could understand consumption both as a source of domestic pleasure and as an arena for political struggle. Thus Jewish mothers of modest means could point with pleasure to their new pots and tinware but also boycott kosher butchers who raised meat prices unfairly. Their daughters, too, liked to buy fashionable clothes and hats, worn to work as well as for the seder, but still took part in strikes against their employers, garment manufacturers.

Just as injecting consumer culture into Passover made the ritual more American and more pleasing, so too adopting American definitions of the holiday provided a secular definition of Passover that broadened its appeal. In 1899 Abraham Cahan referred to Passover as "Israel's Independence Day."[30] Jewish writers described the Covenant with Sinai as a Jewish Declaration of Independence, presented Moses as "an Israelitic Lincoln," and likened the holiday to the Fourth of July. During World War II one father explained that Moses' demands of Pharoah were similar to President Roosevelt's wartime goal to defend the Four Freedoms.[31] Jews in every subsequent generation compared their historical struggle to some contemporary social movement, from civil rights to environmentalism. The redefinition of Passover as a freedom festival also created the kind of bridging of competing values characteristic of ritual—in this instance, helping secular Jews reconcile American loyalties with a Jewish identity.

The Jewish Home Beautiful Movement

Intent on embracing middle-class domesticity, Jewish women who had a foothold on prosperity abandoned their role as guardians of tradition in favor of updating it. They wedded celebration in the home, table decoration, and consumerism to ethnic and religious identity through the purchase and display of ritual objects and the setting of a fine table. German Jews in the late nineteenth century initiated this trend; East European Jews furthered it in the 1920s. In the place of the thrifty homemaker and sharp bargainer stood a fashionably dressed wife and mother with fewer sharp edges, and more silver and crystal goblets on the dining room table.

By the 1920s many of the immigrants had grown prosperous enough to leave the ghetto for roomier apartment houses in more fashionable neighborhoods or single-family houses at the outer edge of cities or in the suburbs. As they did so, they searched for a way to combine their self-definition as Americans rising in status with their desire to remain Jews. The middle-class mother did not toil at a sewing machine; no boarder slept on a cot in her kitchen. As their husbands earned more income, these women tended to leave their jobs in the garment industry and become full-time homemakers or part-time ones who helped in the family business.[32] Successful immigrants built large synagogues, which served as centers of group association as well as temples for religious worship.

Whereas the Gentile home was to be a refuge against corruption and evil, the Jewish home was supposed to function as a bulwark against assimilation.[33] The appeal to the middle-class Jewish mother was that she could diminish the allure of the Gentile world by making her home a sanctuary, "a religious domain," a "miniature temple." The function of the Jewish home, a 1930s "how-to" book to Jewish parenting opined, was to transmit "Jewish civilization" and "instill a love" of the Jewish religion.[34] Relying on then-fashionable behavioral psychology, Jewish cookbooks a decade earlier had insisted that the child's character was formed in the first four years of life. The child needed to be raised in a home with "a truly Jewish atmosphere."[35] These authors gave Jewish women special responsibility for making the home a center of ritual observance, in which women enlarged their own spirits as well as uplifting their family's.[36]

Jews of the shtetl accorded the highest status to the scholar, the rabbi, and the man who devoted his days to studying Torah. In the United States the most respected man had the biggest bank account. Charitable and a good provider, the good Jewish man was no longer a dedicated scholar or the religious instructor of his sons. He remained the ceremonial leader of the seder, but his wife held the responsibility for transmitting Jewish heritage to her children. Even if Hebrew or Sunday school provided religious instruction, she supervised and coordinated it. A mother taught her daughters that the Jewish religion was a way of life linked to maintaining a Jewish home. Jews were adopting the feminized religion of Victorian middle-class Protestants and the domesticated Catholicism of the late nineteenth and early twentieth centuries.[37]

Like the German Jews before them, East European Jews between the 1930s and the 1950s had to be taught their own rituals, since they either no longer knew them or failed to practice them fully. The Lakeville survey in the 1950s, the first systematically to examine Jewish ritual observance, inquired about the practices of respondents and their parents. These were mainly upper-middle-class Jews living in "Lakeville," actually Highland Park, Illinois, a wealthy suburb of Chicago with a large Jewish population. Parents of Lakeville Jews observed on average 5.2 rituals (of 10 mentioned in the survey); the mean number practiced by Lakeville residents was 2.8. The 10 activities named in the study included lighting candles on Chanukah, attending a Passover seder, buying kosher meat, and lighting Sabbath candles on Friday night.[38] The fact that even the parents of Lakeville residents were only celebrating five out of ten ritual practices suggests that the decline in sacramentalism was well under way by the 1930s, the decade when most parents of the Lakeville Jews queried entered their middle years.

The interwar generation of Jewish women published cookbooks, guidebooks, and manuals in English precisely because the middle-class Jewish woman had not mastered such matters in her youth or was looking for a more decorative and up-to-date rendering of them. Mathilde Schechter, the wife of the chancellor of the Jewish Theological Seminary and the founder of the Women's League of Conservative Judaism, believed that Jewish women should create an aesthetically pleasing home. Setting a beautiful seder table with matched plates, silver candlesticks, monogrammed silverware, fresh cut flowers, and a lovely damask tablecloth made the Passover ritual an artistic performance. *The Jewish Home Beautiful,* which went through fourteen editions up to 1941, published photographs of Passover table settings and recipes so that the seder table could be a "thing of beauty as precious and as elevating as anything painted on canvas or chiseled in stone." The book devoted more pages to "the prince of holidays" than to any other festival. The purpose of *Jewish Home Beautiful* was not only to make home-based Judaism modern and tasteful but to dispel the stereotype these women perceived of Judaism as coarse, grace-less, and lacking in charm. Whereas Jewish mothers in small towns were making main dishes and desserts the way their mothers had, Jewish middle-class women in cities and suburbs were the main audience of the *Jewish Home Beautiful*.[39]

The *Settlement Cook Book,* probably the most successful collection of Jewish recipes in the interwar years, went a step beyond *Jewish Home Beautiful* in transforming a religious ceremony in the home into an elegant (but ritually suspect) dinner party. Begun by two Milwaukee Jewish women who had established the Jewish Mission and planned on using the proceeds from the cookbook to provide scholarships for needy students and pay for the mission's nursery school, the *Settlement Cook Book* went through forty editions and sold over a million copies by the 1940s. Recipes for nonkosher food were included, although pork was excluded from the early editions.[40] Sample menus include a main dish with meat followed by a *schaum torte* with whipped cream, a clear violation of the rules of *kashrut* against the mixing of meat dishes and those made with milk. As an additional elegant touch, the cookbook suggested that *harosis* (a diced apple and wine mixture, sprinkled with cinnamon) might be arranged on a bed of watercress with a sprig of parsley, and served as an appetizer. (*Harosis* was supposed to be placed on a ceremonial plate and eaten with matzoh during the reading from the Haggadah.)

As the second generation in cities and suburbs began to shed some of its adherence to ritual, "gastronomic Judaism" became a keynote of Jewish identity. It was an easy, undemanding way to assert a sense of Jewishness. Jewish women brought "a certain playful solemnity to the preparation of certain festive dishes," including the gefilte fish, roast chicken, noodle kugel, and sponge cake so many favored.[41] For the family that usually did not eat Jewish cuisine or kosher food the rest of the year, Passover became the time to savor it.

At the same time, prepared foods began to make the work of preparation easier. Jewish firms met some of the demand, but in the early twentieth century, brand-name food companies operated by Gentiles also sought to profit from the Jewish market for special foods at Passover. Even before the Civil War American Jews had been purchasing matzoh from Jewish bakers. Passover cooking required special goose fat, which had to be kept separate from food that might contaminate it. In place of goose fat, some Jews began to use vegetable oil. Hydrogenated vegetable oil was first marketed under the name Crisco in 1911. Crisco began to publish a Yiddish-English cookbook in the 1930s. An endorsement on the can cited the authoritative words of Rabbi Margolies of New York who declared that "the Hebrew Race has been waiting 4,000 years for Crisco."[42] By the late 1920s families could also purchase jars of ground horseradish.[43]

Jewish-owned wine manufacturers, working with rabbis, succeeded especially well by the 1920s and 1930s. Only a few Jews continued to make their own wine, a time-consuming process involving the squeezing of grapes or ground raisins through sieves. Because yeast was *hametz,* it could not be added to the grapes to produce fermentation. Instead, the grape juice had to be exposed to the air to ferment, a process that took several months. Most families instead began to buy Manischewitz, Mogen David, or Monarch products. Monarch, which did not distribute kosher wine to the public, sold its bottles to rabbis, who in turn sold them to their congregations. Manischewitz bought out Monarch and began marketing wine under the Manischewitz label in 1936.[44]

Haggadot printed by Maxwell House Coffee and offered free with the purchase of cans of coffee were the best example of the merger of the commercial and the sacred. In 1923 advertisements in Yiddish assured Jewish consumers that they no longer had to turn down a cup of coffee at the end of seder. East European Jews had thought that coffee beans, like other beans, were prohibited at Passover. A Jewish publicist, Joseph Jacobs, developed the idea of marketing food products to Jewish consumers in Yiddish newspapers. He found a rabbi who claimed that coffee beans were actually berries and therefore kosher for Passover. In 1934 Jacobs devised the idea of a Maxwell House Haggadah. Since then over 20 million copies have been printed.[45] While businessmen made millions from marketing crosses as jewelry and selling family Bibles, Maxwell House was the first company to use a religious text as a promotional tool to create a sense of identification with a brand name.

Commercial food products for Passover, like those for Easter, became important objects of nostalgia. Moreover, kosher-for-Passover ketchup and preserves made it easier to endure a week of being deprived of favorite foods. Jewish food manufacturers, such as Rokeach, Streit's, Manischewitz, Goodman's, and a variety of mainstream food companies manufactured and sold packaged and bottled foods, from gefilte fish to kosher-for-Passover ketchup, applesauce, tomato juice, and strawberry jam. In the 1940s Barton's introduced chocolate-covered matzohs, and other companies followed suit.[46] Bartons, Rokeach, and Manischewitz capitalized on the association of the holiday with family gathering and sentiment. Barton's chocolate tin and Streit's aluminum container for macaroons became cultural objects themselves. Memories of Passover became intertwined with brand labels. Marnie Bernstein of Brooklyn recalled, "The grocery order would arrive. Boxes of matzohs, packages of multicolored sugar-coated jellies, sacks of walnuts and pecans in their shells, tins of Barton's chocolate miniatures (kosher for Passover), bottles of Manischewitz Malaga wine."[47]

The Suburban Idyll

In the 1950s, as in earlier decades, synagogue sisterhoods assumed that many Jewish women needed to be instructed in ritual. The sisterhoods and religious school PTAs sponsored workshops on how to set the seder table and what dishes to serve.[48] Settled into a ranch house or a split level in the suburbs, the middle-class Jewish mother was supposed to devote herself to homemaking, her children, and Jewish communal organizations. Like Gentile women in the 1950s, most Jewish women married in their early twenties and became homemakers. In 1957 only 12 percent of Jewish women with children under age six worked outside the home, compared to 18 percent for white Protestants. Because of the importance assigned child rearing and the adequacy of most men's earning power, the typical Jewish mother in the 1950s tended to remain outside the labor force until the youngest child entered junior high school.[49]

Consumerism, having made its mark on the kitchen pantry, moved into the place of worship in the postwar years. At the synagogue gift shop the suburban homemaker could purchase a matzoh cover with an embroidered Jewish star or a seder plate made in Israel. If she was a guest at a seder, she might want to buy and gift wrap a wineglass, a silver cup of Elijah, or a handsomely illustrated Haggadah. These shops, tucked in a corner of the synagogue, sprouted up as Jews moved away from urban centers where such objects could easily be purchased in stores. The synagogue gift shop encouraged the trend begun in the 1920s of beautifying the Jewish middle-class home with ceremonial items. The objects offered for sale in the house of worship became talismans that strengthened the link between women's consumerism, Jewish symbolic ethnicity, and ritual observance.[50]

In the child-oriented culture of the 1950s, the primary rationale for Passover changed from maintaining the Jewish family as a unit to the Jewish education of the child. The adult-oriented Judaism of the immigrants gave way to a religion designed to provide children "with a Jewish identity." As early as Ruskay, Jewish women authors had been concerned about providing proper religious training in the home for Jewish children. Moreover, every Jewish mother and father took pride in a son's achievements and success. By the 1950s, however, many Jewish families celebrated Passover and Chanukah more for the sake of the child than for the sake of family solidarity. Mothers enlisted their children to carry the Passover dishes from the storage place in the basement, help make the *harosis,* and set the table. At the seder the child had an assigned part, sang songs, and hunted for hidden treasure, the return of which brought a reward. Even nonreligious Jewish parents could look on these holidays as fun-filled opportunities to transmit Jewish identity and heritage to their children.

First-generation Jews viewed prayer as an adult activity into which children were initiated. Jews in the postwar suburbs often affiliated with a synagogue only when their children were ready for religious school. Such parents often abstained from religious ritual and attending synagogue service except when the event was child oriented.[51] Sklare and Greenbaum argued that "the traditional Jew performs rituals because they are pleasing in the sight of God, while the new Jew, it is said, performs them as a child-rearing device and as a result of secular rather than sacred drives."[52] Just as was true of immmigrant schoolchildren at Thanksgiving, Jewish children learned about Passover at Sunday school and asked their parents why they did not have a seder.[53] Rabbis also used the child-centeredness of their congregants as a rationale to encourage celebration of Passover.[54]

By the 1950s, Passover had become a one-evening family celebration rather than an eight-day holiday. To be sure, some Reform congregations held a seder in the basement of the temple in addition to encouraging their congregants to hold one at home.[55] Virtually no Jewish businesses closed for the holiday by the 1950s, except Jewish bakeries or those in Orthodox neighborhoods. Most of the preholiday ritual and prayer had disappeared. Jews from the shtetl and

Orthodox Jews initially eliminated their surplus *hametz* by selling it to the rabbi. No one did that anymore.[56] Only observant families searched for the *hametz* or burned it the next day. Few families went to evening prayers before the seder meal. Firstborn sons rarely fasted, or even knew they were expected to do so. Because fewer Jews read Hebrew or had been schooled in Jewish ritual, many felt uncomfortable leading the seder ceremony. The Bible forbade inviting noncircumcised men to the seder. Nonetheless, it became common to include non-Jewish friends or, because of intermarriage, Gentile relatives. One Maryland woman at the end of the seder called on her guests to sing songs from their own religious tradition. Her Methodist brother-in-law led the group in singing "Onward Christian Soldiers."[57]

With each successive generation, the number of Jews keeping kosher declined. Maintaining a kosher kitchen, either for a special holiday or throughout the year, required trips to the kosher butcher shop, two separate sets of dishes, extra expenses, and constant vigilance to see that meat dishes were not mixed with milk dishes. For Passover the homemaker had to purify two sets of everyday dishes and pots and pans, or purchase two additional sets. The Reform branch of Judaism decided as early as 1923 that this "practice was not essential to the proper observance of Passover."[58] Moreover, the desire to spend less time cooking and overseeing the kitchen eroded the practice of kosher. Only 22 percent of Lakeville Jews in 1957–1958 kept the dietary laws of Passover, while 54 percent of their parents had done so.[59]

The exceptional stability and endogamy of the 1950s Jewish family came to an end in the 1960s. Divorce began to increase, fertility fell, and women's employment rose. The rate of Jewish intermarriage skyrocketed from about 3 percent in 1940 to 52 percent in 1990.[60] The celebration of Passover among the intermarried, the divorced, and the widowed was not as common as in traditional nuclear families in which both spouses were Jewish. (No statistics were kept about the frequency of celebration among gay people, reflecting the invisibility of homosexuality.) The increase in intermarriage created tension at the seder table. One grandmother maneuvered so as to be able to invite her grandchildren for the first night's seder without having to include her daughter and Gentile son-in-law. The daughter from another mixed marriage felt uncomfortable asking the four questions because she did not feel she was really a Jew.[61] Beginning in the late

1960s, some secular Jews, often unaffiliated with a synagogue, sought spiritual fulfillment through ritual observance. Ironically, this resurgence of Orthodoxy among younger Jews led to the splintering of the multigenerational family. Because of their strict dietary rules, many of the newly Orthodox were unable to eat at their parents' homes on Passover.[62]

Acquiring a professional degree also diminished Jewish ritual observance. Scientific thinking, a cosmopolitan outlook, or a vital network of professional associations and friendships with Gentiles dampened the level of religious involvement among Jewish professionals. But this did not apply to the seder. In fact, the higher the level of educational attainment, the greater the likelihood of celebrating Passover.[63] Among various professionals, those that used lecturing in their work—college professors, schoolteachers, and lawyers—showed a special affinity for the holiday. The feast of Passover allowed them to preside over and express their allegiance to the ideal of freedom at a family "talk feast." Physicians had lower rates of observance, presumably not because of scientific skepticism about the miracle of Exodus, but because of the unusual time demands of their profession.[64]

Detailed descriptions of family seders in the 1970s suggest that the Jewish home beautiful movement dictated the aesthetics of the occasion, and sentimentalism the emotional tenor. Barbara Frankel's description of her family's seder held at her parents' home in 1970 unapologetically makes that point. Frankel observed that celebrating the family was the main function of the seder and the reason it persisted.[65] Before turning to their Haggadot, Frankel's father, a wealthy self-made businessman, gave an extended impromptu speech in which he pointed out that his wife's birthday was the day before, and that the family was looking forward to the wedding anniversary of one child and the birth of a third grandchild. Frankel describes a happy family dinner party at which matzoh balls and chicken soup were served and many dinner guests, including some of the children, became tipsy, having drunk more than the obligatory four cups of wine. Rituals of purification were entirely absent, the narrative of the Exodus was treated as a mythic tale, and the symbols were "viewed without awe and handled casually." The family hurried through the ritual to get to the main event of the evening, the dinner.[66] (Some have claimed that the query "Is it time for dinner yet?" has become central to the modern event.)

Jewish Feminism

Jewish feminism, which emerged in the late 1960s and early 1970s as part of the general feminist resurgence of those years, not only attacked the gender division of labor at the seder but also helped to reshape the ritual. The ordination of Sally Priesand as the first female reform rabbi in 1972 marked the first victory for modern Jewish feminism. Thirteen years later the Jewish Theological Seminary, the home of Conservative Jewry, decided to ordain women rabbis as well. Criticizing anti-Semitism within the women's movement and sexism within the Jewish religion and Jewish organizational life, Jewish feminism sought a more equal place for Jewish women within Judaism and greater recognition of Jewish women as Jews within secular feminism. Jewish feminists took aim at the patriarchal nature of their religion, at stereotypes of Jewish mothers and "princesses," and at the lack of recognition and power of Jewish women in communal life. In the early 1970s, many of the calls for change also came from women in the Havurah movement, informal groups that met to pray without the leadership of a rabbi. Out of one havurah, a group of Conservative Jewish women, most of whom were in their late twenties, formed their own Jewish feminist organization, Ezrat Nashim. It presented a manifesto addressed to the rabbinic assembly of the Conservative movement in 1972, calling for inclusion of women in the *minyan* (the group of adults needed for a prayer service), reform of Jewish divorce procedures, the ordination of female rabbis and cantors, and leadership roles for women in Jewish organizational life.[67]

Jewish feminists regarded the seder as a symbol of the inequality of women in a patriarchal religion and of the burdens Jewish women bore in creating and maintaining a traditional Jewish family. They bristled when girls were not allowed to ask the Four Questions during the seder, or when the wife scurried from the dining room table to the kitchen while the husband conducted the seder. Very few could remember a mother who sat throughout the entire ceremony. One young woman pictured her aunts bringing bowls of water for the men to wash their hands, but not for the women. She also bitterly recalled that only the men had pillows to recline on during the seder. Others complained that the mother did all the cleaning before Passover, while the father performed the symbolic act of gathering up a few crumbs of *hametz* with a feather and offering the blessing.[68]

The contrast between the father's ceremonial role and the mother's exertions rankled. Letty Cottin Pogebrin recalled her youth in the late 1940s and 1950s: "Year after year, the Haggadah, the retelling of Israel's liberation from bondage, came to us in my father's authoritative bass voice, annotated by the symbols, songs, and rituals that he brought upstage like some great maestro conducting the solo parts of the seder symphony. It took me years to see that my father's virtuosity depended on my mother's labor and that the seders I remember with such heartwarming intensity were sanctified by her creation even more than his."[69]

The 1960s generation of highly educated Jewish women included a large proportion of single women. Those who married did so at a later age and had one or two children on average. A high proportion of Jewish women, even married women, were employed, either part or full time, often in the professions.[70] Many prominent leaders of the mainstream women's movement, from Betty Friedan to Bella Abzug, were Jewish, as were Shulamith Firestone, Andrea Dworkin, Robin Morgan, and many others in the more radical wing of the movement. Feminism appealed to educated Jewish women in the 1960s and 1970s, but anti-Semitism and anti-Zionism in the women's movement also repelled them.

Jewish feminists noted the discrepancy between the Jewish ideal of freedom and the special burden of being a homemaker at Passover. Because Passover was so widely celebrated, it was an easy target for criticism.[71] Of course, individual women complained before the 1960s. Many had voted with their feet, by going to a seder at a resort, the temple, or a banquet hall. That remedy—not celebrating Passover at home—had always been available. What was new was that women's grievances were placed within the context of inequality and oppression. Orthodox Jewish feminist Blu Greenberg told the story of the illustrious rabbi, often consulted about proper kosher practice at Passover, whose wife was hospitalized just before the holiday. He had to move himself and his three children to an apartment, because he could not conduct the ritual purification himself. Greenberg's mother taught her the quip "that the Jewish housewife was the only one who didn't go out of bondage on Pesach."[72]

Jewish women in the 1970s began to write feminist Haggadot. These varied from the integrationist (which added female heroines alongside the men) to the matricentric celebration of the bonds of

mother and daughter to the explicitly lesbian.[73] Many Haggadot celebrated Jewish heroines, such as Anne Frank or midwives Shifra and
Purah, who disobeyed Pharaoh's decree to slaughter firstborn Hebrew
sons at birth.[74] Feminist Haggadot made Moses' sister, Miriam, into a
heroine for saving her infant brother by hiding him in the bulrushes as
well as a victim, punished for her lapses by her brother and dying
alone of leprosy. A special cup for her was set at the seder table. Others drank a fourth cup of wine to commemorate modern women's
struggle for liberation.[75] A hostile male at a talk of a Jewish feminist
claimed that women belonged as rabbis as much as bread belonged on
the seder plate. The feminist responded that women rabbis, like an orange on the seder plate, symbolized transformation.[76] Some included
an orange on the seder plate to make good her promise. Prayers added
the matriarchs Sarah, Rebecca, Leah, and Rachel to the prayers honoring the patriarchs Abraham, Isaac, and Jacob. Many Haggadot
included questions of the four daughters instead of those asked of
four sons.

Contemporary feminist politics inspired the creation of feminist seders. Like many other American Jewish seders that preceded it, the
feminist seder fused dueling identities, in this case Jewish and feminist
ones. Jewish feminists invested seders with new meaning, rather than
discarding much of the old ritual as Frankel and her family had done.
Between the 1970s and the 1990s the feminist seder became more
popular and mainstream. It evolved from a home-based ritual to an
organizational seder for Jewish women's groups, and from an American innovation to a global Jewish ritual celebrated in South Africa,
Russia, and Israel as well as the United States and Canada.[77]

The feminist seder attracted only a small group of women, but feminist ideas had an impact on seder ritual and the preparation of the
meal. To be sure, in households where an adult Jewish male was present, it was rare for a woman to be the ceremonial leader of the seder.
Nonetheless, as was true at the postsentimental Thanksgiving, men
were participating in the cleanup, and cooks were buying more packaged foods for the feast.[78] As was true in other postsentimental holidays, some families were also eating the feast at a restaurant. Unlike
the feasts at Delmonico's that Ruskay complained of, restaurants in
New York City more recently claimed to offer meals that were kosher
for Passover.[79]

One may ask why alternative feminist ritual appeared at Passover and not at Christmas, Thanksgiving, or Easter. Because of the over-representation of Jewish women in modern feminism, there was a critical mass of Jewish feminists who had pent-up grievances from their childhood. Moreover, the sexism of the Passover ceremony and the importance of the event afforded an easy target.[80] But other secular and Christian holidays were also ripe for this critique. Passover was unlike these other home-based feasts in that it was a religious ritual with a written text. The patriarchal words of Haggadot gave feminists written evidence of unequal regard, similar to the wedding vows in the Book of Common Prayer. Women could use their imagination and literary skill to rectify the wrongs, and thus reconcile their feminist identity with their religious heritage.

Jewish feminists attacked the patriarchy of the seder because it was the most visible symbol of inequality. They did not much criticize the consumerism of the ritual or the stereotyping of Jewish women in Manischewitz or Monarch ads. Jewish male novelists from Herman Wouk to Philip Roth had consistently lambasted the excesses of Jewish spending and, without tackling the home beautiful movement by name, made fun of its style in *Marjorie Morningstar* and *Portnoy's Complaint*. Perhaps because these male novelists combined their critique of consumerism with hatred of Jewish women as mothers and shoppers, Jewish feminists may have decided to leave this whole side of Passover unexplored.

Unlike Thanksgiving, Christmas, and Easter, Passover was not an invented tradition of the nineteenth century but a central religious ritual of ancient origin as well as a community event open to all Jewish families. With migration to the new world Passover no longer symbolized purification and order. It became a celebration of the Jewish family, ethnic identity, and freedom. Because of these political and modern redefinitions of the holiday, Passover appealed to secular Jews as well as the religiously devout. Overall, the ritual became shorter, simpler, more personalized, and more child-oriented as Jews encountered consumer culture and Christian America.

Over the decades of the twentieth century the majority of American Jews came to celebrate Passover for just one night rather than eight. The purification rituals and food prohibitions mostly disappeared. The celebrants still read from the Haggadah, but they have a variety of texts to choose from. While the seder continued to symbolize love of the child, or warm family feeling, it also acquired some postsentimental features. Women were spending less time cleaning the house and preparing for the holiday. Attending a seder outside the home became a not uncommon way to celebrate the holiday. Feminists offered the greatest critique—and renovation—of Passover. Even among the majority of American Jews who did not seek innovation, the meaning of the holiday became more symbolic and secular, less religious than it was for their grandparents. As Jews became more assimilated— as they intermarried and moved freely in the Christian world—the seder provided them with a familial definition of ethnic and religious identity.

CHAPTER SIX

Eating and Explosives

Long ago, our family stopped getting together for Thanksgiving . . . But
we still gather for Chinese New Year's, the time for renewal and hope.

—BEN FONG-TORRES, 1994

Among the Chinese in America the New Year is the most frequently
observed holiday and the most significant.[1] The New Year, which
Chinese believe should be a time of "only joys and no sorrows," is
actually a long string of separate private and public events—family
gatherings, public performances, temple visits—tied together by the
stated purpose of preparing for and celebrating the arrival of a new
year.[2] "The family, not the individual, is the basic social unit in
China," Wolfram Eberhard points out; "all festivals are essentially
family festivals rather than church or state festivals."[3] Among the central events in the New Year celebration both in China and in Chinese
America are the family feast on New Year's Eve and the subsequent
visits to relatives during the first fifteen days of the New Year.

Chinese New Year is a holiday of ancient origin. Although Passover
is arguably the longest continuously celebrated holiday in human history, Chinese New Year probably ranks second. Scholars suspect that
the New Year's holiday became a sequence of celebrations during the
Han dynasty (206 B.C.E.–220 C.E.). Like Passover, it underwent many
changes over the centuries. My focus is on the purpose and new
meanings that Chinese immigrants in the United States attached to it.
The holiday acquired new meanings because so many early Chinese
immigrants were bachelors or husbands living apart from their wives,
who were left behind in China. They were celebrating a family holiday without their family. The holiday in America was therefore a time

of melancholy, as well as a respite from backbreaking menial work. But the Chinese in America also made their holiday serve new purposes. They actively reinvented it. In the nineteenth century Chinese immigrants created their equivalent of the third seder, a holiday banquet held in public and sponsored by a community organization, sometimes in addition to the home meal on the New Year, sometimes instead of it. Chinese merchants also used the holiday as a time to show hospitality to outsiders.

The Chinese New Year followed the same path toward a sentimental and postsentimental feast as did Passover. The sentimental aspects of the holiday, however, appeared much later among Chinese-Americans than among Jews in the United States because Chinese culture continued to uphold the ideal of the patriarchal family even while men lived apart from their families. Because Chinese, unlike American Jews, did not immigrate as families, they had to adapt their family festival to meet the needs of a mostly male society. The creation of sentimental occasions was usually the work of a middle class. After the end of the World War II, Chinese-Americans entered white-collar occupations and the professions. Courts struck down restrictive racial covenants that had kept Chinese from moving into many neighborhoods. As a result, many Chinese-Americans left Chinatowns for the suburbs. Because of these changes by around the 1950s Chinese New Year became a sentimentalized occasion. At the same time ethnic entrepreneurs in Chinatown promoted the festival as a tourist attraction, which demonstrated both the anti-Communism of the American Chinese and their ethnic pride. The emergence of militant activism and nascent Chinese-American feminism as part of 1960s social activism led to the first critique of New Year festivities and thus to a postsentimental phase in the evolution of the holiday. Activism, as well as the general social interest in ethnic pluralism and the search for roots, led to the New Year celebration's assuming great symbolic weight; the holiday became a cultural performance of emerging ethnic identity. Chinese-American intellectuals, writers, and filmmakers sought to defend the holiday as a key symbol in the definition of Chinese-American identity.

Frequency of Celebration

Because of the Jewish fear of assimilation and the prominence of Jews in the fields of social science, there are more studies of the frequency of the celebration of Passover and other Jewish rituals than of Chinese holidays.[4] Moreover, scholars in general have not devoted as much study to Chinese-Americans as to American Jews because the Chinese form a smaller part of the U.S. population. Chinese in the United States in 1990 numbered 1.6 million people, whereas there were about 5.8 million Jews. Between 60 percent and 89 percent of American Jews observed Passover between 1957 and 1990. The frequency of Chinese celebration of the New Year was lower, between 50 percent and 80 percent. The three studies of the frequency of Chinese New Year observance between the 1950s and the 1980s, however, derive from such different populations that it is difficult to claim that observance is rising or declining.[5]

In the anti-Communist, antipluralist culture of the 1950s many Chinese-Americans called themselves Americans rather than Chinese-Americans and chose not to celebrate the New Year. This was especially likely to have been the case among Chinese immigrants who did not live in California or New York City, the major areas of Chinese settlement. Rose Hum Lee, who interviewed 80 Chicago Chinese families in 1950, found that half observed Chinese and American holidays, whereas the other half celebrated only American ones. Lee did not provide crucial information as to the social class or length of residence in the United States of these interviewees. But it was clear that along with an ignorance of the Chinese language, a failure to worship one's ancestors, and an inability to use chopsticks, not celebrating the New Year ranked as an important index of assimilation, a sign of American, not Chinese, self-definition.[6]

Stanley Fong found a higher rate of observance among 336 Chinese and Chinese-American undergraduates at San Francisco State University in 1963. Most of these students were lower-middle-class, second- and third-generation Chinese-Americans who did not speak Chinese. The typical student lived in a largely white neighborhood, but had mainly Chinese-American friends. When Fong asked the students their "standpoint in viewing things and events," the majority said it was Chinese-American. Fong inquired as to whether the students celebrated Chinese New Year in a "traditional manner at home, e.g., eating lettuce to symbolize longevity, baking Chinese pastry, giving li-shee (red envelopes with money in them), etc.?" Two thirds of the San Francisco State undergraduates, the majority of whom were female, answered yes.[7]

Newcomers from abroad brought their traditions with them, and found much greater reason to celebrate the New Year than American-born Chinese. It is not surprising then that the rate of observance was higher among 100 Taiwanese immigrants living in Flushing, New York in the 1980s. Flushing was a major center for Taiwanese settlement, ethnically diverse but with a large population of recent Taiwanese immigrants. About 80 percent of them celebrated the New Year. Arriving in the United States between the 1960s and the early 1980s, most were living in families. Among these immigrants the New Year was the most frequently celebrated holiday. Professionals and business owners were just as likely as waiters and factory workers to celebrate it. Even though the holiday followed soon after Christmas, Chinese Christians usually attended New Year gatherings, just as Buddhists and practitioners of Chinese folk religion did. (Other Chinese holidays were less frequently celebrated. Whereas the Mid-Autumn Festival was an important family occasion in Taiwan, many single immigrants, living apart from their families, did not observe it.) Many owners of Chinese businesses, however, did not give their employees a vacation day for the New Year and thus discouraged full notice of the holiday.[8]

The pejorative term used among Chinese-Americans for post-1950s Chinese-Americans raised in the suburbs is "banana"—yellow on the outside but white on the inside. Among the "bananas," and the intermarried, also often suburbanites, celebration of the New Year became a one-evening event rather than a two-week-long celebration or disappeared entirely. Non-Chinese women who had intermarried did not prepare a specific meal.[9] Even immigrants living in the suburbs often did not observe New Year's. One couple, who emigrated to the United States in 1978, explained, "When we first arrived, we lived in Chinatown and celebrated Chinese New Year. But now we have a house in an area which is all non-Chinese, so we really don't do much to celebrate. The kids go to school on that day, and I don't make any special dishes. I just tell them that it is Chinese New Year, and that it is a special day. The longer we are here the less we do on the holiday."[10]

Bachelors Celebrate a Family Holiday

The distinguishing feature of the first Chinese New Year's holidays in the United States was that a family festival was being celebrated chiefly by men without families. Throughout the nineteenth century most Chinese immigrants were males, attracted to the United States by the discovery of gold in the hills of California. Chinese laborers, initially welcomed as needed additional workers, built the railroads and worked in the mines; others were ranch hands, cannery workers, loggers, and houseboys. In 1852, there were only seven women among the 11,801 Chinese living in California. By 1870, the Chinese population in the United States had risen to 63,199, but it was only 7 percent female. Even in 1930, the percentage of women was only 20 percent.[11]

The familyless males consisted mainly of young single men, with a smaller group of married men who had left their wives and children behind. Poor peasants from the rural areas surrounding Canton arrived in the "Flowery Flag nation" seeking their fortune, with hopes of returning home, their pockets lined with gold. They came to America so as to be able to support their family: a husband or son emigrated but left his wife and children or kin behind in the home village to maintain the family altar and visit the family graves. Unlike American Jews, the Chinese did not intend to stay, and did not arrange for their families to join them.

Had Chinese men wanted to bring over their wives, they would have been barred from doing so by U.S. law. Fearful of the Chinese, who were seen as an Oriental, inferior race, and worried about the spread of disease and prostitution, Congress approved the Page law of 1875, which required that would-be immigrant Chinese women prove to American consuls in Hong Kong that they were not prostitutes in order to be allowed entry into the United States. In order to reduce competition from low-wage Chinese labor, Congress seven years later enacted the first explicitly racial immigrant legislation. The Chinese Exclusion Act of 1882 reduced Chinese emigration to a mere trickle of merchants, students, and tourists. It also prevented Chinese laborers already living in the United States from bringing their wives to the United States. Only the small merchant class had legal permission to do so. The Exclusion Act also barred most Chinese in America from being naturalized as U.S. citizens and was only repealed in 1943, as China became a wartime ally. Fifteen states also passed laws prohibiting interracial marriage, thus discouraging Chinese men from taking non-Chinese wives.[12]

Most Chinese immigrant men, severely restricted in bringing their family to the United States or forming one in the United States, had special reasons to commemorate the New Year. Most were isolated from American life and had limited cultural contact with American society. Their hairstyle and clothing were different than those of native-born whites. They wore wide black pantaloons that extended to the knees, collarless tunics, black broad-brimmed hats, and slippers with wooden soles. Under a silk cap, their hair hung in a queue, a long braid down their back (tucked into a hat when they ventured outside of Chinatown). For the most part, they saw themselves as temporary migrants who intended to return to China (and often did), and who found in their own culture and religion the psychological security they needed to survive. They preferred to live among and associate with other Chinese. Clinging to their native language, most learned only a few phrases in English. They did business with other Chinese and looked to the institutions of Chinatown for support and comfort. Unless they were forced to, they did not purchase goods from American storekeepers. Importing from China chopping knives and arrowroot, copper pans and dried duck kidneys, Chinese immigrants ate their own cuisine with chopsticks and rarely tasted American food.[13]

The Chinese were isolated not only because of these preferences but also because they faced hostility, prejudice, discrimination, segregation, and even, on occasion, decapitation. In this environment the Chinese looked to their own holidays as a source of solace and a means of preserving cultural ties to their family and China.[14] Migrants in rural areas would travel to San Francisco, Seattle, or another city with a large Chinese population so that they could celebrate the holiday, gamble, perhaps smoke opium, and visit a prostitute. This brief vacation made it more bearable for these men to return to work. Fireworks, gambling, and the sound of gongs, cymbals, bells, and drums transported the immigrant men from their daily routine into a different, more hospitable world.

The New Year's ritual in the United States was not the same as that celebrated in the villages of southern China from which most of the sojourners emigrated. The American Chinese New Year was briefer than that in China because Chinese laborers were permitted no more than a few days of holiday. Most employers in the late nineteenth century gave Chinese workers a one-day vacation, some three days.[15] Chinatown businesses, which depended on a Chinese clientele, usually remained closed for several days, but not the fifteen common in south China.

Rituals or duties that had been performed by men in China were easily retained in the United States. For example, men had been responsible for money matters in China, so immigrants continued tradition at New Year's by paying off their debts and settling their accounts. Similarly, because it had been a man's task in China, migrant men performed the ceremony of bidding farewell to the kitchen god on the evening of the twenty-third or twenty-fourth day of the twelfth month. By performing this ceremony of farewell, they hoped to receive in return from the gods a prosperous and healthy new year. It is unclear whether they also held a family feast at the end of this ceremony, which in China had been prepared by women.[16]

When an immigrant culture is mostly male, it usually makes its ritual into a public event, with some men being put to work as cooks to serve the group. In hosting a New Year's banquet at their headquarters, clan associations invented a new way of celebrating the New Year. Members of these associations (best thought of as social clubs or lodges among extended kin) helped to create and maintain an identity as villagers living abroad. Clan associations functioned as the equivalent of the family for migrant men living in American cities. Members made the clan banquet an alternative to the family feast on New Year's Eve.

While many clans included only those with the same surname, others took in men with a different surname but from the same village or region. Clans often established headquarters in a room or suite above a Chinatown store or restaurant; there unattached men could live, cook, and sleep. In San Francisco clan associations provided private police protection and picked up refuse. A local merchant usually sponsored and led the clan; he might even pay for the banquet. In return, the merchant solicited business from clan members, often enjoying a monopoly on their purchases. Clans helped their members find jobs, provided charity in times of need, and shipped the bones of the dead to families in China. Despite the clear hierarchy in the clan with one merchant at its head, on the New Year the mood was one of fellowship, of common bonds among men.

After the clan banquet ended, men stepped outside to set off firecrackers or went to gambling houses, opium dens, or the Chinese opera or theater. There was no such tradition in China; instead, on the evening before the New Year families would gather. In America successful gamblers spent their winnings on prostitutes; the truly lucky might have enough silver to buy a ticket home.[17] Men at gambling houses, tong headquarters, and bachelor apartments stayed up all night drinking and playing finger guessing games, mah-jongg, and the American game of poker.[18] (The tong was a dues-paying secret society that provided protection for its members. For a time tongs functioned as a Chinese Mafia, controlling opium, gambling, and prostitution in Chinatown.) At the Chinese theater, established in San Francisco in 1879, men would sit on benches in the gallery, smoking and eating oranges or Chinese melon seeds, listening to a Chinese orchestra or the drama on stage. The few women in the theater sat in a segregated section.[19]

Despite these activities, Chinese men were still homesick and melancholy, for they were separated from their families at the New Year. The holiday reminded them of how hard it was to uphold patriarchal values when the family was divided by the vastness of the Pacific. In 1911 a Chinatown bookseller published an anthology of folk songs, written in rhyme, collected from Chinese men in San Francisco. Because the songs often contained typographical errors or incorrectly formed Chinese characters, we can assume that the writers were poorly educated and thus fairly representative of Chinese immigrant men. One song had these lyrics:

> New Year's Day starts a new calendar year.
> The scent of spice fills the air beyond the front door.
> Everywhere, we Chinese sojourners greet each other with
>   auspicious sayings.
> In joyous laughter,
> We wish good luck to others, and to ourselves.
> May this year be prosperous for all walks of life;
> So that, clothed in silk, we can together bid the Flowery Flag
>   [the United States] farewell.[20]

Did these men secretly enjoy the freedom of living apart from their elders, being able to gamble without having to suffer a disapproving look from their mothers or wives? If so, they never confessed as much. Chinese autobiographers and visitors from China noted many sad-looking men. As late as the 1930s, a diplomat with the Chinese consulate who was visiting New Orleans described the poignant atmosphere that hung over the celebration of the New Year there.

The first thing I noticed was there were no women! . . . There was a certain sadness that was reflected in all of the men. I suspect that what truly seemed to make this mood so striking was that there were no children laughing. Chinese New Year is always noisy with the play of children. Here, there was a silence that I've never known to be part of Chinese New Year. It was very different but everyone tried to smile and the lodge was decorated with all of the slogans and pictures that encouraged us to do that . . . Generally, I most remember the banquet. They seemed to always have some special Chinese dishes that you ordinarily did not see in New Orleans . . . I recall some Chinese musicians playing and capturing everyone's attention. There were no lion dances or displays of Kung Fu. No one had the money to import such equipment. Most of the money was spent on food and later we to tried to find a Chinese movie to show.[21]

A Chinese laundryman in Chicago in the 1930s expressed similar sentiments. He noted that at Thanksgiving and Christmas Americans enjoyed family reunions, good food, and good music. "We have the same thing in China," he said, "but not here."[22]

The few Chinese women in the United States in the late nineteenth century may have felt more joy than melancholy. Initially Chinese women brought to the United States were prostitutes, set up in small cagelike "cribs" to provide sexual service. The high-class ones had an exclusively Chinese clientele; the rest accepted customers of all races. Chinese prostitution seems to have peaked in 1870, although rings organizing the trade persisted in San Francisco's Chinatown through 1920.[23] In part because American immigrant law attempted to stem the importation of prostitutes, the few Chinese women living in the United States by the 1880s were mainly the wives of Chinese merchants. Such women by custom were permitted to leave their house only once a year, on the New Year. Even then, they rode with their children in a closed carriage to make their calls, since a woman walking alone on the streets was assumed to be a prostitute. Another reason that respectable women rode in carriages was to avoid kidnap by white gangs or rival tongs.[24] The New Year was the one time of year when women could visit each other. Admiring each other's silk skirt, jacket, embroidered slippers, and jade, women tried to prolong these visits as long as possible. Once the carriage took them home, they had to remain there for the rest of the year, except for the occasional first-month feast to honor the birth of a child born to a member of a clan or the Festival of the Good Lady, which was celebrated once every seven years.[25]

Commercializing the New Year

White American entrepreneurs could have popularized Chinese culture; there were after all silent films showing stereotypical Chinese characters. But the Chinese New Year was a festival celebrated in a segregated neighborhood, where residences were interspersed with ethnic businesses. Thus, it was mainly the Chinese who created their own commercial version of the holiday, drawing white tourists to Chinatown and showing special hospitality and courtesy toward their regular white customers. Chinatown merchants as early as the 1870s discovered that the New Year's celebration drew curious whites, who enjoyed the sights, sounds, smells, and cuisine of what was to them an alien culture. Although Chinatown was seen as a vice district, this did not deter white tourism, but instead encouraged it. Whites wanted to see the prostitutes and opium dens of Chinatown; pickpockets were attracted by the large crowds. Visitors attended morning performances of the Chinese theater or opera. A man might want to take his "best girl" to the celebration. Some white women found the festival so interesting that they returned for tours of the temples. Local newspapers often dispatched a reporter to describe the festivities. Their descriptions were invariably condescending but nonetheless favorable. In New York reporters who traveled to Passaic, New Jersey, for the New Year were surprised by the "scrupulously clean" rooms of Chinese men working in a local laundry, since it was widely believed that foreigners lived in vermin-infested hovels and infected Americans with tuberculosis and other diseases. In the 1920s the *El Paso Herald* commented of the Chinese that "hospitality and generosity are two of his virtues he is seldom given credit for, but which always abide in him to a surprising degree."[26]

Chinese merchants recognized that in order to do business successfully in a foreign land they had to offer bribes or favors. Thus they would extend hospitality to their non-Chinese guests, despite the traditional belief that the New Year's banquet should be reserved for family members. Chinese merchants, dressed in dark blue tights and long blue silk gowns, invited policemen and politicians to their homes, to Chinese restaurants, or to the rooms in which they lived at the back of a store. Gambling houses, which were normally closed to whites, welcomed them at New Year's. In New Orleans, local Chinese hosted white Americans at a banquet the purpose of which was to lobby for the lifting of the Chinese Exclusion Laws.[27] Laundrymen gave their women customers a narcissus and distributed candy or firecrackers to children.[28]

Chinese restaurant owners in the United States learned to adapt their cuisine to American tastes. They invented chop suey and fortune cookies to please their customers. Similarly, the Chinese adapted their rituals of welcome to appeal to whites. Merchants offered their Chinese callers sweetmeats, lotus and melon seeds, and cups of tea as a way of wishing their visitors many sons. To their white customers they gave tea, brandy, sherry, or champagne, cigars, and sweetmeats in lacquered boxes. They spoke to their guests in English and handed them business cards. Chinese merchants and clan associations did not try to conceal the prostitution, opium smoking, and gambling that many Americans found repugnant. Still, the Chinese during the New Year's holiday displayed a pride in their cultural heritage and a quest for social tolerance and mixed generosity with hospitality.[29] (They were mistaken, however, if they believed that these gestures bought a lessening of violence or harassment.)

The Reemergence of the Family Holiday

Between 1911, when the Chinese monarchy was overthrown and Sun Yat-sen established the Chinese republic, and the waning of Red Guard virulence in the 1970s, Chinese America was actually more "traditional" than China. The republic of China forbade the celebration of Chinese New Year, which it associated with superstition. The republic also abolished the ancient Chinese lunar calendar in favor of the Western one. Many mainland Chinese still celebrated the holiday, however, but they did so both on January 1 and on the moveable dates of the lunar calendar. By the 1930s shops in China often closed for only three to five days rather than fifteen. When the Chinese Communists took over, they outlawed ancestor worship and gambling, told families to dismantle their altars, and forbade hanging the picture of the kitchen god above the family stove. Red Guards of the 1960s were to report anyone they saw bowing to the tablets of ancestors.[30]

By contrast, as married men brought their wives over from China in

America the New Year became longer and more traditional. The balance between the sexes was not equalized until the 1950s. But more wives were allowed to emigrate in the 1920s, 1930s, and 1940s. The clan banquet remained and became an important event in the life of the community; some married men brought their wives to it.[31] Some Chinatowns began to stage night parades with lanterns to celebrate the Feast of Lanterns, the holiday at the end of the New Year season.[32] Still, as more women reunited with their husbands in America, the New Year became more home-centered, and the number of family occasions multiplied.[33] In some cases, the clan banquet moved from the hall to the businessman's home, where over two hundred guests might be invited.[34] Maxine Hong Kingston's semiautobiographical novel *China Men* describes four Chinese immigrants who open a laundry in New York City in the 1930s; they rarely celebrate any holidays, Chinese or American, until the wife of one of the partners arrives from China. Kingston writes, "the cooking women, the shopping and slicing and kneading and chopping women brought the holidays."[35] Children stayed home from school; daughters made new clothes for every member of the family for the holiday. In preparation for the New Year, mothers and children scrubbed, dusted, washed, and scoured in one "grand house-cleaning day."[36]

The Chinese mother was both a symbol of tradition and an instructor in it. Mothers transmitted central cultural values to their children, such as respect for elders and belief in familial duty and obligation. Chinese mothers, like Jewish mothers, were supposed to be bulwarks against assimilation. Mothers also taught their children the finer rules of Chinese etiquette, such as how to serve tea and delicacies on New Year's Day. One mother in the 1930s tutored her children in proper behavior: "I want both of you to call everyone by their right names tomorrow. Tomorrow is the New Year, and you must be polite. When anyone comes, you must serve tea and be sure to offer it with both hands."[37]

Women made complicated dishes both for the banquet and for the family altar. Men who had wives no longer needed to cook for themselves. Women's production of sweets, rice flour, nine-layer-high pudding cakes, and doughnuts and turnovers fried in vegetable oil became a symbolic display of the elegance women added to the former bachelor society.[38] The work of the feast and its serving displayed gender roles in exaggerated form. Host and visitors enjoyed each other's company in sex-segregated spaces, and the presentation of the food was done in such a way that proper deference was shown to the males of the household. Men might dictate the menu; they were usually also the first to be served.

As was true for many women at Thanksgiving or Christmas, Chinese women on New Year's Eve enjoyed getting together in the kitchen to chop, slice, and dice.[39] One woman who grew up in the 1950s recalled that in her mother's kitchen "the whole table was covered with plates of different tasty ingredients. I can still remember my aunts running around, yelling and screaming for the ingredients and my mother putting [them] into the wok."[40] Lonely bachelors ate heartily at the family's table. One Chinese-American recalled that for the "uncles" at his family's table in the 1950s the event meant "a joyful, sometimes boisterous time, but, above all, a time when family bonds and a sense of belonging were reinforced."[41]

Among Chinese, as among Jews, women took responsibility for transmitting a cultural heritage, while men took on the job of providing for the family and acting as the ceremonial leader of the household at key rituals. With a husband preoccupied with his business or work, the wife became the main enforcer of values. One Chinese-American raised in Hawaii in the 1930s explained, "In return for her economic security, my mother provided religious security for my father. Mother celebrates the various festivals and holidays, and often goes to the temple to ask blessings for father and his business."[42] Because mothers-in-law were usually absent and husbands were preoccupied with business, Chinese immigrant mothers had more power in the home in America than in China. Certainly women migrants gained from having escaped the domination of mothers-in-law, whom they had been obliged to treat in China as their own mother. In any conflict, a husband was expected to side with his mother rather than with his wife. An old Chinese proverb held, "A son-in-law may perform one-half of the duty of a son, but a daughter-in-law must do twice as much as a daughter."[43] By these measures, the burdens of a wife in America were cut in half. One woman who grew up in Hawaii in the 1930s commented on the increase in maternal power since her mother moved to the islands from China. In China she noted that her "mother had to eat what grandmother bought and like it . . . But as soon as she came to Hawaii and raised a family she was her own boss. Dad gave her money to spend and she was really independent."[44]

Ironically, while Chinese women as wives enjoyed greater freedom from patriarchy, they used their newfound influence to enforce patriarchal values. In China elders had as much right to discipline children as parents. In the absence of the elders, the mother became the strict disciplinarian, administering whippings with the wooden end of a bamboo duster. As historian Judy Yung observes, Chinese women were "strict with their children, demanding unquestioning obedience, adherence to traditional gender roles, and the continued observance of folk religion, Chinese language and food, and celebration of annual festivals."[45] Yung identified the forces that began to create conflict in Chinese-American families and weakened the hold of patriarchal values. While Chinese mothers became enforcers of patriarchy in the home, allegiance to these values was weakening among their children. Public schools and peer culture, fashion, radio, movies, and advertising introduced Chinese-American girls to beliefs quite different from the ones they learned at home. Chinese daughters in the 1920s often had their own versions of the flapper: they were beginning to bob their hair and wear lipstick and nail polish. Young people did not address each other using traditional kinship terminology (older brother, younger brother, older sister, younger sister).[46] They began to chose their own mates without parental consent. Couples even kissed and embraced, acts rarely seen in public among the older generation. American-born daughters wanted smaller families than their mothers, and they were eager for information about birth control. Parents and children fought over dating, girls' education, and even the speaking of English at home.

Christianity, especially the Protestant version preached to and adopted by many immigrant Chinese, also encouraged women to demand greater self-respect in their marriages and even to leave abusive ones.[47] Chinese-American families, sometimes at the behest of Protestant missionaries in U.S. cities, began to celebrate American holidays such as Thanksgiving, Christmas, and Easter along with Chinese festivals. Few of the second generation owned ancestral tablets or worshipped their ancestors. Many American-born children could not speak Chinese and knew virtually nothing about Buddhism, Taoism, or Confucianism. Some American-born Chinese in the 1930s regarded Chinese festivals, including the New Year, as grounded in "medieval superstitions at best."[48]

Chinese-Americans were Americans at the same time that they were "overseas Chinese" who followed changes in the homeland. Political and cultural changes in China were as much of a modernizing force as American influences. After the Chinese republican government was established in 1911, the government outlawed foot binding. The few Chinese women in the United States who had "lily feet" unbound them and stopped binding their daughter's feet. In addition, more Chinese-American women began to wear Western clothes and walk unaccompanied in public. Chinese in America adopted the republican view that girls should be educated and permitted to earn wages outside the home.[49] The new government encouraged women to speak out on behalf of their rights, and a few women activists in Chinatown mounted platforms to demand their rights.[50]

The New Year holiday had always symbolized freedom for women, even when wealthy women were virtually bound to the home. Yung emphasized three major forces for change among Chinese-Americans: Americanization, Protestantism, and republicanism in China. As a result of these forces, women won even greater freedoms at the New Year. Certainly by the 1940s, a wife accompanied her husband and children in making calls on the first day of the year. She no longer followed four steps behind, as had been the practice as late as the 1930s. Even if she still wore embroidered silk tunics and pants on the occasion, her daughter dressed in Western clothes. Her daughter also probably cut and styled her hair in the American fashion and wore American-style makeup, not the white powder, heavy rouge, and hair fixed in place with wax favored by older Chinese women at holiday time.

Celebrating the New Year since the 1980s

With the lifting of immigration restrictions in 1965, many more Chinese newcomers arrived in the United States. In the decade of the 1960s, about 100,000 arrived from the Chinese mainland, Taiwan, and Hong Kong. Although quite a few were political refugees, more were economic migrants, coming to the United States for the economic opportunities it offered. The number of immigrants doubled in the 1970s, and doubled again a decade later. The most common destinations for these Chinese immigrants were New York City's Chinatown, Flushing in Queens, and a suburb of Los Angeles, Monterey Park. Immigrants from Taiwan and Hong Kong reinvigorated the tradition of the New Year even as they celebrated the holiday differently from the way they had in their home countries. Immigrants from mainland China rediscovered the holiday, since it was only since the 1980s that it was observed in Communist China.

Among all these groups of recent immigrants and among Chinese-Americans born in the United States, the New Year holiday was seen as a sentimental occasion. The family, especially among the American-born, was middle class and centered on the mother, but with a discernible gender division of labor and a stronger emphasis on education, filial piety, and respect for the elderly than was common among other Americans. As a family holiday, the New Year still affirmed the importance of family ties, prosperity, health, and companionship, but some of the more male-centered values (sexual prowess and the desirability of having many sons, for example) had disappeared.

Hsian-shui Chen's study of 100 Taiwanese immigrants in Flushing, New York, in the 1980s provides the fullest survey of how the holiday was celebrated by recent immigrants, most of whom arrived in the United States in the late 1970s and early 1980s. Some came as students; others sought work immediately, often with assistance from kin and friends. Seeking economic opportunity and a college education for themselves and their children, Taiwanese immigrants were not sojourners; most intended to stay permanently in the United States. Often a brother would send a ticket home or a husband would establish himself and then bring over his wife and children.

The impact of modern work schedules and the general streamlining that affected all late-twentieth-century rituals led to a reversion to the nineteenth-century pattern of a shortened New Year. Chinese restaurants and bakeries in Flushing would close for two or three days, after proprietors had organized a banquet and had given each of their employees a red envelope containing a year-end bonus. Taiwanese immigrants in Flushing usually celebrated the holiday for one day, or perhaps the evening before and the day of the new year. Chinese travel agents arranged van service to take revelers to the Atlantic City casinos; West Coast and Hawaiian residents often frequented Las Vegas at holiday time. Responding to their holiday patrons, the casinos might arrange for a Chinese band and singers and an outdoor lion dance.[51]

Among the Taiwanese immigrants in Chen's survey the New Year was a holiday for Christians as well as those who practiced traditional religions. Over a quarter of the Taiwanese immigrants were Christian, and about the same proportion prayed, meditated, and burned incense at Buddhist temples. Most of the immigrants did not perform the ceremony of bidding adieu to the kitchen god. In addition, few of the immigrants, whatever their religious preference, burned incense, put up a family altar in the home, or kowtowed to the elders. Only 16 out of the 100 immigrants surveyed had Buddhist inscriptions, amulets, or ancestor tablets in their home.[52]

Middle-class American-born Chinese were becoming more like other Americans and less isolated from non-Chinese, often living outside of Chinatown. To be sure, the rate of intermarriage was still fairly low (about 15 percent in 1990), much lower than among Japanese-Americans.[53] But intermarriage was quite high in Los Angeles and in Hawaii, where the Chinese-American population included many in the second and subsequent generations. As Chinese-Americans entered the American upper middle class, their family ideals became more Western. According to the 1990 census, the median family income of Chinese born in the United States was $56,762, or 61 percent above the national average—the highest family income of any ethnic group in the United States.[54]

Despite a revival of ethnic identity that began in the 1970s, acculturation continued to produce many changes among Chinese-Americans. In addition to the declines in knowledge of Chinese and in adherence to Buddhism, ancestor worship, or Confucian practice mentioned earlier, there were other indicators of acculturation. Children were no longer taught that China was their home; America was. They had little understanding of the rituals—even if they saw their parents performing them—and could not explain what the many symbols stood for. Most could not write Chinese calligraphy well enough to produce New Year's mottoes. Violating custom for the New Year's Eve banquet, families invited not only relatives but also friends and neighbors, many of whom were not Chinese.[55] Very few children or adults wore traditional formal Chinese clothes to greet visitors on New Year's Day. They usually did not serve their guests—or their elders—cups of tea. One grandmother born and raised in Honolulu explained, "I don't expect that of them. I say they're being Americanized."[56]

The disdain for Chinese customs could easily spill over into disdain for a mother's way of viewing and dealing with the world. American-born children were caught in the classic tug-of-war between loyalty to their family on the one hand and American individualism and mass culture on the other. Many American-born youth could not understand the significance of superstition or the customs that called for handing over one's destiny to the gods. It was common for mothers to be called superstitious and fathers to shout, "No more ancestor worship! No more stinking joss sticks!"[57] In the autobiographical novel *China Boy* (1991), the narrator, the son of Hong Kong immigrants, had trouble distinguishing "between the Kitchen God, who lived in Heaven and returned to the call of firecrackers, and General Electric, who operated the ice machine and only worked if money were sent to him in a white envelope with a magic stamp on it every month."[58]

By the 1960s, American-born Chinese regarded the clan association banquet as traditional, too traditional for one third-generation son who confessed to an anthropologist that "all this Chinese jazz is in another world."[59] One of the greatest difficulties for the younger generation was that the banquet was conducted in Cantonese, with some English phrases inserted. Clan associations still held New Year's banquets, often at the association hall or at a restaurant. In some cities they had two seatings to accommodate the large crowd. Men still gambled after they finished their meal, and children received li-shee. A Chinese-American congresswoman at one such banquet gave a carefully prepared speech in Cantonese and English praising her "cousins" of the clan association. But U.S.-born Chinese, who considered the event boring, did not attend, unless their elders insisted.[60]

Despite the fact that a distinctive cuisine is often the last remaining element of ethnic identity, Chinese cuisine was changing. On New Year's Day Chinese men had once prepared a Buddhist vegetarian stew, *tsai*. The stew was a symbolic statement of Buddhist identity, since Buddhist monks were vegetarians. *Tsai* was now served at the New Year's Eve dinner, often with meat added. Indeed, one baby boomer even thought such a meal was traditional.[61] Since the 1970s many families ate at a Chinese restaurant rather than having a feast in the home. Some do not have time to cook, while others are unable to produce the requisite dishes. Parents' chief goal during the banquet is often to keep children from watching television.

By the 1950s the Chinese-American family was becoming less patriarchal as it became more middle-class. Although girls had less graduate education than sons, daughters as well as sons were sent to college. The Chinese-American kinship system became bilateral rather than patrilineal: children recognized relatives on their mother's as well as father's side. Very few mothers-in-law lived with their adult sons.[62] Among immigrants, if a grandmother lived in the home, she assumed the role of a kindly figure, not one inspiring her daughter-in-law's awe or fear. Even though respect for elders was still important, kowtowing had become optional. (Kowtowing involved knocking the forehead on the ground three times and prostrating oneself nine times. It was performed according to birth order and gender, with the eldest son kowtowing first.) Arranged marriages and preference for sons were decidedly out of date. One celebrant at San Francisco's New Year in the 1970s, however, offered a perspective on gender roles that seemed to mimic the version of segregated roles so common in the 1950s. He told a reporter, "For me, the No. 1 priority is the family . . . Some of the elderly Chinese still think it is important for the first born to be a son. I don't care, as long as it is a healthy child. I tell my wife she can do whatever she likes as long as she's seen to the family first."[63]

Student social activism in the late 1960s created the pan-ethnic term "Asian-American," grouping Chinese with their former Japanese enemies. The emphasis on both a new identity and a hyphenated one actually increased the interest in the New Year among educated, acculturated Chinese. Like the Christmas celebrations of Americanized immigrant groups in the 1970s, celebration of the Chinese New Year is a display of symbolic ethnicity, an activity one undertakes to prove one's ethnic identity to oneself and show it off to others. In Chinese-American novels, New Year's celebrations are also an opportunity for nostalgia—to show sympathy toward immigrant mothers in their role as guardians of tradition and to criticize the "bananas" who are embarrassed by being Chinese. Sons and daughters of immigrant parents are portrayed as caught between two cultures, feeling not entirely comfortable with American middle-class life but unable to overcome the cultural gaps between themselves and their parents, especially their mothers, who are described as cold and distant.

Chinese-American filmmakers and writers, who regarded the New Year as a cultural text, scrutinized it for signs of family conflict and the tensions wrought by acculturation. In films and novels the banquet usually functions as a way of showing the erosion of an older sense of kinship obligation. Wayne Wang's film *Dim Sum* (1984) is remarkably similar to Barry Levinson's *Avalon*. Both filmmakers used tension at the family feast as a dramatic symbol of the decline in family feeling among the American-born children of immigrants. In *Dim Sum* the widowed immigrant mother from Hong Kong lives with her dutiful adult daughter in Chinatown. Her other daughter, son, daughter-in-law, and grandchildren reside in the suburbs and are not dutiful at all. They attend the New Year's banquet the mother prepares, but convey their discomfort. After eating hurriedly, they make their excuses and leave quickly. The next day across the clothesline the mother sighs deeply as she explains to her neighbor, "Everybody ate . . . and everybody left."

A Modern Tourist Attraction

Just as Chinese businessmen in the nineteenth century welcomed the New Year as a commercial opportunity, Chinese businessmen of the 1950s and later made the New Year into a staged event for tourists. Festival organizers in San Francisco hoped to encourage Anglos as well as suburban Chinese and Chinese living in other cities to attend that city's parade. Chinese business leaders also cooperated with city officials and members of the chamber of commerce. In San Francisco's Chinatown in the 1950s (as in Lindborg, Kansas, a decade later) merchants' associations and entrepreneurs intent on generating customers for local businesses developed the New Year holiday to appeal to visitors by combining American and ethnic elements. Festival organizers saw themselves as educating others about their traditions and history, but the "traditional" festival was an ersatz one that combined American and ethnic elements. New Year's celebrations were held in most of the larger Chinatowns, but only in San Francisco, the largest area of Chinese settlement, did the festival come to be seen both by Chinese businessmen and the white chamber of commerce as a means of generating tourism.

The Golden Dragon Parade in San Francisco's Chinatown is a Chinese-American invented tradition of the 1950s. Henry Kwok ("H. K.") Wong, a San Francisco businessman, columnist, public relations executive, and president of the Chinatown Chamber of Commerce created the contemporary New Year's Festival in that decade. He wanted to remake the image of the Chinese for American tourists, who tended to think of New Year's as a Chinese gambling holiday and regard his ethnic group as "mysterious." By the 1930s the Grayline Bus Company was offering tours of San Francisco's Chinatown. Travelers in those early days encountered faux lepers and fake opium dens. Although these practices were eliminated by the 1940s, the image of Chinatown as a closer-to-home version of "the wicked Orient" prevailed. Ironically, while Wong promoted tourism in this way, he also wanted both to teach non-Chinese about real Chinese art, music, dance, and fashion and to show how American the residents of Chinatown had become.[64] Moreover, in the immediate aftermath of the Korean War, Chinese-Americans were eager to demonstrate their patriotism and anti-Communism.

San Francisco city officials and businesses funded a publicity budget for a festival in the 1950s. They saw the New Year's festival as a tourist attraction that could "rival Mardi Gras." In fact, the organizers modeled their event on Mardi Gras and the Rose Bowl parade on New Year's Day in Pasadena. As McCarthyites ferreted out Chinese Communists in California, the parade dramatized the loyalty of the average Chinese-American. Chinese-American veterans of World War I, World War II, and Korea marched along with air force, army, navy, and marine bands. The lion and dragon dances became surrounded by the more structured marching bands and floats of the modern parade. Eventually the airlines, the California state lottery, and California banks sponsored major floats, which resembled those at the Rose Bowl.

In 1953 Wong proposed making a beauty pageant, with a contest, coronation ball, and fashion show, part of the New Year's festival. The beauty contest was a distinctively American idea and had no Chinese antecedents, although there had been queens of Chinatown as early as 1915, and Chinese-American organizations had sponsored beauty pageants as far back as 1948.[65] Miss Chinatown rode on her own float in the New Year's parade. Proceeds from ticket sales to the pageant helped fund the New Year's parade. The presence of well-educated Chinese-American contestants showed that the women had become acculturated. Their beauty and poise proved, in the words of a pamphlet for the festival, that they had come a long way "from dim memories of wee bound feet to present day stiletto heels."[66] American-born Chinese thus demonstrated their fealty to the United States and its corporations, as well as to the use of women as a sexual symbol to sell products or promote commerce.

Postsentimental Critique—and Defense

Just as 1960s cultural nationalism was important to the development of Kwanzaa, sixties radicalism contributed to the critique of Wong's festival. The Vietnam War, the growth of the New Left, and the founding of the Black Panther party in 1966 affected the community. Chinese-American activists, some of them students at San Francisco State or Berkeley, others high school students, adopted the language, the fashion (black leather jackets and sunglasses), and the programs (free breakfast programs) of the Black Panthers. Activists at San Francisco State staged a strike in November of 1968 for the establishment of an ethnic studies program.

The postsentimental Chinese New Year can be said to have begun with attacks by these radical activists on the San Francisco pageant in the late 1960s. Chinatown community organizers, some of whom were sympathetic to the Panthers, the Red Guards on the mainland, and Berkeley radicals, with Chinese-American feminists found much to dislike in both the parade and the beauty pageant. White tourists, they argued, showed disrespect for an urban neighborhood with more than its share of overcrowded housing, inadequate medical services, tuberculosis, and suicide when they ripped down posters and lanterns to take home as souvenirs. Activists also protested against the building of a Holiday Inn in Chinatown instead of government-subsidized low-cost housing.[67]

Women attracted to feminism were mainly Chinese-American women college students and recent graduates in the Bay area. They discussed their inferior treatment in the Asian-American movements for social change as well as their own sense of inferiority because of their Asian-American looks.[68] Chinese-American feminists took offense at the beauty pageant, just as radical feminists protested by throwing curlers into a trash can in Atlantic City at the Miss America contest in 1968. Chinese-American feminists argued that the pageant was "a parade of flesh," "a livestock show" at which women competed with each other in displaying their bodies.[69] They wanted instead a contest or program that recognized the problems facing low-wage women workers, such as the garment workers in Chinatown. They attacked both the sexism and the racism of the contest and claimed that to win, a contestant had to meet white standards of beauty:[70] long legs, a large bosom, a narrow nose with a high bridge, and large, more Western-looking eyes with double eyelids and longer eyelashes.[71]

Why did feminists choose to attack the public, rather than both the public and private aspects, of the festival? First, Chinese-American feminists echoed the feminist rhetoric of the time about the exploitation of women as sexual objects. Certainly feminists analyzed "the politics of housework" in the late 1960s, but the "politics of holidays" emerged only as part of the Jewish feminist critique of Passover. Second, Chinese-American feminists saw their mother's cooking at the feast differently from the way Jewish feminists saw their mothers' work. Jewish daughters complained about mothers who were never able to sit down to eat. To Chinese-American daughters a mother's cooking offered symbolic proof of the love a mother did not express directly.

In the 1950s, the Chinese New Year's festival reflected the political allegiances of American Chinese. Bosomy beauty queens and uniformed drum and bugle corps echoed the cultural influence of Pasadena, Atlantic City, and the American remaking of the carnival or procession into a parade. In each subsequent decade the parade echoed the patterns of American society: sixties militants were followed in the 1970s by proud ethnics searching for their identity without having to give up their participation in middle-class, consumer society. In 1969, militant activists disrupted the parade and were hauled off by the police. By the late 1970s parade organizers were searching for "authenticity." The authentic was located in the past and in the homeland. One organizer traveled to Taiwan to bring back bridal carriages and red silk wedding dresses in order to stage an "authentic" wedding procession from the Han period. This search for the authentic was a reaction to overassimilation in the 1950s and 1960s, a reflection of greater sophistication among educated Chinese-Americans, and a marketing ploy for parade organizers. The search inevitably led to a trip to Taiwan or mainland China, since authenticity was defined as a performance identical to one found in those countries.[72] As more immigrants from Taiwan, Hong Kong, and the mainland entered the beauty contest, contestants proudly gave answers to the questions judges posed in fluent Chinese without an American accent.[73]

When Chinese-American culture was put on public display, it mirrored the politics and culture of the times. In the home the feast had lost virtually all of its association with Buddhism, Confucianism, and

ancestor worship. Families made their celebration into a symbol of togetherness. They gathered to affirm good feelings across the generations to strengthen family ties, rather than to venerate ancestors and
to give unquestioned respect for elders and patriarchy. As was common at many postsentimental holidays, many Chinese held their New
Year's feast at a restaurant. The holiday was no longer part of the Chinese festival cycle, but rather a supplement to the American one. Ken
Hom, the author of many Chinese cookbooks who grew up in Chicago's Chinatown, wrote in the 1990s, "Growing up Chinese-American meant that I got to celebrate several extra holidays. After the
Christmas holidays, I could always look forward to the Chinese New
Year, usually a month or two later."[74]

Because Chinese children could explode firecrackers, eat sweets, and
receive li-shee, the lucky money, Chinese New Year has always been a
special holiday for children; but it had once been much more. While
the respect for elders and ancestors diminished, the gaiety of the holiday remained. Like the dough encasing a Chinese dumpling, ethnicity
enfolded the family event. Assertions of ethnic identity were borrowed from older Chinese practices, but many American ones were
added. The hallmark of the postsentimental New Year was a celebration of family solidarity and ethnic identity.

As Chinese in the United States transformed themselves from sojourners and overseas Chinese to Chinese-Americans and then Asian-
Americans, their need for the Chinese New Year has fluctuated and
the meanings they assigned it have changed. Acculturation, increased
education (especially for daughters), loss of the ability to speak the
language of the home village, and the move to the suburbs all led to a
decline in the observance of the new year. The countervailing forces
were the sharp increase in post-1965 immigrants who selected the
holiday as a central ritual they wanted to preserve and the ethnic revival of the 1970s, which defined it as a display of one's identity in a
multicultural society. Thus, it was appropriate that a banner at an
Evanston, Wyoming, New Year's parade in the 1970s spelled out, in
Chinese characters that many Chinese-Americans were unable to
read, "I am an American."[75]

1. A woman stitched these two symbols of mourning, the urn and the weeping willow, using as thread two shades of the brown hair of her beloved dead. A brassmaker probably made the locket, which is dated 1799; the location of his shop is unknown. The woman probably wore this locket as a memento of her loved one. (Courtesy Winterthur Museum, gift of Mr. Roland E. Jester)

Fig. 1.

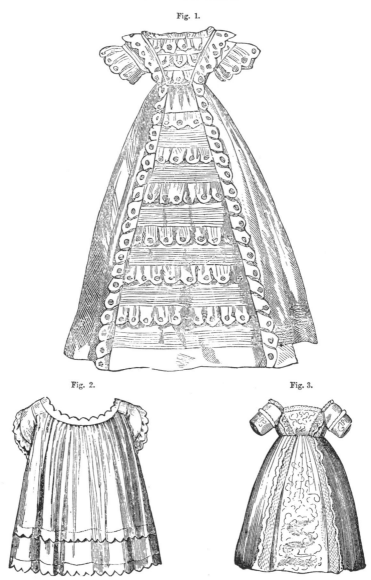

Fig. 2.   Fig. 3.

2. In 1852, *Godey's Lady's Book* was showing its readers how to create facsimiles of family heirlooms if they had not inherited them. A middle-class mother might make this christening gown, but more often she probably hired a seamstress to do the work. The fabric called for prestigious cambric, imported from France; and lace was to be used for the trim. (From *Godey's Lady's Book*, 1852)

THE BIRTH-DAY GIFT.

3. Fancy clothes—party dress, stiff crinoline underneath, white hose, black patent leather shoes—and store-bought gifts made the birthday party a special event. In holding up her gift for her guests to admire, as in this illustration from an 1859 children's book, the birthday girl was demonstrating the pleasure that a purchased, special doll might bring. (Courtesy American Antiquarian Society)

4. Having just arrived from the city, the fashionably dressed young family greets Grandfather, while Grandmother holds her granddaughter. In this Currier and Ives illustration from 1871, the matriarch stands at the threshold of the family's New England farmhouse, inviting the young family to enter the sacred shrine of the ancestral home. This or a similar illustration, which was likely to be hung in the family parlor, suggested the nostalgia for the rural life felt among the middle class, who often lived in the city. (Courtesy Prints and Photographs Division, Library of Congress)

5. At first communion a child might pose for an individual portrait in a studio. Also popular were group portraits of the class with the priest—or the priest and the nuns—usually taken on the front steps of the church, as in this photograph from Muncie, Indiana, in the 1880s. Because photography equipment was heavy to transport, there was no picture-taking at the family party after the church service. (Courtesy Notre Dame Archives)

6. This German-American bride in Michigan in 1887 had her wedding portrait taken in a studio in the traditional German black bridal dress and floor-length white veil. German Lutherans in Germany and the United States wore black to distinguish themselves from Catholics. By about 1900, however, most German-American brides were choosing a white gown and a shorter white veil. (Courtesy Frankenmuth Historical Association)

7. For Chinese New Year in the 1890s family members wore special clothes. The platforms on the girl's shoes provided the look of a "lily" foot without her mother having to bind her daughter's feet. The children's and the mother's clothes were made of silk; the father's clothes, not as important a signifier of family status, were probably made out of cotton. (Courtesy Arnold Genthe Collection, Prints and Photographs Division, Library of Congress)

8. A Victorian mother probably purchased these Easter outfits for her children, colored and hid the eggs, and bought the Easter lilies used to decorate the living room. The girl in the center of the photo is holding up a beautifully decorated large porcelain egg. The photograph was probably taken by a professional, rather than a family member. (Courtesy Corbis-Bettmann)

9. Children wore the same silk embroidered outfits for a birthday party as for Chinese New Year. Taking a family photograph with a hand-held camera was a new activity, which became a significant part of the birthday party. The photograph, the frosted cake, and the lit candles were the American elements at this syncretic birthday party in San Francisco in 1912. The sailor hat on the older boy may have been a symbol of sympathy with the Chinese republican army. The other children's hats—the little boy's rice bowl hat and the crownlike one on the little girl—were worn at New Year's and other special occasions. (Courtesy Arnold Genthe Collection, Prints and Photographs Division, Library of Congress)

10. This bridal shower in St. Paul, Minnesota, was held in a woman's home around 1910. The size of the group, which was probably Scandinavian-American, was relatively small. The guests, agemates of the bride-to-be, brought symbols of her future responsibilities as a wife—the fish, a pot to cook it in, a whisk broom, a shawl, and garters for the bride to wear on her wedding day. The atmosphere appears to be more serious than lighthearted. (Courtesy Minnesota Historical Society)

11. This wedding shower of 1922 among the Jewish middle class was large, commercial, and silly. The emotional climate was warmer: several of the women are touching another's shoulder. The shower was held in the private dining room of a large Miami hotel. One of the organizers probably made the funny hats for the guests. The bride-to-be is seated at the center, wearing the largest paper hat. (Courtesy Florida State Archives)

12. This wake for an Italian-American woman was held in her parlor in Philadelphia in 1929. It was proper style to display several standing wreaths. Florists printed the name of the donor on the wreath's satin ribbon. The mortician has wrapped a rosary around the left hand of the corpse. (Courtesy Balch Institute for Ethnic Studies Library; Benjamin Verdile photo)

13. In this Polish baptismal certificate from Philadelphia in 1923, the mother presents the child to be baptized. Godparents are noticeably absent. Sometimes a family might hang these certificates on the wall of the parlor. (Courtesy Balch Institute for Ethnic Studies Library)

14. In the 1920s the groom usually chose the honeymoon locale, and he seems often to have wanted to go camping. Here the romantic trip to the wilderness is connected to the purchase of an automobile. The Howard Automobile Company, in trying to associate a Buick with romance, was also helping to boost the total cost of the honeymoon. (Courtesy Sam DeVincent Collection of Illustrated American Sheet Music Covers, Archives Center, NMAH, Smithsonian Institution)

15. Unlike most other bar mitzvah boys, this thirteen-year-old in Philadelphia in the 1930s was not given a suit with long pants. The studio pose, with the boy holding a book, was a common one not specific to the bar mitzvah. (Courtesy Philadelphia Jewish Archives Center)

16. On Easter Sunday in the 1940s black parents in Chicago's black section (the "Black Belt") gave children spending money for the movies. Apparently children wore their new outfits the whole day, not just to attend church Sunday morning. (Courtesy U.S. Farm Security Administration collection, Prints and Photographs, Library of Congress)

17. American Jews acquired their sweet tooth from their Christian neighbors, who enjoyed chocolate made in the shape of bunnies for Easter. Bartons, a Jewish-owned firm, introduced chocolate candy and chocolate-covered matzohs for Passover in the 1940s. Tins like this one became objects of nostalgia, repositories of family memories of special kosher-for-Passover foods. (Courtesy National Museum of American Jewish History, Philadelphia; Will Brown photo)

18. In the 1940s Christmas cards with a family photo began to appear. Despite the celebration of motherhood in the 1950s, the wife is missing from this card. Both the type of card and the subject and composition of the photo present a happy American family of the business class.

𝕭est Christmas 𝕸ishes

The Cooneys

19. St. Lucia Day was not a traditional holiday among Swedes in Minnesota. Immigrants from Sweden living in the United States during the war may have introduced this holiday to the Minneapolis area in the 1940s. By the 1960s, when this photo was taken at the Lutheran Bible Institute, the rituals associated with the day had become invented traditions. (Courtesy Minnesota Historical Society)

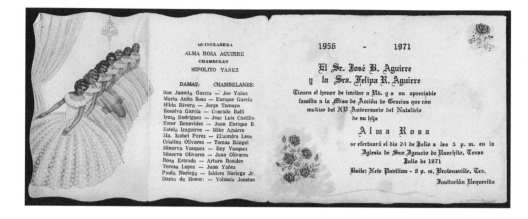

QUINCEAÑERA
ALMA ROSA AGUIRRE
CHAMBELAN
HIPOLITO YAÑEZ

DAMAS: CHAMBELANES:
San Juanita Garcia — Joe Yañez
Maria Anita Sosa — Enrique Garcia
Hilda Rivera — Jorge Tamayo
Rosalva Garcia — Conrado Balli
Irma Rodriguez — Jose Luis Castillo
Ester Benavides — Juan Enrique B.
Estela Izaguirre — Mike Aguirre
Ma. Isabel Perez — Elisandro Leos
Cristina Olivares — Tomas Rangel
Minerva Vasquez — Rey Vasquez
Minerva Olivares — Juan Olivares
Rosa Estrada — Arturo Rosales
Teresa Lopez — Juan Yañez
Paula Noriega — Isidoro Noriega Jr.
Dama de Honor: — Yolanda Jonston

1956 — 1971

El Sr. José B. Aguirre
y la Sra. Felipa R. Aguirre

Tienen el honor de invitar a Ud. y a su apreciable
familia a la Misa de Acción de Gracias que con
motivo del XV Aniversario del Natalicio
de su hija

Alma Rosa

se efectuará el día 24 de Julio a las 5 p. m. en la
Iglesia de San Ignacio de Ranchito, Texas
Julio de 1971

Baile: New Pavilion - 8 p. m. Brownsville, Tex.

Invitación Requerida

20. This 1971 invitation to a quinceañera in Brownsville, Texas, was illustrated with a drawing of seven *damas* (ladies in waiting). The invitation included the names of all the *damas* and their *chambelanes* (ceremonial male attendants). Hispanic-owned print shops found the quinceañera trade a profitable sideline. (Courtesy Alma Rosa Aguirre)

CHAPTER SEVEN

Cakes and Candles

Is there in fact anything quite so near heaven as stuffing yourself with
strawberries and cake and ice cream and wishing on the way home you
could have eaten more?

—WALTER BROOKS, 1915

Ron Popeil, the supersalesman who made millions by demonstrating
the Veg-o-matic on television, was recently interviewed on CNN.
Popeil described how he succeeded in business despite an unhappy
childhood. His uncaring divorced parents had sent him to boarding
school and never visited. In all the years of his childhood not once
had he had a birthday party. His questioner sympathized, responding, "That's rough." Forty years before Popeil's interview, a fictional
character in a musical also complained about parental deprivation.
Ralphie in Clifford Odets's *Awake and Sing* (1935) remarked angrily,
"I never in my life had a birthday party. Everytime I went and cried in
the toilet when my birthday came."[1] Birthday parties are seen as such
an essential part of childhood that the lack of one proves parental in-
difference, if not outright neglect.

The children's birthday party was a sentimentalized occasion of the
nineteenth century, born out of new beliefs honoring the individual,
indulging the child as a demonstration of parental affection, and con-
ceptualizing time and age in new ways. As a gift-giving event for a
special child, the birthday party emerged at the nexus of an affectionate family and a consumer society. Strictly speaking, the birthday
party is a fete for an individual, not a family event. Nonetheless, it undoubtedly is a domestic occasion because of the mother's role in organizing it, the fact that the party is held in the home, and the meaning
of the event and the gifts given at it as symbols of parental love of

the child. Parents also used the party as a means of teaching children proper manners so that these children would eventually be able to assume a place of respectability, honor, and privilege in society.

The children's party was begun by wealthy Protestants in the nineteenth century. By the twentieth century children from every and no religion and from families of even modest means were indulged and given special treats on the day of the anniversary of their birth. With rising standards of living and the growth of compulsory schooling, such children were seen as special and deserving of recognition. Even during its long sentimental phase, the birthday party underwent significant reinventions. The earliest parties were parent-run, had many guests, and were quite formal. Birthday parties for young children remained events controlled by parents for obvious reasons. Parties for older children, while retaining their character as sentimental occasions, changed significantly, especially between 1870 and 1920. Mothers allowed children greater input in deciding the guest list and the games to be played at the party, and the party became smaller and more informal.

Various ethnic traditions surrounded the date or year of birth, although the idea of the children's birthday party was mainly absent outside the Protestant upper and middle class. Immigrants mixed and blended older forms of birthday celebration with Anglo-American (and German) ones. The familiar processes of immigrant adaptation were evident; gradually the newcomers adopted and adapted American forms, partaking of the American ritual and combining it with the unstated aim of affirming the social network of the parents. Immigrant children again served as agents of Americanization; in learning about the American style of birthday party, they begged their parents for it. In its hybrid form immigrants used the party to strengthen ethnic culture and family ties.

The postsentimental party was held outside the home, often at a restaurant or commercial indoor playground, where food and birthday cake were provided. Dating the emergence of a postsentimental phase of birthday celebration is difficult, because it took place gradually. Unlike Thanksgiving and Christmas, there was no distinct change in birthday parties in the 1960s. There were fewer commercial options then for such celebrations, and parental spending was still somewhat restrained, since the number of dual income parents was more limited. The development of family entertainment centers in the

1980s encouraged commercialization of the children's party. In the end, consumer culture no longer reinforced domesticity, but supplanted it.

The Parent-Run Party

The birthday party had only a limited carnivalesque phase. In their public display of excessive eating and drinking, birthday parties of the elite resembled carnivals, with the wealthy handing out food or liquor to male youths who came to their door. The elite held birthday celebrations, but not necessarily on an annual basis. Birthdays of pharaohs, emperors, kings, queens, and nobles might be celebrated as often as twelve times a year. The emperor Augustus held a monthly fete on the anniversary of his birth. Wealthy colonists in America held balls once a year on the king's birthday.[2]

Adults as well as children had birthday parties in the nineteenth century. By the 1840s spouses were giving each other birthday presents, but they apparently did not host large parties for each other.[3] Antebellum families gave parties to honor an elderly parent. As for children, although an American girl had a birthday party as early as 1772—that is, she had a special dance as a commemoration of her date of birth—birthday parties did not become common even among the wealthy until the late 1830s, or about a decade after the domestic Christmas had emerged.

The parent-run party was a sentimental occasion that originated with the English elite and the Germans.[4] It was formal—a party to which as many as forty children might be invited. Some of these were same-sex fetes, others were for both sexes. The first American evidence of a birthday party I have found is from an entry in the girlhood diary of Anna Green Winslow dated November 1772. Her father had left his wealthy Boston family to serve as the commissary to the British regiments in Nova Scotia. Winslow's parents had sent her to school in Boston, where she lived with her aunt. On the day after Anna's twelfth birthday her aunt held a ball for Anna, to which were invited eight girls, including three of Anna's cousins. To the accompaniment of a flute, the girls danced reels and minuets. It was clear that the birthday was also an occasion to give her a few luxury gifts. Anna's mother sent presents, consisting of cloth, a bag to embroider as a purse, ribbons, and a black hat; Anna's aunt gave her ermine with which to trim her red cape.[5] A month and a half later Anna attended the birthday party of a ten-year-old girl, a distinguished "scoller" at the local dancing school. Although less is known about parties for younger children during this period, another diarist recorded one such event. In the 1790s Martha Pintard Bayard, a woman of considerable wealth, hosted a special family dinner for her five-year-old son to which relatives were invited. Conforming to the tradition of the wealthy, her son presented each servant with a gift.[6]

In addition to the English ball and party, the German *kinderfeste* (children's festival) helped shape the modern form of the birthday party. At this somewhat religious family dinner parents gave the child a few presents. Mothers cooked the child's favorite dishes and invited other children and family friends to join the family for supper. For dessert cake was served, but not the round, frosted, double-layer cake now associated with birthdays. Instead, German mothers baked a ring cake with nuts and raisins, and dusted it with sugar. The celebrant was supposed to make secret wishes before blowing out all the candles on the cake with a single puff. On the table was a small tree like the ones used at Christmas, decorated with bonbons and ribbons, under which were piled presents for the child.[7] The Birthday Man, a bearded elf who rewarded good children with gifts but punished the bad, sometimes appeared at German-American birthday parties.[8]

Although much is known about how non-German Americans became interested in the German Christmas tree and Easter Bunny, only one writer, a Mrs. Halbert, told in the 1870s of her visit to a German family's birthday party. She noticed that when a German father entered the threshold of his home, he left his worries about work behind him. Germans somehow were able to combine domestic festivity without going into "wild extravagance." She observed, "we do not believe anywhere else in the world so much good cheer can be managed for so little money."[9] She especially liked the German practice of singing a hymn after the candles were blown out. "What could make a sweeter, holier impression on the heart of a child," Mrs. Halbert wrote.[10] Because a hymn rather than a birthday song was sung, and because the ring cake did not have two layers, these now familiar elements of the birthday party clearly had American, rather than German, sources.

Around 1840 or 1850 several innovations made cake baking easier and led to the emergence of what we now consider the standard type of birthday cake. Cookstoves, freestanding stoves with their own ovens, were invented then. The temperature in the oven of a cookstove could be more easily controlled than in the bake oven of a fireplace. Also, by 1850 a cook could purchase an eggbeater, a wire whisk, a powder mill for grinding sugar, and a syringe for cake decorating. To make the batter lighter, a woman could buy baking powder at the country store (before that she had to use brewers' yeast or baking soda). Peddlers and merchants began to sell round tins for baking instead of the heart-shaped ones women had been using. Before the 1850s it took three or four hours to heat the bake oven; granulate sugar; grate lemons; blanch, grind, and beat almonds into a paste; grate, grind, and pound nutmeg, cinnamon, cloves, and allspice; and dry the flour before sifting it. A cook had to devote several additional hours to making the frosting, since many recipes called for beating twenty egg whites for three hours until properly thickened.[11]

In addition to these factors, changing views of children and the impact of industrial society on attitudes toward age and the life cycle influenced adult-run birthday parties of the 1840s. Enlightenment thinkers had carved out childhood as a distinct and separate stage of life. Swiss educator Johann Pestalozzi, for example, encouraged his readers to recognize the positive benefits in gratifying the child's innocent desires. He argued that play and other childish pleasures children were allowed in their early years nurtured their innate innocence. He also believed that mothers, because of their close relationship with the child, could play a positive role in infant education.

By the 1840s influential Christian writers such as theologian Horace Bushnell, perhaps influenced by Pestalozzi, began to change their attitudes toward children's play. Most premodern people did not believe children needed a special time or space devoted to play, and children were integrated with adults both at work and at play.[12] Roughhousing as much with adults as with each other, children shared with grown-ups their hoops, horns, whips, and balls, though wealthy children did have a few toys of their own. Whether slightly inebriated or half asleep, children frolicked while adults reveled, except at the balls of the elite, from which they were excluded. Poor parents usually did not give children special items for play, but instead allowed them to make their own out of scraps of cloth, sticks, string, or rags.

Bushnell, along with many middle-class parents, believed that children deserved a relatively carefree period in their lives when they could play. Wholesome games, he felt, formed a useful part of child-hood, not a temptation to evil. Special books and magazines, chil-dren's furniture (high chairs, cribs, swings, baby carriages), individual bedrooms (a nursery and separate bedroom for the older child), and new toys (hobbyhorses and board games) were signs of parental re-gard for the young. The birthday party was an opportunity both to honor an individual child and to allow him or her to display proper manners. Christmas served as a model for the birthday party. Antebel-lum publishers, as noted earlier, first offered gift books as presents for New Year's and Christmas. By 1837, they were also advertising gift books as suitable for birthdays.[13]

Educators and physicians, beginning at the end of the eighteenth century, inadvertently contributed to increased age consciousness. Learning, Johann Pestalozzi argues, should proceed according to a child's age. Physicians developed benchmarks for growth and devel-opment appropriate for certain ages. By increasing popular con-sciousness of specific ages, educators and medical doctors helped fur-ther the desire to mark key moments of increased age with ceremony. Life was no longer seen as an unending and ever-turning wheel or as a ladder to be climbed, but instead as a series of steps one ascended un-til reaching middle age and then descended thereafter. Industrial so-ciety also measured time more accurately and placed greater value on sustained effort at work. Thus, employers went to considerable lengths to make sure that workers showed up on time and devoted themselves to the tasks at hand in their hours on the job.

The agricultural cycle had once provided a sense of time: daylight hours were the time for doing work outdoors and seasons were seen as times for planting or harvesting. Most people did not own an alma-nac or a calendar; few knew their birthdate. The premoderns mea-sured time by the seasons, the sun, the moon, the tides, or the outward signs of maturation and aging of the body. Physical size and family status mattered more than chronological age. In farming areas, where a son's ability to do a man's job measured his worth, relatives de-scribed a boy by his size (a "large" or "great" boy) more often than by his age.[14] In addition to strength and physical maturity, knowing that someone was a younger daughter or eldest son revealed more about them than their exact age.[15] Premodern people also paid attention to the religious seasons. Catholics, following the dictates of their church, often ignored birthdays, since the church did not approve of the day-of-birth celebrations of the elite, which it associated with Greek and Roman orgies.[16]

The growth of industrial society, with its proliferation of clocks and wristwatches, helped further the new attitude toward children's play and toward the view of life as having a series of milestones worthy of commemoration. Machines and equipment such as trains and clocks led to a new, more scheduled view of minutes and hours during the daylight hours and into the evening. People began to regard play as a necessary respite from work. Children who delighted in blindman's buff, it was believed, might return refreshed to schoolwork or find it easier to assume adult responsibilities.

As with other domestic occasions, the work of creating the birthday celebration fell to the mother. Shopping, decorating, planning, and organizing the party were woman's work, but not necessarily the mother's, since aunts and grandmothers assisted. The woman in charge supervised and took responsibility for the event, although she did not necessarily do all the cooking, cleaning, and baking. In many homes household servants made the jellies and ironed the damask tablecloth for the party.

Mothers also became the schedule keepers of the home, keeping track of all the significant "times" for the family. A mother made entries in the birthday book, an annual calendar to which she added the names of family members and significant commemorative dates, usually ones that required a note, a gift, or perhaps a party. The birthday book, which appeared first in England in the mid-nineteenth century, created a filing system for organizing family occasions. Later on the book became a woman's inventory of gift-giving, as she would note presents given and their cost.[17] Most birthday books specialized in the quotations of one author. Julia Ward Howe's daughter, for example, selected appropriate sayings of her mother and arranged them in such a book.[18]

The mother-organized birthday party was a display of refined manners, parental wealth, and proper gender roles. It did not exist among the poor. The working class and the poor did not own dining room tables, sideboards, or iceboxes. Children from such families had no parties in their honor. They had to amuse themselves by playing with tin cans, cows' bladders, or homemade rag dolls. Their parents tended to believe that children should contribute economically to the family, make few demands, and obey without question.

Among the middle class and the well-to-do the idea that children should conform to the rules of polite society made the parent-run birthday party into an evaluation of how well a child knew the rules of etiquette. Because knowing etiquette defined one as middle or upper class, it was important that a child be able to perform these rules without error. Mothers were responsible for teaching children such things as when to say thank you and how to greet guests properly. Children were seated with the family at regular meals (as opposed to the English custom of a separate children's table) so as to learn table manners. Dining with company was a test of how well children had mastered their lessons.[19]

The children's birthday party was an event to which other children were issued invitations, rather than being a community festival where the doors were thrown open to all comers. This more private view of a party was characteristic of the sentimental occasion. The invitation-only children's party defined the child's proper peer group. The uninvited were children who did not belong to proper society. Thus, by inviting only children of relatives and family friends, a mother could insure that her children associated with other respectable people.

The form the party took tended to give pleasure to girls more than boys, since it encouraged what were seen as the female pleasures of loving sweets, dressing up, and giving gifts; it taught boys that the formal party was a female art form. Boys, although they delighted in receiving a hobbyhorse or a rifle as a present, probably did not relish these events as much as girls. One little boy winced as he remembered his younger brother's birthday party, probably around the late 1860s. "Awkward and confined in their starch suits," the boys at the party "stood around the doors of what was known as the 'parlor,' and tried to conceal their embarrassment by every now and then thumping or pushing one another. The girls, on the other hand, were entirely at ease and paraded up and down the room in full consciousness and enjoyment of their finery."[20] Although Victorian middle-class boys played hide-and-seek with girls, most preferred to roam freely out-of-doors. At parties boys were not allowed to play the kind of competitive, active, and sometimes physically violent games they preferred when they played among themselves. (One of the favorites was "Rap Jacket," in which boys hit each other with whips or poles made out of beech, until one boy, presumably bruised and perhaps bloodied, gave up.) To enforce the message that conforming to etiquette was unmasculine, other boys called one who had good manners a dandy, Tom Apronstring, or girl-boy.[21]

Meanwhile, girls recorded each present in their diaries as well as the names of the guests at the party and the food served. The birthday party drew the girl from a wealthy family into a world of interior decoration, festivity, gift-giving, shopping, and bonbons. The kissing games at some of these parties initiated boys into the female world of romantic love and male initiative in choosing a female partner in marriage, such as in the kissing game of Post Office. In the game of Pillows and Keys, a boy, carrying these two objects in his hands, marched in time to music played on the piano. When the music stopped, he had to "kneel to the wittiest, dance with the prettiest, and kiss the one you love the best."[22]

W. P. Frith's painting *Many Happen Returns of the Day* (1854) illustrates the significance of gender display and deference to men in the parent-run birthday event.[23] This British artist provides us with the first illustration of a Victorian birthday party. The women at the party are actively monitoring the children, serving them food, or marveling at a gift for the birthday girl. Frith portrayed the party as a woman's event that fathers and grandfathers attended, though remaining slightly disengaged. The seating arrangements at the table, with the father at the head and the mother at the foot, symbolized both the dominance of males in the Victorian household and their removal from its social center. The girls were dressed in their silk party dresses and the boys were wearing their best suits. The grandfather briefly glances up from his newspaper to receive a glass of wine a little girl is handing him so he can make a birthday toast. Frith's painting suggests that men, especially elderly men, were to be waited on and shown deference, but that children's hearts belonged to their female relatives.

In the painting, as in the dining rooms of the American elite, wealthy parents simultaneously indulged their children and controlled them. Amidst all the rules about using the right fork and saying thank you, children received a number of treats. Between 1840 and 1870 several modern innovations in party giving appeared, including the following:

ice cream, which was molded into shapes and surrounded by
    raspberry sherbet and chocolate eggs;
goody bags, made out of a handkerchief the child brought to the

party, the four corners tied together and used to carry home
party candy, such as bonbons wrapped in colored tissue paper;
paid entertainment, such as a storyteller, a Punch and Judy show,
    or performing dogs;
an outing, including rides on Shetland ponies or a merry-go-
    round.[24]

Philip Hone, a wealthy retired businessman, proud grandfather, and
former mayor of New York City, entertained with considerable style.
In a diary entry for 1846 he noted a birthday party for his granddaughter attended by twenty two-year-olds (a group about seven
times the size modern mothers consider manageable). He wrote, "Our
dear little Mary [his granddaughter, age two] gave a *dejeuner à la
fourchette* at Grandfather Hone's. About twenty-odd little Responsibilities, whose joint ages did not amount to the sum of mine, after a
royal romp sat down to a grand banquet of cold chickens, sandwiches, jellies, confectionery, etc. The lady hostess did the honors at
the head of the table, with her usual grace and propriety, and at three
o'clock the dining room had become a banquet hall deserted."[25]
Hone's entry suggests that children played some games ("a royal
romp") before sitting down to eat. We do not know whether his wife
and daughter planned or organized this event; perhaps they worked
on it together, since some grandmothers' diaries mentioned how they
assisted in preparing for such occasions.[26] Presumably the Hones's
black cook, Emily, prepared the meal (note the lack of mention of a
layer cake) and the family's maids served it.[27]

From the time of the Revolution to the downfall of the Confeder-
acy, middle class and wealthy families, North as well as South, rural
as well as urban, hosted elaborate birthday parties for their children,
though not quite on Hone's grand scale.[28] One Georgia plantation
mistress held a big family dinner on the occasion of her child's birthday. At another Southern party, the children of the master had their
cake and presents, then handed out a quarter in silver to each slave as
a gift. Even the Civil War did not hamper the Solomons, a wealthy
Jewish family in New Orleans, from celebrating the birthdays of both
their four-year-old daughter and their nineteen-year-old's later that
year. The family may have decided on a more modest party for the
older daughter, a schoolteacher, because by then war had broken out.
Even so, Mrs. Solomon managed to find a special bottle of champagne for the party.[29]

The Peer-Culture Birthday Party

Sometime between 1870 and 1920 parents began to cede some of the control over the guest lists and the games to be played at the birthday party to their children. The peer-culture birthday fused the older concept of the child as an innocent being with the evolving concept of the child as a consumer capable of making choices among goods or games. The distinctive feature of the peer-culture party was that the child helped to draw up the guest list. In a short story published in 1875, a mother told her daughter, "You may invite just whom you please, daughter."[30] Even etiquette advisors thought this a good idea. Emily Post by 1940 conceded that "letting him [the birthday boy] take full responsibility in managing his own party by himself is the very best training in social ease."[31] As the birthday party became more peer-culture oriented it also became choral: the song "Happy Birthday to You," composed in 1894, began to be sung, probably increasing in popularity after 1934 when the song was incorporated into the Moss Hart musical *As Thousands Cheer.*[32] In sum, the peer-culture party was still organized by women, but children were participating in planning it.

One reason for the advent of peer-culture parties was the development of age grading in American elementary schools. Older, rural schools often consisted of one large room; a child walked to school with his or her siblings and learned alongside them in class. In the 1850s the first urban schools began assigning children to separate classrooms based on age. Educational reformers sought to emulate the efficient organization of factories and to create a more democratic system for learning. They also argued that teachers would find it easier to manage a classroom comprised of children of the same age. By the 1870s, most American urban public schools were age-graded. Children who attended such schools began to select playmates from among their same-age school chums as well as from among neighbors and family members. Parents began to accept the age-grading of children as a "natural" form of sociability among children.[33]

Consumer and popular culture also encouraged the growth of peer-culture birthdays. Early silent films showed adults as well as children celebrating birthdays with a cake and candles. Department stores tried to reach the child consumer directly.[34] By the early 1920s large department stores had their own radio stations or sponsored weekly programs on other stations. Uncle WIP, who hosted Gimbel's *Kiddies'*

Show, read a list of children's birthdays on each program. Schools gave stores lists of students; stores also compiled the names of children who participated in store contests. They then mailed birthday greetings to children whose names appeared on the lists. One California merchant explained the wisdom of this idea in reaching boys: "We send him letters on his birthday. We tell him we have a little present waiting for him at the store. You can imagine how much the average youngster is pleased with this attention."[35]

Popular child psychology of the 1920s also encouraged the development of the peer-culture birthday party. Child-rearing experts in that decade claimed that such an innovation helped develop independence in children. The child should help decide the theme of the party and the games to be played, and he or she should address the invitations. A mother might even bring the child on a visit to a party planner.

Taking charge of one's own party was a good place for a child to start in organizing and managing his or her own affairs. To make this possible, however, a mother had to give up some of her own decision-making power.[36] Party books from the 1920s offered a new principle in party planning, that the number of guests should equal the child's age. To do this, a modern mother usually could invite only the child's friends rather than also inviting the children of *her* friends. The stated age rule was "a guest for each year old."[37] This was a significant departure from Victorian norms. Illustrations and photographs from the late nineteenth century showed parties for twelve to nineteen guests. One grandmother mentioned her preparations for a party of forty boys and girls.[38]

The party books offered several rationales for limiting the number of guests, although the main one was that having too many children put a strain on the child. Advisors thought it easier for children to play with a smaller group of children. Mothers also found it more manageable to serve six rather than sixteen. Children suffered, it was claimed, from being the center of attraction at a party of two dozen.[39] The growth in popularity of the small party occurred at about the same time as the decline of servants in middle-class households. While the vacuum cleaner and the washing machine may have replaced the live-in servant, there was no machine to straighten out the parlor after forty children had finished their games.

The range of birthday parties expanded with the growth of modern adolescence, but all were based on the idea that the young person belonged to a peer group. The growth of junior high schools, which appeared in the first decade of the twentieth century, and of senior high schools a little later contributed to the rise of an adolescent peer group culture by the 1920s. Teenagers were spending an increasing amount of time together, not only in the classroom but also in after-school activities and clubs. During the 1920s girls began to host the slumber party, later called a pajama party. At these parties the guests stayed awake much of the night, engaging in gossip and pillow fights, without parental supervision. Boys of the same age sometimes tried to attend—or disrupt—these parties of girls.[40] By staying awake as late as they chose, the young people were exercising even greater control over the event than merely choosing the games or the guest list.

Although magazine articles in the 1890s referred to "sweet sixteens," these parties for girls first became popular in the 1920s. Their emergence coincides with the opening of coed high schools. The sweet sixteen party provided middle-class girls with a rite of passage into adolescence, dating, and romantic love, less formal than a social debut but more adult than the birthday parties of their younger years. The sweet sixteen was usually an all-girl party or one for mother and daughter pairs, although there were also some coed dance parties. Mothers often hosted these parties at a restaurant or the home of a female friend.[41] The sweet sixteen party was a middle-class version of the debutante ball, which first appeared in the late nineteenth century. In the 1920s a growing social distance opened up between mothers and daughters, as daughters succumbed to the influences of advertising, dance crazes, use of cosmetics, and popular films. The sweet sixteen party seemed to bridge this gap by celebrating female bonds precisely as girls were becoming attracted to boys and engaging in relatively unsupervised dating.

In the 1950s party advisers added another subtype of party for the younger child, the age-appropriate fest. It shared some elements of the peer-group party, in that the number of guests had to be limited according to the child's age. In addition, the age of the guests was still supposed to be about the same as that of the birthday girl or boy. But at the age-appropriate fest, games and activities were fitted precisely to the age of the guests. Arnold Gesell of the Gesell Institute for Child Development at Yale asserted that children passed through distinct stages of physical, cognitive, and emotional development. He urged parents to adapt the party to the child's age and abilities.[42] *Life* magazine turned to Gesell's institute for party advice. They sent a photographer to a home where a mother was hosting a party based on Gesell's principles. The authors of the Gesell party book published their manual, they said, because they had received so many letters from mothers. One wrote them that "a number of years ago I read with a great deal of interest your series of articles on children's parties in *Life* magazine. This week I gave a party for my 4-year-old twins according to your rules. This party was so successful that I would like to have the rules for the other parties if you could send them to me."[43] For every age from three to fifteen, the institute's party manual recommended different decor, refreshments, games, favors, and music. The rigidity of the rules and the emphasis on appropriate activities for each age confirms the stereotype of the 1950s as an exceedingly conformist decade.

Name Days and Party Hats

Except for Germans and some wealthy foreigners from various nations, immigrants to the United States were not accustomed to celebrating a child's birthday with a party for the child's friends.[44] Once in America, however, they embraced the idea of a children's birthday party and made it their own. Immigrant parents took the sentimentalized party and created a hybrid form, looking outward to American society and backward toward the homeland. They adopted the cake, the ice cream, the candles, the song, and the presents of the birthday party, but changed its meaning. Unlike the parent-run parties of the Victorian elite, these parties assembled and affirmed the social networks of adults. Relatives living in the United States, and sometimes close family friends, were invited. In general, parents of the second generation usually dropped these hybrid forms in favor of the standard birthday party with no distinctive ethnic elements.[45]

Some immigrants in America grafted the birthday cake and candles onto religious occasions and used purchased goods and services to create a large, lavish party in place of what had been a more modest event (as explained further in Chapter 8). American Jews, for example, transformed the bar and bat mitzvah from a minor ceremony into a major one, making it both a religious rite and an extravagant birthday party (sometimes with the birthday cake in the shape of a Torah).

Similarly, the *quinceañera,* uncommon among Hispanics until the 1960s, combined a mass at a Catholic church with a reception featuring the cutting of a birthday cake on the girl's fifteenth birthday. Hispanics often described the event using the phrase of the dominant culture ("a sweet sixteen"); Puerto Ricans even sometimes held these events on the girl's sixteenth birthday.

Initially, Catholic immigrants around the turn of the century celebrated the name day of the saint the child was named for rather than the child's birthday.[46] (The saint's day was the date the Church reckoned as the saint's date of death).[47] Just as saints' days became less important in the Catholic calendar (as evident, for example, in the disappearance of special church services on All Saint's Day) so, too, naming children after saints became less common. Name day celebrations disappeared gradually. At first, some immigrant parents chose the more pleasing name of another saint whose feast day fell near, but not on, the child's date of birth. Seeking a compromise between old and new, some parents held parties both on the feast day of the saint and the birth date of the child. They made the name day the more significant event, but invited the child's aunts, uncles, and grandparents to the child's birthday party.[48]

Asians in America had to decide whether to celebrate birthdays according to their own calendars or the Western manner of reckoning time. Japanese-Americans considered one's birthday the first day of the new year in the Western calendar, whereas Chinese who were recent immigrants added a year to their age on Chinese New Year. One Chinese mother in the 1970s made what may have been a typical compromise among more acculturated immigrants. She told her grandchildren they were a year older on both the day of Chinese New Year and their western birth date.[49] Japanese-Americans in the United States rapidly abandoned the idea of considering January 1 the universal birthday. Instead, they began to hold parties for the child on the child's actual date of birth. Nevertheless, Japanese mothers, who only gradually took to baking or buying a birthday cake, initially tried other alternatives. In the 1940s some of these mothers did not serve cake, but instead fried pancakes on the child's birthday, writing the child's name on the pancakes with food coloring.[50]

For Chinese immigrants the "full month" birthday custom became simpler, shorter, and more egalitarian over the course of more than a century. This was a celebration of an infant's birth one month after it occurred. In the nineteenth century families celebrated the full month only for boys, with an especially large party held after the birth of the first son. Since the culture was no longer patrilineal by around the 1930s, it became unnecessary to define family simply in terms of the father's line. Thus, by that date, Chinese-Americans were holding parties for girls as well, although they were usually less elaborate than those for boys. In the 1980s Chinese families no longer distinguished between celebrations for the birth of a boy or a girl. For non-Christians the full month once consisted of a variety of ceremonies at the altar in the home and at a Chinese temple, as well as a banquet. Over time Chinese families compressed the ceremony into a banquet at home or a restaurant and shortened the ritual of cutting the child's hair. This used to be performed by the grandmother in the home before the child was taken to the temple. Using red eggs dipped in water, the grandmother would moisten the child's head and then shave the child's hair and eyebrows with a Chinese razor. The shaved scalp would then be oiled, and the child would be dressed in a bright red outfit. In the 1980s grandparents simply snipped a lock of the infant's hair.[51] By then some parents had become Christians, and most of the others had become less religious.

The children's birthday party for subsequent ages balanced Asian and American elements. Among both the Japanese and Chinese, there were certain auspicious birthdays: the twelfth for a Japanese child, the tenth and fifteenth for the Chinese child. These were always special events. Though the American influence was felt in celebrating the child's birthday on a annual basis, some traditional elements were retained. Chinese parents or grandparents handed the child li-shee along with typical American-style presents. As early as the 1910s, some wealthy parents were taking photographs of their children in front of a cake with candles, a ritual wholly absent in China. Exactly when Chinese children began to wear American play clothes at parties rather than embroidered silk outfits, special shoes, and hats is unclear. Certainly special Chinese dress had disappeared by the period after World War II. As for who was to be invited, sometimes the guests were Chinese children; the more acculturated invited the schoolmates of the child, who might not be Chinese.[52] Children sensed that their parents preferred a party to which other Chinese adults were invited. A ten-year-old Chinese-American girl living in the Chicago suburbs in the 1970s, realized as much. She told an interviewer, "I think our birthday parties are just an excuse for the grownups to get together. They like to cook in the kitchen and talk."[53]

The syncretic, or hybrid, birthday party took the cake and candles, amateur photography, and perhaps the birthday song of the dominant culture but added the cuisine of the homeland (other than the cake), ethnic costumes, and adult sociability. Usually the guests invited were not the child's schoolmates, but the adult friends of the parents, and perhaps the children in this social network. Immigrants would speak to each other in their native language, listen and dance to the music of the home country, and eat foods of the homeland. Mothers talked to the other women at the event, and men mainly conversed among themselves, sometimes in a separate room or a distinct space. Although mothers sometimes instructed children in cultural rules about greeting and serving guests, they did not organize games for the children to play. Immigrants saw themselves preserving tradition by holding such events when they were actually combining their culture with the dominant American one.[54]

This kind of party was designed to cement the bonds of adult immigrants, their kin, and friends from the same ethnicity, but also to recognize the child in the Western manner. Such parents did not want the peer-culture birthday party because it represented the kind of outside American influences they were seeking to minimize. The syncretic party appears in photographs of Chinese-American children in 1910; it has been described among Punjabi immigrants in London in the 1980s and among Haitian immigrants in New York in the same decade. Despite changes over time, the elements of the syncretic birthday party seem to have remained much the same.

As was true of other holidays and celebrations, the immigrant child was often the agent of change, bringing home a demand for the ice cream, cake, and presents other classmates had.[55] Immigrant children in the early twentieth century learned about birthday parties from their friends at school.[56] Schools and other bureaucracies used the birth date as a basis for age grading and classification. Moreover, teachers would single out the birthday boy or girl at school and perhaps would have the class sing the birthday song. Parental responses to their children's demands varied. Some wanted children to have a party "no matter how bad things were" and took photographs of the event as a statement of family success and pride.[57] A few balked at the idea, considering it an extravagance, a foreign custom, or both.

The Postsentimental Birthday Party

Even in the early twentieth century children's birthdays were mainly celebrated in the home. Mothers in the 1920s saw taking the birthday boy or girl to the movies as a form of entertainment that required less work and interested them almost as much as the children. By the 1950s birthday parties might be hosted at a museum, bowling alley, rollerskating rink, or indoor swimming pool. Operators of local fast-food franchises such as McDonald's began to encourage parties at their establishments. But the mother still organized the event and mailed the invitations, and the guests might return to the child's home for cake and ice cream after their excursion. The growth of "family entertainment centers" in the 1980s, such as Chuck-E-Cheese and the Discovery Zone, relocated the party to a business establishment that offered an indoor playground for children. These businesses catered entirely to children, rather than providing recreation that adults could share. For a single price, these for-profit indoor playgrounds furnished the invitations, a cake with candles, and a playground and games for the party, thus largely assuming the responsibility for planning and executing the child's party. Attendants at these centers might even light the birthday candles and cut the cake. None of the activities of the party occurred at the child's home, although some parents might have a second "family party" with a cake at home.

Parent-run and peer-culture birthday parties fitted well with a nuclear family, one with a middle-class male provider and a female homemaker. The mother had time to devote to the preparation of the party and may have found the party affirming of her mothering. But between the 1960s and the 1980s, the American family underwent a number of wrenching changes. The most important one, at least in terms of transforming the birthday party, was the growth of married women's employment. Instead of working temporarily before marriage and after children were of school age, mothers remained more or less committed permanently to paid work.

Still, more of the demand for parties to be held at family entertainment centers came not from the parent but from the child, who attended one or learned about such places from television advertising. The growth of these parties coincided with the increase in dual-earner families. Parents in such families had more money to spend but less time to organize the party or clean up after it. In addition, the smaller average family size in the 1980s—just under two children—made it less of a burden on the family to spend more on a child's party. Finally, the desire for novelty and a sense of competition between parents (sometimes abetted by children's demands) were also factors that caused the birthday party, which was once a celebration of home life, to be moved outside the home. Some parents tried to outdo each other, holding parties at gymnastics centers, art museums, or indoor playgrounds. Since other parents knew the price of these events, such parties made parental affluence visible.

The mother's responsibility for the postsentimental birthday lay in choosing from among the options these centers offered, sending out the invitations, and perhaps making or purchasing cupcakes for the child's event at school. She also bought birthday cards and presents, and she (or her husband) helped transport children to parties they attended. The good father since the 1950s was expected to assist at the child's party and more recently to be present, even if he had to cut short a business trip to attend.[58] He might also have the role of family photographer. However, he was less likely than his wife to shop for cards or presents.[59]

Employed mothers, not fathers, felt guilty or ambivalent about not having a party at home. The definition of being a good mother entailed putting a great deal of time and creativity into staging the party.[60] Being a good mother was a competitive role, because it rested on outdoing the parties other mothers staged. Because the party was not being held in the home, some parents held a second smaller "family party" at home, at which a cake or cupcakes was served. Writers in women's magazines encouraged these feelings of maternal guilt; there were no similar entreaties to fathers. Etiquette advisors had always looked askance at efforts of mothers to avoid the burdens of the party. In 1924, Lillian Eichler cautioned mothers who planned a "motion picture party" to "remember that there is after all not a great deal of art in amusing people when the amusements are furnished by someone else, and also that the art of entertaining charmingly at home is perhaps the greatest art of them all."[61] In the 1990s sociologist Arlie Hochschild took an even sterner attitude. Mothers who held their child's party at a "payground," she concluded, had "outsourced pieces of familial life."[62]

Beginning in the 1980s magazine articles complaining about "birthday party blues" furnished additional evidence of the growth of a postsentimental attitude toward the child's party.[63] The phrase first appeared in the 1980s, but advice books as early as the 1940s had begun to admit that the party could be "overwhelming" and "exhausting" and that after it was over many parents uttered the vow "never again."[64] *Life* in 1946 went so far as to claim that "to most parents the prospect of giving a child's party is about as appetizing as giving a lynching."[65] The metaphor suggested that the birthday party was a bizarre, even immoral, event involving physical torture. Complaints about such parties seem to have appeared just as the feminine mystique of time-consuming mothering was getting under way.

Articles about "battling the birthday party blues" in the 1980s became acceptable as the double burden of employed mothers could not be ignored.[66] Such complaints stemmed from recognizing that the management of many children at a party was a chore rather than a labor of love. Women writers for women's magazines sympathized with a mother's woes and offered a number of principles of party planning—many of them borrowed from the writers of the 1920s and subsequently—to help women make the event more manageable.

Americans who were more affluent were the first to celebrate occasions such as their children's birthdays. There are obvious class differences in birthday parties today, but the dividing line is no longer between having and not having one. As goods have flooded the consumer market and incomes, especially discretionary incomes for the masses, have risen, children in households of modest means, not just rich ones, have come to expect a birthday party with presents. In addition, the concept of the child as an individual deserving of recognition took hold across all strata of American society. The transition was a gradual one, however, and cannot be dated exactly. Certainly during the Great Depression it was rare for children to have any recognition of their birthday, except perhaps for a special cake a mother baked and served as dessert after family dinner.

As children's birthdays came to be recognized, the celebrations took a standardized form of cake, candles, a song, and presents. More American parents today than at any previous time in history honor their child with a yearly party. It is rare to encounter the belief that a child's birthday need not be celebrated. However, groups outside mainstream American culture may use the occasion as an opportunity to affirm the solidarity of their larger kin group rather than simply to recognize the individuality of the child. Within the dominant culture, the peer-culture birthday party, which developed as early as 1870, gave the child greater power to define his or her social network. Indeed, parents seemed to recognize that it was best to do so, since a network of friends as well as family would become a defining feature of middle-class adult life.

The original function of the birthday party was to recognize the child and simultaneously impart the rules of etiquette, a marker of respectable middle-class status. To some extent this is still true. At the same time, the informality of post–World War II American culture and the change in the American diet have had their effects on the birthday party. Children now eat pizza with their cake and wash it down with gulps of carbonated soft drink. The elite's emphasis on showing good manners at the party has largely disappeared, both because the nonelite is now celebrating the event and because most American children are now expected to observe fewer rules of etiquette. It is no longer the wealthy who shape the birthday party as much as popular culture derived from cartoons and movie heroes.

The widespread acceptance of the birthday party as a child's right was the last great victory of sentimentalism. Still, ever since the 1920s children and mothers have sought novelty and amusement in parties held outside the home. Over time it became possible to substitute purchased services for women's unpaid labor. The postsentimental party, the one outside the home, was a victory of sorts for mothers, since it reduced their work. Yet such a party does not give mothers the pleasure of having their creativity displayed and affirmed.

CHAPTER EIGHT

Rites of Passage

I want to preserve my culture, something that's so hard to do nowadays. A lot of people today don't know what nationality they are. They don't have a sense of ethnic roots. I don't know a lot of Hispanic people because I go to school in Niles [Illinois].

—HISPANIC GIRL, 1993

In the American colonies, various rites of passage marked a child's birth or coming of age. These tended to be celebrated by the entire community, rather than being events to which only friends and relatives were invited.[1] Some of these rites marked a biological event, such as the child's birth. Others, such as the child's first communion, confirmation, or bar mitzvah, were religious rites for a child who had reached a certain age. Little advance planning or preparation was required for any of these ceremonies. It was not particularly important for relatives to gather for them, and it was often impossible for them to do so because of the dispersion of kin and the difficulties of travel. Instead, the people living nearby assembled, sometimes at a church or synagogue, often in the home of the family.

Religion was the driving force behind rituals for incorporation of an infant, a child, or an adolescent into the community of believers. It determined what rites were needed, who could preside over them, their location, the participants' script, the equipment used, and the age and gender of the initiate. In rituals for older children and adolescents, religion also prescribed the kind of instruction required prior to the ceremony. But religious doctrine provides only a partial explanation for the presence or absence of a particular ritual. These rituals were practiced because the members of the community often demanded them, even when religious authorities had other priorities.

In the twentieth century the rites of passage became less elaborate.

It is tempting to think that the growing secularism of modern society produced this result. Yet as was noted in Chapter 4, most twentieth-century Americans belonged to a religious institution and considered themselves believers. Instead, in the twentieth century rites became more specialized, either entirely secular or wholly religious. Christening parties were the exception; here a religious rite was usually followed by a family celebration. However, most families in the mid- to late twentieth century held no party whatsoever after a first communion or confirmation. Perhaps because families were hosting *secular* rites for the child—birthday and graduation parties—religious rites did not seem to require embellishment. At any rate, by the 1960s, if not earlier, first communion and confirmation came to be defined mainly as religious events.

Religious rituals for adolescents—the bar and bat mitzvah among Jews, the quinceañera among Hispanics—are the exceptions to this general trend. Both the Jewish and the Hispanic rites evolved from being simple and short religious ceremonies followed by a small party to lengthy religious rituals that preceded one or more elaborate receptions. But there were significant differences between the Jewish rites and the quinceañera. The bar mitzvah was traditionally only for Jewish boys. The first bat mitzvah for a Jewish girl was in 1922. Even after that, the bat mitzvah remained relatively rare among girls until the 1970s. The quinceañera was always a rite for a girl. It became popular with the growth in Chicano consciousness in the 1960s and is mainly found among immigrants from Mexico, many of whom are working class. The bar mitzvah has a longer history among American Jews. It did not decline among third- or fourth-generation Jews and is found among Jews of all social classes. Despite the differences in the two rites, their functions were similar. Both were badges of parental success in raising a child on the threshold of adolescence and of pride in a religious and ethnic identity.

Childbirth and Child Naming

Childbirth rituals ease the transition into a new social role for the parents and incorporate the newborn into a community and a religion. Until the twentieth century birth rituals were twofold: the first was a secular ritual among women, occurring in the home where a woman gave birth; the second involved the child's incorporation into the family's religious faith, taking place in a church or synagogue, or the family's dwelling. The first, the home birth, had some of the characteristics of a woman's party. A colonial woman in the first stage of labor was supposed to provide refreshments—"groaning beer" and "groaning cakes"—for her attendants. "Groaning" referred to the woman's cries of pain, the weight of the table piled high with food, and the sounds of overstuffed women diners. Before Hannah Sewall, a Massachusetts Bay Puritan woman, went into labor she set out for her "gossips" a feast of boiled pork, beef, chicken, roast beef, turkey pie, and tarts.[2] After a successful birth, the attendants, gathered around the bedside, would have another party. Women of wealth, reclining comfortably on their childbed linen decorated with lace, would supply their female neighbors with an elegant dinner; the humble would merely proffer their thanks.[3]

The community of women who gathered for the birth of a child, prevalent in colonial times and throughout the nineteenth century, was part of a cradle-to-grave system of emotional support among women.[4] The support and assistance offered at the birth carried over into feelings of special kinship. A new mother often selected her midwife or afternurse to be godmother at the child's baptism. The same women who attended a birth often made the funeral preparations in the event of the infant's death. As long as women gave birth at home, they held some form of celebration after the birth. However, by the 1940s the majority of births were occurring in hospitals. Nurses and doctors defined childbirth as a medical procedure, at which a woman's guests—friends or even her husband—got in the way. No ritual celebration after childbirth seemed appropriate at a hospital.

For centuries some branches of Christianity offered a ritual to reincorporate the new mother into her faith and her community after she gave birth. "Churching" of the new mother, usually four or six weeks after childbirth, was a religious ceremony of purification and thanksgiving practiced by Greek Orthodox, Russian, Russian-German, Episcopalian, and Irish Catholic immigrant women as late as the 1940s.[5] In this ceremony, often organized by the midwife who presided over the infant's birth, the new mother was blessed and officially welcomed back into the community of her church. Churching was usually followed by a feast, accompanied by drink and sexual banter. Some historians of churching interpret the ritual as a male-dominated ceremony designed to remove the pollution of original sin from a mother before she was allowed to rejoin the church. Others view churching as a female-organized ritual, giving the woman an opportunity to express thanks for surviving childbirth and to gather her community around her. Both meanings could coexist: religious leaders seem to have regarded women and the ritual in negative terms, whereas new mothers tended to view their role more positively, as givers of life who had survived a terrifying ordeal.

Churching eventually disappeared from all religions, beginning with the Protestant reformation and eventually reaching the Catholic church by the 1960s. Calvinists at the time of the Protestant reformation banned it as a papist practice. Later many Protestant denominations seem to have considered churching superfluous. Perhaps women were no longer demanding to be churched. Rituals such as churching can always be redefined in a more positive light, and in modern times women have sought rituals for miscarriage and menopause as well as childbirth. But as the baptismal ceremony became as much a mother's as a child's event, women may have perceived churching as unnecessary.

There is more continuity with the past in the ritual that incorporates the infant into the community of faith. Early Christians borrowed the Jewish ritual of purification through immersion in water and used it to incorporate adults, and then children, into the faith.[6] Among Catholics baptism was a sacrament, its function being to recognize the child as a member of a Christian community, confirm the identity of the parents, and affirm the group's commitment to provide guidance and protection to the infant. Baptism also provided the child with an alternative set of parents (godparents) in charge of his or her religious instruction, and gave the child a name.[7]

Christian faiths had differing views on the reason for baptism. Catholics saw baptism as a means of removing the taint of original sin and insuring that the infant could be admitted into heaven. Without it, the infant's soul was stuck in limbo, never to reach heaven or hell, or even the way station of purgatory. For the Puritans, baptism was merely the first stage in a process that would eventually lead to the individual's becoming an adult member of the church.[8] Christian faiths also differed as to whether baptism should occur at infancy or later in life. Baptists and Mormons baptized only adults, reserving the ceremony for those who could make an informed choice of faith.

Among the wealthy and the middle class, by the mid-nineteenth century the christening began to be defined as a private event, an especially familial and mother-centered one. In colonial times the father, as the head of the household and main religious instructor of the child, arranged the church ceremony, which the mother, recuperating at home, would not attend. By the early nineteenth century, it was more common for a woman or her female relatives to make the arrangements, and for the mother to be present. These changes reflected the general cultural climate, which idealized the mother-child bond and assigned the father the role of titular head of the family.

Among the well-to-do of the nineteenth century the christening party became an elegant luncheon or dinner, its culinary high point the serving of a white iced cake, resembling a wedding cake, and wine. As at a wedding, dainty gifts were spread on a table covered with a white tablecloth; etiquette books advised men to present the child with a gift of silver and women to give a piece of needlework.[9] Because of the sentimentalization of motherhood, the mother and the infant, rather than the godparents, were the center of attention. Such a christening also served the function of displaying family wealth.[10]

The ethnic christening was open to everyone. It was not a domestic occasion, since the child was being incorporated into an ethnic and religious community of believers as much as into an individual family. In the nineteenth century and the first half of the twentieth century German, Italian, and Hispanic parents, even those of limited means, hosted christening parties for hundreds of guests, with plenty to eat and drink. Among Germans the festival was an ethnic tradition as much as a religious one, since it was found among both German Lutherans and German Catholics. The poor Mexican-American family might take out a loan to pay for a *bautismo*.[11] After the Hispanic ceremony in a Catholic church godparents were expected to bestow coins on the children attending. At the fiesta afterward, guests drank, danced, and toasted the parents, the infant, and the godparents. After being serenaded by a guitarist, each guest was expected to acknowledge his or her regard for the child by dropping a donation in the guitarist's hat. Godparents and parents also sang the praises of the infant.[12] While most working-class christening parties were held in the home, some took place in saloons, where a larger group could be accommodated and it was easy to serve liquor.

Even among Mexican-Americans, christenings became smaller and less elaborate by the 1960s.[13] Some godparents treated everyone to a party at a restaurant. More often parents had a small party in the home for friends and relatives. The fact that there tended to be a large celebration for the birth of the first child and smaller ones or none at all for subsequent children suggests that parents had become more conscious of the cost of these events.[14] Also, if godparents were no longer paying for christenings, parents may have been more reluctant to host a lavish event.[15] Among non-Hispanic Catholics the same trend toward increasing simplicity was evident in the ceremony itself. The mother, rather than the godmother, held the baby during the ceremony, suggesting that the mother-child bond, rather than the tie of kinship, was the central one to affirm. Picture-taking, once prohibited, was accepted. Children were also baptized in groups, rather than in individual ceremonies, and as part of the regular mass. These changes were an apparent effort to reduce demands on the priest's time.[16]

Catholic groups had the most extensive system of godparenthood in the United States, since they followed traditions of their homelands. At the Catholic church service the priest usually spelled out the expectation that godparents oversee the spiritual education of the child. Hispanic godparents of the infant were expected to pay for the expenses of the church at baptism, give the baby a christening gown, a gold ring, or gold medallion, and provide gifts for adults who attended the ceremony.[17] Among Hispanics, Italians, and Poles godparents felt obligated to provide gifts for first communion and confirmation, and to assist with the costs of the wedding.

The Mexican-American system of godparenthood, *compadrazgo*, was the most extensive of all. Hispanics created separate sets of godparents for a person's birth, first communion, confirmation, wedding, and even graduation. Godparents were often addressed as *comadre* (comother) or *compadre* (cofather), referring to the special bond between godparents and the child's parents as well as between godparents and the child. Nineteenth-century Hispanic parents selected as godparents nonrelatives, often people of means and standing in the community, who would act as religious guides and protectors of the child, especially in the event of parental death. Poor families sought out wealthy godparents, who could aid them or their child in times of need; the parents were likewise obligated to the godparents. Such a system served to defuse social conflict along class lines, since it bound the wealthy and the poor in lifelong networks of support and obligation. This was a uniquely Hispanic pattern, however, since among other American families in the nineteenth century most godparents came from the equivalent social rank as the parents.[18]

Godparents in the twentieth century generally had fewer responsibilities for the godchild than in previous times. Many honored their obligations perfunctorily: on special occasions they sent the child a greeting card. During the Great Depression family friends were reluctant to take on this added responsibility.[19] By the time prosperity returned in the 1940s, the old pattern had disappeared. Friends moved away and did not maintain contact.[20] It became more common to name blood kin of the parents as the child's godparents. Godparents, if they were nonkin, were no longer expected to provide for the child in the event of the parent's death. Instead, it was assumed that the child's relatives would assume guardianship and provide support if needed, even if friends had been named as godparents. In most cases, there was a separate godparent for each child. In the last two thirds of the twentieth century selecting friends or relatives as godparents came to be seen as an honorific that did not carry any sense of lifelong responsibility for the child.[21]

A new prebirth ritual was invented in the 1930s—the baby shower, which, unlike the religious rituals just mentioned, was entirely secular. Before the 1930s most people believed it was bad luck to provide a pregnant mother with gifts before a child was born.[22] Instead they brought gifts to the christening or brit, or bestowed them in visits to the new mother at home.[23] The baby shower, which signaled the happy assumption that both mother and infant would survive the birth, represented the triumph of anticipation over fear. It made sense only in a world where maternal and infant mortality had become uncommon. Emily Post first offered rules of etiquette for a baby shower, also called a stork shower, in the 1937 edition of her guidebook; she had not mentioned the shower in the original (1922) edition.[24]

The baby shower appears to have been modeled on other woman's parties, such as the bridal shower or the children's birthday party. Like the birthday party, the baby shower might feature a special cake, punch, games (guessing games and quizzes), party hats, and presents.[25] A close woman friend or relative hosted the shower, to which only other women, including the woman's mother and her female relatives, were invited. The baby shower was a rite to initiate a woman

in her maternal role. Bringing together a group of women was designed to affirm and reinforce a female community that would assist
and support the new mother.[26]

The ritual combined gift-giving, the gathering of the female community once present at childbirth, and the nineteenth-century emphasis on good manners. The idea of a sharing female community was reflected in the typical seating arrangement of the guests in a circle. The
passing of each gift around the circle of seated guests pointed to the
centrality of gift-giving. At one side of the expectant mother an attendant wrote down the name of the giver and her gift, so that the
mother would be able to fulfill the expected etiquette of later writing a
thank-you note. As the honoree unwrapped each present, the gift-
giver might explain how the item could be used. These explanations
formed a brief introduction to the consumer goods of modern mothering.

Although the baby shower had its origin among wealthy and middle-class women during the Great Depression, it quickly became common among women of every social class, race, and region. Recent immigrants had them, too, and did not add any distinctive customs of
the homeland. Perhaps it was understood that syncretic customs were
only important for the socialization of the young or at family gatherings. Despite its being a sentimental gift-giving occasion, there were
no criticisms of the materialism of the shower. Unlike Christmas gifts,
which are often criticized as shallow and meaningless, baby-shower
gifts are accepted as the bounty needed for proper mothering and for
the welcoming of an infant into the world. Yet baby gifts also convey
the message that one of the functions of modern mothering is to be a
good consumer, to know and use properly the various products for
the care, comfort, and display of the baby.[27]

In the contemporary United States a postsentimentalist form of
baby shower is found mainly among employed married women. If not
universally feminists, such women were nonetheless affected by the
egalitarian expectations raised by the woman's movement since the
1970s. Showers may now be held at the workplace or a restaurant as
well as at a woman's home. Men might be invited, even regarded as
honored guests, because they are also expected to be present at the
child's birth and generally to be more involved as parents. Like the
birthday cake, the cake for the postsentimental shower is often pur-

chased at a bakery. The playing of games, formerly a central element of the shower, has largely disappeared as women began to take themselves more seriously.

With the development of the baby shower, the secular world seemed to be competing with the religious one as to how to recognize the prospect of birth. Most women had a baby shower, a consumer event, before giving birth in a hospital. Religious ritual took pride of place in the postbirth period; the infant baptism or brit continued to fulfill the function of incorporating the child into a religious community.[28] Parents still hosted a party after these rituals, but these tended to be abbreviated affairs. The kinship system had changed as well, so that less was expected of those family friends thought of as kin or even of relatives named as godparents. In fact, the institution of godparenthood shrunk to being wholly honorific. Children were not going unnoticed, however, since each year their birthdays were commemorated.

Puberty Rites

First communion and confirmation, for many centuries religious, familial, and social events, became in the twentieth century entirely religious. First communion, a sacrament of the Catholic church and a grand ceremony designed to stir emotion, was once a rite of passage from childhood to adolescence. The child consumed a wafer of bread and drank some wine, and this was seen as a symbolic sharing in the body and blood of Christ. In the sixteenth century the age of first communion, supposed to occur at the age of discretion, was between the ages of nine and fourteen. By the nineteenth century the general pattern was for a child to have first communion at age twelve. In some parishes, first communion and confirmation could be the same day—a mass in the morning followed by a second one in the afternoon. However, a papal decree in 1910 held that children should receive communion when they acquired a basic religious knowledge, typically at around age seven. One aim of the decree was to do away with lavish display and reduce the amount of gift-giving at first communion.[29] U.S. priests in the early twentieth century often extracted from young communicants at their first communion a pledge to refrain from drinking alcohol until they reached twenty-one and another pledge not to marry a non-Catholic.[30]

After the papal decree of 1910 a child's first communion took place at age seven, and confirmation, also called "big communion," at twelve or thirteen. By putting an interval of five or six years between the two ceremonies, the church lengthened the period of religious instruction for children. A child of six or seven was not coming of age, but instead leaving early childhood behind to enter a period of formal schooling. First communion symbolized this new stage of childhood and provided implicit instruction in gender roles.

While first communion was available to all Catholic children, some families were unable to afford the new outfit required for the child. Godmothers and other relatives helped working-class and poor families to buy the appropriate clothing. If all else failed, nuns implored merchants to purchase the necessary outfits for the poor. A boy would show up at church for his first communion with a fresh haircut, a new black suit (perhaps with a flower in the buttonhole), a white shirt, dark shoes, white socks, and an oversized white ribbon tied around his arm above the elbow.[31] The ribbon symbolized the purity of his soul, for shortly before communion initiates made their first confession and were absolved of sin. Unless nuns or relatives bought items for the girl, her family was expected to buy the dress or make it. Her family also needed to purchase white shoes and stockings, a white veil, long white gloves, and rosary beads. Dressing girls as little brides socialized them to the standard of a virginal bride dressed in white (or a novitiate in the sisterhood).[32] The photographic portrait of a boy or girl in the first-communion outfit became an important and desired consumer purchase even among working-class families as early as 1910.

In many ways the confirmation ceremony was a reprise of first communion. Girls and boys lined up on opposite sides and filed down the aisle of the church. Girls were dressed in white veils and dresses, boys in suits and ties. Godparents or sponsors attended and gave gifts of prayer books or hymnals.[33] For most Catholics confirmation was primarily a religious group ceremony that involved little preparation, and there was often no family party after the event.[34]

Individual Initiation Rites

In many simple, nontechnological societies, the puberty rite is a group rite, and lasts from a few days to as long as several weeks. Adolescents are usually isolated from adults and undergo a physical ordeal. Initiates take on new names and learn a sacred language. The world of childhood dies, and the child is reborn an adult. It has often been claimed that the United States, like many other Western societies, lacks rites such as these and thereby is failing to provide youth with a sense of historical continuity. For the Gilded Age elite a grand tour of Europe, a trip through the Wild West, or a cotillion for a marriageable daughter could be seen as such a rite.[35]

In the contemporary United States an individual, rather than group, ceremony is used to mark puberty, and is found only among Hispanics, Jews, and Western Indian groups such as the Navaho, the Hopi, and the Apache. The Hispanic ceremony, the quinceañera (fifteenth year), is for girls on their fifteenth birthday. The Jewish ritual, the bar mitzvah, originally for boys on their thirteenth birthday, is now also for girls when they turn twelve. Unlike the quinceañera and the bar mitzvah, the kinaaldá of the Navaho and the Sunrise Ceremony of the Apache can be considered biological, rather than social, puberty rites, in that they occur soon after a girl's first menstruation. These Indian rites generally occur on the reservation, thus requiring urban Indians to return there for it.[36] Except for the buckskin dress of the Apache girl, which could cost thousands of dollars, no special expenses are incurred: Indian families hire no caterers, florists, or photographers.

Initiation ritual played an important part in the creation of modern Jewish and Hispanic identity. Jews and Hispanics also wanted to adhere to the old ways, as the Navaho and Apache did, but sought to embrace, rather than reject, modern consumer culture. Although some Mexican-Americans would return to Mexico for a quinceañera, and some Jews would travel to Israel for a bar or bat mitzvah, for the most part these events were held in the locale where the child's family was living. These rites were not ethnic variations of the mainstream ritual, since there was no mainstream ceremony for the passage into adolescence. An examination of the evolution of each ritual reveals patterns common to both: the emergence of a standard format; the increasing length and complexity of the religious ceremony; and the growing lavishness of the party or series of parties that followed the religious ritual.[37]

The Bar Mitzvah

The bar mitzvah (Hebrew for "son of the commandment") originated among Jews in Europe in the Middle Ages. Jews began to count only adult males in the minyan (the group of ten Jewish males required for a Jewish religious service). Some form of rite was then required to admit a boy to membership in the minyan.

Jews in America made several important changes in the bar mitzvah.[38] Religious authorities favored a standardized format and an increased opportunity for religious instruction of youth. In the format that evolved a boy was required to perform a minimal set of readings in Hebrew. "Bar mitzvah factories" in immigrant Jewish neighborhoods in the early twentieth century offered the necessary preparation. Many immigrant parents, themselves unschooled in ritual, found these establishments the best and easiest source of instruction for their boy.[39] During the service, a rabbi would call the boy to the bimah, the platform at the front of the synagogue, and the boy would read a "portion" of the Torah in Hebrew. After the reading, the boy might also give a speech in English. Although there were some mothers—or even rabbis—who wrote these speeches, it was more common for the boy to select an already composed speech from a bar mitzvah manual (the first of these appeared in 1907).[40]

The bar mitzvah opened up a number of commercial opportunities in America by the 1920s. The boy, dressed in a special suit, with his first pair of long pants, had his photograph taken in a studio. Jewish shops offered "bar mitzvah sets" of tallitot (prayer shawls) and tefillin (phylacteries, a small box strapped to the arm and head, which contained Biblical inscriptions in parchment and were worn by Orthodox Jewish men during morning daily prayers). Relatives gave the boy the obligatory fountain pen, along with watches, wallets, and gloves. (Psychoanalysts liked to point out that the pen was a phallic symbol. Many immigrant parents pictured in their minds their son, the doctor, using his fountain pen to write prescriptions.)[41]

The typical reception after the bar mitzvah in the 1910s and 1920s in the United States was a simple affair. After the service in the synagogue, the boy and his father and the other men at the synagogue would have a small repast (called a kidush) of herring, wine, and whiskey supplied by the father. One boy recalled his bar mitzvah in Hartford in the 1920s: "I read from the Torah, the guys came around and drank some schnapps, and that was it."[42] A mother might also make a dinner for friends and relatives at which the boy would make a speech. Or she might invite the father's friends for cake and whiskey in the family kitchen.[43] Prosperous Jews, often trying to meet or exceed the standards in their social circle, could afford a reception in a hotel or at a restaurant. In the 1910s the usual pattern was to hold a small luncheon after the ceremony or the Sunday after the service. A decade later middle-class families began to host catered affairs at hotels. Intended as both family reunion and proof to peers that a family had "arrived," many parents included more of the parent's business associates than kin or the boy's friends. By the 1920s five- or six-course dinners were standard at the "better class of bar mitzvah."[44]

Even when some families did not serve kosher food at the reception, they still turned to Jewish establishments for the bar mitzvah. Jewish caterers organized the reception and devised new rituals for it. The candle lighting ceremony was one such innovation that became a standard element. While the band played different music for each person named, the bar mitzvah boy, standing next to his parents, called on his relatives one by one to light one of thirteen (or perhaps fourteen, one extra for good luck) candles on a giant white birthday cake. Then the boy and his parents blew out the candles.[45] The cake was usually made in the shape of a scroll or giant set of tefillin. Through this ceremony, as Jenna Weissman Joselit notes, Jewish caterers transformed the cutting of the birthday cake into a "quasi-sacred event," increasing the religious quality of the reception.[46] The balance tipped in favor of the secular in the 1950s when caterers helped to create the theme bar mitzvah, organized around a nonreligious topic and represented in centerpieces and decorations of the hall—a baseball bar mitzvah, a luau bar mitzvah, a vaudeville bar mitzvah. Since all these elaborations were part of Jewish family celebrations, and the sentimentalization of the family was a hallmark of modern Judaism, there was no clear dividing line between secular and the sacred.

As a result of the growth of consumerism and peer culture, children at younger ages were gradually allowed more choices. Perhaps as late as the 1970s, the bar mitzvah reception was a party more for the parents than for the child, to which parents invited their friends, relatives, and business associates.[47] In the 1980s the bar mitzvah boy often had a separate party in the evening, replete with a disc jockey. The child would decide on the guest list for this event and would issue the invitations.[48]

Decade after decade rabbis denounced the lavish receptions following bar mitzvahs as vulgar, crass, and tasteless; Jewish novelists, comics, and even photographers joined in the roast.[49] The standard joke was that at the bar mitzvah the caterer was more important than the rabbi. Mordecai Kaplan, the founder of Reconstructionism, an egalitarian form of Conservative Judaism, believed that the catered affair showed the "disintegration of Jewish life."[50] Some wanted to eliminate the reception entirely. Failing that, others hoped that it could become a more Jewish celebration, which might include Jewish blessings of food and Jewish folk dances.[51]

The attitude of Reform and reform-minded Jews toward the bar mitzvah has invariably reflected changing attitudes toward both religious ritual and the amount and kind of religious instruction needed for girls. Borrowing from Christian tradition, Reform rabbis in the United States in the 1840s inaugurated confirmation explicitly as an egalitarian alternative to the bar mitzvah. They took a dim view of the bar mitzvah, considering it outmoded and unnecessary. For Reform Jews confirmation was the Jewish equivalent of a graduation ceremony. It included a group of boys and girls aged fourteen to sixteen, who attended instructional classes for about a year beforehand. At the ceremony, they would assemble at the pulpit and read from the Torah or from their own compositions. By the 1930s, in lieu of frilly dresses and new suits, many celebrants began to don ceremonial robes for the confirmation ceremony. After the service the boys and girls would change into their party clothes and join in a public group reception.[52]

Having rejected the bar mitzvah as out of date, however, parents in Reform congregations started to demand them soon after World War I. Reform rabbis disapproved, but the parents of adolescent boys preferred what they perceived as an ancient tradition, instead of the recent innovation of confirmation. Besides, the bar mitzvah focused on the individual boy rather than a group. Unwilling to abandon the confirmation, Reform and Conservative congregations accepted both. For Conservative Jews confirmation had at least two advantages: it extended the period of Jewish education by at least three more years, and it was available to girls as well as boys. However, since the thirteen-year-old boy had already had a bar mitzvah, he sometimes chose not to be confirmed. As a result, confirmation sometimes became a female-dominated or even a girls-only religious event.

Despite the fact that Jewish girls were eligible for confirmation, they wanted the bar mitzvah as well, both because they were denied it and because the rite was associated with the prestige of learning.[53] Judith Kaplan, the daughter of Mordecai Kaplan, broke the gender barrier in 1922. At her bat mitzvah (daughter of the commandment) she chanted blessings and read a selection from her own Bible, but her father did not think it fitting for her to read directly from the Torah or chant the haftarah, the weekly portion from the Prophets.

Although Mordecai Kaplan wanted to make Judaism more egalitarian, most Conservative congregations adopted the bat mitzvah for nonfeminist reasons. Supervisors of Hebrew schools found it an attractive incentive for retaining their female students.[54] By the 1940s, one third of Conservative congregations were conducting bat mitzvahs. Although Orthodox Jews first offered this ceremony in 1944, it did not became popular among them until the 1970s, when it took on the aura of being an egalitarian challenge to male privilege. Reform rabbis, who were never in favor of the bar mitzvah in the first place, were lukewarm in their embrace of the equivalent ritual for girls. In 1953 about 35 percent of Reform congregations made the bat mitzvah available to girls. Usually it was held on Friday night, rather than on Saturday morning, when the boys had theirs.[55]

The bat mitzvah of the 1950s offered girls ceremony and religious recognition while upholding the prevailing gender stereotypes about woman's place. Girls might recite prayers only in English or begin by lighting the candles (a female responsibility) or substitute the traditional Jewish paean to womanhood, *Ayshet Chayil* ("Women of Valor") instead of the haftorah reading and traditional blessings. The major gender difference in the 1950s was the reception.[56] Most girls had a fellowship hour in the synagogue or temple after the service, and presents were kept to a minimum.

A few Jewish girls refused to accept the second-class status of the bat mitzvah. Marlene Adler recalled years later that "[I] derailed my own bat mitzvah when I saw how meager it would be compared to my brother's bar mitzvah years down the road."[57] As a result of feminist demands within Judaism, beginning in the 1970s the ceremony for the girl came to be identical with that of the boy in both Conservative and Reform Judaism, and the spending for the party afterward was also on an equivalent scale.[58]

Quinceañera

The quinceañera, like the bar mitzvah, was initially a simple ritual that post-1960s Hispanic families transformed into one as opulent as a wedding.[59] The motives for having one were also similar: the desire to display affluence and economic success, reunite extended kin, and celebrate a child's birthday within a religious and ethnic context. Unlike the bar mitzvah, which evolved into a more egalitarian ritual because of the women's movement, the quinceañera changed little because of feminism. With a few exceptions, it remains a ceremony only for girls. Even in the United States today the quinceañera communicates that the Hispanic girl has become a Catholic woman, fertile, sexual, and destined to become a bride and a good mother. Like the traditional bar mitzvah, the quinceañera was an affirmation of gender, ethnic, and religious identities—an embrace of multiple identities.

Although often claimed to be an ancient Aztec tradition, the quinceañera was likely a Spanish one introduced into Mexico by the Spanish elite in the mid-nineteenth century. Certainly the clothing, gestures, and movements of the quinceañera were Spanish, not Indian. The elaborate dress for the girl suggests a ball gown worn by a wealthy woman at the Spanish court. Prior to the 1960s the quinceañera was rarely celebrated among Hispanics in the Southwest and California except in areas having large Hispanic parishes with Hispanic priests or sympathetic non-Hispanic ones. Among Hispanics in Colorado and in northern cities, such as Chicago, Minneapolis, or Toledo, it was uncommon, even unknown. In general, Anglo priests did not consider the ceremony a sacrament, and therefore were unwilling to perform it.[60]

Since the quinceañera was relatively rare in Hispanic America before the 1960s, it surely qualifies as an invented tradition. Earlier celebrations were more humble, and considerably less didactic. At a Brownsville, Texas, quinceañera in the 1940s, for example, the girl received no formal religious instruction. Some Brownsville families held the party in the backyard; the more affluent hosted a reception in a hotel ballroom, where a trio played Mexican music. While musicians struck up a march, the quinceañera and her escort led a promenade around the ballroom. Then, with the spotlight on her and the lights dimmed, the girl waltzed with her father.[61] In the 1950s the quinceañera was still quite rare, even in the Southwest. In that decade most Hispanics wanted to blend into Anglo culture, rather than celebrate tradition. Some claimed to be Spanish rather than Mexican-American or Puerto Rican.[62] One woman explained that she did not have a quinceañera then and added, "None of my girlfriends had one in those days."[63]

From the 1960s on, the quinceañera was most common among

first- or second-generation immigrants from Mexico who were living close to the border, those who were *muy mexicanos,* perhaps people who went back and forth to Mexico. Among Puerto Ricans, whose relations to the American Catholic church are even more distant than Mexican-Americans, the quinceañera often became entirely secular as a "sweet sixteen party" held on the girl's sixteenth birthday. Cuban-Americans, far more economically successful than other Spanish-speaking migrants, held lavish quinceañeras. These, too, were entirely secular events, but were held on the girl's fifteenth birthday. There are thus quite different practices among Latinos, though the greatest attention has been given to the celebration of quinceañera among Mexican-Americans.

Even since the 1960s most third-generation Mexican-Americans did not have a quinceañera, although some professional families did have small but posh parties, perhaps a group ceremony followed by a cotillion, which served as a fund-raiser for a Hispanic organization or charity. Such celebrations could be identified simultaneously as the Anglo ritual of the debutante ball and as religious and ethnic tradition. The general lack of interest in the quinceañera among the third and subsequent generations of Mexican-Americans can be seen as a sign of acculturation and a mark of a rise in status. (The Mexican elite, which considered a quinceañera vulgar, did not have them, either. They often gave their daughters a trip to Europe as a fifteenth-birthday present.)

While Mexican-American ethnic consciousness since the 1960s increased interest in the quinceañera, the ritual as conducted in the homeland shaped how the ceremony was performed in the United States. Innovations in Guadalajara (rings, medals, satin pillows, and a bouquet of flowers for the girl) were quickly adopted in the United States. Some girls traveled to Mexico to buy their dress, and a few celebrated their quinceañera there.[64] Mexicans had been moving back and forth between Mexico and the United States for several centuries. It was not return to the homeland that led to celebration of this ritual, but rising group consciousness among Hispanic immigrants in the 1960s. The Catholic church, influenced by the civil rights climate of that decade, felt the need to respond to this growing sense of ethnic identification.

Mexican-American families, especially working-class ones, used the extended kinship system to pay for the event. The kin network in the working class tended to be large and lived nearby, often in the same neighborhood. When working-class Hispanic families moved, they tended to migrate near kin. Unlike at the baptism, where one set of godparents was selected, there might be more than a dozen for the quinceañera. As one Houston mother explained, "Frankly, if we didn't have relatives who agreed to share the expense, we couldn't do it."[65] Relatives and friends named as godparents paid for the cake, the photographer, the hall rental, the flowers at the church, the girl's bouquet, the gown, the rental of a tiara, the payment to the priest, the alcoholic beverages, and the religious medallion.[66] Close friends of the girl's family were willing to take on the obligation, but the economic demands of the quinceañera often strained the kinship system. Some found an excuse to be out of town the day of the event so they did not have to contribute to it.[67]

The bar mitzvah at the conscious level celebrated religious manhood, and at the unconscious level it celebrated sexual maturation.[68] Similarly, at the quinceañera a girl's sexuality hung over the ceremony like the necklace she received as a gift. In modern times, the quinceañera served as an announcement that a girl was eligible for dating, although in many cases she had already begun. The older message was that the father was indicating the eligibility of his virgin daughter for marriage. The girl, like a bride, dressed in white, a symbol of purity. In the 1970s the teenage sexual revolution, in which even the "good girl" who attended high school was no longer a virgin, began to affect urban Hispanics. Failure to have a quinceañera in many Hispanic communities was taken as a sign that a young woman was not a virgin and might even be pregnant. Conversely, having one was seen as an effort to prove a girl's virginity, even if the facts were otherwise.[69]

The dress for the quinceañera was in some ways equivalent to the bar mitzvah suit, in that it was a very special outfit signifying a transformation in status. The suit made a boy into a man; the dress made a girl into a fairy princess, or young bride who was marrying her prince charming.[70] The traditional gown was a floor-length white dress, snug at the top, wide at the bottom, with the skirt shaped like a bell and worn with a crinoline. During the reception the father (or grandfather) kneeled in front of the girl and put high-heeled shoes on her feet, symbolizing that the girl was now a woman and that her girlish feet had become transformed into sexual gams.[71] The elaborate gown with the stiff crinoline underneath took a large amount of space, one of the surest ways to demonstrate high status.

Just as rabbis often looked askance at excessive spending on the reception following the bar mitzvah, so, too, many priests roundly criticized the quinceañera. They complained that the ceremony was lavish and ostentatious and contained little religious content. They also worried that working class or poor parents were going into debt to pay for it.[72] The quinceañera also posed a scheduling problem for Catholic churches. The church gave highest priority to performing sacramental rites, such as weddings. Families wanted a high mass at the quinceañera, which might last at least an hour and a half. With a shortage of priests, the quinceañera made it difficult to accommodate weddings at the church.

Because Reform Jewish parents demanded bar mitzvahs, rabbis acceded. So, too, Hispanic Catholic parents wanted the priest to preside over a quinceañera. Most priests agreed, sometimes reluctantly. In the 1980s the archdiocese of Los Angeles first refused to perform the ceremony, because the church leadership felt it encouraged lavish spending among the poor. Eventually they changed their policy, however, because Hispanic bridal shop owners and printers, who depended on the quinceañera trade, insisted.[73] Many Hispanics, denied the ritual by the Catholic church, were even turning to Protestant denominations to perform it. Faced with continuing competition from Protestant faiths for Hispanic souls, archdioceses began to relent.

Catholic priests in the 1970s and 1980s not only created a new liturgy for the quinceañera but also tried to reformulate the definition of the ceremony from an initiation rite for a girl into sexuality and eligibility for marriage into a rite that taught a girl to assume adult responsibility. Priests often refused to perform the ceremony for girls who dropped out of school, were pregnant, were known to use drugs, or belonged to a gang. One priest in Phoenix told girls in his parish, "You want a quinceañera? You get your life straight."[74] Some required that each member of the girl's court go to confession.[75] Many priests preferred ceremonies for a group rather than for the individual girl. In Chicago in the 1980s church officials required that the girl enter the church escorted by both parents, or by her father, rather than the usual young male escort, because they did not want to give the impression that having a quinceañera was giving the church's permission for the girl to think of herself as ready for sexual intercourse.[76]

The effect of the church's rules about eligibility for the quinceañera was to underscore the division in Hispanic culture (indeed, in all western cultures) between good girls and bad ones. The birthday girl was the pure, virginal Eve, who accepted parental norms and parental authority. Her world was bounded by home, school, and church. She obeyed the dictates of her church and was destined to marry, have children, and care for her family. The bad girl took drugs, joined a gang, and got pregnant. Girls clearly understood this division and saw their quinceañera as a reward for their good behavior. The symbolic meaning of being a good girl on the verge of becoming a blushing bride and pious mother fit with the idealization of the Virgin Mary in Hispanic culture.[77]

Some nuns, acting out of feminist egalitarian impulses, tried to design an equivalent ceremony for a boy. Sister Angela Erevia, assistant to the bishop of Dallas and the author of a religious manual on the ceremony, proposed one in the 1970s, and in some Southwest parishes some boys had such ceremonies. Many families hosted a birthday party with a small gathering of friends for the fifteen-year-old boy. Some parents may have planned to have a mass for their son on his birthday, but few seem to have had one.[78] Because the ritual was defined as a celebration of a girl's virginity, it was difficult to make it seem necessary for a boy. Unconsciously the ceremony assumed a sexual double standard. Sexual abstinence among unmarried boys was not expected or particularly valued. If anything, the legacy of *machismo* was that a true man should be sexually aggressive and experienced.

The reception after the ceremony in the church showed the influence of rising standards of consumption, popular culture, new technology, and even changing sexual standards.[79] In the 1960s the girl might be delivered to the church in a low rider (usually a convertible whose chassis had been lowered); in the 1990s she might arrive in a rented limousine. For a proper reception in the 1980s and 1990s a family hired a disc jockey and a photographer with a video camera. In earlier days the music and dancing at the reception represented a compromise between the demands of tradition and those of the peer culture. In addition to the traditional waltz, girls danced to whatever music was currently popular. Later some girls dispensed with the waltz entirely.[80]

*   *   *

If the rituals described in this chapter successfully initiated an adolescent into adulthood, why were they so uncommon in other cultures? Adolescence was a period of great anxiety and lack of self-definition; the ritual, it was argued, helped to relieve parental fears for the future of their adolescent and provided the child with a ceremony that signaled to friends and kin the onset of maturity. The fact that black initiation rites were developed in the 1970s suggests that where anxiety was the greatest, new ritual was developed. The initiation rites for black youth in the 1970s and 1980s, developed by black churches and social organizations, involved lengthy periods of preparation and instruction. Kwanzaa provided the model for these rites, in that the initiations were presented as an updating of African heritage. Churches and social service organizations, in offering these rituals, hoped to attract working-class and poor black youth otherwise destined for teen pregnancy, teen parenthood, gang membership, drug pushing, and drug use.[81] Unlike Kwanzaa, however, these rites never attracted a middle-class constituency, perhaps because they were so clearly defined as attempts to curb behavior seen as prevalent mainly among "at risk" youth.

In putting forth these arguments in favor of initiation rites, it must be admitted that the Jewish and Hispanic rites were less successful than they at first appeared. Observers even in the early twentieth century noted that Jewish boys soon after the bar mitzvah stopped going to synagogue and even refused to come home for Friday night supper. Hispanic parents, not just priests and nuns, often worried that the quinceañera seemed to give the girl permission to date and be sexually active. Nonetheless, many children did seem more mature after their performance, and many parents took pride in organizing, participating in, and being able to pay for a successful event. To some extent, the demand for adolescent ritual was met by secular events—attending the prom, a graduation party, or a debutante ball; obtaining a driver's license; registering for the draft. Except for some black churches, most Christian faiths were unwilling to create new religious ceremonies for an adolescent.

Meanwhile, among Jews and Hispanics once simple religious ceremonies followed by small home receptions had become lengthy rites involving considerable preparation and often very fancy parties. There were several reasons for this development. Performed once in a lifetime, these rituals took place under religious auspices, but permitted secular as well as religious celebration. While the demand for these rituals came largely from parents or the child, rabbis, priests, and nuns recognized an opportunity to provide the child with more religious instruction. Eventually the ritual came to be redefined as a celebration of family success, an expression of ethnic and religious identity as well as the chance to have a very special birthday party for an adolescent. The religious ritual and the reception following it offered a pastiche of traditions and modern innovations that brought pleasure to the parents and to the child, within an ethnic and religious framework. In feasting, dressing up, and bringing the family together Hispanics saw themselves reaching back to the tradition of the Aztecs, and Jews to the Middle Ages. These motives were the prevailing ones, irrespective of the social class or degree of religiosity of the parents. The initiation rite always had as its goal self-transformation, making a child into an adult member of the tribe. These rituals became much like weddings because this age-old goal was united with self-transformation achieved with the help of florists, haberdashers, caterers, musicians, and photographers.

CHAPTER NINE

Please Omit Flowers

> If a man died, shall he live again, is not half so important to some people
> as is, if a man die, will he be buried properly? Funeral Director A. D. Price
> will answer that question.
>
> —ADVERTISEMENT FOR A. D. PRICE FUNERAL HOME, RICHMOND, VA., 1916

Middle-class and wealthy Victorians showed respect for the dead and made the funeral the most spectacular event of life. By the end of the first half of the nineteenth century, the funeral had become a commodity to be purchased, even saved for. Mourners in colonial times had picked flowers to put on the grave; their descendants preferred to buy huge wreaths of roses or lilies. The dead were once buried in a simple pine box (called a coffin) or simply placed in the ground wrapped in a white sheet. In the nineteenth century the burial container for the corpse acquired a new name, the casket; it became longer; and it was made out of sturdier materials, such as mahogany, bronze, or other metals. In colonial days the dead were buried in the town graveyard. The Victorian middle class began purchasing family plots in privately owned cemeteries and marking graves with a manufactured marble or granite headstone. Having injected the body with embalming fluid, and powdered and painted it, Victorian undertakers successfully combined two opposing attitudes toward death: fixation on the corpse and denial of death.[1]

Eventually, the extravagant Victorian code of conduct for acknowledging and mourning a death collapsed. The postsentimental attitude toward funerals arose because of the tragedy of World War I. The social elite began to favor a plainer, shorter, and more private funeral. An increase in life expectancy had an even greater effect on the style of funerals than did the First World War. More and more Americans died in old age, having lived long and full lives. Their kin had less reason to grieve. It might be thought that changes came about during the course of the twentieth century because the funeral was religious ritual, and as religiosity in the United States declined, religious ritual disappeared as well. Actually, liberal Protestant authorities often advocated the less expensive and shorter ceremony as being more spiritual than one with velvet palls. Moreover, even in the 1990s most Americans believed in an afterlife and wanted to bury their dead with religious ceremony.

At the same time, Americans in the late twentieth century had decided that the funeral was not the most important ritual of life. One South Boston undertaker in the 1990s, regretting the disappearance of the Irish wake, said, "it seems the younger generation wants to get on with their lives."[2] Some people saw this attitude as callous, self-absorbed, narcissistic, a product of the 1960s. Actually, there was nothing new in the controversy about whether funerals should be modest and simple or grand. It was a staple of debate during the Protestant Reformation in Europe.

The acculturation of ethnic groups and their increasing entry into the middle class led to a decline in distinctive burial customs, especially since the late 1940s. A review of African American burial customs shows how an ethnic group, even while changing its customs, continued to find meaning in lavish funerals. American blacks, like other ethnic groups, moved in the direction of a simpler funeral, but at a very slow pace. The lavish funeral offered them a means of coping with the indignities they suffered in life. In addition, the increasing urbanization of blacks beginning in the late nineteenth century led to fancier funerals.

Pageant of Woe

The Victorian way of celebrating death endured until about the time of World War I.[3] In Victorian times morticians, florists, monument sellers, and casket manufacturers tried to persuade consumers to spend freely on elaborate, even extravagant funerals. The middle class and the wealthy had their own reasons for doing so. They sought to show their love and respect for the dead, display their wealth, and prove their family's respectability and social standing. The sentimental view of the family and of death also encouraged the desire for a beautiful ceremony that could express sadness and love. Heaven was not commercialized—there were no shops there—but it was certainly domesticated as a place where the family would dwell together. It was no longer simply the place where souls were reunited. Often the living tried to keep the memory of the dead alive by displaying images of the person's face or a lock of hair, by visiting the grave, and by engaging in an elaborate ritual of mourning. Some, especially those who had lost a son or brother in the Civil War, looked to spiritualism and se-ances in an attempt to contact their dead as they tried to make sense of the shocking and untimely deaths on the battlefield.

The Victorians often used domestic occasions as a means of reliev-ing the stress of living during the transformation of an agrarian soci-ety into an urban and commercial one. Similarly, middle-class and wealthy Victorians looked to the funeral as a source of comfort for their anxieties. Yet the Victorians were not particularly worried about whether or not they would get to heaven; they believed they were headed there. What made them more nervous was their standing in the highly uncertain world of the living. One day they enjoyed secu-rity and a happy home; the next the bank failed, and their savings were depleted. A show of worldly success could relieve this particular form of unease.

Victorian Death Rituals

The Victorian funeral was not simply a religious service after death but a sequence of rituals for the entire process of dying, burying the corpse, and mourning. Most people died at home, not in a hospital. A wake would be held there, as in colonial times. The corpse, however, was no longer readied for burial clad in a simple white linen shroud, as was the standard practice of the colonists. Men were instead dressed in their best suits and women in a white burial gown or their wedding dress.[4] White-gloved pallbearers carried the metallic or bronze casket into a church, where the minister preached a long fu-neral sermon. After the funeral of a wealthy man or woman the hun-dreds of mourners, dressed in black crepe, would board their car-riages to follow the hearse to the grave.[5]

Family feeling and the desire to display family status led to the de-velopment of gardenlike cemeteries in the nineteenth century. As part of the reaction against Catholicism, the Puritans had opposed burying their dead in a church graveyard. Instead they established town burial grounds, which in practice were often located next to the church. In rural areas many of the dead were buried on their own farms.[6] Each of these locations proved unsatisfactory. Public health officials warned of the spread of cholera and other epidemics from burying the dead in the center of town, where town burial grounds were located. Farmers who sold their land ended up ceding the family burial plot to strangers. The solution was to create "cities of the dead" at the edge of major population centers. In addition to this change in location, families also began to make cemeteries into parks, where mourners could find consolation in nature. Families purchased the burial plot, along with headstones of marble or granite that were carved with the faces of cherubs, urns, or weeping willows (the weeping willow was a frequent symbol because the willow required constant watering, presumably from tears); occasionally they even procured elaborate family tombs.[7]

Wealthy colonists had handed out mourners' rings as mementos to friends and relatives who attended a funeral. The Victorians had many more mementos, which functioned as mnemonic devices through which survivors could evoke affectionate memories of the dead. They treasured lockets, brooches, and wreaths containing the portrait of the dead as well as strands of their hair. Many mourners wanted to own a likeness of the deceased, even a portrait taken soon after death. The invention of the daguerreotype in 1839 made it possible for a photographer to capture an after-death likeness. Daguerreotypes of the dead usually provided a visual aid to memory and in showing the dead with eyes closed provided additional reinforcement for the belief in death as a form of permanent and peaceful sleep.[8]

Embalming made it possible to preserve the body for a longer period, and so lengthened the wake. During this longer interval between death and burial, faraway kin had time to return home. Thus, embalming helped to make the funeral a family homecoming, like Thanksgiving. During the Civil War, wealthy families paid dearly so that they could transport the body of a soldier to the family plot for a proper burial.[9] Surgeons and chemists, setting up tents at the battlefield, charged outrageous fees to embalm dysentery-ravaged and battle-scarred soldiers' bodies for shipment home. Embalming took on the cachet of prestige after Lincoln was assassinated and his body chemically preserved so that it could be displayed on the long train trip from Washington, D.C., to Springfield, Illinois. As a result of embalming, undertakers were able to define their services as hygienic and scientific. They began to establish professional associations and schools of mortuary science. In addition to embalming, undertakers also started to use techniques of cosmetic restoration to give the corpse a ruddy and lifelike appearance.

By the late nineteenth century the funeral was moving out of the home and into a business establishment. Embalmers were finding it increasingly cumbersome and costly to carry equipment to the family's home. Moreover, they preferred to work in their own premises, where they had more control and privacy. As more people died in hospitals rather than at home, the undertaker had to transport the corpse from hospital to funeral parlor, from funeral parlor to home, from home to church, and from church to grave. Families were used to holding pregravesite rituals at both home and church. It was cheaper and more convenient for the undertaker to eliminate some of the extra trips. Funeral directors who housed both wakes and funerals at their establishment could offer a more lavish ceremony at a lower cost. At the undertaker's establishment one small room came to be used for wakes and another, larger one for funeral services. Because their establishment replaced the family parlor as the site of the wake, undertakers began to call their place of business a funeral "parlor" or funeral "home." Even immigrants of limited means recognized a wake in a funeral home as being prestigious. When Mary Hojnacki's mother, a Polish immigrant to Chicago, died in the 1920s, her last wish was "not to lay in the house."[10] Nonetheless among rural immigrants, blacks in cities and the countryside, and poor Southern whites, women continued to lay out the dead in the home up to the 1930s and 1940s.

A woman's black silk or bombazine dress symbolized a family's prestige as much as a mahogany casket. Worn both in private and in public, such attire showed others that the mourner was to be taken seriously and not tempted by frivolity. Victorians had an elaborate set of rules about mourning. Women were not supposed to attend weddings in the first year of mourning. A proper hostess did not even invite a woman during her period of grief to a festive occasion.[11] There were more mourning restrictions for women than for men, and women felt that propriety required them to conform. At one level, the rules of mourning asserted the sexual privilege of the dead man. His woman remained outside of the (re)marriage market, sexually unavailable to other men and faithful to his memory. At another level, a woman assumed the role of guardian of the family's grief. Society expected men to return to the world of commerce because their work demanded attention and their family needed their earnings. One distraught father in Schenectady, New York, in the mid-nineteenth century decided he must return to his office two days after his daughter's demise. Later, even though his relationship with his daughter was a close one, he did not commemorate the anniversary of her death.[12] Women, seen as emotional by nature, were supposed to feel the loss most keenly. In their clothing and demeanor they expressed the sundering by death of family relationships.[13]

The Evolution of the Postsentimental Funeral

Modernism and disillusionment with the unnecessary carnage of World War I put an end to the Victorian pageant of death. During the war influential American literary magazines argued that conventional funeral customs were pagan. At war's end, the older generation, like mourning post-Civil War families, turned to spiritualism and erected gigantic memorials to fallen soldiers. They also visited graves of U.S. infantrymen who fell in France. Meanwhile, the younger generation danced the Charleston and drowned its sorrows in bootleg liquor. Writers decried the "ostentatious display" of the bronze casket with the corpse in full view and "the hot-house exotics" of floral wreaths, which encouraged mourners in "false emotion."[14] No longer did many people feel the need to spend lavishly or endure a lengthy ceremony. Gradually the funeral receded in importance—and the wedding became the grandest event of all.

Except for the funerals of public figures, most families came to believe that a sad occasion should be a simple one. By the 1930s, they had decided that it was as important to be happy as to display respect for the dead—or, as Ira Gershwin wrote, it was "madness to be always sitting around in sadness, when you could be learning the Steps of Gladness." Spending on funerals as a percentage of gross domestic product has been falling steadily since 1929, when statistics on such matters were first collected. Meanwhile, the price of weddings was rising. In the 1930s, for example, the average funeral cost a little less than the typical wedding. By the 1950s the price of a funeral was just

17 percent of the cost of a typical wedding. Similarly, in the 1990s, the bill for a funeral was just 16 percent of the total price of the average formal wedding.[15]

As the location of the funeral moved outside the home, families paid for professional services to care for their dead. The funeral director played an increasingly large role in orchestrating the event. The ritual of death became centralized at the funeral parlor; eventually, no part of the ceremony took place in the home of the deceased. The body was prepared for burial in the funeral home, where mourners assembled for a visitation or viewing of the body and the funeral service. Families often held the postburial feast at a restaurant or public hall rather than at their home.

Funeral directors, preferring regular business hours, discouraged all-night or several-day-long wakes. The visitation (the modern term for the wake) usually lasted several hours on one day, or perhaps an evening. Some of the earlier customs of the wake also disappeared. It was no longer a place for young people to court. There were no more professional (that is, hired) mourners. Young children were not lined up to carry the casket of their friends or siblings to the grave. By the 1950s politicians rarely paid an obligatory call at the Irish wake, and heavy drinking or drunkenness was rare.[16] As funeral directors took charge of the service and burial, they sought uniformity by eliminating these and other distinctive customs, such as the marching bands that accompanied the procession to and from the grave. They also urged the minister to avoid a lengthy sermon that might frighten the congregation in favor of a short one that would relieve "the tortures of the bereaved."[17] Writers of etiquette manuals argued that because the "eulogy was harrowing to the feelings of mourners" it should be eliminated.[18]

Hoping to minimize the pain of the grief-stricken, funeral directors wanted to shield the family from other mourners. They led them into a private room before the service at the funeral home. They also encouraged a smaller party to accompany the family from the funeral home to the gravesite. Some funeral directors even urged the family to have private funerals and burials, in which only the immediate family and relatives participated—and some families preferred it this way. The aim of excluding the general public and fellow parishioners from burial services was to reduce contacts with onlookers, which might bring pain to the family.[19] Too much emotion expended in grief was self-indulgent, funeral directors told their customers as early as the

1930s. Some rebuked loud crying; others called in a physician and offered tranquilizers. The public seemed to concur that grief should occur in private.[20]

Families often asked friends to make a donation to a favorite charity rather than sending an elaborate standing wreath to the funeral.[21] Many families began to insert the phrase "Please omit flowers" in the funeral notices they placed in newspapers. To be sure, some Puritan ministers in colonial America had urged families to make a charitable contribution for the education of poor children rather than spending lavishly on a funeral.[22] Critics had been castigating the fancy funeral for centuries. What was new was that the middle class had come to perceive the standing wreath with its satin ribbon as a symbol of excess and tastelessness.[23]

Perhaps the most important feature of the postsentimental attitude toward the funeral is that families no longer wanted to practice the more elaborate customs of the sentimental era, in part because they sought to keep death, and the corpse, at bay. Due to unfamiliarity, or even fear and disgust, with dead bodies, people refrained from touching or kissing the corpse—and funeral directors discouraged it. By the 1920s the middle class had decided that postmortem photographs of the dead lying in the padded casket were morbid and psychologically unhealthy. Some families still snapped these pictures themselves but concealed them from others, or contacted a photographer who discreetly took a few photos at the funeral home. Mainly lower-middle-class families, especially African Americans, Asians, Poles, Russians, Italians, Scotch-Irish, and German Lutherans, wanted these portraits as proof of their respect for the dead.[24]

Despite the changes in the funeral service, however, mourners still felt that through its natural surroundings the cemetery might provide consolation. The memorial park, with its uniform grave markers flush against the ground and barely visible and its trees and well-manicured lawns, constituted the preferred burial place in postwar America. This modern cemetery was a democratic society's way of remembering the dead: the markers were uniform, and few distinctions of rank or status were visible. In addition, the modern memorial park provided more gender equality, since it had invariably been men who had been honored with large tombstones in garden cemeteries. Catholic cemeteries also modernized; the Catholic church in the 1950s began to oppose the use of photographs on gravestones.[25]

Frequent visits and the decorating of graves became practices found mainly among particular ethnic groups, such as Italians, Hispanics, Japanese, and Chinese, who went to cemeteries on their distinctive days of the dead (such as All Souls Day) as well as on national holidays, such as Memorial Day. Even in these groups, the younger generation, especially those living outside areas of ethnic concentration, rarely visited graves.[26] Families might go to the cemetery when a monument was unveiled. However, family picnics at the gravesite or family gatherings to clean the graves became uncommon. In the South, newspaper notices announcing community work days at cemeteries to replace broken markers, rake and sweep, and mow the grass disappeared by around World War II. Cemeteries instead either hired a groundskeeper or abandoned maintenance altogether. Sunday family picnics at the graveyard among Italian-American families began to disappear at about the same time. Brooklyn College undergraduates in the 1980s told their professor they had rarely visited a family grave in the last five years. Adults in Los Angeles in another survey in the same decade gave the same response. One Los Angeles man expressed the typical modern attitude when he told an interviewer, "Don't keep running there. There's nothing there. I guess it's okay on Decoration Day."[27]

Most of American society had no explicit mourning period and no ceremonies to mark its end and the resumption of normal life. The Jewish shiva stands out as an organized period of mourning. Stopping all work for seven days after the burial, and not washing during that week, mourners gathered in the home of the deceased or their own home to pray, grieve, and accept visits from friends and neighbors. At the modern shiva, a catered affair of potato chips, soda, and fruitcakes, mourners no longer expected a "doleful occasion," but instead engaged in "an exercise in conviviality." In observing shiva, postwar Reform Jews ended mourning after three days or less. Conservative men often returned to work after three days, while their wives continued to "sit shiva" the full seven.[28] The work schedules of the office, factory, and school were incompatible with a lengthy period of grieving.

During the first year after a relative's death, a Jewish male was supposed to attend the synagogue daily to recite the kaddish, a prayer for the dead. In addition, mourners in the first and subsequent anniversaries of a loved one's death were to attend a yearly memorial service in the synagogue at which the deceased's name was mentioned. Unlike

Passover and Chanukah, which had great appeal as holidays for children, and the bar and bat mitzvah, which were rites for the adolescent, these rituals persisted despite the fact that they were observed entirely by adults, some of whom attended synagogue only rarely otherwise. The main explanation for the persistence of these customs is that grown Jewish sons and daughters, remembering parental sacrifices and warmth, acted out their own version of filial piety.[29]

Most women after World War I put away their mourning clothes shortly after the funeral because they were no longer required: widows were ready to resume their lives. But several ethnic groups deviated from this overall pattern. Until the 1960s widows in the rural South and first- and second-generation women from Mediterranean and Iberian groups—Mexican-Americans, Portuguese, Italians, and Greeks—dressed in black for a lifetime. In these patriarchal cultures a widow was upholding family honor. Some widows covered their heads with a black veil, even in the home. Expectations for widows in these groups began to change by the 1970s. It became unheard of for a Mexican-American widow, for example, to wear black for an entire year. Men also decided that the etiquette of mourning was out of date. Mexican-American men in Austin, Texas, in the 1980s told an interviewer that they did not want their wives to mourn as their mothers and grandmothers had done.[30]

The most important reason for these changes in funeral and mourning practices in modern America was that death came mainly to the elderly. Advances in public health and sanitation, improvements in the standard of living, better diet, and the eradication of many infectious diseases led to major declines in infant and maternal mortality and increases in life expectancy. As the old proverb said, "Death keeps no calendar," but in the second half of the twentieth century it did. In the late twentieth century almost two thirds of all American deaths occurred to people over the age of sixty-five. That the dead were mainly old, rather than infants or young adults, helps to explain not only the shift in mortuary customs, but also why these deaths had come to be regarded, in sociologist Robert Blauner's words, as "low grief losses."[31]

Many of the elderly had succumbed to a "social death" before physically expiring—that is, they had retired from work and were living separately from adult children and grandchildren. No longer active workers, their deaths did not disrupt the proper functioning of society. There was a direct relationship between the style of funeral services and the fact that so many of those dying were elderly. Social surveys indicated that adult children were less likely to observe the anniversary of their parent's death than were mothers and fathers whose young children had died or grieving spouses. At funerals of the elderly it was also less common for a corpse to be available for viewing.[32]

The majority of gay men who died of AIDS in the 1980s and 1990s were cremated. After the body had been disposed of, the friends and relatives gathered for a "memorial service" (a term that best applies to a postburial gathering, but is often used as well in referring to a preburial one in which the body is not present). The frequency of simple cremation followed by postburial memorial services for gay men who died of AIDS appears to refute the association of age with simplicity of ceremony, since deaths of men in the prime of life were indeed "high grief losses." The nontraditional religious beliefs of many gay men, the rejection of homosexuality by many traditional religions, and the cosmopolitanism of gay culture may explain the preference in the gay community for cremation and memorial services.[33] At the same time, the rituals of death for those who died of AIDS showed a great deal of innovation and desire for celebration. Men dying of AIDS often planned their own funerals as a celebration of their life. In 1987, friends and family began memorializing those who had died of AIDS by making a large fabric square as part of the Names Project Quilt. Some dying men wanted mourners to forsake a funeral in favor of making a square for the quilt. This memorial project was a modern form of *memento mori,* larger and more collective than Victorian brooches and lockets, but similarly designed to evoke the memory of the dead for mourners.[34]

Critics of the Lavish Funeral

Just as different brands of automobile were created for different levels of consumption—a Chevy for the masses, a Cadillac for the wealthy—different styles of funeral were also used for various classes, except that the standard of consumption was inverted. The top of the class structure came to want the Chevy, while the bottom wanted the Cadillac. The postsentimental funeral developed as an alternative to the lavish one. Brevity and simplicity were valued more, theatricality and emotionalism less. Americans have criticized excessive spending at funerals since Puritan times. From Mark Twain to Evelyn Waugh writers have portrayed the mortician as a suspicious smooth talker, out to take advantage of the bereaved and the poor. In the twentieth century social workers, Protestant ministers, church groups, labor unions, and even insurance companies have investigated the practices of funeral directors and called for simpler funerals. Social workers and unions opposed the exploitation of worker's families at the moment when they were most vulnerable.[35] Life insurance companies, especially in the 1920s, investigated the cost of funerals. The companies may have wanted to demonstrate the need for more life insurance, since burial costs were depleting sums needed for survivors.

The demise of the Victorian pattern of elaborate mourning during World War I was only the first stage in the development of the post-sentimental funeral. The second was the effort to simplify the funeral service. Between the two world wars rabbis and Protestant ministers, writing in *The Nation, The American Mercury*, or in Christian (Protestant) magazines, took the lead in criticizing the aggressive sales tactics of funeral directors, the high cost of funerals, and the focus on the display of the corpse. Rabbis' criticisms were muted, since they generally formed cooperative relationships with Jewish funeral home directors. Priests, like their Protestant counterparts, urged Catholics to donate to charity in the name of the deceased and avoid "the costliest casket, the richest floral piece"; but their advice, published in Catholic journals, did not reach a large audience. The most influential critics were liberal Protestant clergy because Protestant services were often held in a funeral home, rather than a church, where clergy often felt the display of the corpse overwhelmed the spiritual character of the ceremony. The undertaker wanted the casket open to show his work; the minister wanted it closed so as not to distract from the solemnity of the service. Protestant clergy found themselves quarreling with the funeral director about who would choose the hymns.[36] They perceived a battle between spirituality, simplicity, and family privacy, which they favored, and display of the corpse, materialism, and public spectacle, which they opposed.

Congregants from Unitarian and liberal Protestant churches in the interwar years formed social action committees, funeral cooperatives, and memorial societies to encourage simple and private funerals and to assist people in arranging for their own funeral. Funerals did not have to be costly, members of these societies argued. They did not approve of embalming and display of the corpse at a visitation or funeral service. Some favored cremation, with a memorial service following at a suitable interval after death. Others wanted a private funeral, restricted to relatives and close friends. Even in late-twentieth-century United States regional and religious differences that had defined the interwar period continued to shape attitudes toward funerals. Those most critical of the funeral home ceremony were nonchurchgoers and members of memorial societies; those most satisfied were Catholics and Midwesterners.[37]

Textbook writers about changing attitudes toward death often consider the publication of Jessica Mitford's *The American Way of Death* (1963) a watershed event. Viewed in the light of the extensive criticism of the lavish funeral dating back to World War I, Mitford mainly repeated the rebukes of others. Nonetheless, she reached a large audience and even influenced Congress to pass consumer legislation against deceptive funeral home practices. In the same decade other authors were urging a more frank recognition of the process of dying. In publishing *On Death and Dying* in 1969, psychiatrist Elisabeth Kubler-Ross suggested that physicians needed to attend as much to the psychological state of dying patients as to their medical needs.[38] Her work helped develop the academic subject of thanatology and initiate the "death awareness" movement. The number of academic articles about death and dying increased tenfold, from 400 to about 4,000, between 1965 and 1975. Kubler-Ross's writings also spurred the growth of the hospice movement. The first hospice program was a nursing service for patients who wished to die in their own homes in New Haven, Connecticut, in 1974. Hospices acknowledged the reality of dying and sought to wrest control of the process of dying from hospitals and physicians. Many hospice volunteers were women who, in feeling a womanly obligation to care for the dying, were reviving female tradition.[39]

By the time the first hospice was founded, death was beginning to be widely discussed, even while dying was still hidden away in hospitals and nursing homes.[40] In 1937, 37 percent of all deaths in the United States took place in a hospital or a convalescent home. By 1949, the figure was nearly half; in 1992, 77 percent of all deaths occurred in a hospital or nursing home.[41] In the last two decades of the twentieth century the public debated death and dying endlessly, from the merits of assisted suicide to recognition of a new mortal disease, AIDS. There were even how-to books for people who wanted to lay out their own dead.

In 1963 as a grieving widow in a shoulder-length black veil and suit, Jacqueline Kennedy had led the nation in mourning, setting the standard for dignified, even stoic, demeanor in public. More than thirty years later, suffering from incurable lymphoma, she requested release from a New York City hospital so she could die at home in her Manhattan penthouse. Her preferences, so widely approved of, showed the public's yearning for the "good death," at home, surrounded by loved ones. Her death also illustrated another valued feature of modern dying: having full knowledge of her condition, she made decisions about her care up to the very end.

Living wills became popular as the public came to fear dying while being connected to feeding tubes in the intensive care unit even as they sought the cures hospitals and doctors offered.[42] Many Americans also wanted a more meaningful, albeit brief, ceremony, at which family or friends would speak, poetry would be recited, and live or recorded music would be played. Even the eulogy was back in favor. Religious manuals of major faiths argued that viewing the body at a funeral service was not pagan after all and might even help the family face the reality of death. Some Protestant churches were urging congregants to observe the anniversaries of death with special services.[43]

Cremation, once seen as a violation of religious teaching, became a viable alternative to burial. The percentage of bodies that were cremated more than tripled between 1975 and 1994 (from 7 percent to 22 percent). Rates of cremation were highest in Hawaii and on the West Coast. Except in Hawaii, where the lack of available land curbed the development of cemeteries, cremation was most common on the West Coast because so many people there were uprooted from kinfolk and were often unaffiliated with churches. Residents of the West Coast also preferred nontraditional and simpler funerals.[44] One important objection to cremation was removed when the Catholic church gave its approval in the late 1970s. The main reason for the growth in cremation was that it was cheaper than burial. Cremation was usually accompanied, in the words of a representative of the funeral industry, by "less than complete funeral services" and sometimes by no funeral at all.[45] Usually there was no wake or viewing of the body before cremation. Thus, through cremation, a considerable part of the population had in effect eliminated contact with the corpse.

African American Burials

In the twentieth century, funerals of Protestants, Catholics, and Jews have become less lavish and quite similar.[46] Nonetheless, many ethnic groups, including Japanese and Chinese Americans, Muslims, and Orthodox Jews continue to have distinctive customs of death. The "ethnic" funeral arose out of a desire to be buried according to the practices of one's group and one's faith. The performance of the rituals also helped maintain group identity and solidarity. The evolution of black funerals is traced here as an example of this, though it is an exception to the general trend toward simpler, briefer funerals.

Black funerals remain the most sentimentalized of all funerals. The reasons why this is so reveal a great deal about African American religious beliefs and culture. As chattel and subsequently as recently emancipated former slaves, blacks had a highly emotional style of grieving. But because they were poor, they could not afford expensive caskets and fancy hearses to deliver the casket to the grave. Nonetheless, beginning around the late nineteenth century, and sometimes before that in free black communities, African Americans held lavish funerals both to express their grief and to compensate for the indignities they suffered in life.[47]

Distinctive attitudes toward death originated in Africa and persisted among the Christianized slaves in America. First converted to Christianity in the 1700s in a wave of religious revivals, slaves adopted the Christian concept of heaven and hell, although they tended to view heaven as a place of freedom, where masters had to earn the right to be admitted. The descendants of Africans in America continued to hold that after a person had expired, his or her spirit dwelled in an afterworld. Christianity offered eternal salvation and consolation, but Africans in America often believed in spirit possession, that spirits protected the living and could bring harm to one's enemies.[48]

It is difficult to know how many African funerary customs survived the Middle Passage because West and Central African burial customs differed widely. The N'debele (from what is now part of Zimbabwe and Zaire), for example, placed their dead in the earth aligned from east to west, but the Dogon (from what is now Mali) buried their dead facing north to south.[49] Even if one could arrive at a single checklist of African burial customs, it is impossible to show that such customs were unique to the Africans in America. Many white Southerners also buried their dead lying east to west. As another example, slave burials often occurred at night; but Anglican internments took place then as well.[50] One possible reason for this coincidence of black and white customs is that the African customs most likely to survive were those that resembled European practices. It has also been argued that African burials shaped white practice in the South. But, as noted later, white practices similar to black ones could be found in the Upland South, where few blacks lived and the likelihood of black influence on whites was slim.

Africans brought to the New World in chains had more need of their customs than ever before, but their white masters did not allow the slaves to practice most of them. Even if slave owners had not believed in the superiority of the Christian funeral, they would not have permitted their chattel to recreate the lengthy burial ceremonies of West Africa. The LoDagaa of northern Ghana, for example, devoted three days to public ceremonies to bury the corpse and another three or four days to private ceremonies for the kinship group. Most West African societies organized three ceremonies after the burial service. Masters usually did not interfere with the first postburial ceremony since it was held on Sunday, a day the slaves were not required to work. In theory, the slaves could have held the other two ceremonies on Sundays as well. But not every ritual was passed down. Moreover, these ceremonies were harder to fit within the kind of Christian worship masters would permit. Masters were reluctant to allow elaborate ceremonies even on Sunday because they feared that large crowds assembled at slave funerals might plan or even undertake rebellions. From slave testimony it seems that most masters did permit slave burials—some took pride in furnishing a postburial feast, and the wood and nails for a coffin—but a few showed no respect whatsoever for the slave dead.[51]

Because Africans in America retained their belief in spirits, they continued to regard the body in special ways. The spirit had to be treated properly—and needed food—to embark on its journey into the spirit world. A hungry spirit could linger near the grave and wander from there to cause harm to the living. Two important ways of propitiating the spirit were the "second burial" and distinctive forms of grave decoration. The purpose of the West African second burial was to inquire into the possibly disturbed human relationships and the spiritual reasons that caused a person's death. The ceremony was said to comfort the hovering spirit by showing that the living had not forgotten it.[52] Second burials also functioned as memorial services and were held from six weeks to a year after the death.[53]

Grave decoration was another way of propitiating the spirits. Slave burial practices were influenced by West African or Congolese customs, even though the actual graveyard was usually a field set aside by masters. Mourners placed familiar objects, the last objects touched by the deceased, on top of the grave, because, as one black Southerner explained, "unless you bury a person's things with him he will come back after them."[54] Mourners broke glass and pitchers so that the spirit in them could be released to enter the spirit world. Some practices believed to be characteristic of blacks, such as burying the dead in mounds, placing lamps or lights on the grave, planting trees on the grave, decorating the grave with seashells, and scraping the grass near the grave have been found in Southern white cemeteries as well as in black graveyards. It is doubtful that Southern whites derived these practices from blacks since anthropologists and folklorists have noted these customs in the Upland South, where slavery was uncommon and blacks were few in number. Instead, it seems likely that these forms of graveyard decoration were common in West and Central Africa as well as in the highlands of Scotland and Ireland, from which many Appalachian whites had originated.[55]

The combination of African and Christian mortuary customs persisted among former slaves and their descendants in the rural South even into the first third of the twentieth century. Among poor blacks in the South during these decades the funeral was a community event. Women neighbors continued to lay out the dead as neighborly obligation rather than for pay. Neighbors and relatives participated in the "settin' up," an all-night vigil of song and prayer held in the home. People told stories about the dead person, and women sang ("All Dat Ah Got Done Gone" or "We'll All Rise Togedder, to Face de Risin' Sun!"). Men dug the grave as a sign of respect. Mourners at the church service and at the grave danced the ring shout, an African shuffle dance in which dancers bent their knees and moved clockwise slowly in a circle, while singing hymns. Women served a hearty feast at the church after the burial. Little money, if any, was spent on a grave marker. Blacks were denied burial in many cemeteries. At cemeteries that admitted black corpses, caskets were frequently reburied, stacked on top of each other, or vandalized. There was thus less reason to spend money on a marker than on the funeral.

Families held a second burial, called "stirring up the dead," in a church. It was open to everyone in the community and was a chance to reunite the family, since kin living far away had time to assemble.[56] The second burial was more of a community event than a display of worldly status. It had some dramatic elements, such as when the congregation stood and swayed back and forth as they listened to a vocalist. In the funeral sermon a black preacher could display his verbal art. A family might bring in a preacher who was noted for his beautiful baritone and power to move his listeners, or several preachers might speak. The good qualities of the deceased would be highlighted and defects transformed into merits. A gifted preacher played his congregation like a virtuoso played a violin. He began slowly, using conventional prose and increased the pace, chanting his words to a regular beat. When he reached a crescendo his words became lyrical and the congregation responded by singing, clapping, and shouting. At the end the preacher slowed down and reverted to conventional speech. Most of the emotionally stricken mourners were women, who groaned, wept openly, and sometimes fainted.[57] Women let out their tears at funerals and then went on with their lives, especially after the second burial service, which functioned as an official end to mourning. The community did not scorn a widow who remarried soon after a husband's death. Southern whites could not understand what they perceived as "quick recovery from grief" among blacks, but they also did not much respect black emotionalism.[58]

The middle-class interest in the lavish funeral grew out of Victorian fondness for sentiment and display of status. Because most African Americans lived in poverty throughout the nineteenth century and well into the twentieth century, display of status was not the main factor in their funeral customs. In addition, blacks were not trying to compete with whites in the kinds of funerals they held, nor were they trying to outdo each other.[59]

Having a proper, even fancy, burial was common among many poor and working-class peoples in the United States and Western Europe and was by no means unique to American blacks. Many families

of modest means wanted to avoid the ignominy and feelings of worth-
lessness the pauper burial symbolized.[60] At a pauper burial no family
sentiment was displayed; the absence of ceremony and pomp symbolized earthly failure and shame for one's survivors. The pauper burial
consisted of wrapping the corpse in a sheet or placing it in the cheap-
est kind of coffin. Pallbearers carried the corpse to the grave, rather
than transporting it in a hearse or wagon. The grave was usually dug
in a field on the edge of town, called a potter's field (which simply
meant a burial place for the poor), or in a separate section of a burial
ground or of a religious or municipal cemetery. Interred in these fields
were criminals, strangers, stillborn babies, infants, and African Americans of all ages. The pauper could be buried in an individual or mass
grave, but the grave was always unmarked.[61] An absence of funds did
not demonstrate the absence of grief. Poems about death in working-
class newspapers, however, were written in the same sentimental language as those of Harriet Beecher Stowe or Elizabeth Phelps. With
limited means, these families chose not to put sentiment ahead of the
practical need for living, so they buried infants or stillborn children in
the paupers' section of the cemetery.[62] If a working-class family did
not have enough money to pay for a funeral, people passed the hat;
lodge and church members were asked to contribute.

When they chose to use their savings for a proper burial, the poor
were motivated primarily by the desire to avoid the indignity of a pauper burial. Sojourner Truth, for example, who had no savings, mort-
gaged her house in Battle Creek, Michigan, in 1876 and went $300 to
$400 in debt to pay for her grandson's funeral. While burial associa-
tions developed almost as early as black churches were founded, they
grew most rapidly between the 1880s and the 1930s. Members were
required to attend the funerals of all the association's members. Black
life insurance companies, which began by selling policies simply to
cover the cost of a funeral, evolved out of burial associations. In the
early twentieth century, it was common practice for blacks, usually
women, to set aside weekly sums as "coffin money" earmarked to pay
for a funeral.[63]

On average, blacks spent less than whites on funerals—and still
do.[64] But since the income of blacks was considerably lower than that
of whites, the expense constituted a larger share of black families'
income. The truly lavish black funeral was an urban phenomenon,
which began in the late nineteenth century. Black middle-class fami-

lies began to engage photographers to take postmortem photos of their dead. In New Orleans and other cities, ten- to twenty-five-piece funeral bands played dirges as they accompanied the procession to the grave, and returned from the cemetery dancing to the tune of "When the Saints Go Marching In."[65] Photographer James Van Der Zee created a visual record of lavish black funerals in Harlem in the 1920s.[66] Most of his photos show the elegant metallic casket with its silken quilted padding, the elaborate wreaths with roses and satin ribbons that indicated the donor's name, the dead embalmed and dressed in their Sunday best, and the assembled kin swathed in black.[67]

The female attendant, first referred to as the mortician's nurse and later called the "first lady," was a unique employee at black funeral homes, beginning around 1900. Considered the "backbone of the black funeral service," she provided consolation for women during the service and visited the family in the first week of mourning. Fanning the distraught woman mourner, giving her sips of juice, the first lady reassured the grief-stricken that "God knows best." Among whites, the undertaker replaced the female layer-out of the dead in the nineteenth century; among blacks, women's nursing roles were folded into the funeral home business. The mortician's nurse, who might actually have been his wife, could also be a religious woman with some nursing skills. She might also serve as a soloist at the funeral, read the obituary, and even say a few words at the gravesite service.[68]

Black deathways have become more like those of whites in the United States since the 1960s, as more blacks have entered the middle class. At contemporary black funerals attended by middle-class and professional blacks today few mourners wail, faint, or need to be helped to their seats. The urban black middle class was also more likely to adopt the white notion that the entire extended family was no longer expected to gather for a funeral. The majority of black funerals in modern-day Detroit occur in funeral homes rather than churches. The practice of decorating graves with seashells or bits of crockery has disappeared in the North and is dying out even on the South Carolina Sea Islands. Sea Island families in the 1980s were buying large stone markers and burial vaults. The homogenizing influence of American popular culture has also affected the black funeral. Instead of requesting "Lay This Body Down" and "Hark from the Tomb a Doleful Sound," families in the 1980s were asking that the choir sing the Frank Sinatra hit "I Did it My Way." The all-night wake has been replaced by an evening visitation, and the day-long funeral in the rural South has disappeared.[69] No one mentions fears of a returning spirit.

Even so, there is abundant evidence that black deathways remain unique, in part because blacks have more occasions to grieve, since their overall death rate is higher than whites. Infant mortality among blacks still remains higher, and gang stabbings or shootings cease to shock. Some poor mothers buy burial insurance for children because they fear their child might die from gunfire.[70] They dread the indignity of the kind of funeral public aid can furnish, one that pays for a wooden, but not a metal, casket. The urban poor have even used consumer culture to create *memento mori*. In poor black neighborhoods in New Orleans in the 1990s, family and friends were purchasing T-shirts bearing the photograph of the deceased, along with a prayer or poem.[71]

Additional evidence of unique deathways exists among black Americans in general, not just among those in ghettos plagued by drugs and drive-by shootings. In contemporary America blacks have an extremely low rate of cremation because most consider it cheap, "second-rate," un-Christian, and sinful.[72] Black funeral homes in the 1970s still hired female attendants to attend to women mourners.[73] Black funeral services are longer than white ones and are filled with the readings of telegrams from people who could not attend the event, recitation from Scripture, solo singing, choral music, the eulogy, the sermon, and the procession past the open casket. Usually all of the mourners at the funeral also take part in the procession to the grave.

The lavish black funeral highlights the fault lines in attitudes toward the modern funeral. On the one side are those who claim that, unlike whites, black people "respect their dead," know how to grieve, and acknowledge the end of life with ceremony. Black people, it is said, affirm the importance of community and the obligations of kinship. On the other side are those who believe that lavish spending on funerals results from the denial of opportunity in life. They argue that black people orchestrate elaborate funerals to compensate for the wounds inflicted by racism and poverty, and that black funeral home directors, in concert with black ministers, encourage these displays, since they depend on the segregation of black society for their livelihood. In short, as with many other rituals, black business enterprises encourage the elaboration of black rituals. But it was also true that their experience of racial discrimination and poverty has made many blacks receptive to the businesspeople's entreaties. In short, the persistence of African beliefs and American blacks' experience of slavery, racism, and discrimination have combined to reinforce the African American view that the "funeral is the true climax of life."[74]

Critics in the 1980s and 1990s took a dislike to the postsentimental funeral, mainly because they did not approve of the values that seemed to lie beneath it. They saw the loss of the funeral attended by an entire community as a metaphor for the disappearance of the wholesome values of a small-scale society with its reciprocal obligations and community ties. They argued that Americans were worshipping youth instead of reverencing age, that family privacy was replacing community, and that people were putting individualism ahead of duty and obligation. Families have lost their moral compass, the critics complained. Experts, institutions, and paid professionals have taken over many of the functions of the family; physicians have replaced ministers as voices of moral authority. There was some truth in these charges. But individualism, materialism, and worship of youth extend far back in American history.[75]

The moralists fail to mention the gains from increased life expectancy and the advances brought by modern medicine. The elderly often live near their relatives in their own quarters, actively choosing to combine proximity and independence. Few children die an early death, and death in childbirth is rare. Many people prefer the brief funeral because it is less of an ordeal. By eliminating the Victorian etiquette of mourning, women shed the burden of lengthy grieving and the related restrictions on their social life.

The battle between those who want a show and those who want to be buried "without any manner of pomp" has a long history. From World War I to the 1970s, Protestant ministers and left-of-center critics such as Jessica Mitford favored a simplified ritual and a cheaper one. In the 1980s and 1990s right-of-center Catholic writers, specifically historian Philippe Ariès, Michigan undertaker Thomas Lynch, and social analyst Richard Gill, favored a longer, more dramatic ritual, something akin to the Victorian funeral—and were presumably willing to pay for it.[76] They decried the postsentimental funeral and its brevity—what some critics dubbed the McFuneral. The living, they claimed, needed a last gaze before the corpse was interred.

The loss of a structured period for mourning deprived people of the time and social support they needed to grieve, they argued. Of course, no one favored young girls staging mock funerals for their dolls or widows and widowers pinning brooches to their suits containing the hair of a dead spouse or wearing mourning clothes for a lifetime. In other words, the critics were calling for a selective reinvention of Victorian culture, not an entire restaging of the nineteenth-century Western process of death and dying.

Florists and owners of funeral homes, fearing competition from chains and lower-cost cremations, joined the critics of cremation and the no-frills funeral. Adopting the language of therapy, funeral home directors argued that mourners needed funerals as a psychologically healthy structure in which to express grief.[77] The American way has been to embrace both points of view, so that people can "do their own thing"—after all, they have a "right" to choose their own ritual. Religion, race, class, region, and sexual orientation divided Americans in the choice they made. On the one side were highly educated, nonreligious professionals who favored cremation, or a private service and burial, followed by a memorial service or donation of the body to science. On the other were Catholics, most African Americans, and people of modest means who wanted a funeral, a visitation, and a gravesite service. The rapid growth in cremation indicated that the simple ceremony was winning out over the lavish.[78]

The great transformation over the last several centuries in the United States has been from opulent funerals and cheap weddings to modest funerals and lavish weddings. Families began to justify splurging on a wedding because it was a once-in-a-lifetime occasion. A funeral fits that description even better, yet families wanted to keep spending on funerals to a respectable minimum. Consumer advocates and social critics complained much more about the lavish funeral than the lavish wedding.[79] People often justify spending as a means of achieving personal happiness. If this is so, it makes sense to spend most on the ritual that promises to bring the most happiness. On the basis of that principle, the funeral fell short.

CHAPTER TEN

The Bride Once Wore Black

Your happiness is our business.

—MOTTO OF A LAS VEGAS WEDDING CHAPEL

Trailed by twelve trainbearers, Queen Victoria walked down the aisle to marry a man she barely knew but would come to love. Her wedding to her German cousin Albert in 1840 set a new standard for ceremony in the United States as well as in Britain. Usually royal brides dressed in rich brocades and stately robes of velvet and ermine. Victoria's simple but elegant pure white satin gown was trimmed with orange blossoms and had capped laced sleeves. Around her neck she wore the royal diamond necklace, and on her bodice was pinned a sapphire broach Albert had given her as a wedding present. Her face was covered by a white lace veil, and she carried a sprig of myrtle.[1] Two hundred women worked feverishly from March to November to make the exquisite lace and flounce for Victoria's gown. Although a few American brides had been wearing white satin dresses since at least 1785, Victoria was easily the most influential bride in white. Thousands of newspapers and magazines described the event.

Soon American etiquette books trumpeted Victoria's wedding as "the proper style" for a wedding; others came to call it "the white wedding."[2] The "white rules" at such a wedding dictated that the bridal gown, the veil, the shoes, and the frosting on the cake had to be white. The white wedding also incorporated older traditions, such as the father's giving away the bride, the groom's exchanging a ring with the bride in the ceremony, and the couple's being showered with rice as they left the church. The white wedding of the nineteenth century added new elements, especially the groom's giving the bride a diamond engagement ring and the couple's taking a postwedding trip, called a honeymoon, to a romantic, secluded spot. Americans made no unique contribution to this ritual; they simply copied it from Victoria's wedding and those of other British royalty.

The white wedding and the Victorian Christmas were two of the most significant invented traditions in the first half of the nineteenth century, and the most lasting. The history of weddings follow that of funerals in this book because while both rituals have become postsentimental, they have done so in quite different ways—the funeral by becoming simpler, the wedding by becoming more lavish. In spending so much on weddings, Americans are indicating that the wedding is their most valued ritual.

Heralded as the proper way to marry, the white wedding has been enormously popular, filtering down from the well-to-do to the working poor, from Yankees to immigrants and people of color, and from British and Americans to couples in virtually every part of the globe. Although the Protestant upper class invented the white wedding, the ritual captivated common people from many other cultures who had quite different marriage customs. In most cases, couples gradually discarded many of the most colorful customs of their own group, replacing them with those of the white wedding. Since the 1950s the few ethnic dishes and dances at a wedding served mainly as token assertions of group identity among people who have embraced a cultural form not initially theirs.

The white wedding affirmed several Victorian beliefs about marriage and the family. Having the ceremony in a church symbolized the sacredness of marriage and religious recognition of the union. In attending the wedding and reception and giving gifts, the community stated its belief in the appropriateness of the marriage and in the ideal of the happy home.[3] The white wedding especially celebrated romantic love, that fairy tale of the prince charming and his young virgin beauty, who chose each other freely because of mutual attraction and then lived happily ever after. The white wedding transformed the bride into a fairy princess and made the transition to a married state glamorous, indeed the most significant event in a woman's life.

Although the white wedding expressed a large number of ideas of recent and ancient vintage, as a ritual it had always been designed to resolve certain perennial issues in the union of two people. The wedding marked the passage from the single to the married state, and it incorporated a wife into her husband's family and a husband into his wife's. A wedding involved the couple, their families, and a larger social group.[4] The event was usually followed by feasting.

Wedding ritual has changed much more than it has remained the same. Like Christmas, the modern version has become a commercial and gift-giving extravaganza, using goods and services for purposes of display, prestige, competition, self-transformation, and the attainment of happiness. As far back as the Puritans, critics have disliked the lack of attention to spiritual values in many weddings.[5] Others complained about wasteful spending. A writer in a woman's magazine in 1868 attacked the "baneful" custom of giving expensive wedding gifts, singling out for scorn those families who rented silver to display along with the actual wedding presents the couple had received.[6]

Ceremonies from colonial settlement days to the mid-nineteenth century seemed to fall into one of two distinct types, the serious and the boisterous. The serious wedding was often a civil marriage, such as among the Puritans and Quakers, who wanted to simplify and eliminate many annual rituals and rites of passage. They criticized many customs then common in England, from the exchange of rings to dancing at the reception. They often served bridal cake and sack posset (mulled wine with bread floating in it) at a reception, while trying to avoid the sins of gluttony and drunkenness and the singing of "unchaste" ditties. By contrast, the boisterous wedding was the "traditional" form, the one Protestant reformers sought to avoid. It began with a religious service in a church. The reception that followed was noisy, drunken, ribald, and long. Guests remained, sometimes for several days, for a feast of roasted meat, drink, and bridal cake and danced to the music of a fiddler.

Elements of the White Wedding

The civil marriage, the only kind of marriage available in colonial New England, had lost favor by the early nineteenth century. Fashionable couples wanted to be married in a church. By 1860 in Philadelphia, for example, nine out of ten brides were married in a religious wedding.[7] For Catholics, matrimony was a sacrament, celebrated by a priest in front of two witnesses.[8] Nonetheless, many Catholics marrying within their faith had two ceremonies: a civil wedding, presided over by a justice of the peace, followed by a wedding and a mass in a Catholic church, officiated by a priest. More modest Jewish weddings and receptions usually took place in a catering or fraternal hall, while tonier ones were held at hotels or the ballrooms of large restaurants. Having the wedding ceremony in a synagogue and the reception at a hotel or restaurant developed only in the twentieth century because up to then it had been Jewish practice not to profane the sacredness of the synagogue with a wedding. Jews were not permitted to marry in the sanctuary because to do so was considered a desecration of the Torah.

The emergence of the church wedding as the Christian urban elite's proper wedding created a hierarchy of ceremonies. At the top was the white wedding, a religious and legal ceremony, which was supposed to involve couples marrying for the first time. It was assumed that the bride was a virgin, although the husband was not required to be sexually uninitiated. Catholic and Episcopalian services often explicitly stated that the purpose of marriage was procreation, and the couple would agree to raise the offspring of the marriage in the religious faith.

The second-tier wedding was a ceremony at which a justice of the peace officiated. It was usually held in the bride's home or a public space. Widowed, divorced, pregnant, interfaith, and interracial couples were generally married in such ceremonies, as were most couples in frontier or rural areas. Since most Americans lived on farms in the nineteenth century, the second-tier wedding was probably the most common type in that era.

The weddings of slaves belong in a third tier, not because of their form, but because such weddings had no legal standing. As for the form, there was great variation, from white weddings hosted by a kindly master, to simpler affairs presided over by a justice of the peace, to marriages in the slave quarters. Even the ceremony in the quarters varied from those where a slave preacher or elderly woman officiated, to self-marriage, where a couple jumped over a broomstick and considered themselves married.[9] The significant common feature in these otherwise diverse ceremonies was that master and slave alike recognized that, no matter how lavish, the ritual offered no guarantee of permanence and none of the rights to legitimacy of offspring and guardianship of children that legal marriage provided.

Many cohabiting couples had no formal ceremony at all, and thus fall at the bottom of the hierarchy of weddings. Some did so out of choice, and others because they were not legally allowed to marry or could not afford it. A large number of couples, homosexual and heterosexual, lived in this manner—from college-educated women in the Northeast, who resided with another woman in a "Boston marriage" to fur trappers who took Indian wives "according to the custom of the country" to Hispanic couples in the Southwest, who often could not afford to pay for a priest to marry them or had no access to one. In all these cases, the couples regarded themselves as married. While judges recognized the legality of common-law marriages among heterosexuals (the question was never raised about marriage among homosexuals), reformers and ministers by the late nineteenth century tried to stamp out these unions and encourage legal marriage.[10]

The first-tier ceremony for Christians, as was mentioned, occurred in a church. Well-to-do Victorian women preferred to marry there for several reasons. Because a woman sensed she was risking much, she wanted the reassuring presence of her minister at her family's church. Many churches had an organ, a long aisle for a dramatic processional to the altar, a large number of pews (guests no longer had to stand) and a formal, or perhaps quaint, setting. Churches were sacred spaces, but more practically, they were also larger than homes and could accommodate more guests.[11]

Victorian families of wealth often added significant elements to the ceremony, which made it more emotional, romantic, and focused on the bride.[12] The engagement, for example, emerged as a distinct preliminary stage leading to marriage, replacing the older process of posting or publishing the banns. (Banns were public notices of impending marriage to prevent bigamy and other illegal marriages; the inquiry into whether such impediments existed was published, posted, or announced in church.) Wealthy families also sent printed invitations to the wedding or published an announcement in the newspaper.[13] (The practice was limited to whites. Because of racial prejudice, newspapers tended not to publish announcements of black engagements or marriage.) New elements were added to the wedding reception as well. For the first time the bride, wearing a "going away" costume, climbed a staircase and tossed her bouquet to the unmarried female guests. The girl who caught the bouquet was said to be next in line to marry.[14] The custom of dressing bridesmaids in white gowns identical to the bride's was still being recommended as late as 1911. Subsequent advice to dress only the bride in white and her attendants in gowns of other colors gave the bride "an opportunity of shining singly."[15]

British royals created another innovation, the full choral processional from the church entrance to the altar. When Princess Victoria, the daughter of Queen Victoria and Prince Albert, married in 1858, music was played as she walked up the aisle—a change from the usual practice of having music only at the reception. A patron of opera who loved Mendelssohn and Wagner, the princess chose the music for her ceremony.[16] As she walked to the altar, the organist played the Bridal Chorus from Wagner's opera *Lohengrin* (later known as "Here Comes the Bride"). After the ceremony as she and her husband walked hand in hand down the aisle, the organist played Mendelssohn's "Wedding March."[17] Brides by the 1880s were often selecting the song "Oh, Promise Me" for the processional because it evoked the vision of marriage as a paradise.[18]

Weddings had always involved economic exchanges between propertied families. In many cultures the bride's family provided her husband with land, livestock, money, bedding, and furniture at the time of the marriage. In many parts of Europe, a large proportion of people never married, or married relatively late because they had not the means to acquire such property. In sixteenth-century England many parents presented their daughter's dowry (the gifts from her family to the husband) at the ceremony. Wealthy neighbors gave the couple money or silverware, and guests brought food and ale for the feast.[19] Until around the middle of the nineteenth century in England and America, girls too poor to afford a dowry often had a "bidden" wedding, at which friends and neighbors contributed to a small fund for the couple. Also around this time, relatives began to buy the couple wedding presents rather than simply showering them with coins. Later, guests as well as relatives were expected to buy the couple a gift.

By the 1870s arranging gifts of crystal, china, and silver on a table covered with a white damask tablecloth in a separate room, each with the donor's name attached, was a common feature of middle- and upper-class weddings and a clear indication of the view that the wedding was supposed to be a conspicuous display of wealth.[20] For that reason, the goods set out for view had to be luxury items, not practical ones. Originally, the idea for giving gifts to the couple was the same as at the bidden wedding—to provide the couple with the necessities for setting up independent housekeeping.[21] But the wealthy had always wanted to provide the couple with items to prove the status of the donors. Gifts of little practical value also showed that the bride did not require the contribution of the community in order to marry.

Nonetheless, brides received practical gifts for the kitchen and the bedroom at a separate ritual, the bridal shower, which emerged in the 1890s.[22] It became fashionable for the bride's female friends to give parties in her honor to which friends and a few relatives brought gifts. At the shower, the bride received money and gifts of basic household goods from neighbors. The term "shower" seems to have originally referred to a Japanese parasol, which, when opened, showered the bride with gifts. Guests were supposed to bring the bride something she could use in her married life, usually gifts for the bedroom or the kitchen. The shower was a female ritual, usually held at the home of a female friend or relative, which underscored the responsibility of the woman's community in helping the bride acquire the necessary goods for homemaking. But friends sometimes hosted showers for men, at which the groom received gifts of dustpans, aprons, brushes, and household tools.[23] The urban upper middle class, with their greater access to stores and higher incomes, first embraced the ritual of the bridal shower. It did not appear in rural areas until the 1930s.[24]

The growth in the prosperity and social aspirations of the urban middle class is one of several explanations for the development of the white wedding in the nineteenth century. A girl from a middle-class family could afford to hire a seamstress to make her own dress and one for her mother. Did these more lavish weddings become popular because the bride's father wanted to make a show of his daughter's wedding to prove his success? Or was it the mother's wish, since she now regarded her own wedding as too simple and homespun? Thorstein Veblen in *Theory of the Leisure Class* argued that the main purpose of excessive spending was to display wealth in an economic and social system based on status competition. A family served imported champagne to show that they had more than enough money to splurge—to attract attention to themselves, as well as to the bride, who became the main object for the display of status.[25]

The white wedding also gave added emphasis to values highly cherished in the nineteenth century: romantic love; the sanctity of marriage; the home and woman's place within it; female innocence and sexual purity; privacy (in the honeymoon); and love of ostentation. The irony, however, was that at the same time the white wedding took many patriarchal customs that treated the woman as her father and husband's property and as a sexual object necessary only for producing the man's legitimate heirs (customs such as veiling the bride, surrounding the bride with girlfriends to thwart her capture, having the father deliver the bride to her husband, requiring a vow of obedience from the bride, putting a ring on the bride's finger, displaying many symbols of fertility). In the white wedding these customs were incorporated into a ceremony that made the bride the star performer.

As Ellen Rothman argues in her study of American courtship, the white wedding expressed not only the values of the Victorian age but also its anxieties—namely, the woman's anxieties about her fate in marriage. If romantic love gave a woman free rein to choose the man of her heart, it also raised the stakes if she chose wrongly. If the home was a sacred place and a refuge from a corrupt world, it could also be a gilded cage, imprisoning the unhappy wife and sealing her off from protectors and companions she might need. The more that the conjugal relationship was expected to be an intimate romantic pairing rather than a straightforward economic partnership, the greater the anxiety if all should not work out as hoped. If emotion was now so central to the nature of companionate marriage, how better to represent it than with a ritual designed to heighten such feelings?

Women's anxieties were greater than men's, Rothman further notes, because as economic dependents they risked more, placing their future in the hands of the chosen partner. Whether she could afford a servant or had to do without, whether she owned a Brussels carpet or had only the bare floor to sweep, whether she married a companion or dined with a stranger at the dinner table all depended on making the right decision. If a suitor was gentle and respectable now, might he not, like so many others, acquire "vicious" habits later? With so much at stake, women sought from ritual some reassurance—"some support and direction," in Rothman's words, a "predictable beginning for a life that appeared unknowable and risky."[26] Far from providing reassurance, the free choice of a partner relatively unfettered by parental interference heightened the risk. The ritual of the white wedding helped to affirm the rightness of the choice of partner, as parents and guests symbolically nodded approval. The formality, religiosity, and seriousness of the ceremony was designed to shore up marriage, and insure its permanence.

Rothman further points out that sex taboos also increased women's anxieties at the time of the wedding, especially for the bride who was a virgin.[27] The formality of the wedding was both a reward for having remained a virgin and an anodyne for the sexually inexperienced girl who was worried about the tribulations of the wedding night. Courting couples enjoyed kissing, hugging, even a certain amount of petting, but there was no expectation that such familiarities would eventually lead to intercourse.[28] The whiteness of the veil and dress, the satin shoes, the white stockings and kid gloves, even the frosting on the cake, not to mention the modesty of the high-necked gown that covered the body down to the ankles, were all symbols of the bride's sexual purity.[29]

A young American woman looked forward to her wedding as the greatest moment in her life and the sign that she had become an adult woman. The formality and the length of the ritual were designed to make the wedding endure permanently in her memory. The groom's role was mainly that of an escort for the bride. Men did not seem to care much about the kind of ceremony or their attire at it. The man's outfit was not a symbol of his sexual status the way a woman's was; his virginity was not a matter of note.

In the middle and upper classes in the second half of the nineteenth century the bride and her mother made most of the decisions about the event, leafing through etiquette books for advice about seating arrangements or the order of the processional. Mother and daughter even decided what the groom should wear. While the mother had left the couple alone while they courted in the parlor, she now emerged discreetly out of the shadows to enforce a variety of rules. Ellen Rothman observes that "few young people chose to fight this alliance between social custom and maternal authority."[30] Some explained the mother's domination of the event as her last opportunity to exert control over her daughter. A mother could also live vicariously through the extravagance of her daughter's wedding.[31]

Among all the patriarchal customs in the white wedding, the one that drew the most criticism from advocates of woman's rights in the middle of the nineteenth century was the bride's promise to obey her husband. Far from being an age-old custom, Protestant reformers substituted the wife's promise to obey in place of the verbal pledge of the bride in the medieval Catholic pledge to be "bonair and buxom in bed and at board."[32] A minister asked the bride to promise her husband obedience, but the groom was not asked to do likewise. Like so many other customs of the Western wedding, the marriage vow reflected the view of the wife as her husband's property. Advocates of woman's rights, including Amelia Bloomer, Elizabeth Cady Stanton, Abby Kelley, and Angelina Grimké, each protested this ritual utterance at their own weddings. Henry Stanton and his bride Elizabeth Cady left out the word over the objections of the Presbyterian minister.[33] Other advocates of woman's rights spoke out against the ritual of the father's giving away the bride, and even against the bride's being given housekeeping items rather than a book "filled with elevating thoughts."[34]

Growth of the Lavish Wedding

All the fundamental elements of the white wedding had emerged by the 1870s and have persisted to this day. Yet while many of the details of the ceremony remained the same, in the twentieth century the white wedding has become more expensive as well as more popular. Wedding consultants, guidebooks, and bridal magazines—the first of these, *Modern Bride,* founded in 1931—set a national standard for the white wedding, defining what was "tradition" and following precepts of consumer culture, making purchasing and decorating changes appear simultaneously novel and traditional. The development of the bridal industry led to an increase in the use of manufactured products, rather than handmade goods, in the wedding ceremony. Some garment manufacturers began to specialize in making wedding gowns in the 1930s; the store-bought gown was by then of sufficiently high quality so that it was no longer regarded as inferior.

The work of preparing for the wedding moved out of the home, as new service occupations replaced what had been women's work. Caterers not only cooked the meal but began making many of the arrangements for the wedding—before bridal secretaries took over. In 1947 there were about five hundred "bridal secretaries" in the United States, usually found in the bridal shop of a department store. (The secretary later was called a director, planner, consultant, or counselor, and was not necessarily affiliated with a store.) The bridal secretary served as a free adviser about etiquette, home furnishings, even destinations for the honeymoon; and helped arrange the flowers, caterer, and photographer for the wedding. Nevertheless, this degree of professionalization did not reduce women's burden, but rather changed the nature of their tasks. As one exhausted bride from the 1960s recalled her preparations, "I flitted from one catering encounter to another."[35]

Another trend was the growth of the sumptuous wedding, which spread from the urban upper middle class, where it was concentrated in the nineteenth century, to couples of more modest means in the twentieth century, especially since the 1960s. Sociologist Martin Whyte, who surveyed Detroit couples, found that those marrying between 1965 and 1984 were far more likely than those marrying between 1925 and 1964 to have had a bachelor party for the groom, a bridal shower, a wedding in a church, a reception, and a honeymoon. He also noted that the guest list grew longer between 1925 and 1984. Detroit couples who had been married between 1925 and 1944 usually had about 50 people at the reception; for the generation marrying between 1945 and 1964 the average number was 100, and at the typical Detroit reception between 1965 and 1984, there were 150 guests.[36]

The shift in the day of the week on which the wedding occurred was another indication of a grander style of marrying. The typical wedding in Minnesota in the 1920s was held during the week because churches did not encourage weekend weddings. Moreover, the couple usually had to return to work the next day or the day after that. Many a groom and bride stayed in a city hotel for the honeymoon night before returning to work the next day. By the 1970s the ceremony usually took place on a Saturday or Sunday. The weekend wedding made it easier for guests from out of town to attend. The couple then immediately departed for their honeymoon at an out-of-town location, and the average honeymoon lasted seven to nine days.

The increasing number of attendants, ring bearers, and flower girls served as further evidence that wedding ceremonies were growing more formal and elaborate. Newspaper wedding notices in small towns in Minnesota mentioned an average of three attendants in 1925 and nine from 1973 to 1975. The reception became larger and more elegant and was no longer held in the parlor of the home of the bride's parents. Couples from Minnesota small towns even began to perceive the church parlor as too small and sparse for their needs. They preferred the country club, a reception hall, or a restaurant where a catered meal was served and guests had room to dance.[37] In the interwar years couples who married at city hall or in a judge's chambers rarely offered their guests a postwedding feast. By the 1960s even couples who had such simple ceremonies as this were hosting receptions afterward at a restaurant or a hall. The social events before the wedding were also more extensive. Most brides before their ceremony had a bridal shower and a rehearsal dinner, and more grooms than ever before were having bachelor parties. Couples in the 1980s not only attended all these events, but also concluded that to marry in style one needed a live band at the reception and a stretch limousine to transport the bride to the ceremony.[38]

Every guest, even the polite ones, secretly wanted to know how much these galas cost. Since the 1930s, when the first study of wedding expenses was conducted, the average cost of weddings (including engagement expenses and honeymoons) rose from $392 in the period 1933–1937 to $22,750 in the period 1990–1995. The more pertinent question, however, is not the overall cost, but the total expense in relation to the average family's ability to pay. Despite rising family incomes, the formal wedding has taken an increasingly large bite out of family finances. In the 1930s, a wedding cost about a third of average family income; by 1967, about half; and by the 1990s, a little less than two thirds.[39]

It is sometimes claimed that couples since the 1960s preferred these elaborate events because they were more conservative and materialist than their parents and grandparents. In the Age of Aquarius, Yippies, hippies, and even those who did not own a tie-dyed shirt rejected conformity. The stereotype of a 1960s wedding was a wedding like that of Anita Kushner and Abbie Hoffman in 1967. After pledging their love, barefoot in New York Central Park, they joined their guests at a picnic, where they shared joints of marijuana. Such weddings served as symbols of the anti-establishment attitudes of that decade and youth's rejection of formal dress and rules of etiquette. American movies of the 1960s, such as *The Graduate* (1967) loved the rebels, not the conformists. Yet interviews with Detroit area couples show that even in the 1960s most couples married in a religious service, which was followed by a reception with a sit-down dinner, a live band, and a multitiered wedding cake. Those married between 1964 to 1969, the most turbulent years of a tumultuous decade, were just as likely to have a wedding with these elements as those married earlier in the decade.[40] The one major regional exception seems to have been in the South, where there was a preference for buffets rather than sit-down dinners.

Without a doubt, one reason for the growth of the opulent wedding was the bridal industry, which succeeded in convincing the public to spend more. Ads in *Modern Bride* or *Bride's Magazine* for tropical resorts, Waterford crystal, and satin bridal gowns with seed pearls conveyed the message that the highest-quality and most expensive choices were best for a "once in a lifetime" occasion.[41] The N. A. Ayers advertising firm developed the market for a diamond engagement ring in the 1940s with its slogan "A diamond is forever." Other advertisers followed their lead. The bigger the stone in the engagement ring, the deeper, more romantic, and more enduring the love, advertisers implied. Splurging proved one's seriousness about the wedding, and taking a wedding seriously showed commitment to the marriage. (The implicit threat was that not doing so might portend divorce.)[42] Vendors of silverware, diamond rings, and wedding albums claimed that their products were unique, prestigious, and proof of enduring love, and that they fanned the embers of romance. Advertisers suggested that in marrying lavishly a couple was beginning a married life that would be lived in similar "good taste" and style. By the 1960s the number of ads skyrocketed—bridal magazines became as thick as phone books.[43] At the same time, the wedding and honeymoon market helped to create new businesses, such as resorts that catered to honeymooners or travel agencies selling air and resort travel packages.[44]

Another reason for the growth of the lavish wedding since the 1960s is that Americans had more money to spend. The age at first marriage was rising during this period, and both parties were usually employed and could help handle the cost of the wedding. Here was an exception to the rule that women's employment led to the streamlining of ritual. Women who were employed had more elaborate weddings. Moreover, many fathers of brides—who customarily were supposed to foot the bill for most of the expenses of the white wedding—as well as the couple being married were not taking care of wedding expenses out of current income but were obtaining loans or second mortgages, or running up charges on credit cards.[45] To be sure, immigrant parents in the early twentieth century borrowed from loan sharks or pawned their valuables to pay for a lavish wedding. It was not the willingness to go into debt that was new, but the size of the loans.

The main culprits for the increases seem to have been the bride's parents, who wanted to expand the guest list and make the reception larger and more extravagant, although surely many brides acceded to or encouraged parental wishes. Some parents sought to emulate the wealthy or show off their success and "good taste." Keeping up with or even exceeding the standard of the weddings of others they knew was certainly a motive. Also, unconsciously parents may have been trying to incur feelings of obligation in the wedding couple. Perhaps, as mentioned earlier, a mother may simply have wanted to compensate for her having had to marry simply, in her parents' front parlor, dressed in a blue suit.[46]

A third reason for the growth of the lavish ceremony was the wedding of postsentimental attitudes with rising incomes. Popular belief in the value of personal self-fulfillment (itself partly the creation of a consumer culture) and the pursuit of happiness encouraged couples and their parents to make the ceremony special, memorable, and lavish. When sociologist Francesca Cancian analyzed the content of women's magazines from 1900 to 1979, she found that in the 1920s, and again in the late 1960s and early 1970s, an increasing number of articles evaluated marriage according to the emotional and sexual satisfaction the union gave the woman. During periods when feminism was in the air, she speculates, women were emboldened to demand more from their marriage than simply an economic partnership. The growth of prosperity, especially in the postwar years, made it possible for women to focus on fulfilling their fantasies for a storybook wedding. Sentimental novels, and later films, encouraged young women to believe in the dream of romantic love and a happy marriage. By purchasing a special gown or imported champagne, it was thought, the young bride—and her family—would help make dreams come true. Even in the working class in the early twentieth century, many girls wanted this kind of wedding but had to settle for a more modest affair. At the same time, popular expectations for a wedding were indeed rising. "Doing it perfectly" cost a good deal more than merely "doing it right."

Magazine articles in women's magazines suggest that in the 1950s the bride had come to acquire more power over spending, even in choosing the destination for the honeymoon. Up through the 1930s, grooms in these articles were portrayed as the ones who decided on the destination for the honeymoon. The men often opted for a hunting, fishing, or camping trip or a vacation that combined a stay at a hotel with the pursuit of a few business contacts. By the 1950s women's magazines increasingly described the woman choosing the locale of the honeymoon, although usually after she consulted with her future spouse. Not surprisingly, a camping vacation in the wilderness became less popular, since most brides preferred comfort, a romantic setting, and a respite from cooking and cleaning.[47]

Consequences of the Lavish Wedding

In addition to the bills, the extravagant wedding had other consequences. A sexually experienced girl's dressing up as a virgin and fairy princess has often been regarded as the last gasp of tradition before the couple embarks on their married life as equals.[48] Since the 1970s male and female statements about their belief in equality in marriage are more than mere lip service. Yet the white wedding also encouraged traditional gender roles in seemingly egalitarian couples. The woman, as has been noted, usually took on most of the responsibility for arranging the wedding and the honeymoon trip, thus affirming the view that women were the main consumers in the family; and after the wedding, the new wife traditionally carried most of the responsibility for home decorating, cleaning, cooking, child care, kin contact, shopping, and organizing family occasions and vacations.[49] In postsentimental times, however, women cut back on these responsibilities, and men began to do more. Even so, women more often than men would shop for birthday cards for children, buy the turkey and roast it, and purchase most of the couple's joint Christmas presents.

The wedding "with all the trimmings" also stirred up an enormous range of family tensions and conflicts. Ruffled feelings, personal slights, disputes over money, disagreements over the ceremony or the guest list, family problems caused by interfaith and interracial marriages—any one or more of these sometimes erupted into open quarrels the day of the wedding or resulted in bitter feelings that endured long after. The honeymoon now functioned as a time to recuperate from months of exhausting planning and acrimonious premarital fights.[50] One psychiatrist offered the less than scientific observation that four out of five prospective brides became physically ill around the time of the ceremony.[51]

It is more difficult to locate the exact origin of "wedding blues" than of complaints about depression during the Christmas season. Certainly the film *Father of the Bride* (1950) made the trials explicit.

The narrator was a weary middle-class father, perplexed by the spiraling costs of the his daughter's wedding (albeit one quite modest by modern standards, lacking a sit-down dinner or even the now essential element of a white frosted wedding cake). As time has passed the list of complaints has grown longer, involving not only the father of the bride, the groom, and the bride, but also virtually every member of the wedding party. Modern brides disliked being ignored or dictated to at bridal salons. Pushed around by caterers, shop owners, religious authorities, and their relatives, many couples felt their wedding plans spin out of control.[52]

To what extent did modern feminism change the wedding ritual? The short answer is "somewhat," but probably no more than antebellum feminism. A few women involved in the women's liberation movement in the 1970s complained about "going the rounds of showers, shopping, money worries, invitation lists." They also disliked having to invite family they hardly knew and objected to both the idea of having to promise to obey their husband and a minister's pronouncing them "man and wife."[53] A more subtle indicator of the extent of the support for more egalitarian weddings was the number of women who did not take their husband's name at marriage: in 1990, 5 percent of women hyphenated their last name with their husband's; 2 percent kept their maiden name; and 3 percent used some alternative (for example, using their maiden name as a middle name, as in Hillary Rodham Clinton). The percentages were higher for women with a postgraduate degree.[54]

Radical feminists of the 1960s attacked the bridal fair—an exhibit of consumer goods (silverware, china, wedding gowns), with booths for service providers such as bridal consultants and photographers—as an example of how consumer culture imposed false ideals and standards of beauty on women. The New York radical feminist group WITCH (Women's International Terrorist Conspiracy from Hell), along with women from the Brooklyn branch of Students for a Democratic Society (SDS) leafleted and picketed a Manhattan bridal fair in 1969. They expressed critiques similar to those of antebellum feminists, using the language of the antiwar movement ("Confront the Whoremakers") and the politics of socialist feminism (denouncing the "Dracula face of American capitalism"). Wearing black veils and carrying signs that read "Always a Bride, Never a Person," WITCH protesters stated their view that the bourgeois family "oppresses everyone, and particularly women." Inside the fair, the women from WITCH and SDS surreptitiously entered the trousseau fashion show, where they released 150 live white mice.[55]

Modern feminism attacked women's obsession with beauty and narcissism, attempted to minimize distinctions between men and women, and ridiculed the idea of romantic love. The white wedding, by contrast, transported a girl from her everyday reality to a beautiful, glamorous, and special fantasy and made her the center of attention. Having played with bridal dolls and dressed up in long white gowns in girlhood, and having read romance magazines and watched hundreds of films with the theme of boy meeting girl, a woman dreamed of her one special day. If the choice came down to puritanism or indulgence, reality or romance, androgyny or being a beauty queen, most women had an easy time deciding.[56]

The growth of gay commitment ceremonies in the 1980s combined the sentimentalism and lavish spending of the white wedding with postsentimentalism in an explicit critique of the legal and cultural privileges of the heterosexual wedding. There had always been tax and legal advantages to being married, but these had never surfaced as a rationale for legal marriage among homosexuals until the rise of the modern gay liberation movement. In addition, the lesbian baby boom of the 1980s may have made a marriage ceremony seem more appealing. But undoubtedly the largest single reason for greater interest in same-sex ceremonies was the change in gay attitudes toward monogamy. The appearance of AIDS in the 1980s made having fewer, rather than more, sexual partners respectable. Marriage and commitment among gay people was no longer seen as an undesirable mimicking of the institutions of the straight world.[57]

Advice books for gay commitment ceremonies critiqued traditional gender roles and responsibilities in preparations for the white wedding, and some of the ritual itself, suggesting that the gendered script of the white wedding did not apply to gay men and lesbians. Although parents of the couple might be present, the couple invariably paid for the ceremony themselves. There was little in the straight world to compare with the wounds inflicted by parents who found an excuse not to attend the couple's ceremony, or the gay person's pain of feeling that parents had been much more excited about, and approving of, the wedding of a heterosexual child than about the gay child's commitment ceremony.[58] The very existence of such a ceremony, long forbidden by church and state, with perhaps the addition of a lesbian or gay male minister or rabbi, had an air of protest to it. Still, planning books for gay ceremonies tended to recommend (while putting a more positive interpretation on) a variety of traditional practices, from orange blossom wreaths to a tiered wedding cake with marzipan frosting and a best man in a tuxedo.[59] These weddings also were exercises in consumption, including concerns over choosing the right champagne, the proper caterer, and a good disc jockey.

The Bride Once Wore Black, Green, or Red

In the cultures from which many U.S. immigrants came, community and kin were more important than the individual. Romantic love stood rather low on the list of reasons for marrying, since above all else marriage was an economic arrangement. The purpose of marriage was procreation, to produce children who would tend the fields, look after the shop, work around the house, and care for parents in old age. Many of the customs of these sorts of weddings expressed a view that the wife was the property of her husband.[60] Marriage in these cultures was as much a process as a specific event, from the betrothal to negotiations surrounding the marriage contract and its signing, to payment of the dowry, to a ceremony for the bride as she left her family, to the wedding ceremony and the feasts before and after it.[61] Nevertheless, the process usually was stretched out at most a couple of months, since the couple had to get on with the business of setting up housekeeping. In agricultural societies the best time to marry was before spring planting or after the harvest. Because of the slow pace of life and the lack of pressing tasks at those times of year, wedding festivities could last for days. Lengthy weddings also made sense when marriages were arranged, since it gave the couple more time to get acquainted.

However conservative immigrant mothers were, there was something of the rebel in many unmarried immigrant daughters, even in the early twentieth century. Some had refused to marry the man their father had selected even before they arrived in the United States. In European cities from Paris to Warsaw the ideal of romantic love was spreading. In the United States peer culture and popular media encouraged a belief in romantic love. Women workers in factories or in domestic service took pleasure simply from talking about fashion and their dream of a rich suitor who would take them away from menial labor, poverty, and parental control. As early as the 1880s working-class girls were purchasing dime novels, which conveyed and reinforced the belief in romantic love and finding a prince charming. Advice to the lovelorn columns in the immigrant press, often in the native language, accepted a woman's quest for an ideal partner. Movies, film posters, and magazines of the 1920s depicted passionate embraces and couples kissing. Advertising during this period also changed its format from an argument about the product's features to a narrative of a consumer who was rewarded with success, popularity, and romance as a result of buying the product. An American girl thus came to expect that she would not have to settle for a loveless arrangement; she could marry a man almost as dashing as Rudolph Valentino.[62] Those who learned these lessons best and rejected the idea of arranged marriage were urban, employed, English literate, and able to meet men outside of chaperoned situations.[63] To be sure, arranged marriage was common among the immigrant generation, from Greeks to Germans, from Russians to Japanese. What was relatively uncommon—at least until post-1965 migration from India or Pakistan—was for arranged marriage to persist among adult children born in the United States.

The list of all the ethnic wedding customs that have faded is a very long one. Because the dowry disappeared, special ceremonies for signing an agreement and actually handing over the goods or money of the dowry also vanished. Prewedding feasts, bridal leave-taking ceremonies, ritualized personal invitations to kin and neighbors, obligatory bows to parents before the wedding, capping and crowning ceremonies, and rituals putting the couple to bed after the ceremony and feast also fell out of favor, as did communal walks to the church, to the bride's home, or around the reception hall. Showing a bloody sheet or some other proof of the bride's deflowering on the wedding night was usually left behind in the old country.[64] German Lutherans dispensed with their tradition of all-male attendants by the 1890s.[65] Some customs were too patriarchal or too communal. Others were simply too much of a departure from the standard of the white wedding.[66] At Polish-American weddings, for example, brides no longer danced with other women and women ceased singing their bawdy songs.

Immigrants recently arrived in America cast off distinctive hair styles and dress because these customs made it difficult to earn a living in America. One candy manufacturer in New York City preferred to hire women who arrived at job interviews wearing a hat, which he took as a sign that the woman aspired to being an American lady. He often rejected Italian applicants who wore the characteristic shawl.[67] Similarly, employers of domestics also took a girl's dress as a sign of whether she knew how to stir a white sauce. To the immigrants, wearing a hat signaled both the desire to be an American lady and relief at having escaped Old World class distinctions, where in some countries only women of high rank could wear hats.[68] Ethnic wedding costumes quickly gave way to the white bridal dress.[69] Putting away the old bridal costume was an indication of women's assimilation to American consumer and romantic ideals. In Spain, Denmark, and Germany brides wore black, as did Galician Jewish brides; in Norway brides wore green.[70] Many East European brides and many native-born brides in rural America wore a shawl with their wedding costume. It symbolically protected the virginity of the bride during the nuptials until her wedding night.[71] It, too, was discarded by assimilating immigrants.

Abandoning the traditional wedding costume indicated that the bride was entering a new life on American terms, dressed like an American girl. Immigrant women in cities were window shoppers. Domestics also observed their stylish, wealthy American mistresses. As Barbara Schrier points out, "immigrants exchanged the garments of the Old World for the fashions of the New World with the passion of individuals intent on self-transformation."[72] The desire to rent, if not own, a white satin dress was the immigrant girl's vote in favor of American culture, consumerism, and American notions of beauty and fashion.[73] Indeed, marrying for love became a metaphor for Americanization. After all, America was a land of freedom. Marrying for love was a woman's form of freedom, best symbolized in the white wedding. Therefore, in choosing the man of her dreams and marrying in the American style, an immigrant girl would become a true American. Sometimes, as in films or novels, the girl had to marry a native of the United States; but in reality immigrant girls seem to have believed that becoming an American could be demonstrated in how one married rather than whom one married.[74]

The parents of the girl and the immigrant press never urged girls to wear the embroidered wedding costume of the homeland. Few in the immigrant generation could readily afford a white wedding, but many nonetheless often went into debt to pay for it because such an event symbolized success in America. The immigrant press encouraged these desires, even telling its readers where they might rent cutlery, decorations, the white dress, and wedding cakes for display, not eating. Wedding couples' desire for fancy things could not be sated. They wanted an automobile to bring them to the church, music during the processional, a portrait taken at a photographic studio, and a catered banquet—all of which were uncommon or nonexistent in other cultures.[75] They especially desired a photograph of themselves in their wedding clothes to send to relatives in the Old Country.

At the immigrant wedding between around 1900 and 1940 the food, music, and dancing at the feast after the wedding might resemble a wedding in the Old Country, where all the neighbors were invited, sometimes by personal invitation. Immigrants held receptions at their apartment, a neighborhood hall, or sometimes at a saloon. At the Italian "peanut wedding," guests ate peanuts or threw them at the groom. Women made hundreds of sandwiches and filled buckets with homemade cookies, which were served with beer, root beer, and peanuts.[76] The immigrant wedding could last for days. Of course, the men returned to work during the day and women carried on their responsibilities in the home, but the feast resumed each evening; by the 1950s, however, the multiday wedding had begun to disappear.[77]

A unique feature of ethnic weddings was the manner in which guests handed the couple money during the festivities. The exchange was a public presentation, not a discreet gift, and was an organized feature of the reception, usually part of the dancing. At a Croatian wedding guests would place their donation on a platter in front of the bride.[78] At Hispanic weddings parents of both the bride and the groom would begin the Dollar Dance, during which men would pin a dollar to the bride's dress.[79] The money gathered in this manner helped to defray the cost of the wedding and provided a nest egg for the newlyweds.[80]

As post–World War II families became affluent and third-generation immigrants entered the middle class, a lavish wedding reception at a restaurant or the country club became obligatory. These weddings not only rivaled but also often exceeded in number of guests and expense those of the white Protestant upper middle class.[81] The accordion player at the Italian-American wedding was replaced by a live band, which played the hokey-pokey rather than the Sicilian tarantella. The bride and groom greeted guests in a reception line, rather than the bridegroom and his father-in-law pouring shots of *rosolio* (homemade liquor) for the male guests while the bride and her mother served sweet liqueur to the women. The buffet table piled high with sandwiches, homemade cookies, and pitchers of beer was gone; guests were seated for a multicourse dinner and champagne was served by waiters in bow ties and white jackets.[82] Families no longer displayed the bride's trousseau before the wedding. Customs calling for the bridegroom or his family to pay for some of the bride's trousseau, the feast, the music, and the hall disappeared.[83] In most cases, third-generation immigrants adopted the assignment of wedding expenses the etiquette books decreed. The growth of ethnic intermarriage, residence in multiethnic neighborhoods, the prevalence of changes in religious affiliation, and the entreaties of caterers and consumer culture generally all contributed to the rise of the white wedding among ethnic couples.

Whyte's survey of Detroit couples from the 1920s to the 1980s found that fancy weddings were especially common among Catholics who had gone to parochial schools and considered themselves religious.[84] It may have been a wedding of a Pole to an Italian, but the Catholic wedding, even if interethnic, became the first-tier wedding; the interfaith wedding was usually smaller and cheaper. In opting for a lavish wedding Catholic couples were signaling their commitment to a marriage they expected to be long-lasting.

Arbiters of bridal etiquette criticized the presentation of money at the ethnic wedding as inegalitarian and insulting to the bride. Many children and grandchildren of immigrants agreed. Claudia de Monte, who was married on Long Island in the late 1960s, was embarrassed by the presentation of money to the bride. At her wedding she told her mother, "'Ma, I'm doing the wedding and forget about the booster bag. There is no way I'm doing that.' What happened? I did not have the bag, and the Italian guests came to the wedding with envelopes for Ed and me. They placed the envelopes in front of us, and in desperation we ended up using a black plastic bag that my aunt brought her old shoes in, in case her feet hurt. At the end of the day, the bag was filled with money."[85]

The revival of ethnic consciousness in recent times has led to increased assertion of group identity at weddings. But the degree to which old ethnic customs were readopted has varied. At one extreme were the weddings where the bride and groom had reverted to wearing ethnic costumes and tried to pattern the entire ceremony on the customs of the homeland. Much more typical were couples who splashed a few ethnic colors onto the standard canvas, creating a hybrid ritual, one in which the customs of the ethnic culture were clearly subordinate in number and significance to those of the dominant culture. This was not so much truly syncretic, as at birthday parties, but instead was closer to symbolic ethnicity, the couple asserting that they would not allow their ethnicity to intrude on their full participation in the American consumer economy.

American Jewish weddings became so culturally complex as almost to defy categorization. In the increasing popularity of marrying in a synagogue (which was once seen as defaming the sanctity of the synagogue), 1950s Jews were actually copying Christians. (The same had been true of German Jews, who had married in synagogues as early as the 1860s.) By adding symbolic elements of tradition in the 1950s—among them signing the *ketubah* (wedding contract), marrying under a canopy, and the husband's smashing a glass after the couple were pronounced husband and wife—American Jews, especially Southern ones, reincorporated elements that had been abandoned. In dancing the hora, an Israeli dance unknown in Eastern or central Europe, at the reception, they were defining themselves as postwar American Jews, who made identification with Israel a central part of their identity.[86] American Jews until the 1960s had managed to maintain a boundary between themselves and Gentiles by incorporating the idea of romantic love, consumer culture, and both Christian and Israeli cultural elements with a strong taboo against intermarriage. Even that barrier fell in the 1970s. Reform rabbis became willing both to marry interfaith couples even if the Gentile member of the couple had not converted to Judaism and to participate in an interfaith marriage with a member of the clergy from the other faith.

The rise of black nationalism in the 1960s had an impact on African American weddings in that decade and subsequently, with new features incorporated into a wedding ceremony with a black Christian minister presiding. The televised drama of Alex Haley's family saga, *Roots,* showed Kunta Kinte and his bride, Bell, marrying by jumping the broom. Some African American couples, influenced by the television series, began to incorporate jumping the broom, or African drumming or music during the processional.[87] One could even find the groom wearing a bit of colored cloth to symbolize "kinte" cloth (strip-woven colored cloth, made by peoples from the Gold Coast of West Africa) on his tuxedo or the bride wearing a head wrap or a white wedding dress decorated with cowrie shells.[88] Jumping the broom was also an implicit statement that African Americans could adopt traditions from American slavery, rather than having to claim "ancestral" African origins for customs, as was done for Kwanzaa.[89] The Afrocentric trend led to the rise of bridal consultants specializing in this style of wedding and, in the 1990s, to the appearance of a new magazine devoted to African American brides. Just as Kwanzaa was most popular among the black middle class, these African elements appeared most commonly in the weddings of professional, urban couples.

As in the case of Christmas, the rediscovery of ethnicity among African Americans inspired group consciousness among other groups. Many couples sought to display their ethnic heritage—or heritages. To accommodate two cultures, some couples had two wedding ceremonies. Thus, a bride in the 1990s might wear a sari for her Hindu ceremony and a white gown for her Catholic one the next day. (Chinese-Americans had developed this form of accommodation as early as the 1920s.) At the reception, the disc jockey or band would play music from both cultures as a way of signaling the union of the pair from two different ethnic groups.

The couple wishing to incorporate ethnic elements into their wedding often had no direct knowledge of tradition to draw on. They turned to bridal books that advised them "to rediscover your roots and . . . revive some of the signs and symbols that have special meaning for you, your families, and your community."[90] One book listed three or four distinctive customs for each group. While some of these customs affirmed old notions of patriarchy or community, distinctly missing from these modern lists were the customs most unlike Western ones and some of the most patriarchal ones.

Since the 1960s more couples than ever before have married in the grand manner. The white wedding swept aside other forms of ceremony, as people of even modest means in the United States and throughout the world embraced it. At a time when most people believe tradition is dying out, the desire for a white wedding is a ringing vote in favor of what people take to be tradition, even if it is not their own. The white wedding functioned as a symbol of success, prestige, and affirmation of the belief that in buying and personalizing a standard package, one might be able to achieve self-transformation and personal happiness.

The bride-to-be and her female relatives would leaf through bridal magazines with one hand and wipe their brow from exhaustion with the other. The increased number of shopping trips and arrangements to be made more than compensated for the decrease in time spent in the kitchen. Parental and societal pressure pushed couples to chose the standard package, the white wedding. But having done so, were they not also conforming to expectations about gender roles and the division of labor between husband and wife?[91] There is something ominous in receiving a thank-you note in the bride's hand, with both of the wedding couple's names on it, for it suggests that the white wedding has had an effect, encouraging the couple to think of the home, kinship, and consumer spheres as women's domain, to which a husband is merely an interested spectator, a beneficiary of the invisible work his wife has assumed.

Some couples kept their plans simple and their costs low by eloping or being married at city hall. Still, the majority wanted what was defined as right, proper, and perfect. Of all the rituals considered in this book, the white wedding is the most lavish and the most rigid in form. The demise of the ethnic wedding costume serves a metaphor for Americanization, since it reveals extensive acculturation occurring even among first-generation immigrants in the early twentieth century and among working-class as well as middle-class couples. Nonetheless, the trend did not become full blown until after World War II, as consumer income finally began to match consumer desires. The revival of ethnicity in the 1970s has made ethnicity into a kind of spice to flavor a homogenous culture; having a wedding favor of sugared almonds proves one is different, but not that different, from the rest.

There is no escaping the conclusion that the white wedding is wasteful, extravagant, patriarchal, heterosexist, and anachronistic, and that it obliterates traditional cultures. Nonetheless, the public's— especially women's—love of the white wedding shows the continuing appeal of prestige and romantic fantasy, the marriage of consumer culture and Victorian invention, the capacity of a dominant culture to overwhelm traditional cultures while incorporating a few customs from these cultures. Women grew up wanting this event even before they picked up their first bride's magazine. The white wedding was the culmination of their having played dress-up as a little girl. At the white wedding a woman could transform herself and her everyday world through flowers, fashion, photography, music, and (in the twentieth century) cosmetics. Gay commitment ceremonies, feminist ones that critiqued patriarchy, hippie unions in a park, marriages in the middle of a lake or at the top of a bungee jump platform, and nuptials of couples in ethnic costumes might poke fun at or critique the standard ritual; but these were relatively rare exceptions to the "white rule." Spending and the quest for true happiness were inextricably bound together. Many of the values encouraging the white wedding—transformation and the desire for self- and personal fulfillment—were formed in relation to consumer culture. The lavish wedding represented the realization of the dream consumer culture authorized.

CHAPTER ELEVEN

Rituals, Families, and Identities

To answer the question of "who I am" correctly, then, is to know and live one's history and practice one's culture.

—MAULANA KARENGA, 1988

When the public laments the loss of tradition, they do not have in mind gander pulling on Shrove Tuesday or Easter Monday, or black-face on Christmas, New Year's, Thanksgiving, and the Fourth of July. Nor are they thinking of children begging at Thanksgiving, sexual orgies on Pinkster, or shooting matches on Christmas Day.[1] These examples of the carnivalesque style of celebration are gone, although vestiges of the style can be found at Halloween, Mardi Gras, April Fool's Day, New Year's Eve, and during the Christmas season. Americans still enjoy some of the pleasures of masking, costuming, and excess, and children take pleasure from costumed begging for candy at Halloween.[2]

Despite these traces of an earlier style of holiday celebration, the carnivalesque diminished as two other approaches to family ritual were added, the first in the nineteenth century, and the second in the twentieth, particularly in the second half of the twentieth century. Momentous change took place as domestic ritual, reconceptualized and matched to a new age, took hold. The carnival approach receded because the middle class no longer was willing to tolerate routine rowdiness as a form of cathartic release among the lower orders, especially lower-class men. They sought to defend and protect their own family's privacy, and they wanted a more orderly and humanitarian society, one devoid of blood sports, dueling, and public hangings. Such an orderly world, it was believed, could reinforce the timeliness and work discipline an industrial society needed. Seeking a more domestic festive life and special times for far-flung kin to gather, middle-class Victorians fused religious piety, familialism, and spending. Impelled by these varied motives, and responding to complaints about sexual license, noise, drunkenness, child begging, and destruction of property, politicians and reformers, particularly in the nineteenth and the first third of the twentieth centuries, tried to eliminate misrule at Christmas, Easter, and Thanksgiving.[3] To a great extent the centers of change were the centers of wealth—the Northeast and the Mid-Atlantic states—but Southern planters and urbanites also began to celebrate in this more subdued manner. Although the domestic occasion was intended to replace carnivalesque festivals, the two continued to coexist for many decades.

The Protestant middle class was not the first social group to hold family feasts, but they were the first to see the family occasion as a solution to the social changes created by the industrial revolution. The middle and upper classes of the mid-nineteenth century were made anxious by the growth of commerce and industry and by their fear that greed and the pursuit of self-interest were being put ahead of community and religious piety. Experiencing economic dislocations as a decline in morality, they worried about the loss of the national religious mission and about young people leaving the family farm to move to the city or the frontier. Sentimental domestic occasions provided an orderly way of celebrating and made people feel more comfortable with modernity by reassuring them that they were engaged in something truly old-fashioned.

Once created, the family rituals of the Victorians functioned as active agents of social change, helping to shape middle-class and national identity, sideline distinctive regional or ethnic customs, and disseminate the ideal of domesticity. The ultimate irony was that middle-class Victorians had conceptualized the family as a private world separate from and purer than the marketplace. Yet luxury goods purchased in the marketplace came to symbolize the idea of family affection. Thus, the middle-class family was not so private after all, but was instead a ready market for family Bibles and baubles. While in reality there was no real barrier between the market and the home, the idea of family privacy did reinforce class distinctions. The elite, then the middle class, began to favor private family events.

Because of the emphasis on family privacy in the ideology of domesticity, some events shut out the public and were by invitation only. In excluding the uninvited guest and the larger community, the middle-class domestic occasion reinforced the social distance between one's own kin and the rest of the community. But the peer culture birthday party, a development begun in the 1870s, also recognized that the parent could no longer exercise complete control over the child's world. Because children were educated with age peers and were entering a world in which they would have to depend on friends as well as relatives, parents in the last third of the nineteenth century began to accept the child's peer culture—his or her own chosen friends—as a necessary adjunct to the private family.

Victorian writers and editors, from Sarah Josepha Hale to Charles Dickens, created the ideology of domesticity and wrote poems, stories, and songs enshrining it. The new kind of family envisaged in this ideal seemed to require rituals that symbolically affirmed its values— domestic warmth, intimacy, romantic love, special affection for children and grandparents, and a familial and feminized view of religion. Relatives made pilgrimages to the secular shrine of the grandparent's house in the country to partake of a form of spiritual renewal before returning to a more hectic life in a town or city. Even heaven was fashioned as a family environment, where kin would be reunited. The domestication of festival increased Protestant religiosity, since many Calvinists had taken a dim view of ritual and sought to limit its scope. While this "home religion" was initially Protestant and middle class, it also developed similarly, though at later times, among middle-class Catholics and Jews.

Department store owners, florists, sellers of greeting cards, confectioners, and coffin makers had much to gain from making domestic occasions more elaborate, and getting people to celebrate more often. But they were neither especially manipulative or acute in recognizing social trends and exploiting them. However inept at anticipating public demand for celebration, merchants nonetheless responded to festivals already popular by offering a cornucopia of goods and services to enhance them. Candy and desserts, presents, flowers, photographs, and fancy family table settings made domestic events more beautiful, emotional, luxurious, memorable, and satisfying for the sweet tooth. Greeting cards helped family members maintain kin contact; gifts symbolized the donor's affection for the recipient. After about 1910 it was difficult to name a holiday or rite of passage that was devoid of all four of the most common elements—presents, flowers, cards, and candy. At the same time, many critics then—as now—saw the abundance of goods and the emphasis on buying them as profaning the sacred meaning of the occasion. It was this debate about the merits of commercialized festivity that drained some of the enthusiasm from the domestic occasion.

The idea of binding local, regional, and particularistic ties into love of nation through commemoration of its founding events also contributed to the growth of family ritual in the nineteenth century. (I have not discussed the major national holidays, such as Fourth of July, at length, because these were largely public festivals and secondarily or incidentally times for family gathering.) Thanksgiving became a historical commemoration like July Fourth, but one that was a family gathering as much as a national celebration. A regional holiday until the Civil War, Thanksgiving became truly national in the Progressive era. In that period of greater centralization, educated professionals and Americanizers became more aware than ever before of the conflicting allegiances of the masses and the need to make them into loyal citizens. As a huge influx of foreigners disembarked at U.S. ports, reformers turned to the calendar and the flag as a means of including new immigrants and the rural poor in the polity and socializing them as citizens. Through celebrating the family the symbol of national unity became reality.

Schools began to use Thanksgiving and other holidays as instructional tools during this period, when the socialization of immigrant children acquired special urgency. Most teachers believed that newcomers' learning about the dominant culture's holidays helped produce a sense of patriotism. This view of the calendar as a form of education in citizenship has become a prevailing educational principle. Schools succeeded quite well in their attempts at Americanization, since the agent of change in many immigrant families was the child, who wanted the ritual learned about in school observed at home. Later, spectator sports have also served a nationalist function. Even the football game, an entirely secular event, when listened to or viewed on Thanksgiving, New Year's Day, or (since the mid-1960s) on Superbowl Sunday, imparted feelings of national unity and loyalty. Nonetheless, on national days some Americans protested their exclusion, while others felt they simply did not belong.

Love of the nation also came to mean celebrating in the manner of the middle class, with birthday candles, gift wrap, bows, plastic Easter eggs, and Coca-Cola, which even had its own version of Santa. It also meant acquiring middle-class etiquette and table manners—individually greeting one's guests and sending thank-you notes. Gift-giving and shopping became elements of this way of life. Late-nineteenth-century immigrants wrote home that true Americans bought presents on Christmas and birthdays and married for love in church weddings. Gradually new consumer items were added to the list, from custom photography to printed invitations.

Ever since the early nineteenth century, middle-class women put the idea of the domestic occasion into practice. They cleaned and cooked, shopped, mailed cards, decorated the home and the church, and acted as the family's chief mourner. By teaching the rules of etiquette and table manners, they trained children to take their proper place as members of a privileged class. Men became increasingly marginal figures in many sentimental occasions, even as they seated themselves at the head of the table (and took on a new role in the twentieth century, that of family photographer). Their main role, however, was as family breadwinner. The outside world regarded the man who could pay for a Thanksgiving turkey and provide his wife with a generous allowance for Easter finery and Christmas gifts as a good provider; a prosperous father spent generously on his daughter's wedding.

The work of women tested their worth as homemaker and mother. Occasions varied greatly as to the level of exertion required, with Thanksgiving, Christmas, Easter, Passover, and weddings being among the most demanding. At all of these events women derived satisfaction and even power in the family for their efforts. For every woman who complained about the crush of holiday shoppers were two or three who enjoyed leaving the house to browse in department stores or to take children to visit Santa. Women's shopping combined leisure and work and gradually came to give them increasing power over the family purse. One of the many pleasures of the domestic occasion for women was that it convened a female community. At feasts in the home women cooked with other women and girls, displayed their creativity, artistry, and skills, received praise for their efforts, and basked in their self-image as being caring, nurturant, and charitable. Ritual can survive without women, but it cannot be very elaborate. When holidays were celebrated by mostly male groups, as in festivals of the Chinese New Year among nineteenth-century immigrants, the feast would be held at the headquarters of group associations or at restaurants.

The domestic occasion not only sanctified the middle-class woman as the queen of the home but also underscored the importance of displaying status and wealth in making an occasion memorable. Rituals that celebrated the home also made visible a system of social ranking. People of higher status had always used ritual as a way of distinguishing themselves from everyone else. In consumer rituals positive judgments were based on the ability to use purchased goods and services creatively, while negative judgments were made if one were unable to provide a necessary show of beauty and wealth. Thus, marriage in the judge's chambers, burial in a pine box, or Christmas with a single orange in the stocking were seen as second rate.

The need for fresh symbols and rituals not seen in English culture led the American middle class between 1830 and 1870 to copy the birthday parties, Easter egg hunts, and Christmas customs of the Germans. Searching for new customs with which to create child-oriented festivals, American writers and travelers reported on German customs that made holidays familial and festive rather than drunken, and that allowed children to be indulged without being spoiled. Native-born Americans adopted some features of German ritual and ignored the rest. So successful was the cultural transfer that by the late nineteenth century the German origins of many holiday customs were forgotten. Similarly, in the twentieth century, immigrants and blacks—Israel Baline (Irving Berlin) and Frank Capra, Bing Crosby and Nat King Cole—have spun out modern secular hymns and visual paeans to holiday sentimentality. Just as the German contributions to American festivals were invisible, the ethnic and racial backgrounds of these modern cultural creators went unnoticed.

Ethnicity and Ritual

Who are we and where do we come from? Ritual seemed to provide Americans with the answer to this question. It helped to define one's identity but also indicated changes in identity. The relationship between ritual and ethnic identity was multifaceted.

The prevailing social climate affected the way people chose to define and express their ethnic identity. The restriction of the flow of immigration in the mid-1920s (and earlier for Asian immigrants), for example, encouraged a steady dissolution of ethnic identity along generational lines. The first generation adhered more closely to tradition, while the second often wanted to "do things more the way it was done here." Many ethnic groups, even Hispanics and Chinese-Americans, were trying to blend into American culture from the 1920s through the 1950s. They wanted to be Americans, not hyphenated ones. In the 1950s, the conformity imposed by Cold War fears, the crusades to root out Communism, the mass marketing of consumer goods, and the new medium of television encouraged many Americans to minimize, or even conceal, their ethnic roots.

Many rituals disappeared as immigrants resided for longer periods of time in the United States and as they raised a new generation. Acculturation was evident for every group and every ritual. In examining U.S. ethnic groups in the course of the twentieth century, such signs of ethnicity as knowledge of a foreign language or dialect, residence in an ethnic enclave, and membership in a group association have fallen away. Many rituals disappeared entirely or were practiced only in a few towns or cities with unusually large ethnic populations. If a church did not encourage a practice, it was less likely to survive. In general, religious institutions, especially ones that combined ethnicity and religion, were important in preserving traditions. Ritual was especially likely to vanish among immigrants or their children who did not live in an ethnic enclave but instead resided in multiethnic neighborhoods and attended multinationality parishes or had changed their religious affiliation.

For every group the acculturation process was accompanied by a streamlining of the religious and agricultural calendar once observed. For example, in 1870s Galicia, thirty-four districts had 100 to 120 nonworking days per year, twenty-two districts had 120 to 150 nonworking days, and sixteen districts had 150 to 200. In the United States legal holidays varied from state to state. Nonetheless, in 1900 it was common for there to be only four: Christmas, New Year's Day, the Fourth of July, and Thanksgiving.[4] Most groups found it difficult to clear space for their own holidays within this public calendar. Feast days and celebrations that occurred on a day that did not coincide with an American legal holiday tended to fade away. Immigrants selected a few holidays to observe, either the ones considered most important or those that fell at the same time as an American holiday. They thus preserved a few rituals while abandoning the wider range of rituals that had once been theirs.[5] More important, celebration of the holidays of the Old Country acquired the added meaning of being a rear-guard action to preserve one's culture against the onslaught of American influences. Immigrant mothers especially took this view and redefined their role to include instructing children in their religious and ethnic heritage.

Who are we and where do we come from? This question became even more puzzling as a family rose in status and entered the middle class. Such families began to adopt more American rituals and dress up their ethnic occasions. The simple repast—a party in the backyard—no longer sufficed. Many of these events followed the Protestant middle-class pattern of excluding the public, reserving the event for family and friends. The middle-class family could have very large parties, but it made a distinction between its own social circle and a wider community. Middle-class women in these groups took on a new role as updaters of tradition, crafting not the authentic and homey but the aesthetic and fancy. (A notable exception to this class rule was among Hispanics, where the working class was more likely than the middle class to have quinceañeras.) The timing of the emergence of a fancier occasion varied for each holiday and each ethnic group. Nonetheless, the late 1940s and 1950s saw a great homogenizing of the ritual for weddings and funerals, and a decline in distinctive deathways and wedding rituals.

Race was another important factor in how celebrations were handled. Non-white races developed their rituals in such a way as to solve some of the problems caused by inequality and racial prejudice. The lack of interest until recently in black, Chinese, and Hispanic consumers provided a protected market for ethnic entrepreneurs, including minority-group funeral directors, grocery owners, and manufacturers of religious objects and ethnic foods. Racial restrictions also led to the invention of the clan banquet for the many bachelors in the Chinese immigrant population. Black families were more likely to spend freely on a funeral than a grave marker or family tomb. Burial grounds discriminated against blacks, and those open to them were not well maintained. Meanwhile, black funeral directors and ministers encouraged urban black families around the beginning of the twentieth century to think of embalming and a padded casket as prestigious.

One feature of ethnic adaptation was the invention of entirely new rituals that arose not from the storehouse of tradition but from the perceptions and needs of people living in the United States. The actual creation of a new ethnic tradition was relatively rare, and thus especially noteworthy: the bat mitzvah, St. Lucia Day, and Kwanzaa are some examples. The egalitarian impulse was behind the development of the bat mitzvah, as well as more practical considerations about the religious instruction of girls. A small number of nationalist leaders interested in increasing their group's allegiance to their homeland helped introduce St. Lucia Day and create Kwanzaa. Ethnic businesses became important in the growth of these holidays, which appealed mainly to the ethnic middle class. Creation of such new rituals appears to have been especially common at the Christmas season, where the ethnic ceremony served as a supplement to or an alternative to the Christmas of the dominant culture.

Initiation rites for adolescents, once minor ceremonies, became family extravaganzas, as early as the 1920s for the Jewish middle class and in the 1960s for the Hispanic working class. These initiation rites were used to allay parental anxieties about the approach of adolescence and to bridge the gap between participation in American consumer culture and allegiance to a distinct ethnic and religious identity.

Syncretization, a blending of cultures to produce a new result, was more common than the invention of wholly new rituals or the fancifying of minor ones. It allowed immigrants to inject some elements of ethnic life into the rituals of the dominant culture and thus symbolized their desire to forge a dual identity, ethnic and mainstream. Ethnic music, food, and dancing—features evoking the earliest and most positive memories of childhood—were fused with the dominant culture. Ethnic food, for example, was added to American cuisine at Thanksgiving, sometimes as side dishes. At birthday parties, ethnic food, costumes, and adult sociality were combined with the mainstream American (originally German) cake and candles.

Domestic rituals also crossed into the public sphere, as in the clan banquet or third seder. Chinese immigrants at Chinese New Year were the first to use their holidays as a means of extending hospitality to otherwise hostile Americans, in order to increase mutual understanding and to develop businesses and tourist attractions. A taste for the exotic close to home has been characteristic of Americans at least since white tourists in the late nineteenth century flocked to Chinatown for Chinese New Year. Despite the social discrimination many groups faced (or, in the case of minority-group funeral preparations, because of it), each ethnic and racial group has been able to use its rituals for commercial gain. In the twentieth century national firms as well as ethnic entrepreneurs sought to profit from ethnic rituals, prepared foods, and tourism.

The fancy funeral falls in a special category, since it did not grow out of the status striving of the middle class. At least since the late nineteenth century, Greeks, Italians, Irish, blacks, and the poor in general have usually scraped together the money and passed the hat in order to pay for a lavish funeral. Those interested in such funerals were not concerned about rising in status so much as about not falling into ignominy. They dreaded the anonymity and lack of respect for the dead the pauper's burial conveyed. The fancy funeral gave the deceased the kind of dignity that was denied in life. If the fancy wedding symbolized economic and social success, the fancy funeral showed that survivors, even poor ones, respected their dead. Spending on a funeral served not to signal family status but to preserve family honor.

Between the 1910s and the 1940s, children of immigrants learned the values of individualism, romantic love, and consumerism through their participation in mass culture. They attended baseball games and boxing matches. They developed a fondness for the rhythms of ragtime, jazz, and the songs of Tin Pan Alley. Working girls bought the latest fashions and went on dates unchaperoned. American-born Chinese in San Francisco frequented Chinatown's nightclubs in the 1940s. Immigrant parents, especially immigrant mothers, often shrugged their shoulders. The immigrant mother came to be seen as the preserver of tradition, the bulwark against assimilation. Nonetheless, she was also an active consumer, who joined a Christmas club and saved to give her children new clothes for Easter or first communion. It is an oversimplification to conclude that consumer culture, with its emphasis on luxury, novelty, and an altered and improved self, simply overpowered ethnic, racial, or even class identity. In some cases, it served to enhance these identities. Moreover, having wishes, fantasies, and daydreams did not preclude having multiple definitions of the self.

The Postsentimental Approach to Family Ritual

It is best to think of the postsentimental approach to ritual as a third layer, added on top of the carnivalesque and the sentimental approaches, and as a stance in a debate, which presumes that others will argue and make visible the merits of sentimentality. Postsentimentalism is both a way of talking about ritual and a style of practicing it. Cynical and critical, postsentimentalism uses sentimentality as a foil. It requires the persistence, not the total disappearance, of sentimental occasions.

Funerals during and after World War I were the first rituals to show evidence of postsentimentalism. The simpler funeral was an explicit rejection of the sentimental view of death, burial, and mourning. World War I shattered the elaborate mourning customs of the Victorians. Influential Americans no longer believed that the funeral should be the grandest occasion of all. Americans, especially the middle class and liberal Protestants, wanted them to be brief, simple, and emotionally sparse, as they sought to push death aside. In addition, as increasing life expectancy led to the concentration of deaths among the elderly, deaths of kin older than seventy came to be defined as "low grief losses."

Increasingly in the second half of the twentieth century, rituals were celebrated outside the home.[6] This change mainly occurred when a service industry took over women's unpaid work, which had usually been performed in the home. Again, funerals set the pattern. Even in the late nineteenth century, funerals were increasingly held outside the home, at a church or funeral home, and were arranged by a funeral director. Gradually, other ceremonies were moved to outside the home. This new location did not necessarily lead to a decline in women's work. In hiring a wedding caterer, for example, a women and her neighbors no longer had to cook for the wedding feast; but it was equally time consuming to engage and supervise the work of others, from florists and photographers to musicians and party planners.

Postsentimentalism was also a result of major changes that affected the family during three decades, beginning in the 1960s. The social and sexual revolutions of that time spurred sweeping family changes: an increase in divorce, a growth in cohabitation as an alternative to marriage, and a greater willingness of women to bear and rear children as single parents. Forced to confront a growing diversity of marital and family patterns, some responded with understanding, others with regret or disgruntlement. There was nothing new in the postmodern condition of discontinuity and doubt, instability and uncertainty. That had been the experience of families living through the Black Death, the slave trade, or the Great Depression. What was different about the decades between 1960 and 1990 was that dramatic social changes were accompanied by the steady march toward woman's independence from lifelong marriage and a renegotiation of gender roles for couples along egalitarian lines.

Women's wage earning had been rising throughout the twentieth century, but by the 1970s it caused a loud crash in the kitchen. Many women were beginning to recognize that they suffered from double duty, attending to both the work of the family and the demands of their paid job. To be sure, married women's employment brought increased money for presents and party goods as well as for more practical items. But it also contributed to women's discontent, since paid work fueled the resurgence of feminism and contributed to a surging divorce rate. Women, better educated than ever before and more committed to paid work throughout their lifetimes, pared down family size and complained about the holiday blues. Their response to the blues was often to reduce the amount of ritual work. Many women began to encourage husband and children to help cook or clean for family feasts, or to ask guests to bring dishes for a pot luck buffet. Another solution was to substitute services for women's unpaid labor—to purchase birthday cakes at a bakery or to dine at a restaurant on Easter Sunday.

Equally important in shaping postsentimental ritual was the changing attitude toward racial integration and the issue of minority groups' participation in the American mainstream. Disenchantment as a result of stalled progress in civil rights in the mid-1960s led to a resurgence of black nationalism. Initially, blacks who celebrated Kwanzaa intended to symbolically demonstrate their support of black nationalism. Maulana Karenga, the creator of Kwanzaa, believed that American blacks needed to celebrate the holiday to learn and affirm their African identity. Christmas, he contended, confirming the suspicions that many American blacks had long held, was a white people's holiday. Many blacks began to wear the Afro hairstyle, take an African first and last name, and give their children African names. Much black invented tradition, from Kwanzaa to African drumming at weddings to initiation rites for youth at black churches, sprang from a desire on the part of American blacks to recover an African heritage.

Black nationalism had as much influence on nonblacks as on peoples of African descent. The growth of racial identity among Asians, Hispanics, native Americans, and many other ethnic groups owes much to black power. Families were encouraged to recapture lost customs or add ethnic elements to their celebrations; they rediscovered rarely practiced traditions and invented new ones. Local chambers of commerce and businesses developed ethnic parades and festivals. Some festivals, such as the New Year celebration in San Francisco's Chinatown, which had had an assimilationist slant in the 1950s, took on a more "authentic" Chinese flavor in the 1970s.[7]

In the decades since the 1960s more Americans than ever before were intermarrying and associating with neighbors and workmates from other groups. Even many recent immigrants were living in the suburbs and intermarrying. People no longer recognized taboos on marrying someone from a different ethnic, religious, or racial background. Families increasingly invited members from other groups to their ethnic feasts. Wedding rituals were often used to send a signal that the two families would accommodate the different cultures of the bride and groom.

Instead of affirming an ideal of the family, celebrations in postsentimental times upheld a set of values that can best be described as individualist, pluralist, therapeutic, and consumerist. With the exception of the therapeutic, these values had long flourished on American soil. By the end of the nineteenth century, urban workers had come to believe that purchased goods and services brought magic to one's life. The growth of real wages for ordinary working families, boosted by World War II wartime industry and American postwar prosperity, made consumer dreams a reality for ordinary folk, not just the urban middle class. Rising farm incomes during the postwar years closed the urban-rural gap, except for pockets of regional and racial poverty. It became possible for rural people to consume in the manner of their city cousins.[8] In an abundant twentieth-century America, chocolate candy became an everyday treat, birthday parties an expected rite, and sending a greeting card an assumed obligation.

Twentieth-century American popular culture was mainly optimistic and happy, upholding the belief that it was more important to celebrate happiness than to wallow in death. In an increasingly abundant society, many thought that in spending freely they could find happiness, express love, and make a joyous occasion perfect. Some came to this conclusion because of the influence of advertising and the mass media, which portrayed spending as the way to achieve happy holidays. Encouraging dreams of fulfillment through purchased goods was an aim of advertising as early as the nineteenth century, which even then depicted children asleep, dreaming of the toys Santa was going to bring them. Irving Berlin was simply adding to this image of Christmas as a time of reverie when he wrote about "dreaming of a white Christmas."

Spending for certain rituals was one particular kind of dream, that of self-transformation. The making of a fantasy world was particularly suited to rites of passage, since these rituals had always been concerned with how individuals might transform themselves from one stage in life to another. By hosting a big reception for relatives from out of town at a bar or bat mitzvah, a Jewish family could help a child make the passage into adolescence truly memorable. Similarly, an expensive quinceañera offered a way for young adolescent Hispanic girls to realize their dream of being a fairy princess. The lavish wedding was intended to achieve the greatest transformation of all, waving a magic wand over a plain girl and making her into a radiant queen for a day. The honeymoon that followed, often at a tropical resort, the desired honeymoon location of couples since the 1980s, brought to life fantasies of two beautiful people experiencing romance and sensual pleasure on a white-sand beach.

Anthropologist Mary Douglas has argued that with increased individualism and the disappearance of many tightly knit communities, the amount of ritual in a society would decline.[9] Contrary to her prediction, the opposite appeared to be the case in the United States in the 1970s. Ritual was seen as a creative solution to personal and social problems. It became one of several means to achieve the dominant ethos of the decade, self-realization through therapeutic self-help. The kind of ritual then in vogue was supposed to be personally meaningful, experimental, derived from some "authentic" ancient tradition, and perhaps non- or even anti-institutional. Since the 1970s Americans have invented a number of new rituals—initiation rites for black youths at black churches or social service organizations, home childbirth ceremonies, gay coming-out and commitment ceremonies, child-naming events, ceremonies for menstruation and menopause, even for divorce and miscarriage.[10] Feminism, New Age spirituality, black nationalism, gay and men's liberation, divorce, intermarriage—all of these developments have led to the creation of new rituals and provided a rationale for the need for new ceremonial events.

The language of psychology, especially the often-repeated metaphor of "healing" a wound, provided another important rationale. Funeral directors defended the funeral as a form of grief work. Therapists endorsed the view that many family rituals had become static and obligatory and called for new, more meaningful ones that would reflect the many changes in modern American families. Many people were searching for new rituals with which they could express transcendent meaning. In the secular language of therapy, people were looking for a way to "maintain and alter important relationships, to facilitate complicated life-cycle changes, to heal losses, to express [their] deepest beliefs, and to celebrate life."[11]

Yet if the therapists are correct that the older rituals lack meaning for today's Americans, how do we explain the growth of that anachronism, the white wedding? What do we make of a couple who have a wedding reception at a hotel for two hundred guests, complete with a vocalist and a seven-piece band, and two years later hold a "dedication ceremony" for their infant, written by themselves, with a Protestant minister and a Buddhist priest officiating? Ethnic intermarriage and contact between cultures, even the popularity of ethnic food and music, have promoted experimentation and liberal cultural borrowing from religious or ethnic traditions not one's own. Great anxiety, insecurity, and nostalgia have coexisted with the quest for meaning and the desire to create new rituals. The work of blending the traditional and the new continues, as the technologically proficient construct web pages with photos of their child's birthday party, their own wedding, and their family Christmas tree with presents under it, and the cosmically oriented have their ashes sent into space.

These new practices follow the patterns of the rituals of the past, but what of the future? Do we need a larger and more varied set of rituals, ones that do not impose an unfair burden on women, or exclude and alienate minorities who do not share the faith or values of the dominant culture? John Gillis defined a new standard for a just cultural life. He wrote, "We must strive toward new family cultures that will not unduly burden or privilege either sex or any age group, or ignore the creativity of any class or ethnic group. Men must be willing finally to pick up their share of the cultural work involved, but women must be prepared to make a place for them in this endeavor."[12] Philosopher Nancy Fraser proposes that cultural justice would consist of "the wholesale transformation of societal patterns of representation, interpretation, and communication in ways that would change *everybody's* sense of self."[13] The political theory of Michael Walzer implies that the freedom *not* to go home for Thanksgiving—not to feel you must go there (what he calls the "freedom to leave the groups and sometimes the identities behind")—constitutes the "liberal idea of voluntary association."[14]

If we took any of these utopian standards seriously, we would have to eliminate most of the ways we currently celebrate the life cycle and organize the calendar! Gillis, Fraser, and Walzer offer quite different standards of fairness. None of their proposals is workable, let alone acceptable, for the majority of families. What is significant is that they raise questions of cultural justice. Gillis calls for gender equity and sees ethnicity and class as a matter of pluralist tolerance and inclusion. Fraser wants to democratize American popular culture. Walzer openly questions the fiction of ethnic identity, even suggesting that the freedom to escape from its burdens and demands is a fundamental liberty.

Meanwhile, women continue to be the main consumers of advice about etiquette and party planning. Martha Stewart was the most important expert on ritual in the United States in the 1980s and 1990s. The transformation of Martha Stewart, née Martha Kostyra, from Nutley, New Jersey, the daughter of Polish-American parents, whose father was a pharmaceutical salesman and whose mother was a housewife, to modern America's Sarah Josepha Hale—a triumph of self-reinvention as well as business acumen—showed that one did not have to come from the dominant culture to become a expert on how to create it. Bursting on the national scene in 1982, not long after the defeat of the Equal Rights Amendment, she seemed almost single-handedly to stimulate a revival of domestic crafts and reinvigorate the cultural quest to make the home a sanctuary. As part of the turn toward social conservatism, women's magazines of the 1980s heralded a "new traditionalism" among women.

Through marriage, Martha Kostyra became Martha Stewart and took on the identity of a WASP. (Her father-in-law was in fact Jewish, having changed his name to Stewart in the 1930s as a way of avoiding anti-Semitism on Wall Street.) A scathing unauthorized biography suggested that Stewart's evocation of her happy family in her magazines, cookbooks, videos, housewares advertisements, mail order catalog, web site, TV shows, and radio programs is an illusion developed to cover up the reality of a stern, parental home and a conflict-filled marriage, which eventually ended in divorce. Stewart, however, never sought to conceal her Polish-American background, and even sentimentalized it in some of her books.[15]

Stewart combined a celebration of female (commercialized) craft skill with concepts of display (defining what good taste was) and consumption. Like Currier and Ives or Irving Berlin, she understood that nostalgia for the simple country life—for fresh vegetables from the garden, home-cooked food, domestic crafts, and a loving family set in a country kitchen in rural Connecticut—sells. Seeking to convey information about how to celebrate in an upper-class manner, she offered instruction to Americans who lacked confidence in their own taste and style. Her frequent use of the word "perfect" made Martha Stewart an exemplar of the modern approach to entertaining and domestic occasions. Martha Stewart—as iconic figure, celebrity, media personality, and name brand—inspires praise, respect, and parody. Gift stores offer wall plaques that read "Martha Stewart doesn't live here." That one can both love and laugh at Martha Stewart reveals how we Americans continue simultaneously to shape and reshape the dominant culture, and critique it. To parody Martha Stewart reveals the cynicism so characteristic of postsentimental discourse. To notice that the form of parody is a consumer object for sale in a party goods store shows the continuing significance of consumer culture in a postsentimental age.

Notes

1. Festivals, Rites, and Presents

1. For an example of the unhappiness felt on holidays by homosexuals who are estranged from their families, see Kath Weston, *Families We Choose: Lesbians, Gays, Kinship* (New York: Columbia University Press, 1991), p. 2.

2. Theodore Caplow and Howard H. Baur, *Middletown Families: Fifty Years of Change and Continuity* (Minneapolis: University of Minnesota Press, 1982), p. 225.

3. Leigh Eric Schmidt, *Consumer Rites: The Buying and Selling of American Holidays* (Princeton: Princeton University Press, 1995), pp. 16–17; *New York Times*, Oct. 28, 1997, p. C1; Shannon Durtch, "Greetings America," *American Demographics* 19 (February 1997): 4.

4. "Supermarkets Find Once-Joyful Holidays are Now the Time to Give Away the Store," *Wall Street Journal*, Dec. 8, 1992, p. B1.

5. Judith Stacey, *Brave New Families: Stories of Domestic Upheaval in Late Twentieth Century America* (New York: Basic Books, 1990). For an argument that the central characteristic of postmodern ritual is a "fragmented" identity, see David Parkin, "Ritual as Spatial Direction and Bodily Division," in Daniel de Coppet, ed., *Understanding Rituals* (London: Routledge, 1992), pp. 11–25.

6. Robert N. Bellah, Richard Marsden, William M. Sullivan, Ann Swidler, and Steven M. Tipton, *Habits of the Heart: Individualism and Commitment in American Life* (New York: Harper and Row, 1985), p. 90. In this book I study the "discourse" of occasions, a term introduced by French historian and philosopher Michel Foucault. By discourse, Foucault meant not simply rhetoric or discussion but also social practice, cultural imagery, and the relationship between representations, discussions, and reality. As Foucault

pointed out, ideas and practice are related, but may fit together poorly. Rituals may express contradictory views, or may contradict the ideas prevalent in magazines and newspapers. Michel Foucault, *The History of Sexuality,* vol. 1, trans. Robert Hurley (New York: Pantheon Books, 1978), pp. 100–102.

7. See Cary Carson, Ronald Hoffman, and Peter J. Albert, eds., *Of Consuming Interests: The Style of Life in the Eighteenth Century* (Charlottesville: University Press of Virginia and U.S. Capital Historical Society, 1994).

8. Stephen Steinberg, *The Ethnic Myth: Race, Ethnicity, and Class in America* (New York: Atheneum, 1981), p. 63.

9. Eric Hobsbawm, "Introduction: Inventing Traditions," in Eric Hobsbawm and Terence Ranger, eds., *The Invention of Tradition* (Cambridge: Cambridge University Press, 1983), pp. 1–14.

10. Ibid., p. 2.

11. For more about the development of Victorian rituals, see John R. Gillis, *A World of Their Own Making: Myth, Ritual, and the Quest for Family Values* (New York: Basic Books, 1996), pp. 61–132.

12. Peter Burke, "The Repudiation of Ritual in Early Modern Europe," in Peter Burke, ed., *The Historical Anthropology of Early Modern Italy: Essays on Perception and Communication* (Cambridge: Cambridge University Press, 1987), pp. 223–238; Edward Muir, *Ritual in Early Modern Europe* (Cambridge: Cambridge University Press, 1997), pp. 155–228.

13. Victor Turner studied ritual inversion in *The Ritual Process: Structure and Anti-Structure* (Chicago: Aldine, 1969).

14. Natalie Zemon Davis, *Society and Culture in Early Modern France* (Stanford: Stanford University Press, 1975), pp. 97–123.

15. Roger D. Abrahams, *Singing the Master: The Emergence of African American Culture in the Plantation South* (New York: Pantheon Books, 1992).

16. I discuss only in passing family reunions, family vacations, wedding anniversaries, and graduation parties. Moreover, in order to limit the scope of the study, I have not analyzed New Year's Day, St. Patrick's Day, Memorial Day, Labor Day, Columbus Day, or July Fourth. Although one might classify some of these holidays as national days, families sometimes celebrated these days with feasts, picnics, or parties.

17. Anthropologists have written extensively about the distinctions between ritual, rite, ceremony, and festival. Some anthropologists and students of ritual define ceremonies as events with multiple rituals and festivals as multiple ceremonies. Others define a ceremony as a secular, nonmagical ritual. As will be clear in this book, there is no fixed boundary dividing the secular and religious worlds. I have not found these distinctions meaningful, so I use the terms *ritual, rite, ceremony, celebration,* and *occasion* synonymously.

18. *Feast* comes from the Latin, meaning "public joy," but the word is as often associated with a private banquet as with communal eating in a public place.

19. Mary Douglas and Baron Isherwood, *The World of Goods* (New York: Basic Books, 1979), pp. 114–127.

20. For much of the 1980s, historians tended to see immigrants "transplanting" their customs, and they deemphasized the process of acculturation. Recent statements about the history of ethnicity in the United States, however, are once again giving attention to the process of acculturation. See Gary Gerstle, "Liberty, Coercion, and the Making of Americans," *Journal of American History* 84 (September 1997): 524–569; Russell A. Kazal, "Revisiting Assimilation: The Rise, Fall, and Reappraisal of a Concept in American Ethnic History," *American Historical Review* 100 (April 1995): 437–471; James R. Barrett, "Americanization from the Bottom Up: Immigration and the Remaking of the Working Class in the United States, 1880–1930," *Journal of American History* 79 (December 1992): 996–1020; Ewa Morawska, "In Defense of the Assimilation Model," *Journal of American Ethnic History* 13 (Winter 1994): 76–87; Elliott R. Barkan, "Race, Religion, and Nationality in American Society: A Model of Ethnicity—from Contact to Assimilation," *Journal of American Ethnic History* 14 (Winter 1995): 38–75.

21. Of the one hundred six ethnic groups that received separate entries in the *Harvard Encyclopedia of American Ethnic Groups*, I could trace the changes in particular rituals for fourteen: Navahos, English, Chinese, Japanese, Germans, Italians, German Jews, East European Jews, African Americans, Mexican-Americans, Mormons, Poles, Swedes, and Scotch-Irish. Anthropologists and folklorists found the traditions of these groups exotic, or believed these traditions were dying out, so they recorded them in order to preserve them. Jews and Mormons often studied their own groups, actively collecting folklore, family letters, and photo albums. The absence of detailed information about the other groups cannot be easily explained. The Irish were a large immigrant population, but I found surprisingly little information about Irish weddings or St. Patrick's Day feasts. From the group of fourteen about which there was sufficient information I selected six for more detailed treatment: Jews, Chinese, African Americans, Mexican-Americans, Swedes, and Poles. For the sake of variety, some of my chapters relate the history of several groups, while others concentrate on the history of a single group. In some cases, the nature of the source material helped define my focus. I have more to say about the celebration of Chinese New Year in San Francisco than in Honolulu, for example, because more documents are available for San Francisco. Similarly, my account of the reinvention of St. Lucia Day since the 1960s depends on Larry Danielson's ethnography of his hometown, Lindsborg, Kansas. In general, I was able to note some class distinctions between the styles of celebration within different ethnic groups. However, students of ethnicity have shown that major differences in such things as language retention and group identity relate to ethnic clustering or dominance, isolation in a rural area or in a single-group neighborhood, the founding of churches or synagogues, and the presence of religious schooling for children. I would have needed much more information about the practice of ritual in different settings in order to explain differences within an ethnic group. Stephan Thernstrom, ed., *Harvard Encyclopedia of American Ethnic Groups* (Cam-

bridge: Harvard University Press, 1980); Larry William Danielson, "The Ethnic Festival and Cultural Revivialism in a Small Midwestern Town" (Ph.D. diss., Indiana University, 1972).

22. For the view that political, social, and cultural forces shape how we define what is a race, see Michael Omi and Howard Winant, *Racial Formation in the United States* (London: Routledge and Kegan Paul, 1986).

23. Erving Goffman, "Gender Display," *Studies in the Anthropology of Visual Communication* 3 (1976): 69–77.

24. Jeanne Boydston, *Home and Work: Housework, Wages, and the Ideology of Labor in the Early Republic* (New York: Oxford University Press, 1990), pp. 120–141.

25. Denise A. Segura and Jennifer L. Pierce, "Chicana/o Family Structure and Gender Personality: Chodorow, Familism, and Psychoanalytic Sociology Revisited," *Signs* 19 (Autumn 1993): 62–91.

26. Douglas and Isherwood, *The World of Goods;* Russell W. Belk, Melanie M. Wallendorf, and John F. Sherry, "The Sacred and the Profane in Consumer Behavior: Theodicy on the Odyssey," *Journal of Consumer Research* 16 (1989): 1–38.

27. Daniel Horowitz, *The Morality of Spending: Attitudes toward the Consumer Society in America, 1875–1940* (Baltimore: The Johns Hopkins University Press, 1985), p. 168. See also James G. Carrier, "Gifts in a World of Commodities: The Ideology of the Perfect Gift in American Society," *Social Analysis* 29 (December 1990): 19–37. On how goods acquire symbolic meanings, see Mihaly Csikszentmihalyi and Eugene Rochberg-Halton, *The Meaning of Things* (Cambridge: Cambridge University Press, 1981), pp. 65–91; and Igor Kopytoff, "The Cultural Biography of Things: Commoditization as Process," in Arjun Appadurai, ed., *Social Life of Things: Commodities in Cultural Perspective* (Cambridge: Cambridge University Press, 1988), pp. 77–90.

28. Eugene Rochberg-Halton, *Meaning and Modernity* (Chicago: University of Chicago Press, 1986), p. 176.

29. Leigh Eric Schmidt, "Practices of Exchange: From Market Culture to Gift Economy in the Interpretation of American Religion," in David D. Hall, ed., *Lived Religion in America: Toward a History of Practice* (Princeton: Princeton University Press, 1997), pp. 73–74.

30. Schmidt, "Practices of Exchange," pp. 69–91; David Cheal, *The Gift Economy* (New York: Routledge, 1988).

31. Leigh Eric Schmidt notes that "gifts and visits thus served as interrelated vehicles of attachment, affection, and exchange." Schmidt, "Practices of Exchange," p. 80.

32. David Kertzer, *Ritual, Politics, and Power* (New Haven: Yale University Press, 1988); Barry Schwartz, "Mourning and the Making of a Sacred Symbol: Durkheim and the Lincoln Assassination," *Social Forces* 70 (December 1991): 343–364.

33. Ramona Faith Oswald, "Gay, Lesbian, and Bisexual People's Experiences at

Family Weddings: An Exploration of Heterosexism" (Ph.D. diss., University of Minnesota, 1998).

34. For this point in relation to ethnic traditions, see Kathleen Neils Conzen, David A. Gerber, Ewa Morawska, George E. Pozzetta, and Rudolph J. Vecoli, "The Invention of Ethnicity: A Perspective from the U.S.A.," *Journal of American Ethnic History* 12 (Fall 1972): 5.

35. Gillis, *A World of Their Own Making*, pp. 225–240.

2. Family, Feast, and Football

1. *Washington Post*, November 26, 1981, p. A-1.

2. As secular national holidays, July Fourth and Thanksgiving have much in common. Yet July Fourth never became a time for family homecoming. The day-long family picnic was one of many activities on the Fourth, but never the rationale for the day or the central focus of festivities. Most of the organizers and sponsors of early July Fourth celebrations, beginning in the 1790s, saw the holiday as a public one, with occasional additional private celebrations. These originally were all-male dinners for politicians or the militia. Even in the nineteenth century, civic leaders, who organized the public events for the holiday, saw the Fourth as a public celebration. Antebellum women writers, such as Sarah Hale, never challenged this view. Len Travers, *Celebrating the Fourth: Independence Day and the Rites of Nationalism in the Early Republic* (Amherst: University of Massachusetts Press, 1997).

3. Robert Bellah, "Civil Religion in America," in Robert Bellah, ed., *Beyond Belief: Essays on Religion in a Post-Traditional World* (New York: Harper and Row, 1970), pp. 168–192.

4. Thanksgiving finished a distant second to Christmas in a holiday popularity poll in 1989. A whopping 72 percent of Americans considered Christmas their favorite holiday; only 8 percent gave Thanksgiving their vote. Roper Center for Public Opinion, Princeton Survey Research Associates, Great American TV poll no. 5 (December 4, 1989). Dialog, File 468. Public Opinion Online, Storrs, Connecticut.

5. Sarah Josepha Hale, *Northwood; or Life North and South* (New York: H. Long and Brother, 1852), p. 91.

6. Caroline Howard King, *When I Lived in Salem, 1822–1866* (Brattleboro, Vt.: Stephen Day Press, 1937), p. 108.

7. Sally F. Moore and Barbara G. Myerhoff, "Introduction: Secular Ritual: Forms and Meanings," in Sally F. Moore and Barbara G. Myerhoff, eds., *Secular Ritual* (Amsterdam: Van Gorcum, 1977), p. 24.

8. Nell Irving Painter, *Sojourner Truth: A Life, A Symbol* (New York: W. W. Norton, 1996), pp. 182–183.

9. Hale, *Northwood*, p. 90; diary of Almira McDonald, November 30, 1882, Strong Museum, Rochester, New York; Susan Williams, *Savory Suppers and Fashionable Feasts: Dining in Victorian America* (New York: Pantheon, 1985), pp. 196–201, 239–241.

10. Jeanne Boydston, *Home and Work: Housework, Wages, and the Ideology of Labor in the Early Republic* (New York: Oxford University Press, 1991), chaps. 6 and 7.

11. An excellent introduction to women's holiday preparations as a form of women's unpaid work is Micaela di Leonardo, "The Female World of Cards and Holidays: Women, Families, and the Work of Kinship," *Signs* 12 (Spring 1987): 440–453. See also Carole M. Counihan, "Female Identity, Food, and Power in Contemporary Florence," *Anthropological Quarterly* 61 (April 1988): 51–62.

12. Harriet Beecher Stowe, *Oldtown Folks* (Boston: Fields, Osgood, 1869), p. 338.

13. E. H. Arr, "Thanksgiving Dinners," in Robert Haven Schauffler, ed., *Thanksgiving: Its Origin, Celebration, and Significance as Related in Prose and Verse* (New York: Moffat, Yard, and Co., 1908), pp. 94–95.

14. Jane C. Nylander, *Our Own Snug Fireside: Images of the New England Home, 1760–1860* (New York: Alfred A. Knopf, 1993), p. 279; King, *When I Lived in Salem*, p. 113; Sarah Connell Ayer, *Diary of Sarah Connell Ayer* (Portland: LeFavor Tower Co., 1910), p. 28; Karen V. Hansen, *A Very Social Time: Crafting Community in Antebellum New England* (Berkeley: University of California Press, 1994), pp. 114–136.

15. E. Anthony Rotundo, *American Manhood: Transformations in Masculinity from the Revolution to the Modern Era* (New York: Basic Books, 1993), pp. 4–5.

16. [No author], *Foods That Made New England Famous* (Boston: privately published, 1946), p. 106.

17. Juliana Smith, Diary (1779), as quoted in Schauffler, ed., *Thanksgiving*, p. 141.

18. Anna Fuller, *Pratt Portraits, Sketched in a New England Suburb* (New York: G. P. Putnam's Sons, 1892), pp. 240–241.

19. John R. Gillis, "Ritualization of Middle-Class Family Life in Nineteenth Century Britain," *International Journal of Politics, Culture, and Society* 3 (Winter 1989): 223.

20. Elizabeth Stone, *Black Sheep and Kissing Cousins: How Our Family Stories Shape Us* (New York: Times Books, 1988).

21. Amy J. Kotkin and Steven J. Zeitlin, "In The Family Tradition," in Richard M. Dorson, ed., *Handbook of American Folklore* (Bloomington: Indiana University Press, 1983), p. 93. Kotkin and Zeitlin also found that African Americans were less likely than others to tell "lost fortune" stories about their families, apparently because they were less likely to believe that the rules of the game were fair enough to permit any of them to make a fortune.

22. W. E. B. Du Bois, *The Philadelphia Negro* (New York: Schocken, 1967), p. 196; Jon Gjerde, *The Minds of the West: Patterns of Ethnocultural Evolution in the Rural Middle West, 1830–1917* (Chapel Hill: University of North Carolina Press, 1997), p. 230.

23. On hunting on Thanksgiving, see Eleanor Arnold, ed., *Voices of American Homemakers* (Bloomington: Indiana University Press, 1985), p. 35.

24. Elizabeth Fox-Genovese, *Within the Plantation Household: Black and White Women of the Old South* (Chapel Hill: University of North Carolina Press, 1988), p. 364; Stephen Nissenbaum, *The Battle for Christmas* (New York: Alfred A. Knopf, 1996), p. 271; interview with James August Holmes by Mrs. J. H. Walsh, in George P. Rawick, ed., *The American Slave: A Composite Autobiography,* suppl. ser. 1, vol. 8, Mississippi Narratives, Part 3 (Westport, Conn.: Greenwood Press, 1972), p. 1046; interview with Robert Young by Iris England, in Rawick, ed., *The American Slave: A Composite Autobiography,* suppl. ser. 1, vol. 10, Mississippi Narratives, Part 5 (Westport, Conn.: Greenwood Press, 1977), p. 2409; Gjerde, *Minds of the West,* p. 230.

25. Holly Garrison, *The Thanksgiving Cookbook* (New York: Macmillan, 1991), p. 207; Harpo Marx with Rowland Barber, *Harpo Speaks* (New York: B. Geis Associates, 1961), pp. 27–28. For the practice by Brooklyn Democratic politicians in the 1930s, see Shirley Chisholm, *Unbought and Unbossed* (Boston: Houghton Mifflin, 1970), p. 50. Immigrants who were not politicians also left turkeys on the doorsteps of needy families. Theresa F. Bucchieri, *Feasting with Nonna Serafina* (New York: South Brunswick Press, 1966), p. 125.

26. For varying political uses of this song, see Robert James Branham, "'Of Thee I Sing': Contesting 'America,'" *American Quarterly* 48 (December 1996): 623–652.

27. Michael Kammen, *Mystic Chords of Memory: The Transformation of Tradition in American Culture* (New York: Vintage Books, 1991), pp. 206–211.

28. W. DeLoss Love, Jr., *The Fast and Thanksgiving Days of New England* (Boston: Houghton Mifflin, 1895), p. 429.

29. Clarice Whittenburg, "Holiday Observance in the Primary Grades," *Elementary School Journal* 35 (October 1934): 193–195.

30. Ronald Sanders, *Reflections of a Teapot* (New York: Harper and Row, 1972), p. 132. See also Stephan F. Brumberg, *Going to America, Going to School: The Jewish Immigrant Public School Encounter in Turn-of-the-Century New York City* (New York: Praeger, 1986), p. 126. Segregated black schools in the South also had Thanksgiving programs, and Booker T. Washington encouraged them at Tuskegee as well. For an example of the Thanksgiving program in a segregated black Southern school, see Chris Mayfield, ed., *Growing Up Southern: Southern Exposure Looks at Childhood, Then and Now* (New York: Pantheon Books, 1972), p. 24.

31. Marion S. Blaisdell, "Thanksgiving in the Past and Present," in Schauffler, ed., *Thanksgiving,* pp. 221–265; and Dorothy Canfield Fisher, "A New Pioneer," in Wilhelmina Harper, ed., *Stories of Thanksgiving Yesterday and Today* (New York: E. P. Dutton, 1938), p. 186; Whittenburg, "Holiday Observance in the Primary Grades," pp. 199–237.

32. Angelo Pellegrini, *American Dream: An Immigrant's Quest* (San Francisco: North Point Press, 1986), p. 21.
33. Jeff Kisseloff, *You Must Remember This: An Oral History of Manhattan from the 1890s to World War II* (New York: Schocken Books, 1989), p. 499.
34. For an example of immigrants who were eager to embrace Thanksgiving, see T. T. Nhu, "Crab-and-Guilt for Thanksgiving Dinner," in De Tran, Andrew Lam, and Hai Dai Nguyen, eds., *Once Upon a Dream: The Vietnamese-American Experience* (Kansas City, Mo.: Andrews and McMell, 1995), p. 90.
35. One anthropological study of Taiwanese immigrants in Flushing, New York, in the 1970s found that professionals (accountants, lawyers, scientists, and so forth) and the well-educated celebrated Thanksgiving, but waiters, factory workers, and store clerks did not. Among Taiwanese newcomers noncelebrants viewed Thanksgiving as an American holiday that had nothing to do with them. Instead they transformed the holiday with gambling, a Chinese way to celebrate a special day. Hsiang-shu Chin, *Chinatown No More: Taiwan Immigrants in Contemporary New York* (Ithaca: Cornell University Press, 1992), pp. 83, 84.
36. Pearl Kazin, "We Gather Together," *New Yorker* 31 (November 26, 1955): 51–56. But Orthodox Jewish synagogues held special services on Thanksgiving, at which a prominent Gentile was often invited to speak. Moreover, Shonie B. Levi and Sylvia R. Kaplan included a section on Thanksgiving in their *Guide for the Jewish Homemaker* in 1959. They described it as a holiday that "all the American people have taken to their hearts" and mentioned that synagogues joined with churches in holding Thanksgiving services. Levi and Kaplan did not look favorably on the celebration of Halloween and St. Valentine's Day, because these holidays, they contended, had their origins as saints' days. Shonie B. Levi and Sylvia R. Kaplan, *Guide for the Jewish Homemaker* (New York: Schocken Books, 1959), p. 150; Jenna Weissman Joselit, *New York's Jewish Jews: The Orthodox Community in the Interwar Years* (Bloomington: Indiana University Press, 1990), p. 44.
37. Pardee Lowe, *Father and Glorious Descendant* (Boston: Little, Brown and Co., 1943), p. 66.
38. Gloria Braggiotti, *Born in a Crowd* (New York: Thomas Crowell Co., 1957), p. 237.
39. Richard White, *Remembering Ahanagran: Storytelling in a Family's Past* (New York: Hill and Wang, 1998), p. 188; Ken Hom, *Easy Family Recipes from a Chinese-American Childhood* (New York: Alfred A. Knopf, 1997), p. 146.
40. Swedes were the exception in that they did not serve Swedish side dishes at the Thanksgiving meal. See Phebe Fjellstrom, *Swedish-American Colonization in the San Joaquin Valley in California: A Study of the Acculturation and Assimilation of an Immigrant Group* (Upssala: Almqvuist and Wiksells

Boktryckeri AB, 1970), p. 125. For examples of the cultural and culinary melting pot, see Silvio Torres Saillant, ed., *Hispanic Immigrant Writers and the Family* (Jackson Heights, N.Y.: Ollantay Press, 1989), p. 39; Ruth Horowitz, *Honor and the American Dream: Culture and Identity in the Chicano Community* (New Brunswick, N.J.: Rutgers University Press, 1983), p. 58; unpublished interview, Carole Holmes, February 4, 1977, Smithsonian Family Life Folklore Collection; unpublished interview, Mary Louise Ortenzo, Smithsonian Family Life Folklore Collection, June 20, 1976; Arlene and Howard Eisenberg, "Thanksgiving with a Lebanese Flavor," *Good Housekeeping* 178 (November 1971): 84, 86, 88, 93; Raj Mehta and Russell W. Belk, "Artifacts, Identity, and Transition: Favorite Possessions of Indians and Indian Immigrants to the United States," *Journal of Consumer Research* 17 (March 1991): 398–411.

41. W. D. Howells, *Through the Eye of the Needle* (New York: Harper and Brothers, 1901), p. 9.

42. Jack Santino, *All Around the Year: Holidays and Celebrations in American Life* (Urbana: University of Illinois Press, 1994), pp. 164–167; Robert J. Meyers, *Celebrations: The Complete Book of American Holidays* (Garden City, N.Y.: Doubleday and Co., 1972), pp. 114–115.

43. Mike Beno, *When Families Made Memories Together* (Greendale, Wisc.: Reiman Publications, 1994), p. 157; Alfred L. Shoemaker, "Fantasticals," *Pennsylvania Dutchman* 4 (1953): 16. Al Smith wrote that in his childhood a fancy dress ball was held several days after the parade. Alfred E. Smith, *Up to Now: An Autobiography* (New York: Viking Press, 1929), p. 30.

44. Smith, *Up to Now*, p. 30.

45. *New York Times,* November 27, 1885, p. 18; *New York Times,* November 29, 1895, p. 4.

46. George Chauncey, *Gay New York: Gender, Urban Culture, and the Making of the Gay Male World, 1890–1940* (New York: Basic Books, 1994), p. 294; Alfred L. Shoemaker, "Fantasticals," *Pennsylvania Folklife* 9 (Winter 1957–58): 28–31. William R. Leach argues that the Macy's Thanksgiving parade was the commercial inheritor of the Fantastic and ragamuffin parades because the two events occurred on the same days. Moreover, as Leach shows, the department store parade was copied from circus parades. Department stores had been staging small-scale parades since around 1900. By World War I they were holding them to welcome home the troops. Child welfare agencies organized alternative activities to begging. Store executives at Macy's were not interested in such matters, and instead were preoccupied with making their event a "Christmas parade." Finally, it is true that the tradition of ragamuffin begging was disappearing gradually. However, even after Macy's first parade in 1924, child begging continued on a small scale for about fifteen years. William R. Leach, *Land of Desire: Merchants, Power, and the Rise of a New American Culture* (New York: Pantheon Books, 1993), pp. 331–336.

47. *New York Times,* November 25, 1938, p. 7.
48. King, *Salem,* p. 111.
49. *New York Times,* November 22, 1930, p. 17.
50. Howells, *Through the Eye of the Needle,* p. 49.
51. Tad Tuleja, "Trick or Treat: Pre-Texts and Contests," in Jack Santino, ed., *Halloween and Other Festivals of Death and Life* (Knoxville: University of Tennessee Press, 1994), pp. 82–104. Tuleja argues that Thanksgiving begging was only one of several origins of trick-or-treating.
52. Mikhail M. Bakhtin, *Rabelais and His World* (Cambridge: M.I.T. Press, 1968), p. 7.
53. Marjorie Garber, *Vested Interests: Cross-Dressing and Cultural Anxiety* (New York: Routledge, 1992), p. 10.
54. Stephen Nissenbaum, *The Battle for Christmas* (New York: Alfred A. Knopf, 1996), p. 153.
55. *Saturday Evening Post* 204 (November 28, 1931), pp. 42–43.
56. Leach, *Land of Desire,* pp. 331–336.
57. Ibid., p. 336.
58. Louis Carlat, "'A Cleanser for the Mind': Marketing Radio Receivers for the American Home, 1922–1932," in Roger Horowitz and Arwen Mohun, eds., *His and Hers: Gender, Consumption, and Technology* (Charlottesville: University Press of Virginia, 1998), pp. 115–137.
59. S. W. Pope summarizes the various claims made on behalf of football in S. W. Pope, *Patriotic Games: Sporting Traditions in the American Imagination, 1876–1926* (New York: Oxford University Press, 1997), pp. 85–100; Rotundo, *American Manhood,* p. 241.
60. Barre Toelken, *The Dynamics of Folklore* (Boston: Houghton Mifflin, 1979), pp. 132–135.
61. Michael Messner, *Power at Play: Sports and the Problem of Masculinity* (Boston: Beacon Press, 1992), pp. 168–170. The high ratings of televised football on Thanksgiving are reported in "Thanksgiving Ratings Are Consistently High," *Atlanta Journal Constitution,* November 22, 1990, G2.
62. Stuart Murray and Norman J. McCabe, *Rockwell's Four Freedoms* (Sturbridge, Mass.: Berkshire House, 1993), p. 50.
63. Bob Morris criticized models at a Thanksgiving shoot for *Ladies' Home Journal* who posed as an ideal family when they were not actually married and did not live together. "A Model Family," *New York Times Magazine,* November 12, 1995, Sec. 6, p. 93.
64. Roger Abrahams, "The Language of Festivals: Celebrating the Economy," in Victor Turner, ed., *Celebration: Studies in Festivity and Ritual* (Washington, D.C.: Smithsonian Press, 1982), p. 176.
65. Julia Hirsch, *Family Photographs: Content, Meaning, and Effect* (New York: Oxford University Press, 1981), p. 28; Robert Westbrook, "Fighting for the American Family: Private Interests and Political Obligations in World War II," in Richard Wightman Fox and T. Jackson Lears, eds., *The Power of Cul-*

ture: Critical Essays in American History (Chicago: University of Chicago Press, 1993), pp. 195–201.

66. *New York Times,* March 12, 1995, p. 37.

67. Janet Siskind, "The Invention of Thanksgiving: A Ritual of American Nationality," *Critique of Anthropology* 12 (1992): 187.

68. Vine Deloria, Jr., *Custer Died for Your Sins: An Indian Manifesto* (New York: Macmillan, 1969), p. 2. Sunny Nash, *Bigmama Didn't Shop at Woolworth's* (College Station: Texas A&M University Press, 1996), p. 100. For an example of the critique that Thanksgiving is ethnocentric and fails to take into account the Indians' loss of culture and land, see Fayth M. Parks, "Transforming Thanksgiving: A Harvest of Cultures," *The Octopus,* November 29, 1996, pp. 6–7.

69. Brent Staples, *Parallel Time: Growing Up Black and White* (New York: Pantheon Books, 1994), p. 226.

70. Gray is quoted in Jane Howard, *Families* (New York: Simon and Schuster, 1978), p. 23. Nostalgia could operate in reverse in the 1990s. The present was now better than the past because families in the 1950s had been hypocritical. For an example of popular discourse that contrasts the false Thanksgiving of one's childhood with the true family in one's adulthood, see "Counting Our Blessings," *Boston Globe,* November 25, 1993, pp. A57, A58.

71. "Thanksgiving Rituals," *Chicago Tribune Magazine,* November 22, 1987, p. 11.

72. Loretta Lynn, *Coal Miner's Daughter* (Chicago: Henry Regnery, 1976), p. 42.

73. Ruth Baetz, *Lesbian Crossroads* (Tallahassee, Fla.: Naiad Press, 1988), pp. 90–91.

74. Stephen J. Whitfield, "Making Fragmentation Familiar: Barry Levinson's *Avalon,*" in Peter Y. Medding, ed., *Coping with Life and Death: Jewish Families in the Twentieth Century* (New York: Oxford University Press, 1998), pp. 49–64. Contemporary discourse about Thanksgiving expresses conflict, anger, and loneliness. Now the prodigal is rejected at the front door. In the film *Nobody's Fool* (1994) a divorced father who shows up for the feast on Thanksgiving never sits down to eat with his ex-wife. In *Scent of a Woman* (1992) a blind veteran, seeking a rapprochement with his brother, at least manages to take a few bites before a violent argument breaks out, forcing him to leave. *Home for the Holidays* (1995) adds the crazy aunt, another staple of the Thanksgiving tale, to the story of the lonely prodigal. In this film a recently fired single mother returns home to her parents' house in Baltimore for the holiday. There she finds a married sister who insults and hates her and is homophobic toward her gay brother, and an overbearing and hostile mother. After surviving her family homecoming, the woman returns home to her daughter in Chicago and finds romantic love. The film thus reverses the stories of love found at Thanksgiving in *Godey's Lady's Book.*

75. Garrison, *Thanksgiving Cookbook,* p. 212.
76. Melanie Wallendorf and Eric J. Arnould, "'We Gather Together': Consumption Rituals of Thanksgiving Day," *Journal of Consumer Research* 18 (June 1991): 25.
77. *Wall Street Journal,* November 23, 1993, pp. B1, B10; November 15, 1995, p. B1.
78. Ibid., November 15, 1995, p. B1.
79. Richard Gibson, "Company Cafeterias Create Dinners to Go," *Wall Street Journal* (January 13, 1999), pp. B1, B4.
80. Marilyn Kluger, *Country Kitchens Remembered: A Memoir with Favorite Family Recipes* (New York: Dodd, Mead, and Company, 1986), p. 142.
81. *Wall Street Journal,* November 23, 1993, pp. B1, B10.
82. These callers may have been people who rarely cooked and simply reheated food in a microwave oven. One suspects that these uninformed callers were mainly young people who were living away from home for the first time. (Proving that technology is compatible with, not alien to, ritual, Swift's established a Butterball web site in 1996 that offered advice on roasting a turkey. *Chicago Tribune,* December 2, 1996, Sec. 4, 3.)
83. *Wall Street Journal,* November 22, 1992, p. A1. (Of course, this mother was not the only one who knew this trick—I have done it myself.)
84. Wallendorf and Arnould, "We Gather Together," p. 27.
85. Rotundo, *American Manhood,* p. 24.

3. Holiday Blues and Pfeffernusse

1. The major scholarly studies of Christmas in America are Stephen Nissenbaum, *The Battle for Christmas* (New York: Knopf, 1996); Penne L. Restad, *Christmas in America: A History* (New York: Oxford University Press, 1995); William B. Waits, *The Modern Christmas in America: A Cultural History of Gift Giving* (New York: New York University Press, 1993), and Leigh Eric Schmidt, *Consumer Rites: The Buying and Selling of American Holidays* (Princeton: Princeton University Press, 1996), pp. 105–191. Restad, Nissenbaum, and Schmidt emphasize the history of Christmas in the nineteenth-century United States. An earlier scholarly study of Christmas is James H. Barnett, *The American Christmas: A Study in National Culture* (New York: Macmillan, 1954).
2. William Frances Dawson, *Christmas: Its Origins and Associations* (London: E. Stock, 1902), p. 22; J. M. Golby and A. W. Purdue, *The Making of the Modern Christmas* (Athens: University of Georgia Press, 1986), p. 24.
3. Golby and Purdue, *Modern Christmas,* pp. 26, 28; Reginald Nettel, *Christmas and Its Carols* (London: Faith Press, 1960).
4. Allen H. Moore, *Mustard Planters and Printer's Ink: A Kaleidoscope of a Country Doctor's Observations about People, Places, and Things* (New York: Exposition Press, 1959), p. 56.
5. On the "safety valve" interpretation of ritual, see Max Gluckman, *Politics,*

Law, and Ritual in Tribal Society (Oxford: Oxford University Press, 1965), chap. 6; Victor W. Turner, *The Ritual Process: Structure and Anti-Structure* (Chicago· Aldine, 1969), chap. 5; Peter Burke, *Popular Culture in Early Modern Europe* (New York: New York University Press, 1978), pp. 199–204; Melvin Firestone, "Christmas Mumming and Symbolic Interactionism," *Ethos* 6 (Summer 1978): 92–113.

6. The law was repealed in 1681. Barnett, *American Christmas,* p. 3; Ivor Debenham Spencer, "Christmas the Upstart," *New England Quarterly* 8 (December 1935): 498; Philip Snyder, *December 25th: The Joys of Christmas Past* (New York: Dodd, Mead and Co., 1985); Schmidt, *Consumer Rites,* p. 176; Nissenbaum, *Battle for Christmas,* p. 4.

7. Golby and Purdue, *Modern Christmas,* p. 35.

8. Schmidt, *Consumer Rites,* p. 122; Nissenbaum, *Battle for Christmas,* pp. 42–48; Alfred Shoemaker, *Christmas in Pennsylvania* (New York: Houghton Mifflin, 1890), p. 8; Jack Larkin, *The Reshaping of Everyday Life, 1790–1840* (New York: Harper and Row, 1988), p. 282; Lucy Larcom, *A New England Girlhood* (Boston: Houghton Mifflin, 1889), p. 99; Barnett, *American Christmas,* p. 2; Abram English Brown, "The Ups and Downs of Christmas in New England," *New England Magazine* 29 (December 1903): 479–484; Restad, *Christmas in America,* p. 25; Barbara Miller Solomon, *Ancestors and Immigrants: A Changing New England Tradition* (Chicago: University of Chicago Press, 1956), p. 45.

9. Philip Snyder, *The Joys of Christmas Past* (New York: Dodd, Mead, and Co., 1985); Golby and Purdue, *Modern Christmas.* Alfred Shoemaker argues that the hanging of Christmas stockings was not a Pennsylvania Dutch custom, as is commonly believed. See his *Christmas in Pennsylvania,* p. 7.

10. For a more detailed record of the literary and social influences on Moore, including the lithograph of Saint Nicholas commissioned by John Pintard and several other poems about Saint Nicholas prior to Moore's, see Stephen Nissenbaum, "Revisiting 'A Visit from St. Nicholas': The Battle for Christmas in Early Nineteenth-Century America," in James Gilbert, Amy Gilman, Donald M. Scott, and Joan W. Scott, eds., *The Mythmaking Frame of Mind: Social Image and American Culture* (Belmont, Calif.: Wadsworth Publishing, 1993), pp. 25–69.

11. Shoemaker, *Christmas in Pennsylvania,* p. 53; Herman Bokum, ed., *The Stranger's Gift: A Christmas and New Year's Present* (Boston: Light and Horton, 1836); Nissenbaum, *Battle for Christmas,* pp. 195–198; Restad, *Christmas in America,* pp. 58–65, 111–112.

12. Gavin Weightman and Steve Humphries, *Christmas Past* (London: Sidgwick and Jackson, 1987), p. 84.

13. Restad, *Christmas in America,* p. 40; Susan G. Davis, *Parades and Power: Street Theatre in Nineteenth-Century Philadelphia* (Philadelphia: Temple University Press, 1986), pp. 105–107; Nissenbaum, *Battle for Christmas,* pp. 27–28.

14. Snyder, *December 25th,* pp. 43–55, 189, 272; "Old Time Holidays," *Foxfire*

7 (Winter 1973): 326–338; Shoemaker, *Christmas in Pennsylvania*, pp. 112–113.

15. Rudi Laermans, "Learning to Consume: Early Department Stores and the Shaping of the Modern Consumer Culture (1860–1914)," *Theory, Culture, and Society* 10 (1993): 79–102.

16. Waits, *Modern Christmas in America*, p. 73.

17. Schmidt, *Consumer Rites*, p. 152.

18. Margaret Deland, "Save Christmas!" *Harper's Bazaar* 46 (December 1912): 593; Jennifer Scanlon, *Inarticulate Longings: The Ladies' Home Journal, Gender, and the Promises of Consumer Culture* (New York: Routledge, 1995), pp. 2–5.

19. Waits, *Modern Christmas in America*, p. 227. Children were also urged to earn some of the money they spent on Christmas presents. Viviana Zelizer, *The Social Meaning of Money: Pin Money, Paychecks, Poor Relief and Other Currencies* (New York: Basic Books, 1994), p. 87.

20. Penne L. Restad gives an alternative explanation, that the box was a container in the church to collect money to pay for special Christmas masses. *Christmas in America*, p. 176.

21. Nissenbaum, *Battle for Christmas*, p. 111.

22. Schmidt, *Consumer Rites*, pp. 108–122.

23. Sociologist Theodore Caplow argued that people gave Christmas gifts to cement relationships in the family and between friends who were becoming distant. In his view, gift giving helps soothe anxieties about the fragility of the family life he observed in the 1970s. One could make the same claim about the Victorians, since their family ties were often cut short by the high death rate of children and of women in childbirth. Yet family relationships suffered from the same risks of mortality in colonial times, when few gifts other than food or drink were given. Moreover, the truly insecure relations were those of kin who had moved away from home, who may not have received any gifts at all. If anything, the antebellum middle class believed that the family was threatened by the immorality of commercial and public life. It might seem then that the major way to stabilize the family would be to give no gifts at all, or at least to give homemade ones, since such gifts would be unsullied by the marketplace. Theodore Caplow, "Christmas Gifts and Kin Networks," *American Sociological Review* 47 (June 1982): 242–245. For criticism of Caplow, see David Cheal, "Ritualization of Family Ties," *American Behavioral Scientist* 31 (July–August 1988): 633–643.

24. Quoted in Nissenbaum, *Battle for Christmas*, pp. 147, 161. For similar views, see Mrs. H. Bloomfield Moore, *Sensible Etiquette of the Best Society, Customs, Manners, Morals, and Home Culture* (Philadelphia: Porter and Coates, 1878), p. 393.

25. David Cheal, "'Showing Them You Love Them': Gift Giving and the Dialectic of Intimacy," *Sociological Review* 35 (1987): 150–169.

26. Gifts of religious and secular books were not gender coded. In the mid-nine-

teenth century boys played with dolls, for example, and presumably received them as presents as well. William Waits argues that gender differentiation became much stronger in the 1890s because of the cult of manliness prevalent then. As a result, many boys were often given a rifle, a symbol of masculinity, as a Christmas present. Waits, *Modern Christmas in America*, pp. 133–140.

27. As David Cheal notes, such unequal gift giving is a "means of symbolic control; it reaffirms the system of sexual stratification in the family and the dependence of women upon men." David Cheal, *The Gift Economy* (London: Routledge, 1988), p. 109; Gregory J. Moschetti, "The Christmas Potlatch: A Refinement on the Sociological Interpretation of Gift Exchange," *Sociological Focus* 12 (January 1979): 1–7.

28. Shoemaker, *Christmas in Pennsylvania*, p. 60; Katherine Lambert Richards, *How Christmas Came to the Sunday-Schools: The Observance of Christmas in the Protestant Church Schools of the United States* (New York: Dodd, Mead, 1934), p. 195; Elizabeth Silverthorne, *Christmas in Texas* (College Station: Texas A&M University Press, 1990), p. 17.

29. Golby and Purdue, *Modern Christmas*, p. 104; Albert J. Menendez, *Christmas in the White House* (Philadelphia: Westminster Press, 1983), p. 40.

30. Richard M. Dorson, *Folklore and Fakelore: Essays toward a Discipline of Folk Studies* (Cambridge: Harvard University Press, 1976), p. 5; Richard M. Dorson, *American Folklore* (Chicago: University of Chicago Press, 1959), p. 4; Richard M. Dorson, *American Folklore and the Historian* (Chicago: University of Chicago Press, 1971), pp. 3–14.

31. Barnett, *American Christmas*, pp. 108–114.

32. Ibid., p. 114.

33. For an analysis of Christmas films and television specials, see Russell W. Belk, "Materialism and the Modern U.S. Christmas," in Elizabeth C. Hirschman, ed., *Interpretive Consumer Research* (Provo, Utah: Association for Consumer Research, 1989), pp. 115–135.

34. The occasional Christmas scene in a film, such as in King Vidor's *The Crowd* (1928), showed relatives fighting on Christmas Day.

35. Elizabeth C. Hirschman and Priscilla A. LaBarbera, "The Meaning of Christmas," in Hirschman, ed., *Interpretive Consumer Research*, p. 123; Cynthia Crossen, "Does 'Deck the Halls' Make You Want to Deck Someone?" *Wall Street Journal*, December 19, 1997, pp. A1, A10.

36. Jane Addams, *Twenty Years at Hull-House* (New York, 1910; New York: New American Library, 1960), p. 180.

37. John Francis Maguire, *The Irish in America* (New York: D. and J. Sadlier, 1868), p. 317.

38. Zelizer, *Social Meaning of Money*, pp. 76, 110, 117.

39. "Special Consumer Survey Report," unpublished report, The Conference Board, December 1997. See also Cheal, *Gift Economy*, pp. 176–177; Thesia I. Garner and Janet Wagner, "Economic Dimensions of Household Gift Giving," *Journal of Consumer Research* 18 (December 1991): 368–379;

Eileen Fischer and Stephen J. Arnold, "More than a Labor of Love: Gender Roles and Christmas Gift Shopping," *Journal of Consumer Research* 17 (December 1990): 333–343.

40. James T. Patterson, *America's Struggle against Poverty, 1900–1980* (Cambridge: Harvard University Press, 1981), pp. 16, 39; Stanley Lebergott, *Pursuing Happiness: American Consumers in the Twentieth Century* (Princeton, N.J.: Princeton University Press, 1993), p. 101.

41. Carl T. Rowan, *Breaking Barriers: A Memoir* (Boston: Little, Brown and Co., 1991), p. 14. See also Mrs. Medgar Evers, "Black Christmas," *Ladies' Home Journal* 85 (December 1968): 83–84.

42. Rowan, *Breaking Barriers,* p. 14.

43. Henry Louis Gates, Jr., "An Amos 'n' Andy 'Christmas,'" *New York Times,* December 23, 1994, p. A35; Melvin Patrick Ely, *The Adventures of Amos 'n' Andy: A Social History of an American Phenomenon* (New York: The Free Press, 1991), pp. 237–238; Dave Marsh and Steve Propers, *Merry Christmas, Baby: Holiday Music from Bing to Sting* (Boston: Little, Brown and Co., 1993), p. 9. For black children who saw Santa as black, see Beverly Daniel Tatum, *Assimilation Blues: Black Families in a White Community* (Northampton, Mass.: Hazel-Maxwell Publishing, 1987), pp. 82–83.

44. *Time* 88 (December 23, 1966): 44.

45. Samuelson did not find as much of an increase in *Ladies' Home Journal.* There were several reasons for this difference. Edward Bok, the *Journal*'s founder, had editorialized against excessive spending at the holiday and favored giving presents only to children. Bok was also sympathetic to the excessive demands on women shoppers (and women salesgirls) at holiday time. By the 1960s, however, the *Journal* lagged behind other magazines in diagnosing the ills of the American family and taking seriously women's liberation. The editors, concerned about the financial status of the magazine, were afraid of alienating more conservative readers by appearing to be too feminist. After a feminist sit-in at the editor's offices, the magazine began to include more articles critical of the family and sympathetic to women's discontent. Susan Camille Samuelson, "The Festive Malaise and Festival Participation: A Case Study of Christmas Celebrations in America" (Ph.D. diss., University of Pennsylvania, 1983), pp. 184–187.

46. Ibid., p. 126.

47. Richard Sterba, "On Christmas," *Psychoanalytic Quarterly* 13 (1944): 79–83; L. Broyce Boyer, "Christmas 'Neurosis,'" *Journal of American Psychoanalytic Association* 3 (1955): 467–488; James Cattell, "The Holiday Syndrome," *Psychoanalytic Review* 42 (1955): 39–43.

48. Jule Eisenbud, "Negative Reactions to Christmas," *Psychoanalytic Quarterly* 10 (1941): 639–645.

49. Edwin Diamond, "Singing the Christmas Holiday Blues," *New York Times Magazine,* December 17, 1961, pp. 32–33. The rowdy Christmas was a time of sexual license, the 1960s version a season of sexual frustration. Psychia-

trists Diamond interviewed claimed that women, exhausted from shopping and doing holiday errands, were not in the mood for sex. It was also more difficult for a couple to find time alone because during the Christmas vacation children were home from school.

50. Subsequent articles about holiday blues claimed that suicide attempts were more common during Christmas. Amitai Etzioni, "Christmas Blues," *Psychology Today* 10 (December 1976): 23. David P. Phillips studied official death statistics for 1973 to 1979. He found suicide rates to be low at Memorial Day and Thanksgiving. As to whether people postponed dying until after they celebrated Christmas, the evidence was mixed. David P. Phillips, "A Drop in Suicides around Major National Holidays," *Suicide and Life Threatening Behavior* 17 (Spring 1987): 1–12. For the view that suicides decrease at holiday time, see Albert A. Harrison and Neal E. A. Kroll, "Variations in Death Rates in the Proximity of Christmas: An Opponent Process Interpretation," *Omega* 16 (1985–1986): 181–192; and Friedrich V. Wenz, "Seasonal Suicide Attempts and Forms of Loneliness," *Psychological Reports* 40 (June 1977): 801–810.

51. *U.S. News and World Report* 87 (December 17, 1979), p. 68; *New York Times*, December 17, 1980, Sec. II, pp. 22–25.

52. Richard Gelles, *The Violent Home: A Study of Physical Aggression between Husbands and Wives* (Beverly Hills: Sage, 1972), pp. 30, 106–107.

53. Maulana Karenga, *The African American Holiday of Kwanzaa: A Celebration of Family, Community, and Culture* (Los Angeles: University of Sankore Press, 1989), pp. 32–34; M. Ron Karenga, *Kwanzaa: Origin, Concepts, Practice* (Inglewood, Calif.: Kawaida Publications, 1977), p. 21; Desda Moss, "A Special celebration," *Ladies' Home Journal* 111 (December 1994): 95.

54. Omonike Weusi-Piryear, "How I Came to Celebrate Kwanzaa," *Essence* 10 (December 1979): 117.

55. Louise Stallard, *The Holiday Cookbook* (New York: Berkeley Books, 1992), p. 127.

56. Mary C. Waters, *Ethnic Options: Choosing Identities in America* (Berkeley: University of California Press, 1990), p. 122.

57. Anne R. Kaplan, Marjorie A. Hoover, and Willard B. Moore, *The Minnesota Ethnic Food Book* (St. Paul: Minnesota Historical Society Press, 1986), p. 12.

58. Robb Walsh, "A Ruthenian Christmas," *Natural History* 105 (December 1996–January 1997): 71.

59. Richard D. Alba, *Ethnic Identity: The Transformation of White America* (New Haven: Yale University Press, 1990), pp. 78–80, 87. The special occasions mentioned most frequently were Christmas, Easter, Thanksgiving, and St. Patrick's Day.

60. H. Arnold Barton, "Cultural Interplay between Sweden and Swedish-America," *Swedish-American Historical Quarterly* 34 (January 1982): 13; Henry

Hanson, "The Vasa Order of America: Its Role in the Swedish-American Community, 1896–1996," *Swedish-American Historical Quarterly* 47 (October 1996): 236–244.

61. The influx of recent immigrants helped to refresh tradition, as did trips to Sweden. A group at the local Lutheran church or travel to Sweden led to the adoption of St. Lucia Day outside Lindsborg. Wishing to pass along the culture of their childhood, Swedish women who were postwar immigrants helped to popularize St. Lucia Day by introducing celebrations at home or in a church or community center.

62. Larry William Danielson, "The Ethnic Festival and Cultural Revivalism in a Small Midwestern Town" (Ph.D. diss., Indiana University, 1972), p. 197.

63. Jews are only one of several American groups who have religious reasons for not celebrating Christmas. Mennonites and Jehovah's Witnesses do not put Christmas on their religious calendar because the holiday is not mentioned in the Bible. Seventh-Day Adventists hold religious services on Christmas but do not have any family events. Eastern Orthodox Christians celebrate Epiphany rather than Christmas. About five percent of Americans in the 1980s were non-Christian; mostly they were Hindus, Buddhists, Muslims, Jews, and Sikhs. Christmas was not their holiday, but many of these religious groups did in fact practice it. The paucity of historical documents or even contemporary accounts makes it difficult to gauge Hindu, Buddhist, Sikh, and Muslim responses to the American Christmas. In Trinidad Muslims and Hindus join in Christmas celebrations. Hindus in Trinidad justify celebrating Christmas as part of their holiday of Diwali. Some Muslims in contemporary America have Christmas trees in their homes. In the 1930s Japanese Buddhists in Hawaii did not observe Christmas at home, but they exchanged gifts with friends. John F. Embree, *Acculturation among the Japanese of Kona, Hawaii* (Menasha, Wisc.: American Anthropological Association, 1941), pp. 129–130. On Muslim celebrations, see Venetia Newall, "A Muslim Christmas Celebration in London," *Journal of American Folklore* 102 (April–June 1989): 186–190.

64. Jonathan D. Sarna, "The Problem of Christmas and the 'National Faith,'" in Rowland A. Sherrill, ed., *Religion and the Life of the Nation* (Urbana: University of Illinois Press, 1990), pp. 172–174. Sarna described three responses that Jews had to Christmas; I have added a fourth, imitation.

65. On the revival of Jewish interest in Chanukah, see Jenna Weissman Joselit, "'Merry Chanuka': The Changing Holiday Practices of American Jews, 1880–1950," in Jack Wertheimer, ed., *The Uses of Tradition: Jewish Continuity in the Modern Era* (New York: Jewish Theological Seminary of America, 1992), pp. 303–325; James G. Heller, *Isaac M. Wise: His Life, Work, and Thought* (New York: Union of American Hebrew Congregations, 1965), p. 564; Jonathan D. Sarna, "The Problem of Christmas," p. 172. The founder of Reform Judaism, Isaac Mayer Wise, opposed lighting Chanukah candles because the festival was not mentioned in the Bible.

66. *American Israelite,* January 10, 1888, p. 5, as quoted in Kenneth N. White, "American Jewish Responses to Christmas" (ordination thesis, Hebrew Union College–Jewish Institute of Religion, 1982), p. 19.
67. Andrew R. Heinze, *Adapting to Abundance: Jewish Immigrants, Mass Consumption, and the Search for American Identity* (New York: Columbia University Press, 1990), p. 73.
68. *American Israelite,* January 10, 1888, p. 5, as quoted in White, "American Jewish Responses to Christmas," p. 103.
69. Sidney Goldstein, "Profile of American Jewry: Insight from the 1990 National Jewish Population Survey," *American Jewish Year Book 1992* (New York: Jewish Publication Society, 1992), pp. 77–173. See also Bruce Phillips, "Children of Intermarriage: How 'Jewish'?" in Peter Y. Medding, ed., *Coping with Life and Death: Jewish Families in the Twentieth Century* (New York: Oxford University Press, 1998), pp. 94–97. The 1990 survey did not distinguish between Reform, Conservative, and Orthodox Jews. The 1962 survey of Kansas City Jews found that Reform and unaffiliated Jews were much more likely to have a tree than other Jews. Most Kansas City Reform Jews also exchanged gifts at Christmas.
70. Melissa Fay Greene, *The Temple Bombing* (Reading, Mass.: Addison-Wesley, 1996), pp. 102, 121; Leonard Gross, "The Jew and Christmas: To Observe or Not? From a New Generation, a New Answer," *Look* 29 (December 28, 1965): 22–28; Alice Ginnott, "Can a Jewish Child Celebrate Christmas?" *Ladies' Home Journal* 95 (December 1978): 94.
71. *New York Times,* December 21, 1978, Sec. III-1.
72. Letty Cottin Pogebrin, *Deborah, Golda, and Me: Being Female and Jewish in America* (New York: Crown Publishers, 1991), p. 105.

4. Easter Breads and Bunnies

1. John Riley and Marica Staimer, "USA Snapshots," *USA Today,* December 1, 1993, Sec. D1.
2. Gary Putka, "No One Ever Said 'Please Pass Me a Turkey Figurine," *Wall Street Journal,* November 22, 1989, pp. A1, A4; "Where Chocolate Bunnies Come from," *New York Times,* March 22, 1989, pp. C1, C6; *Wall Street Journal,* February 13, 1986, p. 1-1; Amy Sancetta, "Chocolate: A Sure Sign Easter's Here," *Chicago Tribune,* April 3, 1996, Evening p. 7; Peter Steinfels, "Family Holiday Isn't What It Used to Be," *New York Times,* March 23, 1988, pp. C1, C6. But 1990s figures put Mother's Day ahead of Easter in terms of greeting cards sold. Jim Carlton, "Greeting Cards Are Addictive for Some Folks," *Wall Street Journal,* April 14, 1995, p. B1. Sociologists in the 1980s, however, claimed that Easter was the second most commonly celebrated holiday in Muncie, Indiana. Theodore Caplow, Howard M. Bahr, and Bruce A. Chadwick, *All Faithful People: Change and Continuity in Middletown's Religion* (Minneapolis: University of Minnesota Press, 1983), p. 182.

3. Stephen Nissenbaum, *The Battle for Christmas* (New York: Alfred Knopf, 1996), p. ix. In the 1990s newspapers published a few articles about the dual celebrations of Passover and Easter among interfaith families. Pamela Warwick, "Meeting Faith to Faith," *Los Angeles Times,* April 13, 1995, p. E1; Martha Woodham, "Juggling holidays," *Atlanta Constitution,* April 13, 1995, p. B1. Nancy Ross, an illustrator, created the syncretic character of the Matzo Bunny, a folk figure who visited children of interfaith couples. Richard Weizel, "Hippety-hoppity, Matzo Bunny is on her way," *Boston Globe,* April 9, 1995, p. 69.

4. For an exception, see Faye Moskowitz, *Her Face in the Mirror: Jewish Women on Mothers and Daughters* (Boston: Beacon Press, 1994), p. 110.

5. Even Jewish intermarried families in the 1980s rarely went to church on Easter Sunday. Bruce Phillips, "Children of Intermarriage: How 'Jewish'?" Peter Y. Medding, ed., *Coping with Life and Death: Jewish Families in the Twentieth Century* (New York: Oxford University Press, 1998), pp. 97–98.

6. Leigh Eric Schmidt, "The Commercialization of the Calendar: American Holidays and the Culture of Consumption, 1870–1930," *Journal of American History* 78 (December 1991): 915.

7. As American Greeks have become more acculturated, Christmas has become at least as important as Easter. A survey of twenty Hispanic women in the San Francisco Bay area found that eleven thought Christmas the most important holiday, but nine put Easter first. Church-going was as common on Easter as on Christmas. Jeanette Rodriguez, *Our Lady of Guadalupe: Faith and Empowerment among Mexican-American Women* (Austin: University of Texas Press, 1994), pp. 102, 104.

8. Almanacs published in colonial New England, however, noted several feast and fast days, such as Shrove Sunday and Tuesday, Ash Wednesday, and Whitsunday. David Cressy, *Bonfires and Bells: National Memory and the Protestant Calendar in Elizabethan and Stuart England* (London: Weidenfeld and Nicolson, 1989), p. 199.

9. Elizabeth Clarke Kiefer, "Easter Customs of Lancaster County," *Papers of the Lancaster County Historical Society* 52 (1948): 56.

10. Peter Burke, *Popular Culture in Early Modern Europe* (Cambridge: Scolar Press, 1978), p. 190.

11. George William Douglas, *The American Book of Days* (New York: H. Wilson Co., 1948), p. 105.

12. Samuel Kinser, *Carnival, American Style: Mardi Gras at New Orleans and Mobile* (Chicago: University of Chicago Press, 1990), pp. 17–74. For African American influences on the carnival in Mobile, see William D. Piersen, *Black Legacy: America's Hidden Heritage* (Amherst: University of Massachusetts Press, 1993), pp. 121–136. On the celebration in the countryside, see Harry Oster, "Country Mardi Gras," in Richard M. Dorson, *Buying the Wind* (Chicago: University of Chicago Press, 1964), pp. 274–281.

13. George P. Rawick, ed., *The American Slave: A Composite Autobiography,*

Supplement, Series 1, vol. 3, Georgia Narratives, Part 1 (Westport, Conn.: Greenwood Press, 1977), p. 85; vol. 13, Parts 3 and 4, p. 223; Series 2, vol. 4, Texas Narratives, Part 3 (Westport, Conn.: Greenwood Press, 1979), p. 1307; Eugene D. Genovese, *Roll, Jordan, Roll: The World the Slaves Made* (New York: Random House, 1972), p. 576; James Oliver Horton and Lois E. Horton, *In Hope of Liberty: Culture, Community, and Protest among Northern Free Blacks, 1700–1860* (New York: Oxford University Press, 1997), p. 31; Elizabeth Keckley, *Behind the Scenes* (New York: G. W. Carleton and Co., 1868), p. 22.

14. On slave Easters, see Sarah H. Hall, interview with James Bolston, September 10, 1937, in Rawick, *American Slave,* Supplement, Series 1, vol. 3, p. 85; Fred Dibble, interview with Louis Evans, September 13, 1937, in Rawick, *American Slave,* Supplement, Series 2, vol. 4, p. 1307; Hennig Cohen and Tristam Potter Coffin, eds., *The Folklore of American Holidays* (Detroit: Gale Research Co., 1987), p. 137. Black churches, mainly in Louisiana, celebrated "Easter Rock," a joyous, all-night service of prayers, singing, and liberal imbibing of angelica wine. Exactly why this distinctive service was found only in Louisiana is unclear. Lea and Marianna Seale, "Easter Rock: A Louisiana Negro Ceremony," *Journal of American Folklore* 55 (January–June 1942): 212–218.

15. David D. Gilmore, in *Manhood in the Making: Cultural Concepts of Masculinity* (New Haven: Yale University Press, 1900), pp. 30–55, argues that "performative excellence," the idea that deeds spoke for themselves, was central to masculinity.

16. Augustus B. Longstreet, *Georgia Scenes, Characters, Incidents, etc. in the First Half Century of the Republic* (Savannah: Beehive Press, 1992), pp. 124–134; Edward Alfred Pollard, *The Virginia Tourist* (Philadelphia: J. B. Lippincott, 1870), p. 124. For Dutch colonial efforts to prohibit gander pulling, see David Steven Cohen, *The Dutch-American Farm* (New York: New York University Press, 1992), pp. 159–160. In Hispanic California Easter week was celebrated with bullfighting, horse racing, and dancing. William Kelly, *An Excursion to California over the Prairie, Rocky Mountains, and Great Sierra Nevada* (London: Chapman and Hall, 1851), chap. 20; Nancy L. Struna, "Sport and the Awareness of Leisure," in Cary Carson, Ronald Hoffman, and Peter J. Albert, eds., *Of Consuming Interests: The Style of Life in the Eighteenth Century* (Charlottesville: University Press of Virginia, 1994), p. 407. The other Easter Monday sports were cockfights, which pitted the cocks against each other, or cockshailing, in which apprentices or laborers often lashed a cock to a pole and threw rocks, stones, and sticks at it before killing it.

17. Alfred Shoemaker, *Eastertide in Pennsylvania: A Folk Cultural Study* (Kutztown, Pa.: Pennsylvania Folklife Society, 1960), p. 43.

18. Kieffer, "Easter Customs of Lancaster County," 54.

19. Ibid., 45.

20. Ibid.
21. Graham Russell Hodges, *Slavery and Freedom in the Rural North: African Americans in Monmouth County, New Jersey, 1665–1865* (Madison, N.J.: Madison House, 1997), pp. 56–58.
22. A. J. Williams-Myers, "Pinkster Carnival: Africanisms in the Hudson River Valley," *Afro-Americans in New York Life and History* 9 (January 1985): 7–18; David Steven Cohen, "In Search of Carolus Africanus Rex: Afro-Dutch Folklore in New York and New Jersey," *Journal of the Afro-American Historical and Genealogical Society* 5 (Fall–Winter 1984): 149–162; Alice Morse Earle, *Colonial Days in Old New York* (New York: Charles Scribner's Sons, 1896), pp. 188–203; Shane White, *Somewhat More Independent: The End of Slavery in New York City, 1770–1810* (Athens: University of Georgia Press, 1991), pp. 97–106.
23. Guion Griffis Johnson, *Antebellum North Carolina: A Social History* (Chapel Hill: University of North Carolina Press, 1937), p. 180; David Hackett Fischer, *Albion's Seed: Four British Folkways in America* (New York: Oxford University Press, 1989), pp. 363–364, 746; Cressy, *Bonfires and Bells,* p. 19; Horton and Horton, *In Hope of Liberty,* p. 32.
24. Shane White, "'It Was a Proud Day': African Americans, Festivals, and Parades in the North, 1744–1834," *Journal of American History* 81 (June 1994): 13–50.
25. Victoria Newell, *An Egg at Easter: A Folklore Study* (London: Routledge and Kegan Paul, 1971), p. 324.
26. Jennifer M. Russ, *German Festivals and Customs* (London: Oswald Wolff, 1982), p. 51.
27. In Germany the animal who laid the eggs was called a hare, not a rabbit or bunny. Although both are mammals, the hare is slightly larger and has longer ears and hind legs than the rabbit, and its young at birth are born with their eyes open and covered with hair, while the newborn rabbit is not covered with hair and is blind and helpless.
28. Cindy Dell Clark, *Flights of Fancy, Leaps of Faith* (Chicago: University of Chicago Press, 1995), p. 73.
29. Ibid., pp. 54, 55, 58.
30. "The Easter Hare," *Atlantic Monthly* 65 (May 1890), p. 666; Shoemaker, *Eastertide in Pennsylvania,* p. 32.
31. Theodore Caplow and Margaret Holmes Williamson point out that the Easter Bunny is a less interactive magical figure than Santa. He receives no letters—indeed has no speech. They further note that children usually come to the conclusion that it is parents who are hiding the colored eggs several years before they realize that Santa does not shimmy down the chimney to bring them their Christmas presents. "Decoding Middletown's Easter Bunny: A Study in American Iconography," *Semiotica* 32 (1980): 224.
32. Kieffer, "Easter Customs of Lancaster County," p. 57; Judene Divone, *Chocolate Moulds: A History and Encyclopedia* (Oakton, Va.: Oakton Hill Publications, 1987), p. 45.

33. A relatively modern form of Easter candy, the Marshmallow Peep, was invented in the 1950s. These colored replicas of chicks were made out of marshmallow plunged into a bed of dyed sugar. *USA Today,* March 1, 1988, p. D1.

34. Gail Cooper, "Love, War, and Chocolate: Gender and the American Candy Industry, 1880–1930," in Roger Horowitz and Arwen Mohun, eds., *His and Hers: Gender, Consumption, and Technology* (Charlottesville: University Press of Virginia, 1998), pp. 67–74.

35. Leigh Eric Schmidt, *Consumer Rites: The Buying and Selling of American Holidays* (Princeton: Princeton University Press, 1995), p. 195; William S. Walsh, *Curiosities of Popular Customs and of Rites, Ceremonies, Observances, and Miscellaneous Antiquities* (Philadelphia: J. B. Lippincott Co., 1897), p. 364; Shoemaker, *Eastertide,* p. 38.

36. Jane M. Hatch, *The American Book of Days* (New York: H. W. Wilson Co., 1978), p. 308.

37. Schmidt, *Consumer Rites,* p. 217.

38. Steinfels, "Family Holiday."

39. "Easter Flowers," *Harper's New Monthly Magazine* 27 (July 1863): 189–194.

40. Schmidt, "The Commercialization of the Calendar," p. 891.

41. Schmidt, *Consumer Rites,* p. 214; Leigh Eric Schmidt, "The Easter Parade: Piety, Fashion, and Display," *Religion and American Culture: A Journal of Interpretation* 4 (Summer 1994): 150; Ralph M. Hower, *History of Macy's of New York, 1858–1919: Chapters in the Evolution of the Department Store* (Cambridge: Harvard University Press, 1946), p. 170.

42. Mary Helen Ponce, *Hoyt Street: An Autobiography* (Albuquerque: University of New Mexico Press, 1993), p. 145.

43. Daniel Scott Smith, "A Higher Quality of Life for Whom? Mouths to Feed and Clothes to Wear in the Families of Late Nineteenth-Century American Workers," *Journal of Family History* 10 (1994): 30. As late as the 1930s seamstresses were still making Easter dresses. Elaine Latzman Moon, *Untold Tales, Unsung Heroes: An Oral History of Detroit's African American Community, 1918–1967* (Detroit: Wayne State University Press, 1994), p. 293.

There are two explanations for the origin of the custom of new clothes at Easter. One is that it derived from Jewish practice at Passover. The other is that early Christians dressed religious initiates in new white garments to baptize them en masse at Easter.

44. Samuel Pickering, "Easter Sunday: A Reminiscence," *Southwest Review* 70 (Winter 1985): 128.

45. Smith, "A Higher Quality of Life for Whom?" p. 20.

46. Ibid., p. 17; Sarah Booth, "The Finery Things in Life," *Washington Post,* April 1, 1996, p. D2.

47. Karla Pazzi, interview with Julia Pazzi, November 28, 1995; Joan Sherlock, interview with Gertrude Sherlock, November 26, 1975, University of California at Berkeley Folklore Archives, Holiday Lore, Easter, Folder F3;

Charlayne Hunter-Gault, *In My Place* (New York: Farrar, Straus, Giroux, 1992), pp. 54–55; interview with Dorothy Steward Fry (no interviewer mentioned) in Leslie G. Kelen and Eileen Hallet Stone, *Missing Stories: An Oral History of Ethnic and Minority Groups in Utah* (Salt Lake City: University of Utah Press, 1996), p. 79.

48. A.C. to Eleanor Roosevelt, Port Morris, New Jersey, March 20, 1934, Eleanor Roosevelt Papers, Material Assistance Requested Files, FDR Library, Hyde Park, New York.

49. Robert Tomes, *The Bazaar Book of Decorum: The Care of the Person, Manners, Etiquette, and Ceremonials* (New York: Harper and Brothers, 1873), p. 164.

50. Schmidt, *Consumer Rites,* pp. 235–236.

51. Ibid., p. 235.

52. Angelo B. Henderson and Robert McGough, "An Easter Bonnet with Frills upon It Is Decidedly Old Hat," *Wall Street Journal,* April 7, 1998, pp. A1, A6.

53. "Novel Gifts for Easter," *New York Times,* March 28, 1882, p. 2.

54. "Greetings for Easter," *New York Times,* April 5, 1885, p. 14. Gift giving in France at Easter disappeared around World War I. Anne Martin Fugier, "Bourgeois Rituals," in Michelle Perrot, ed., *A History of Private Life,* vol. 4, *From the Fires of Revolution to the Great War* (Cambridge: Harvard University Press, 1990), p. 295.

55. Schmidt, "The Commercialization of the Calendar," p. 905; Francis Weiser, *Handbook of Christian Feasts and Customs: The Year of the Lord in Liturgy and Folklore* (New York: Harcourt, Brace, 1958), p. 236. Another version of the origin of the Easter lily is that Mrs. Thomas Sargent of Philadelphia brought bulbs from Bermuda, and a nurseryman in Philadelphia then popularized the flower. Robert J. Myers, *Celebrations: The Complete Book of American Holidays* (Garden City, N.Y.: Doubleday and Co., 1972), p. 108.

56. Quoted in Schmidt, *Consumer Rites,* pp. 208–209.

57. Ibid., p. 210.

58. Schmidt, "The Commercialization of the Calendar," pp. 895–896.

59. Nada Gray, *Holidays: Victorian Women Celebrate in Pennsylvania* (University Park: Pennsylvania State University, 1983), p. 57; Frances Bransten Rothmann, *The Haas Sisters of Franklin Street: A Look Back with Love* (Berkeley, Calif.: Judah L. Magnes Museum, 1979), p. 12.

60. Throughout France and in the Mediterranean, a feast of lamb at springtime was common even before the early Christians. John F. Baldwin, "Easter," in Mircea Eliade, ed., *The Encyclopedia of Religion,* vol. 4 (New York: Macmillan, 1987), p. 558; "Lamb Dishes of Old World Affirm Tradition," *New York Times,* March 23, 1988, p. C1. On the origin of the belief in Jesus as the lamb of God, see Alan W. Watts, *Easter: Its Story and Meaning* (New York: Schuman, 1950), p. 67.

61. Clarice Whittenburg, "Holiday Observance in the Primary Grades," *Elementary School Journal* 35 (October 1934): 193–204.
62. Easter had to make do by relying on imported literary characters rather than inventing new ones. Whereas Rudolph the Red-Nosed Reindeer was an important new folk figure for Christmas in the 1930s, Easter took its folk figures from children's stories, such as Peter Rabbit or Peter Cottontail. Mother Goose became the rabbit's companion in children's Easter stories.
63. *USA Today,* March 28, 1991, p. D1.
64. Information for 1959 and 1989 came from Gallup polls, as quoted in Steinfels, "Family Holiday," p. C1. The 1994 data can be found in "Religion in America," *American Demographics* 16 (March 1994): 4.
65. Birthdays are the most frequent occasion for restaurant meals, with Mother's Day second. On Easter 16 percent of people eat at restaurants, compared to 10 percent on Thanksgiving, and 6 percent on Christmas. Judith Waldrop, "Here Come the Brides," *American Demographics* 12 (June 1990): 4.
66. Interview with Anonymous (Anon-117), Pauline Golembiewska, Teodozia Malinowski, Frank Broska, Lillian Cwik, Julia Madro, John Gapinski, 1977, Oral History Archives of Chicago Polonia, Chicago Historical Society.
67. Isaac Guzman, "Objects d'egg," *Los Angeles Times,* April 15, 1995, B1.
68. Thomas Burgess, *Greeks in America* (New York: Arno Press, 1970), p. 97.
69. Private communication from Margaret Walsh, April 15, 1997.
70. Interview with [no first name given] MacCurre, 1938–1939, WPA Life Histories Collection, Library of Congress.
71. Theresa F. Bucchier, *Feasting with Nonna Serafina* (New York: South Brunswick Press, 1966), p. 62.
72. There are two other explanations for these customs. Switching, it was claimed, originated as a means of controlling the crowds at Christ's tomb. Another explanation was that the switches represented lashes that Christ received as he carried the cross to his crucifixion. There were other Easter Monday customs as well. One, of English origin, was Easter "lifting." One man or many lifted up girls, who were seated on chairs; the next day the girls took their turn. The lifting was done three times, and the person who was lifted was expected to bestow a kiss on the man who had done the lifting. Watts, *Easter,* p. 116; Newell, *An Egg at Easter,* p. 322.
73. David Steven Cohen, *The Folklore and Folklife of New Jersey* (New Brunswick, N.J.: Rutgers University Press, 1983), p. 206. In Poland the switching was done on Good Friday or Palm Sunday. The two days of switching, first by boys, then by girls, were also sometimes called Dingus-Smigus. M. Mark Stolarik, "Slovak Easter Customs in the United States," *The World and I* 5 (April 1990): 693; Margaret F. Byington, *Homestead: The Households of a Mill Town* (Pittsburgh: University of Pittsburgh Press, 1910), p. 150; Robert Maziarz, "Polish Customs in New York Mills, N.Y.," *New York Folklore Quarterly* 24 (December 1968): 304; Eugene E. Obidinski and Helen Stankiewicz Zand, *Polish Folkways in America* (Lanham, Md.: University

Press of America, 1987), p. 69; Fred L. Holmes, *Old World Wisconsin: Around Europe in the Badger State* (Eau Claire, Wisc.: E. M. Hale and Co., 1944), p. 352; Cohen and Coffin, eds., *The Folklore of American Holidays,* p. 138.

74. Mary C. Waters, *Ethnic Options: Choosing Identities in America* (Berkeley: University of California Press, 1990), pp. 122–123; Janusa Mucha, *Everyday Life and Festivity in a Local Ethnic Community: Polish-Americans in South Bend, Indiana* (New York: Columbia University Press, 1996), pp. 179–182.

75. The numbers were even lower among Polish-American high school students taking a class in Polish at a Buffalo, New York, high school. Obidinksi and Zand, *Polish Folkways in America,* p. 133.

76. Susan Starr Sered, "Food and Holiness: Cooking as a Sacred Act among Middle-Eastern Jewish Women," *Anthropological Quarterly* 61 (July 1988): 129; Bucchier, *Feasting with Nonna Serafina,* p. 57.

77. It had been an English custom to make hot cross buns (a bun with icing in the shape of a cross) on Good Friday. Bakers continue to sell hot cross buns at Easter.

78. Sheryl Julian, "Easter with Mama Magliozzi," *Boston Globe,* March 27, 1991, p. 73; Russ, *German Festivals and Customs,* p. 54; Evanthea Keriazes, interview with "A Greek Mother," New Hampshire Federal Writers Project, 1938–1939, WPA Life Histories Collection, Library of Congress. In many groups a godmother gave a godchild a present at Easter.

79. Interview with Elizabeth Jetter Reimers, June 17, 1996, Family Folklore Interviews, Smithsonian Institution; Lucille Ziesenhenne, interview with George Kelleghan, October 19, 1977, University of California at Berkeley Folklore Archives, Holiday Lore, Easter, Folder F3.

80. Anne R. Kaplan, Marjorie A. Hoover, and Willard B. Moore, *The Minnesota Ethnic Food Book* (St. Paul: Minnesota Historical Society Press, 1986), p. 167.

81. Ibid., p. 185.

82. Greeks most active in the Orthodox church seem to be most likely to retain the old ways.

83. Irma M. Feldman, "Three Generations of Easter Dinner," Folklore 307, Folk Foodways, unpublished paper, no date, Balch Institute for Ethnic Studies.

84. Marie Louise Ardinia, interview with Helen Gannon, November 26, 1976; Willi Rudowsky, interview with himself, November 22, 1975, University of California Berkeley Folklore Archives, Holiday Lore, Easter, Folder F3; Obidinski and Zand, *Polish Folkways in America,* p. 69; Dorotoa Praszalowicz, "The Cultural Changes of Polish-American Parochial Schools in Milwaukee, 1866–1988," *Journal of American Ethnic History* 13 (Summer 1994): 36.

85. Jacek Nowakowski and Marlene Perrin, ed., *Polish Touches: Recipes and Traditions* (Iowa City: Penfield Press, 1996), p. 93.

86. Obidinski and Zand, *Polish Folkways in America,* p. 119.

87. Maria Anna Knothe, "Recent Arrivals: Polish Immigrant Women's Response to the City," in Christiane Harzig, ed., *Peasant Maids—City Women* (Ithaca: Cornell University Press, 1997), p. 321.

5. Festival of Freedom

1. Marshall Sklare, *Observing America's Jews* (Waltham, Mass.: University Press of New England, 1993), pp. 262–274.
2. George Gallup, Jr., and Jim Castelli, *The People's Religion: American Faith in the 90's* (New York: Macmillan, 1989), pp. 116–118. Barry Kosmin puts the comparison this way: "The Jews are too old, too well-educated, too liberal, too secular, too metropolitan, too wealthy, too egalitarian, too civic-minded to be normal Americans when compared to the overall U.S. population." Barry Kosmin, "Exploring and Understanding the Findings of the 1990 National Jewish Population Survey," quoted in Deborah Dash Moore, *To the Golden Cities: Pursuing the American Jewish Dream in Miami and L.A.* (New York: Free Press, 1995), p. 273.
3. Moore, *To the Golden Cities*, p. 273.
4. Marshall Sklare, *Conservative Judaism: An American Religious Movement*, 2nd ed. (Glencoe: Free Press, 1955), p. 204.
5. Sidney Goldstein, "Profile of American Jewry: Insights from the 1990 National Jewish Population Survey," *American Jewish Year Book 1992*, vol. 92 (New York: Jewish Publication Society, 1992), pp. 77–173.
6. Jenna Weissman Joselit, *The Wonders of America: Reinventing Jewish Culture, 1880–1950* (New York: Hill and Wang, 1994), p. 5, 6.
7. Men were also expected to use the *mikveh* after nocturnal emissions.
8. Jenna Weissman Joselit, *New York's Jewish Jews: The Orthodox Community in the Interwar Years* (Bloomington: Indiana University Press, 1990), p. 101.
9. They are Shabbat, Rosh Hashonah, Yom Kippur, Pesach, Shavuot, Sukkoth, and Shemini Atzereth.
10. Jenna Weissman Joselit, "'Merry Chanuka': The Changing Holiday Practices of American Jews," in Jack Wertheimer, ed., *The Uses of Tradition: Jewish Continuity in the Modern Era* (New York: Jewish Theological Seminary of America, 1992), pp. 303–326.
11. The *mikveh*, for example, disappeared precisely because it could not be redefined as modern. Marshall Sklare and Joseph Greenbaum, *Jewish Identity on the Suburban Frontier: A Study of Group Survival in the Open Society* (New York: Free Press, 1967), pp. 50–55.
12. Joselit, *Wonders of America*, pp. 219, 220.
13. Hayyim Schauss, *The Jewish Festivals: History and Observance* (New York: Schocken Books, 1938), pp. 38–47.
14. Mary Antin, *The Promised Land* (Boston: Houghton Mifflin, 1912), p. 8.
15. Rumors of the blood libel crossed the Atlantic and were spread in American Polish and Slavic neighborhoods, sometimes by Polish priests. In small Amer-

ican towns Jews were the merchants to their East European Christian neighbors, as they had been in Poland. The old stereotypes and hatreds were abetted by the fact that Jewish merchants often extended credit to their Christian customers. At Passover some U.S. Jews closed their stores because they were afraid of mobs. Anti-Semitism flourished at Passover because the holiday coincided in time with Easter, and thus stimulated the Christian prejudice that Jews were responsible for the crucifixion of Jesus. Moreover, Protestant ministers in their Easter sermons described "the trial of Our Lord at the hands of the Jewish crowd." Despite all this, most U.S. Jews associated the Passover with freedom rather than persecution. Ann Friedman, "Life among the Poles in Old South Chicago: Memories of a Jewish Family in Business in 'the Bush,'" *Chicago History* 12 (June 1989): 1–5; Ewa Morawska, *Insecure Prosperity: Small Town Jews in Industrial America, 1890–1940* (Princeton: Princeton University Press, 1996), p. 194; Abraham G. Duker, "Twentieth-Century Blood Libels in the United States," in Alan Dundes, ed., *The Blood Libel Legend: A Casework in Anti-Semitic Folklore* (Madison: University of Wisconsin Press, 1991), pp. 233–260.

16. Edna Ferber, *A Peculiar Treasure* (Garden City, N.Y.: Doubleday, Doran, and Co., 1939), p. 73; Jacob Rader Marcus, ed., *The American Jewish Woman: A Documentary History* (New York: Klav Publishing, 1981), p. 361; Albert I. Gordon, *Jews in Transition* (Minneapolis: University of Minnesota Press, 1949), pp. 282–283; Reva Clar, "Jewish Acculturation in California's San Joaquin Valley: A Memoir," *Western States Jewish History* 19 (October 1986): 56. During the Civil War, Southern Jews had difficulty securing matzoh; see Elliott Ashkenazi, ed., *The Civil War Diary of Clara Solomon: Growing Up in New Orleans, 1861–1862* (Baton Rouge: Louisiana State University Press, 1995), pp. 326–331.

17. Barbara Kirshenblatt-Gimblett, "Kitchen Judaism," in Susan Braunstein and Jenna Weissman Joselit, eds., *Getting Comfortable in New York: The American Jewish Home, 1880–1950* (New York: Jewish Museum, 1990), p. 78.

18. Esther Ruskay, *Hearth and Home Essays* (Philadelphia: Jewish Publication Society of America, 1902), p. 75; Mary M. Cohen, "The Influence of the Jewish Religion in the Home," in *Papers of the Jewish Women's Congress, Held at Chicago September 4, 5, 6, and 7, 1893* (Philadelphia, 1894), pp. 115–121, as quoted in Kirshenblatt-Gimblett, "Kitchen Judaism," p. 77.

19. Ruskay, *Hearth and Home Essays*, p. 75.

20. Ibid., p. 76.

21. Mary Douglas explains that such preparations were attempts to create an orderly universe. She wrote, "There is no such thing as absolute dirt; it exists in the eye of the beholder. Nor do our ideas about disease account for the range of behavior in cleaning and avoiding dirt. Dirt offends against order." Mary Douglas, *Purity and Danger* (London: Pelican Books, 1978), p. 12.

22. Ruth Gruber Fredman argues that the purpose of the extensive preparations was to "focus the mind" and teach Jews that the universe could be perfected, but only in accord with God's law. Ruth Gruber Fredman, *The Passover*

Seder: Afikoman in Exile (Philadelphia: University of Pennsylvania Press, 1981), p. 77.

23. *Hebrew Standard,* March 19, 1915, 5, 11, as quoted in Jenna Weissman Joselit, "A Set Table," in Braunstein and Joselit, eds., *Getting Comfortable in New York,* p. 43; Beatrice S. Weinreich, "The Americanization of Passover" in Raphael Patai, Francis Lee Utley, and Dov Noy, ed., *Studies in Biblical and Jewish Folklore* (Bloomington: Indiana University Press, 1960), p. 351.

24. Taking a Passover vacation at Grossingers in the Catskills or at a hotel in Atlantic City or Miami Beach (or in Israel after 1948) became an alternative for the affluent in subsequent generations.

25. Joselit, *Wonders of America,* p. 225.

26. Weinreich, "The Americanization of Passover," pp. 357–359; David Shuldiner, "The Celebration of Passover among Jewish Radicals," in Stephen Stern and John Allan Cicala, eds., *Creative Ethnicity: Symbols and Strategies of Contemporary Ethnic Life* (Logan: Utah State University Press, 1991), pp. 159–170; and Judith J. Shapiro, *The Friendly Society: A History of the Workmen's Circle* (New York: Media Judaica, 1970). See also Anita Schwartz, "The Secular Seder: Continuity and Change among Left-Wing Jews," in Jack Kugelmass, ed., *Between Two Worlds: Ethnographic Essays on American Jewry* (Ithaca: Cornell University Press, 1988), pp. 105–127. Linda Lehrhaupt examines a secular seder in a nursing home, a restaurant, and a hotel in "The Organization Seder in American Jewish Life," *Western Folklore* 45 (1986): 186–202.

27. *American Hebrew,* April 8, 1909, 611, as quoted in Joselit, "A Set Table," p. 43.

28. Joselit, *Wonders of America,* p. 221; Weinreich, "Americanization of Passover," p. 350.

29. Andrew Heinze, *Adapting to Abundance: Jewish Immigrants, Mass Consumption, and the Search for American Identity* (New York: Columbia University Press, 1990), p. 84.

30. *Commercial Advertiser,* March 16, 1899, reprinted in Irving Howe and Kenneth Libo, ed., *How We Lived: A Documentary History of Immigrant Jews in America, 1880–1930* (New York: New American Library, 1981), p. 119.

31. Weinreich, "Americanization of Passover," p. 352; Joan Nathan, *Jewish Cooking in America* (New York: Alfred A. Knopf, 1994), p. 381; Heinze, *Adapting to Abundance,* p. 81.

32. Paula E. Hyman, "Culture and Gender: Women in the Immigrant Jewish Community," in David Berger, ed., *The Legacy of Jewish Migration: 1881 and Its Impact* (New York: Brooklyn College Press, 1983), pp. 157–168; Deborah Dash Moore, *At Home in America: Second Generation New York Jews* (New York: Columbia University Press, 1981).

33. Betty Greenberg and Althea O. Silverman, *The Jewish Home Beautiful* (New York: The National Women's League of the United Synagogues of America, 1941), p. 14.

34. Jacob Kohn, *Modern Problems of Jewish Parents: A Study in Parental Atti-*

tudes (New York, 1932), as quoted in Joselit, "A Set Table," pp. 5, 51; Mrs. Abraham I. Schechter, *Symbols and Ceremonies of the Jewish Home* (New York: Black Publishing Co., 1930), p. 15.

35. Mignon L. Rubenovitz, "The Jewish Home," in *The Center Table,* rev. ed. (Boston, 1929), pp. 1, 7, as quoted in Kirshenblatt-Gimblett, "Kitchen Judaism," p. 100.

36. Joselit, "A Set Table," p. 50.

37. Colleen McDannell, *The Christian Home in Victorian America, 1840–1900* (Bloomington: Indiana University Press, 1986), pp. 77–107; Paula E. Hyman, *Gender and Assimilation in Modern Jewish History: The Roles and Representation of Women* (Seattle: University of Washington Press, 1995), p. 154.

38. Respondents were asked which rituals were practiced in the home when your parents "were about your present age." Sklare and Greenbaum, *Jewish Identity on the Suburban Frontier,* p. 50. On the decline in *kashrut,* see Joselit, *Wonders of America,* pp. 176–177.

39. Joselit, "A Set Table," p. 53; Joselit, *Wonders of America,* p. 186; Morawska, *Insecure Prosperity,* p. 163.

40. Marcus, ed., *American Jewish Woman,* p. 517.

41. Ruth Glazer, "West Bronx: Food, Shelter, Clothing," *Commentary* 54 (June 1949): 584; Joselit, *Wonders of America,* p. 171; Sydney Stahl Weinberg, *The World of Our Mothers* (Chapel Hill: University of North Carolina Press, 1988), p. 140. On the relation of food to group identity, see Mary Douglas, "Standard Social Uses of Food," in Mary Douglas, ed., *Food in the Social Order* (New York: Russell Sage, 1984), pp. 1–40.

42. Kirshenblatt-Gimblett, "Kitchen Judaism," p. 94.

43. Gloria Kaufer Greene, *The Jewish Holiday Cookbook: An International Collection of Recipes and Customs* (New York: Times Books, 1985), p. 252.

44. Sam Levenson, *Everything but Money* (New York: Simon and Schuster, 1949), p. 91; and Reuben Coppeman, "Passovers Past: A Passover Memory," in Society for Humanistic Judaism, *Humanistic Judaism: A Passover Manual* (Farmington Hills, Mich.: Humanistic Judaism, 1984), n.p. Manischewitz and Rokeach published kosher cookbooks in order to persuade Jews to buy their products throughout the year. Kirshenblatt-Gimblett, "Kitchen Judaism," p. 92.

45. Joselit, "A Set Table," p. 58; Nathan, *Jewish Cooking,* p. 22.

46. On the rabbinic supervision required in the making of kosher-for-Passover chocolate, see Weinreich, "Americanization of Passover," p. 348; Joselit, "A Set Table," pp. 56–57; Marc Tull, "Kosher Brownies for Passover," *New York Folklore* 4 (1978): 81–88; Joselit, *Wonders of America,* p. 189.

47. Myra Katz Frommer and Harvey Frommer, *Growing Up Jewish in America* (New York: Harcourt, Brace, and Co., 1995), p. 77. For a bitter memory of Barton's box of chocolate pops in the image of four sons, see Elana Dykewomon, "The Fourth Daughter's Four Hundred Questions," in Evelyn

Torton Beck, ed., *Nice Jewish Girls: A Lesbian Anthology* (Watertown, Mass.: Perspehone Press, 1982), pp. 149–150.

48. Moore, *To the Golden Cities*, p. 103.
49. Sylvia Barach Fishman, "Triple Play: Deconstructing Jewish Women's Lives," in T. M. Rudavsky, ed., *Gender and Judaism: The Transformation of Tradition* (New York: New York University Press, 1995), p. 259.
50. Moore, *To the Golden Cities*, p. 104.
51. Herbert J. Gans, "The Origin and Growth of a Jewish Community in the Suburbs: A Study of the Jews in Park Forest," in Marshall Sklare, ed., *The Jews: Social Patterns of an American Group* (Glencoe, Ill.: Free Press, 1958), pp. 214–225; Shonie B. Levi and Sylvia R. Kaplan, *Guide for the Homemaker* (New York: Schocken Books, 1959), p. 113.
52. Sklare and Greenbaum, *Jewish Identity on the Suburban Frontier*, p. 74.
53. Albert Gordon, *Jews in Suburbia* (Westport, Conn.: Greenwood Press, 1959), p. 130; Judith R. Kramer and Seymour Leventman, *Children of the Gilded Ghetto: Conflict Resolution of Three Generations of American Jews* (New Haven: Yale University Press, 1961), pp. 159–160.
54. Moore, *To the Golden Cities*, p. 108.
55. Ibid., p. 107.
56. In the shtetl families often sold their *hametz* to a non-Jew who, for a small sum, kept the food during the holiday and returned it at the end of Passover. The custom of writing a contract to sell food to a Gentile dates back to sixteenth-century central Europe. Sometimes a rabbi acted as a middleman who received the *hametz* and sold it to a willing Gentile. Gordon, *Jews in Transition*, p. 108. Hasidic Jews left the *hametz* in a locked cupboard and did not physically remove it from the house. Lis Harris, *Holy Days: The World of a Hasidic Family* (New York: Summit Books, 1985), p. 157.
57. Steven J. Zeitlin, Amy J. Kotkin, and Holly Cutting Baker, *A Celebration of American Family Folklore* (New York: Pantheon Books, 1982), p. 171; Eric Liu, *The Accidental Asian* (New York: Random House, 1998), p. 146.
58. *Union Haggadah* (1923), as quoted in Weinreich, "Americanization of Passover," p. 364.
59. Sklare and Greenbaum, *Jewish Identity on the Suburban Frontier*, p. 52. Boston Jews even as late as 1975 were more observant. Asked whether "you yourself observe special dietary rules for Passover," 57 percent answered yes. What did it mean to observe the rules? Some must have meant that they did not eat *hametz* during the holiday. Whatever the meaning, however, with each generation the percentage observing the dietary rules for Passover declined. Two thirds of first-generation Jews in Boston did so, whereas a little less than half of fourth-generation Jews did. Steven M. Cohen, *American Modernity and Jewish Identity* (New York: Tavistock, 1983), Table 3, pp. 2, 56.
60. The 1990 figure applied to individuals born Jewish who were married between 1985 and 1990. Jack Wertheimer, Charles S. Liebman, and Steven M.

Cohen, "How to Save American Jews," *Commentary* 101 (January 1996): 47–51. J. J. Goldberg argued that the 1990 National Jewish Population Survey overcounted Southern, black, rural, and poor Jews, and counted as Jews those who had a Jewish parent but were practicing another religion. Goldberg claims if these biases were corrected, the true rate of Jewish intermarriage in 1990 would fall to 38 percent. "Interfaith Marriage: The Real Story," *New York Times*, Aug. 3, 1997, p. A13.

61. Private communication, October 25, 1993; Sharon R. Sherman, "The Passover Seder: Ritual Dynamics, Foodways, and Family Folklore," in Theodore C. Humphrey and Lin T. Humphrey, eds., *"We Gather Together": Food and Festival in American Life* (Logan: Utah State University Press, 1988), p. 39.

62. Cohen, *American Modernity and Jewish Identity*, Table 6, pp. 4, 126; Sidney Goldstein, "Profile of American Jewry: Insights from the 1990 National Jewish Population Survey," *American Jewish Year Book, 1992*, vol. 92 (New York: Jewish Publication Society, 1992), p. 135.

63. This principle held true among Boston Jews in 1975. A decade earlier, college-educated Jews were more likely to celebrate Passover than those whose education had not gone beyond high school or grade school; those with postgraduate degrees were somewhat less likely to observe Passover than the college-educated. Cohen, *American Modernity and Jewish Identity*, p. 82.

64. Ibid., pp. 90–91.

65. Barbara Frankel, "Structures of the Seder: An Analysis of Persistence, Context, and Meaning," *American Behavioral Scientist* 23 (March–April 1980): 625; Sharon R. Sherman, "The Passover Seder: Ritual Dynamics, Foodways, and Family Folklore," in Humphrey and Humphrey, *"We Gather Together,"* pp. 26–42. See also Sharon R. Sherman, "'That's How the Seder Looks': A Fieldwork Account of Videotaping Family Folklore," *Journal of Folklore Research* 23 (January–April 1986): 53–70. For a description of a seder among a blended family in Minneapolis with a former and a current spouse attending, see Marjorie Leigh McLellan, "Bread and Glue: Celebration and Ritual in Four American Families" (Ph.D. diss., University of Minnesota, 1991), chap. 6.

66. In contrast, Lis Harris attended a seder among Hasidic Jews in Crown Heights. They started at eight-thirty in the evening and did not serve the meal until eleven o'clock. The first half of the seder took so long because the rituals were performed "meticulously and reverentially." Harris, *Holy Days*, p. 168.

67. Joyce Antler, *The Journey Home: Jewish Women and the American Century* (New York: The Free Press, 1997), pp. 285–308; Pamela S. Nadell, "'Top Down' or 'Bottom Up': Two Movements for Women's Rabbinic Ordination," in Jeffrey Gurock and Marc Lee Raphael, eds., *An Inventory of Promises: Essays on American Jewish History in Honor of Moses Rischin* (Brooklyn: Carlson, 1995), pp. 197–208; Paula Hyman, "Ezrat Nashim and the Emergence of New Jewish Feminism," in Robert M. Seltzer and Norman J. Cohen, eds., *The Americanization of the Jews* (New York: New York Uni-

versity Press, 1995), pp. 284–295; Anne Lapidus Lerner, "'Who Hast Not Made Me a Man': The Movement for Equal Rights for Women in American Jewry," in Morris Fine and Milton Himmelfarb, eds., *American Jewish Year Book*, vol. 77 (New York: American Jewish Committee, 1976), pp. 3–38. On the origins of Jewish feminism, see Reena Sigman Friedman, "The Jewish Feminist Movement," in Michael N. Dobkowski, ed., *Jewish American Voluntary Organizations* (New York: Greenwood Press, 1986), pp. 575–601.

68. Dykewomon, "The Fourth Daughter's Four Hundred Questions," p. 150; Adrienne Baker, *The Jewish Woman in Contemporary Society: Transitions and Traditions* (New York: New York University Press, 1993), p. 142; Anne Roiphe, *Generation without Memory: A Jewish Journey in Christian America* (New York: Linden Press, 1981), p. 144; Doris Friedensohn, "Yom Kippurs at Yum Luk: Reflections on Eating, Ethnicity, and Identity," in Jeffrey Rubin-Dorsky and Shelley Fisher Fishkin, eds., *People of the Book: Thirty Scholars Reflect on Their Jewish Identity* (Madison: University of Wisconsin Press, 1996), pp. 245–257.

69. Letty Cottin Pogebrin, *Deborah, Golda, and Me: Being Female and Jewish in America* (Garden City, N.Y.: Doubleday, 1991), p. 18. See also Bert Greene, *Bert Greene's Kitchen: A Book of Memories and Recipes* (New York: Workman Publication, 1993), p. 69. Sylvia Barack Fishman assesses the impact of feminism on Jewish ritual in *A Breath of Life: Feminism in the American Jewish Community* (New York: Free Press, 1993), chap. 6.

70. The overall rate of labor force participation among Jewish women was no higher than for Gentile women in 1990, except for women over forty-five. Those in midlife had more formal education than other women of their age and were employed in white-collar occupations, where workers retired later than in blue-collar ones. Moshe Hartman and Harriet Hartman, *Gender Equality and American Jews* (Albany: State University of New York Press, 1996), pp. 115–164.

71. Jack Wertheimer, *A People Divided: Judaism in Contemporary America* (New York: Basic Books, 1993), p. 73.

72. Blu Greenberg, *How to Run a Traditional Jewish Household* (Northvale, N.J.: Jason Aronson, 1989), p. 418. A Jewish physician in Minneapolis detected changing attitudes as early as the 1940s. After childbirth his patients used to ask him to release them early, so that they could at least supervise, if not cook, the seder meal at home. By the 1940s they were begging him to keep them in the hospital, so that they did not have to prepare for Passover. Gordon, *Jews in Transition*, p. 109.

73. Evelyn Torton Beck, "Naming Is Not a Simple Act: Jewish Lesbian-Feminist Community in the 1980s," in Christie Balka and Andy Rose, eds., *Twice Blessed: On Being Lesbian, Gay, and Jewish* (Boston: Beacon Press, 1989), pp. 177–178; Rebecca Alpert, *Like Bread on the Seder Plate: Jewish Lesbians and the Transformation of Tradition* (New York: Columbia University Press, 1997).

74. Susan Weidman Schneider, *Jewish and Female: Choices and Changes in Our Lives Today* (New York: Simon and Schuster, 1984), p. 110. E. M. Broner and Naomi Nimrod wrote a Haggadah in Israel in 1975; it was published in *Ms.* magazine two years later and subsequently published as *The Telling*. Maida E. Solomon, "Claiming Our Questions: Feminism and Judaism in Women's Haggadot," in Joyce Antler, ed., *Talking Back: Images of Jewish Women in American Popular Culture* (Hanover: University Press of New England, 1998), pp. 228–229.

75. Judith Plaskow, *Standing Again at Sinai: Judaism from a Feminist Perspective* (New York: Harper Collins, 1990), p. 58; Penina Adelman, "A Drink from Miriam's Cup: Invention of Tradition among Jewish Women," in Maurie Sacks, ed., *Active Voices: Women in Jewish Culture* (Urbana: University of Illinois Press, 1995), pp. 109–124.

76. Antler, *Journey Home*, p. 381.

77. Solomon, "Claiming Our Questions," pp. 220–241.

78. Susan Gubar, "Eating the Bread of Affliction: Judaism and Feminist Criticism," in Rubin-Dorsky and Fishkin, eds., *People of the Book,* pp. 15–36; Shelley Fisher Fishkin, "Changing the Story," in Rubin-Dorsky and Fisher, eds., *People of the Book,* pp. 47–63; "Making Your Own Tradition: Redefining Seders for the '90s," *New York Times,* April 10, 1998, pp. A1, A16.

79. "Holding a Nontraditional Seder with a Prix Fixe Feast," *New York Times,* April 1, 1998, p. B11.

80. Riv-Ellen Prell-Foldes, "Coming of Age in Kelton: The Constraints on Gender Symbolism in Jewish Ritual," in Judith Hoch-Smith and Anita Spring, ed., *Women in Ritual and Symbolic Roles* (New York: Plenum Press, 1978), pp. 76–99; Shulamit S. Magnus, "Re-inventing Miriam's Well: Feminist Jewish Ceremonials," in Wertheimer, ed., *Uses of Tradition,* pp. 331–347; Rela Geffen Monson, "The Impact of the Jewish Women's Movement on the American Synagogue, 1972–1985," in Susan Grossman and Riva Haut, eds., *Daughters of the King: Women and the Synagogue, a Survey of History, Halakhah, and Contemporary Realities* (Philadelphia: Jewish Publication Society, 1992), pp. 227–236.

6. Eating and Explosives

1. Gunther Barth, *Bitter Strength: A History of the Chinese in the United States, 1850–1870* (Cambridge: Harvard University Press, 1964), p. 83; William Hoy, "Native Festivals of the California Chinese," *Western Folklore* 7 (July 1948): 240–250.

2. The phrase "only joys and no sorrows" is Pardee Lowe's. See his *Father and Glorious Descendant* (Boston: Little, Brown and Co., 1943), p. 69.

3. Wolfram Eberhard, *Chinese Festivals* (New York: Henry Schuman, 1952), p. 4.

4. There may have been significant differences between the celebration of Chi-

nese New Year in Hawaii and on the mainland, and even in the continental United States between the more populous and smaller Chinatowns. The San Francisco celebration was the largest and most well developed. Hawaii did not enforce the exclusion laws, and as a result there were more Chinese families on the islands than on the mainland until about the 1950s. Although the higher concentration of Chinese-American families in Hawaii probably led to a more elaborate feast and to more extensive patterns of visiting, there is not enough information to verify this assertion, or to compare the celebration in San Francisco with those elsewhere.

5. For frequencies of Passover observance, see Marshall Sklare and Joseph Greenbaum, *Jewish Identity on the Suburban Frontier: A Study of Group Survival in the Open Society* (New York: Basic Books, 1958; rev. ed., Chicago: University of Chicago Press, 1967), p. 63; Max Vorspan and Lloyd P. Gartner, *History of the Jews of Los Angeles* (Philadelphia: Jewish Publication Society of America, 1970), p. 257; Avron C. Heiligman, "The Demographic Perspective," in Joseph P. Schultz, ed., *Mid-America's Promise: A Profile of Kansas City Jewry* (Kansas City: Jewish Community Foundation of Greater Kansas City, 1982), p. 365; Steven M. Cohen, *American Modernity and Jewish Identity* (New York: Tavistock, 1983), p. 56; Steven Martin Cohen, "The 1981–1982 National Survey of American Jews," *American Jewish Year Book, 1983* (Philadelphia: Jewish Publication Society of America, 1982), p. 91; Steven Martin Cohen, *American Assimilation or Jewish Revival?* (Bloomington: Indiana University Press, 1988), p. 121; Sidney Goldstein, "Profile of American Jewry: Insights from the 1990 National Jewish Population Survey," *American Jewish Year Book 1992*, vol. 92 (New York: Jewish Publication Society, 1992), pp. 77–173; Andromeda Romano-Lax, "Being Jewish in Alaska," *Anchorage Daily News Magazine*, August 20, 1995, p. 5. On the frequency of the observance of Chinese New Year, see Rose Hum Lee, *The Chinese in the United States of America* (Hong Kong: Hong Kong University Press, 1960), p. 5; Stanley L. M. Fong, *The Assimilation of Chinese in America: Changes in Orientation and Social Perception* (San Francisco: R and E Research Associates, 1974), p. 23; Hsian-shui Chen, *Chinatown No More: Taiwan Immigrants in Contemporary New York* (Ithaca: Cornell University Press, 1992), pp. 81–82.

6. Lee, *The Chinese*, p. 5.

7. Fong, *Assimilation of Chinese*, p. 23.

8. Chen, *Chinatown No More*, pp. 81–82.

9. Maria Hong, ed., *Growing Up Asian American: An Anthology* (New York: William Morrow and Co., 1993), p. 368.

10. Interview with Kenny and Siu Wing Lai in Joann Faung Jean Lee, *Asian American Experiences in the United States: Oral Histories of First to Fourth Generation Americans from China, the Phillipines, Japan, India, the Pacific Islands, Vietnam, and Cambodia* (Jefferson, N.C.: McFarland and Co., 1991), p. 75.

11. Judy Yung, *Unbound Feet: A Social History of Chinese Women in San Francisco* (Berkeley: University of California Press, 1995), p. 293.

12. Some Chinese men entered into common-law marriages with white women or married Anglo women in Mexico and returned to the United States. The Exclusion Laws were not enforced in Hawaii, and laborers there frequently married native women. New York state did not ban interracial marriage, and as a result Chinese men in New York often married non-Chinese women. How marrying non-Chinese women affected the Chinese immigrants' celebration of the New Year is a subject not yet investigated. David T. Courtwright, *Violent Land: Single Men and Social Disorder from the Frontier to the Inner City* (Cambridge: Harvard University Press, 1996), p. 158. On the exclusion of Chinese women, see Sucheng Chan, "The Exclusion of Chinese Women, 1870–1943," in Sucheng Chan, ed., *Entry Denied: Exclusion and the Chinese Community in America, 1882–1943* (Philadelphia: Temple University Press, 1991), pp. 94–146; George Anthony Peffer, "Forbidden Families: Emigration Experiences of Chinese Women under the Page Law, 1875–1882," *Journal of American Ethnic History* 6 (Fall 1986): 28–46; and George Anthony Peffer, "From Under the Sojourner's Shadow: A Historiographical Study of Chinese Female Immigration to America, 1852–1882," *Journal of American Ethnic History* 11 (Spring 1992): 41–67.

13. Robert F. G. Spier, "Food Habits of Nineteenth-Century California Chinese," *California Historical Society Quarterly* 37 (1958): 79–84.

14. For a perspective that emphasizes the acculturation of the nonsojourning population, see Raymond Lou, "The Chinese American Community of Los Angeles, 1870–1900: A Case of Resistance, Organization, and Participation" (Ph.D. diss., University of California at Irvine, 1982).

15. Arthur Bonner, *Alas! What Brought Thee Hither? The Chinese in New York, 1800–1950* (Madison, N.J.: Farleigh Dickinson University Press, 1997), p. 27.

16. William C. Wu, *Chinese New Year: Fact and Folklore* (Ann Arbor, Mich.: Ars Ceramica, 1991), p. 74.

17. Victor G. and Brett de Bary Nee, *Longtime Californ': A Documentary Study of an American Chinatown* (New York: Random House, 1972), p. 180.

18. Hoy, "Native Festivals of California Chinese," p. 245.

19. Ronald Takaki, *Strangers from a Different Shore: A History of Asian Americans* (Boston: Little, Brown and Co., 1989), opposite p. 274.

20. Marlon K. Hom, ed., *Songs of Gold Mountain: Cantonese Rhymes from San Francisco Chinatown* (Berkeley: University of California Press, 1987), p. 195.

21. Interview with Dr. C. C. Chien, July 15, 1988, as quoted in Lou Ilar, *The Americanization of Chinese New Year: A History of Traditional New Year Customs of the Louisiana Chinese* (Dubuque, Iowa: Kendall/Hunt Publishing, 1993), p. 101.

22. Paul Siu, *The Chinese Laundryman* (Chicago: University of Chicago Press, 1953), p. 154.

23. Yung, *Unbound Feet,* p. 72.
24. Judy Yung, *Chinese Women of America: A Pictorial History* (Seattle: University of Washington Press, 1986), p. 30; Feelie Lee and Elaine You, "Traditions and Transitions," in Asian American Studies Center, *Chinese American Women of Los Angeles* (Los Angeles: Chinese Historical Society of Southern California, 1984), p. 56; Courtwright, *Violent Land,* p. 160.
25. Yung, *Unbound Feet,* pp. 100–101.
26. Bonner, *Alas!,* pp. 27, 32; Lou, "The Chinese American Community of Los Angeles," pp. 277–278; Nancy Farrar, *The Chinese in El Paso* (El Paso: Texas Western Press, 1972), p. 29.
27. The political nature of New Year's was evident in the negotiations with authorities necessary before Chinese were permitted to set off firecrackers in Chinatown. Neighbors invariably complained about the noise and tried to ban firecrackers or at least limit the number of days they could be used.
28. Sandy Lydon, *Chinese Gold: The Chinese in the Monterey Bay Region* (Capitola, Calif.: Capitola Book Co., 1985), p. 244.
29. James F. Rusling, *Across America: Or, The Great West and the Pacific Coast* (New York: Sheldon and Co., 1874), pp. 310–312; Sylvia Sun Minnick, *Samfow: The San Joaquin Chinese Legacy* (Fresno, Calif.: Panorama West Publishing, 1988), p. 100.
30. Lee, *Asian American Experiences in the United States,* p. 165; Carol Stephanchuk and Charles Choy Wong, *Mooncakes and Hungry Ghosts: Festivals of China* (San Francisco: China Books and Periodicals, 1991), n.p.; George Kin Leung, "Peiping's Happy New Year," *National Geographic Magazine* 70 (December 1936): 749–792.
31. Farrar, *The Chinese in El Paso,* p. 29; Eberhard, *Chinese Festivals,* p. 4; Thomas W. Chinn, *Bridging the Pacific* (San Francisco: Chinese Historical Society of America, 1989), p. 232.
32. Tin-Chiu Fan, "Chinese Residents in Chicago" (Ph.D. diss., University of Chicago, 1926), p. 50; Cone, *Two Years in California* (Chicago: S. C. Griggs, 1876), p. 188.
33. Hoy, "Native Festivals of California Chinese."
34. Lowe, *Father and Glorious Descendant,* p. 67.
35. Maxine Hong Kingston, *China Men* (New York: Vintage, 1977), p. 72.
36. Jon Lee, as quoted in Hennig Cohen and Tristram Potter Coffin, ed., *The Folklore of American Holidays* (Detroit: Gale Research, 1987), p. 46; Jeff Kisseloff, *You Must Remember This: An Oral History of Manhattan From the 1890s to World War II* (New York: Harcourt Brace, 1989), p. 51; interview with Ruth Wong, November 29, 1976, San Francisco, Combined Asian American Resources Project, Bancroft Library, University of California at Berkeley.
37. Jon Lee, as quoted in Cohen and Coffin, eds., *Folklore of American Holidays,* p. 46; Ron Chew, ed., *Reflections of Seattle's Chinese Americans* (Seattle: University of Washington Press, 1994), p. 10.
38. E. N. Anderson, Jr., and Margo L. Anderson, "Modern China: South," in

K. C. Chang, ed., *Food in Chinese Culture: Anthropological and Historical Perspectives* (New Haven: Yale University Press, 1977), p. 380; Chew, ed., *Reflections of Seattle's Chinese Americans*, p. 34.

39. Chang, "Ancient China," in Chang, ed., *Food in Chinese Culture*, p. 26.
40. As quoted in Dorothy and Thomas Hoobler, *The Chinese American Family Album* (New York: Oxford University Press, 1994), p. 117.
41. Ken Hom, *Easy Family Recipes from a Chinese-American Childhood* (New York: Alfred A. Knopf, 1997), p. 15.
42. Clarence Elmer Glick, *Sojourners and Settlers: Chinese Migrants in Hawaii* (Honolulu: University Press of Hawaii, 1980), p. 166.
43. Norman S. Hayner and Charles N. Reynolds, "Chinese Family Life in America," *American Sociological Review* 2 (October 1937): 630; Laurence Yep, *Tongues of Jade* (New York: HarperCollins, 1991), p. 38; Yung, *Unbound Feet*, p. 79.
44. Glick, *Sojourners and Settlers*, p. 166.
45. Yung, *Unbound Feet*, p. 83.
46. Bernard P. Wong, *Chinatown: Economic Adaptation and Ethnic Identity of the Chinese* (New York: Holt, Rinehart, and Winston, 1982), p. 62.
47. Peggy Pascoe, "Gender Systems in Conflict: The Marriages of Mission-Educated Chinese American-Women, 1874–1939," in Vicki L. Ruiz and Ellen Carol DuBois, ed., *Unequal Sisters: A Multi-Cultural Reader in U.S. Women's History* (New York: Routledge, 1994), pp. 139–156.
48. Hoy, "Native Festivals of the California Chinese"; Lisa See, *On Gold Mountain: The One-Hundred-Year Odyssey of a Chinese-American Family* (New York: St. Martins, 1995), pp. 104–105.
49. Yung, *Unbound Feet*, pp. 100–101.
50. Paul G. Chace, "Returning Thanks: Chinese Rites in An American Community," Part 2 (Ph.D. diss., University of California at Riverside, 1992), p. 378; Chinn, *Bridging the Pacific*, p. 66.
51. Chen, *Chinatown No More*, pp. 29–30.
52. Ibid., p. 85.
53. The rate was 16.8 percent for wives and 13.1 percent for husbands. Betty Lee Sung, *Chinese American Intermarriage* (New York: Center for Migration Studies, 1990), pp. 14–15.
54. Stephan Thernstrom and Abigail Thernstrom, *America in Black and White: One Nation, Indivisible* (New York: Simon and Schuster, 1997), p. 542. The figures did not include religious-ethnic groups such as Mormons and Jews.
55. Melford S. Weiss, *Valley City: A Chinese Community in America* (Morristown, N.J.: Schenkman Publishing Co., 1974), p. 128.
56. Joyce Chapman Libra, *Women's Voices in Hawaii* (Niwot: University Press of Colorado, 1991), pp. 58–59.
57. Gus Lee, *China Boy* (New York: Dutton, 1991), p. 70.
58. Ibid., p. 41.
59. Weiss, *Valley City*, p. 128.
60. Ibid., p. 179; Chew, ed., *Reflections of Seattle's Chinese Americans*, p. 10.

61. Ben Fong-Torres, *The Rice Room* (New York: Hyperion, 1994), p. 275; "One Family's New Year," *San Francisco Chronicle,* February 7, 1979, p. 13.

62. Glick, *Sojourners and Settlers,* p. 178; Weiss, *Valley City,* p. 254.

63. "One Family's New Year," p. 13.

64. Since the 1960s owners of martial arts studios in many cities made a substantial part of their yearly income from New Year's performances. They instructed students in the lion dance, which was performed in Chinatown celebrations and at local public schools. In other cities the Christian churches and high school Asian clubs performed the lion dance at the local auditorium. Similarly, Chinese parent associations in public schools staged lion dances for a largely non-Chinese audience to promote appreciation of Chinese culture. Edward B. Warburton, "The Lion in Boston's Heart: An Exploration of the Lion Dances during Boston's Chinese New Year, 1968" (B.A. honors thesis, Harvard University, 1986); Minnick, *Samfow,* p. 306.

65. Nee and Nee, *Longtime Californ',* pp. 244–245; Chinn, *Bridging the Pacific,* p. 79; Takaki, *Strangers from a Different Shore,* pp. 246–251.

66. Judy Tzu-Chun Wu, "'Loveliest Daughter of Our Ancient Cathay!' Representations of Ethnic and Gender Identity in the Miss Chinatown U.S.A. Beauty Pageant," *Journal of Social History* 31 (Fall 1997): 5–31.

67. Ibid., pp. 21, 28–29.

68. William Wei, *The Asian American Movement* (Philadelphia: Temple University Press, 1993), p. 77.

69. Ibid., p. 15.

70. In the 1950s the *Chinese Pacific Weekly,* a Chinese language newspaper published in San Francisco, made the same charge. Chinese-American feminists differed from the previous decade's critics in that they framed their arguments in relationship to feminism and rising ethnic consciousness. Private Communication from Chio-ling Yeh, December 18, 1997.

71. Wu, "Loveliest Daughter of Our Ancient Cathay!" p. 23.

72. Charles Taylor, *The Ethics of Authenticity* (Cambridge: Harvard University Press, 1991), p. 17.

73. Ibid., p. 21.

74. Hom, *Easy Family Recipes,* p. 253.

75. Mary M. Wong, "Chinese Folklore in Evanston, Wyoming," Box 31, Folder 13, n.d., Oral Histories of Chinese Americans in Utah, University of Utah.

7. Cakes and Candles

1. Linda Rannells Lewis, *Birthdays: Their Delights, Disappointments, Past and Present, Worldly, Astrological and Infamous* (Boston: Little, Brown and Co., 1976), pp. 10–11.

2. Cynthia A. Kierner, "Genteel Balls and Republican Parades: Gender and Early Southern Civic Rituals, 1677–1826," *Virginia Magazine of History and Biography* 104 (Spring 1996): 185–210.

3. Mary Pierce Poor to Jon and Lucy Tappan Pierce, January 13, 1842, as

quoted in Ronald J. Zboray and Mary Saracino Zboray, "Books, Reading, and the World of Goods in Antebellum New England," *American Quarterly* 48 (1986): 587–622.

4. On the history of the birthday party, see Howard P. Chudacoff, *How Old Are You? Age Consciousness in American Culture* (Princeton: Princeton University Press, 1989), chap. 6; Karin Lee Fishbeck Calvert, "To Be a Child: An Analysis of the Artifacts of Childhood" (Ph.D. diss., University of Delaware, 1984), pp. 196–201; and Ralph and Adelin Linton, *The Lore of Birthdays* (New York: Henry Schuman, 1952). For analysis of the song "Happy Birthday to You," see Bess Lomax Hawes, "The Birthday: An American Ritual" (master's thesis, University of California, 1970). Theodore C. Humphrey analyzed the symbolic meaning of the birthday cake in "A Family Celebrates a Birthday: Of Life and Cakes," in Theodore C. Humphrey and Lin T. Humphrey, eds., *"We Gather Together": Food and Festival in American Life* (Logan: Utah State University Press, 1988), pp. 19–26. On the socialization of girls to be gift-givers and hostesses and the emphasis boys place on games at contemporary birthday parties, see Cele Otnes and Mary Ann McGrath, "Ritual Socialization and the Children's Birthday Party: The Early Emergence of Gender Differences," *Journal of Ritual Studies* 8 (Winter 1994): 73–93.

5. Alice Morse Earle, ed., *Diary of Anna Green Winslow: A Boston School Girl of 1771* (Boston: Houghton, Mifflin and Co., 1894), pp. 5–8, 18.

6. S. Bayard Dod, ed., *The Journal of Martha Pintard Bayard: London, 1794–1797* (New York: Dodd, Mead, and Co., 1984), pp. 79–80. The Bayard party was held in England, where the family resided. Benjamin Franklin also celebrated the second birthday of his grandson there, even though his grandson was living in Philadelphia. Jeffery A. Smith, *Franklin and Bache: Envisioning the Enlightened Republic* (New York: Oxford University Press, 1990), p. 49.

7. Barbara Rinkoff, *Birthday Parties around the World* (New York: M. Barrows and Co., 1967), p. 4; Linton and Linton, *Lore of Birthdays,* p. 18. Anti-German hysteria around World War I seems to have led to the disappearance of the Birthday Man.

8. Stationery stores sold small images of the Birthday Man, which could be placed on the table. There is no satisfactory explanation as to why Americans did not adopt the Birthday Man as a symbol of the event or use a tree on the table as a good visual way to display the gifts the child received.

9. Mrs. C. A. Halbert, "Festivals and Presents," *The Ladies' Repository: A Monthly Periodical Devoted to Literature, Arts, and Religion* 7 (January 1871): 43; David A. Gerber, " 'The Germans Take Care of Our Celebrations': Middle-Class Americans Appropriate German Ethnic Culture in Buffalo in the 1850s," in Kathryn Grover, ed., *Hard at Play: Leisure in America, 1840–1940* (Rochester: Strong Museum, 1992), pp. 39-60.

10. Halbert, "Festivals and Presents," p. 43.

11. Louise Conway Belden, *The Festive Tradition: Table Decoration and Desserts in America, 1650–1900* (New York: W. W. Norton, 1983), pp. 184–186.

12. Calvert, "To Be a Child," p. 199.

13. "Scriptural Anthology," *Southern Literary Messenger* 13 (October 1837): 594; "Notices of New Works," *Southern Literary Messenger* 10 (September 1844): 573; Benjamin Blake Minor, "Notices of New Works," *Southern Literary Messenger* 12 (October 1846): 640; "Gift Books and Annuals for 1852," *Southern Quarterly Review* 5 (January 1852): 176.

14. Joseph F. Kett, *Rites of Passage: Adolescence in America, 1790 to the Present* (New York: Basic Books, 1977), p. 13.

15. John R. Gillis, *A World of Our Own Making: Myth, Ritual, and the Quest for Family Values* (New York: Basic Books, 1996), p. 49.

16. Chudacoff, *How Old Are You?*, p. 127; Linton and Linton, *Lore of Birthdays*, p. 42.

17. Nancy Tuckerman and Nancy Duman urged women to do this in *The Amy Vanderbilt Complete Book of Etiquette* (New York: Doubleday, 1978), p. 431.

18. Laura E. Richards, ed., *The Julia Ward Howe Birthday Book* (Boston: Lee and Shepard, 1889).

19. Jonn F. Kasson, *Rudeness and Civilization: Manners in Nineteenth-Century Urban America* (New York: Hill and Wang, 1990); Karen Halttunen, *Confidence Men and Painted Women: A Study of Middle-Class Culture in America, 1830–1870* (New Haven: Yale University Press, 1982).

20. Walter Brooks, *A Child and a Boy* (New York: Brentano's, 1915), p. 75.

21. This description of "boy culture" summarizes information in E. Anthony Rotundo, *American Manhood: Transformations in Masculinity from the Revolution to the Modern Era* (New York: Basic Books, 1993), pp. 31–55. For a description of Rap Jacket, see Andrew Gulliford, "Fox and Geese in the School Yard: Play and America's Country Schools, 1870–1940," in Grover, ed., *Hard at Play,* p. 193.

22. Mabel Osgood Wright, *My New York* (New York: Macmillan, 1926), pp. 133–134.

23. There were no similar paintings by American artists. Like Norman Rockwell, Frith used his own family as models in this painting, with the exception of the elderly gentleman who posed as the grandfather, whom he located at a workhouse. His own daughter was the model for the birthday girl and his wife for the grandmother. He painted himself as the distracted father. W. P. Frith, *My Autobiography and Reminiscences* (London: Richard Bentley and Son, 1887), p. 264; Christopher Wood, *Victorian Panorama: Paintings of Victorian Life* (London: Faber and Faber, 1976), p. 61.

24. Wright, *My New York*, pp. 133–142.

25. Philip Hone, *The Diary of Philip Hone* (New York: Dodd and Mead, 1936), vol. 2, p. 753.

26. Susan Williams, *Savory Suppers and Fashionable Feasts: Dining in Victorian America* (New York: Pantheon Books, 1985), p. 200.

27. Hone, *Diary of Philip Hone,* vol. 1, p. xvii.

28. Interview with Alice Battle (no interviewer named), in George P. Rawick, ed., *The American Slave: A Composite Autobiography,* Georgia Narratives, Part 1, Supplement Series 1 (Westport, Conn.: Greenwood Press, 1977), vol. 3, p. 40; Elliott Ashkenazi, ed., *The Civil War Diary of Clara Solomon: Growing up in New Orleans, 1861–1862* (Baton Rouge: Louisiana State University Press, 1995), pp. 85, 280; Joan L. Severa, *Dressed for the Photographer: Ordinary Americans and Fashion, 1840–1900* (Kent, Ohio: Kent State University Press, 1995), p. 186; interview with John Sneed (no interviewer named), n.d., in Rawick, ed., *American Slave: A Composite Autobiography, Texas Narratives,* Parts 3 and 4 (Westport, Conn.: Greenwood Press, 1972), vol. 5, p. 49; Susan Eppes, *Through Some Eventful Years* (Macon: J. W. Burke, 1926), p. 176; Mary D. Robertson, ed., *A Confederate Lady Comes of Age: The Journal of Pauline De Caradeuc Heyward, 1863–1868* (Columbia: University of South Carolina Press, 1992), p. 60.

29. Howard Chudacoff claimed that the birthday party did not emerge until the late nineteenth century. The first example he provides is that of Mabel Osgood Wright in the 1870s. Chudacoff argues that before then people were not very conscious of birthdates. Only at the turn of the century, he writes, did Americans come to recognize age as a characteristic of the individual that explained "an individual to self and to others." He dates self-reflection at the time of one's birthday to the late nineteenth century; in fact, however, one can find several examples of girls pondering the significance of their birthdays between 1790 and the 1810s. Chudacoff, *How Old Are You?,* p. 129; Severa, *Dressed for the Photographer,* p. 186; Harvey J. Graff, *Conflicting Paths: Growing Up in America* (Cambridge: Harvard University Press, 1995), p. 58; Francis Everett Blacke, *History of the Town of Princeton, in the County of Worcester and Commonwealth of Massachusetts, 1759–1915* (Princeton, Mass.: Published by the town, 1915), as quoted in Margo Culley, ed., *A Day at a Time: The Diary Literature of American Women from 1764 to the Present* (New York: Feminist Press, 1985), p. 76; Laura Hadley Moseley, *The Diaries of Julia Cowles* (New Haven: Yale University Press, 1931), p. 90.

30. "Sideboard for the Young," *The Ladies' Repository: A Monthly Periodical Devoted to Literature, Arts, and Religion* 2 (1875): 376.

31. Emily Post, *Children Are People* (New York: Funk and Wagnalls Co., 1940), p. 266.

32. Singing "Happy Birthday to You" is a necessary element of the modern birthday party. It was composed by two women, a college president and a homemaker mother, both daughters of a Presbyterian minister, who organized a kindergarten in Louisville to demonstrate the educational value of early schooling. One of them, Mildred Hill, a Kentucky church organist, concert

pianist, and authority on black spirituals, wrote a song for the students to begin the school day, which she called "Good Morning to All." The younger sister, Patty Hill, a teacher in the kindergarten and student of John Dewey's philosophy of progressive education, wrote the lyrics. (Patty became a professor of education at Columbia University in 1905.) When "Good Morning to All" was published in a songbook in 1896, it had only one stanza. The lyrics described an adult greeting children ("Good morning dear children, good morning to all.") One of the pupils at the Hills' kindergarten reported that the guests at her birthday party had serenaded her with this song, but changed its words. Thereafter the Hill sisters recognized each child's birthday by singing "Happy birthday to you." In 1924 a Dallas, Texas, publisher included "Good Morning to All" in a collection, *Harvest Hymns,* but added a second stanza, which included the words "Happy birthday to you." After Irving Berlin and Moss Hart introduced the song in their Broadway musical *As Thousands Cheer* (1934), the Hills' tune entered popular culture and soon became the world's best-known song. The Hills' song, however, was frequently sung and played without the sisters receiving appropriate royalties. Patty Smith Hill's lawyers sued the publisher of *As Thousands Cheer* for copyright infringement and settled without going to court. In 1935, Clayton Summy of Chicago, the original publisher of "Good Morning to All," reissued the song under a new title, "Happy Birthday to You." Hawes, "The Birthday," p. 27; Chudacoff, *How Old Are You?,* pp. 117–118.

33. Chudacoff, *How Old Are You?,* pp. 29–48; David Tyack, *The One Best System: A History of American Urban Education* (Cambridge: Harvard University Press, 1974), pp. 30–32, 44–45; William Bullough, *Cities and Schools in the Gilded Age: The Evolution of an Urban Institution* (Port Washington, N.Y.: Kennikat Press, 1974), p. 45.

34. William Leach, "Child-World in the Promised Land," in James Gilbert, Ann Gilman, Donald M. Scott, and Joan W. Scott, eds., *The Mythmaking Frame of Mind: Social Imagination and American Culture* (Belmont, Calif.: Wadsworth Publishing, 1993), p. 226.

35. *Advertising World* (April 21, 1924), 12, as quoted in Leach, "Child-World in the Promised Land," p. 217.

36. Josephine Pounter, "Whose Birthday Party Is It, Anyway," *Better Homes and Gardens* 26 (June 1948): 219–220; Madeline Snyder, *My Book of Parties* (Garden City, N.Y.: Doubleday, Doran, and Co., 1929), p. 5. Emily Post argued that children's involvement gave them "training in social ease." Post, *Children Are People,* p. 267.

37. Helen Powell Schauffler, "Cakes and Candles," *Good Housekeeping* 84 (April 1927): 79.

38. Harvey Green, "Scientific Thought and the Nature of Children in America, 1820–1920," in Marylynn Stevens Heininger, Barbara Finkelstein, Harvey Green, Karin Calvert, Anne S. Macleod, and Kathy Vandall, eds., *A Century*

of Childhood, 1820–1920 (Rochester: Margaret Woodbury Strong Museum, 1984), p. 136; John F. Kasson, "Rituals of Dining: Table Manners in Victorian America," in Kathyrn Grover, ed., *Dining in America 1850–1900* (Amherst: University of Massachusetts Press, 1987), p. 124; Williams, *Savory Suppers,* p. 200.

39. Pounter, "Whose Birthday Party Is It Anyway," pp. 219–220.
40. Julia Woodbridge Oxreider, "The Slumber Party: Transition into Adolescence," *Tennessee Society Bulletin* 43 (1977): 128–134; Gertrude Brassard, "Sweet Sixteen Whirl," *American Home* 40 (September 1948): 100–103; Emily Rose Burt, *Planning Your Party* (New York: Harper and Brothers, 1927), pp. 288–294; "*Life* Goes to a Sleepless Slumber Party," *Life* 36 (April 16, 1954): 186–188.
41. Hawes, "Birthday," p. 68; Chudacoff, *How Old Are You?*, p. 146.
42. Frances L. Ilg, Louise Bates Ames, Evelyn W. Goodenough, and Irene B. Andresen, *The Gesell Institute Party Book* (New York: Harper Brothers, 1956), pp. x–xi. For similar advice, see Mary Grosvenor Ellsworth, *Birthday Parties for Boys and Girls from One to Fourteen* (New York: Woman's Press, 1951), p. v. A more recent example of advice for holding different kinds of parties for children from ages one to ten is Leslie Kane, "Happy Birthday Parties," *Parents* 70 (May 1995): 60.
43. Ilg et al., *Gesell Institute Party Book,* p. ix. Jay Mechling contends that parents base their child-rearing practices on their own childhood or on observing other parents, not on written advice. Jay Mechling, "Advice to Historians on Advice to Mothers," *Journal of Social History* 9 (1975): 44–63.
44. Gerd Baumann provides an excellent ethnography of a Punjabi birthday party in London in "Ritual Implicates 'Others': Rereading Durkheim in a Plural Society," in Daniel de Coppet, ed., *Understanding Rituals* (London: Routledge, 1992), pp. 97–116. We do not know whether Germans who had parties for children were working class as well as middle class. A Norwegian immigrant in twentieth-century North Dakota recalled that "birthdays were never mentioned." Aagot Raaen, *Grass of the Earth: Immigrant Life in the Dakota Country* (Northfield, Minn.: Norwegian-American Historical Association, 1950), p. 89.
45. Joan Jacobs Brumberg, "The 'Me' of Me: Voices of Jewish Girls in Adolescent Diaries of the 1920s and 1950s," in Joyce Antler, ed., *Talking Back: Images of Jewish Women in American Popular Culture* (Hanover, N.H.: University Press of New England, 1998), p. 57.
46. The quinceañera is the exception: it is a religious celebration on a girl's fifteenth birthday, rather than a secular party on her name day.
47. The name day was an important occasion in the Old Country. The newcomer was expected to send money home for a relative's name day; failure to do so could result in a letter from home listing the names of dutiful kin who had sent money home.
48. Interview with Anna di Benedetto, Italians in Chicago project, 1979–1981,

University of Illinois at Chicago. Colleen Leahy Johnson, *Growing Up and Growing Old in Italian-American Families* (New Brunswick, N.J.: Rutgers University Press, 1985), p. 101. Polish newspapers in the 1940s encouraged the commemoration of name days by offering congratulations on a saint's day to all those bearing the saint's name.

49. Carol Ann Bales, *Chinatown Sunday* (Chicago: Reilly and Lee Books, 1973), n.p.

50. Japanese-Americans in the United States continued, however, to have special celebrations on one's sixtieth, seventy-seventh, and eighty-eighth birthdays, as was done in Japan. Richard Chalfen, *Turning Leaves: The Photograph Collections of Two Japanese American Families* (Albuquerque: University of New Mexico Press, 1991), pp. 194–196; Valerie J. Matsumoto, *Farming the Home Place: A Japanese American Community in California, 1919–1982* (Ithaca: Cornell University Press, 1993), p. 78; Paul Radin, "Japanese Ceremonies and Festivals in California," *Southwestern Journal of Anthropology* 2 (1946): 154. The sixtieth birthday was also an important Chinese-American ritual.

51. Pamela B. Nelson, ed., *Rites of Passage in America: Traditions of the Life Cycle* (Philadelphia: Balch Institute for Ethnic Studies, 1992), pp. 6–7; Carolyn Kozo Cole and Kathy Kobayashi, *Shades of LA: Pictures from Ethnic Family Albums* (New York: New Press, 1996), p. 101; Pardee Lowe, *Father and Glorious Descendant* (Boston: Little, Brown and Co., 1943), pp. 274–275; Clarence E. Glick, *Sojourners and Settlers: Chinese Migrants in Hawaii* (Honolulu: Hawaii Chinese History Center and the University Press of Hawaii, 1980), pp. 169–170; Paul G. Chace, "Returning Thanks: Chinese Rites in an American Community," Part 1 (Ph.D. diss., University of California, Riverside, 1992), pp. 78–79.

52. Bales, *Chinatown Sunday*, n.p.

53. Ibid.; interview with Juanita Mortan, July 31, 1975 (no interviewer named), Mexican Americans in Minnesota Oral History Project, Minnesota Historical Society; Laurence Yep, *The Lost Garden* (Englewood Cliffs, N.J.: Julian Messner, 1991), p. 56.

54. Krishnendu Ray, "Meals, Migration, and Modernity: Domestic Cooking and Bengali Indian Ethnicity in the United States," *Amerasia Journal* 24 (Spring 1998): 105–127.

55. Interview with Hilda Polacheck, July 6, 1939, Works Progress Administration Life Histories Collection, Library of Congress. On Filipino birthday parties, which could be quite lavish, see Edwin B. Almiral, *Ethnic Identity and Social Negotiation: A Study of a Filipino Community in California* (New York: AMS Press, 1985), pp. 168–169.

56. Schoolmates also Americanized the names of immigrant children at school. Prior to television or radio, the immigrant child in the early twentieth century first made contact with the nonimmigrant American world at the school. Susan Cott Watkins and Andrew S. London, "Personal Names and Cultural

Change: A Study of the Naming Patterns of Italians and Jews in the United States in 1910," *Social Science History* 18 (Summer 1994): 169–209.

57. Dorothy and Thomas Hoobler, *The Cuban American Family Album* (New York: Oxford University Press, 1996), p. 91.

58. Monte Williams, "Praise of Victim of Helicopter Crash," *New York Times,* April 17, 1997, A19.

59. A survey conducted by American Greetings in 1995 found that about half of mothers bought their children a birthday present during the previous year and about a third of fathers did so. Camala Brown, "Cakes, Cards, and Candles," *American Demographics* 17 (March 1995): 210–211.

60. Sharon Hays, *The Cultural Contradictions of Motherhood* (New Haven: Yale University Press, 1996).

61. Lillian Eichler, *The Book of Etiquette,* vol. 1 (Garden City, N.Y.: Nelson Doubleday, 1924), p. 267.

62. Arlie Hochschild, *Time Bind: When Work Becomes Home and Home Becomes Work* (New York: Henry Holt and Co., 1977), p. 232.

63. Mary Campbell, "Birthday Party Blues," *Country Living* 12 (June 1989): 130–132.

64. Ellsworth, *Birthday Parties for Boys and Girls from One to Fourteen,* p. vii; Lillian Eichler Watson, *The Standard Book of Etiquette* (Garden City, N.Y.: Garden City Publishing, 1948), p. 460.

65. "*Life* Goes to an Ideal Child's Party: Child Psychologist's Rules Give Rochester Kids a Wonderful Time," *Life* 20 (May 20, 1946): 80–82. Wendy Kozol examines how *Life* portrayed the middle-class white family as the bedrock of the nation, a vital component in the fight against Communism, in *Life's America: Family and Nation in Postwar Photojournalism* (Philadelphia: Temple University Press, 1994).

66. Campbell, "Birthday Party Blues."

8. Rites of Passage

1. Jews had two ceremonies: the circumcision of an infant boy on the eighth day after birth; and a rite called the Redemption of the Firstborn, which occurred on the thirty-first day following the birth of a firstborn male child. Reform Jews eliminated the second ceremony because it was only for boys.

2. Richard W. Wertz and Dorothy C. Wertz, *Lying-In: A History of Childbirth in America* (New York: Free Press, 1977), p. 5.

3. Laurel Ulrich, *A Midwife's Tale* (New York: Vintage Books, 1990), p. 183.

4. Carroll Smith-Rosenberg, "The Female World of Love and Ritual: Relations between Women in Nineteenth-Century America," *Signs: Journal of Women in Culture and Society* 1 (Fall 1975): 1–30; Judith Walzer Leavitt, *Brought to Bed* (New York: Oxford University Press, 1986), pp. 89–91.

5. English Puritans opposed churching as a relic of Catholicism, and Puritans in the American colonies seem to have held the same opinion, declining to offer

such a ritual. Private communication from Paula Rieder, July 9, 1996; John R. Gillis, *A World of Their Own Making: Myth, Ritual, and the Quest for Family Values* (New York: Basic Books, 1996), p. 164; Michael M. Davis, Jr., *Immigrant Health and the Community* (New York: Harper and Brothers, 1921), p. 192; Linda Schelbitzki Pickle, *Contented among Strangers: Rural German-Speaking Women and Their Families in the Nineteenth-Century Midwest* (Urbana: University of Illinois Press, 1976), p. 88; Olwen Hufton, *The Prospect before Her: A History of Women in Western Europe, 1500–1800* (New York: Knopf, 1996), pp. 103–104; Merry E. Weisner, *Women and Gender in Early Modern Europe* (Cambridge: Cambridge University Press, 1993), p. 70; Edward Muir, *Ritual in Early Modern Europe* (Cambridge: Cambridge University Press, 1997), p. 24.

6. Muir, *Ritual in Early Modern Europe*, pp. 20–21.

7. Ibid., p. 22.

8. There was—and is—no standard distinction between a baptism and a christening. Dictionaries tend to define christening as the naming part of the ritual of baptism. To some extent Protestants tend to prefer the term "christening" over "baptism." For Catholics, baptism is a sacrament of the church, although they, too, often use the term "christening."

9. S. L. Louis, *Decorum: A Practical Treatise on Etiquette and Dress of the Best American Society* (New York: Union Publishing House, 1882), p. 370; *The Good Housekeeping Hostess* (New York: Phelps Publishing, 1904), p. 152.

10. M. E. W. Sherwood, *Manners and Social Usages* (New York: Harper and Brothers, 1884), pp. 169–172; Elizabeth L. Gebhard, *The Parsonage between Two Manors: Annals of Clover-Reach* (Hudson, N.Y.: Hudson Press, 1925), pp. 93–95.

11. John E. Baur, *Growing Up With California: A History of California's Children* (Los Angeles: Will Kramer, 1978), p. 73.

12. Shirley Fischer Arends, *The Central Dakota Germans: Their History, Language, and Culture* (Washington, D.C.: Georgetown University Press, 1989), p. 12; Norma Williams, *The Mexican American Family: Tradition and Change* (Dix Hills, N.Y.: General Hall, 1998), p. 25; interview with Matthew Castillas, June 23, 1975 (no interviewer specified), Mexican Americans in Minnesota Oral History Project, Minnesota Historical Society.

13. For the view that Mexican-American families in the 1980s mainly turned to biological kin, not close family friends, for aid, see Anne R. Roschelle, *No More Kin: Exploring Race, Class, and Gender in Family Networks* (Thousand Oaks, Calif.: Sage, 1977), p. 40.

14. Norma Williams, *The Mexican American Family* (Dix Hills, N.Y.: General Hall, 1978), pp. 51, 69–70; interview with David Limon, August 5, 1975, Mexican Americans in Minnesota Oral History Project, Minnesota Historical Society.

15. Williams, *Mexican American Family*, p. 70. If acculturation led to the decline in a distinctive Mexican-American christening, how does one explain the

growth of another Mexican-American ritual, the quinceañera? First, the greater anxiety of adolescence seemed to require more ritual elaboration. Second, parents of adolescents tended to be wealthier than parents of newborns, and therefore may have been more inclined to want to display their wealth.

16. Williams, *Mexican American Family,* pp. 48, 49. Reformers in the United Methodist church advocated combining the rites of baptism, first communion, and confirmation. Joseph T. Reiff, "Nurturing and Equipping Children in the 'Public Church,'" in Nancy Tatom Ammerman and Wade Clark Roof, eds., *Work, Family, and Religion in Contemporary Society* (New York: Routledge, 1995), p. 207. Jewish-Protestant couples in the 1990s occasionally had a "dedication" ceremony at a church, with a rabbi and a minister officiating, as a religious compromise for children who were going to be raised in two faiths. Jerry Adler, "A Matter of Faith," *Newsweek* 130 (December 15, 1997): 51.

17. Frances Jerome Woods, *Cultural Values of American Ethnic Groups* (New York: Harper and Brothers, 1956), p. 125; Williams, *Mexican American Family,* p. 24; Baur, *Growing Up with California,* p. 73.

18. Williams, *Mexican American Family,* p. 26; Paul Kutsche, "Household and Family in Hispanic New Mexico," *Journal of Comparative Family Studies* 14 (Summer 1983): 151–166.

19. Phyllis H. Williams, *South Italian Folkways in Europe and America* (New Haven: Yale University Press, 1938), p. 94.

20. Fredda Gregg Martinez, "Familism in Acculturated Mexican Americans: Patterns, Changes and Perceived Impact on Adjustment to U.S. Society," (Ph.D. diss., Northern Arizona State University, 1993), p. 111.

21. Colleen Leahy Johnson, *Growing Up and Growing Old in Italian-American Families* (New Brunswick, N.J.: Rutgers University Press, 1985), pp. 93–94.

22. On the attitude of Jewish immigrants, see Ruth Gay, *Unfinished People: Eastern European Jews Encounter America* (New York: W. W. Norton, 1996), p. 55.

23. Gillis, *A World of Their Own Making,* p. 160; Katharine Morris McClinton, *Antiques of American Childhood* (New York: Bramhall House, 1970), p. 38.

24. Irene Sege, "The Baby Shower: Where Women Gather," *Boston Globe,* March 28, 1994, Sec. 3, p. 30. Jews are still not supposed to have baby showers because it is considered bad luck.

25. For some of the games recommended for 1950s all-female baby showers, see Helen Emily Webster, *Shower Parties for All Occasions* (New York: Woman's Press, 1953), pp. 84–121.

26. Eileen Fischer and Brenda Gainer, "Baby Showers: A Rite of Passage in Transition," *Advances in Consumer Research* 20 (1993): 320–324.

27. Ibid., p. 321. Fischer and Gainer observed workplace showers as well as "feminist" baby showers in the 1990s. Workplace showers were usually held at a place of employment, to which coworkers, sometimes males and females,

brought gifts. Most were for the pregnant woman, but there were some for expecting fathers as well. A "feminist" shower could be all-female or sexually integrated. Guests often brought small gifts for the mother (such as gift certificates for a massage or a day at a spa) rather than gifts for the baby. Givers wanted to indicate in their gifts that a woman needed a separate identity from that of being a mother, and that she required time away from her children.

28. Gillis, *A World of Their Own Making,* p. 170.

29. Michelle Perrot and Anne Martin-Fugier, "The Actors," in Michelle Perrot, ed., *A History of Private Life: From the Fires of Revolution to the Great War,* trans. Arthur Goldhammer (Cambridge: Harvard University Press, 1990), pp. 324–330.

30. Leslie Woodcock Tentler, *Seasons of Grace: A History of the Catholic Archdiocese of Detroit* (Detroit: Wayne State University Press, 1990), pp. 167–168.

31. Edward Rivera, "First Communion," in Harold Hugenbraum and Ilan Stavans, *Growing Up Latino: Memoirs and Stories* (Boston: Houghton Mifflin, 1993), p. 231; S. P. Breckinridge, *New Homes for Old* (New York: Harper and Brothers, 1921), p. 104.

32. Breckinridge, *New Homes for Old,* pp. 104–105.

33. Carol Coburn, *Life at Four Corners: Religion, Gender, and Education in a German-Lutheran Community, 1868–1945* (Lawrence: University Press of Kansas, 1972), p. 105; Arends, *The Central Dakota Germans,* pp. 113–114.

34. Interview with Gloria Bacci, BAC-72, Italians in Chicago Oral History Project, 1979–1981, University of Illinois, Chicago Circle.

35. Mircea Eliade, *Rites and Symbols of Initiation* (New York: Harper and Row, 1958). Usually those who argue in favor of puberty rites also make the claim that boys need such rites to escape from their overly protective mothers or that the absence of such rites is part of the reason for the aimlessness and amorality of modern youth. Anthony Stevens, *Archetypes: A Natural History of the Self* (New York: William Morrow, 1982), p. 159; Eric Neumann, *The Child: Structure and Dynamics of the Nascent Personality* (New York: Putnam, 1973), p. 186; Jerome S. Bernstein, "The Decline of Rites of Passage in Our Culture: The Impact of Individuation," in Louise Carus Mahdi, Steven Foster, and Meredith Little, eds., *Betwixt and Between: Patterns of Masculine and Feminine Initiation* (La Salle, Ill.: Open Court, 1987), pp. 135–158. On the debutante cotillion in Gilded Age Manhattan society, see Maureen E. Montgomery, "Female Rituals and the Politics of the New York Marriage Market in the Late Nineteenth Century," *Journal of Family History* 23 (January 1998): 47–67.

36. The best descriptions of the Navaho ritual are Edward S. Curtis, *The North American Indian* (New York: Johnson Reprint, 1970), pp. 124–125; Charlotte Johnson Frisbie, *Kinaaldá: A Study of the Navaho Girl's Puberty Ceremony* (Middletown, Conn.: Wesleyan University Press, 1967); Gladys Reich-

ard, *Social Life of the Navajo Indians* (New York: Columbia University Press, 1928); Leland Wyman and Flora Bailey, "Navajo Girl's Puberty Rite," *New Mexico Anthropologist* 25 (January–March 1943): 3–12; Bruce Lincoln, *Emerging from the Chrysalis: Studies in Rituals of Women's Initiation* (Cambridge: Harvard University Press, 1981), pp. 17–33. See also Shirley M. Begay, *Kinaaldá: A Navajo Puberty Ceremony* (Rough Rock, Ariz.: Navajo Curriculum Center, Rough Rock Demonstration School, 1983).

37. In the bar mitzvah, for example, before about 1910 the reading of a haftarah portion, a selection from the Prophets, was optional. Boys might read the entire weekly portion of the Torah, or just a section of it, depending on how good their Hebrew was. In some families boys gave a speech, in which, among other things, they thanked their parents for all they had done and promised to be a dutiful son, while other congregations did not require a speech. Hyman B. Grinstein, *The Rise of the Jewish Community of New York 1654–1860* (Philadelphia: Jewish Publication Society of America, 1945), pp. 247–249.

38. Even so, not every Jewish boy had one. Among Cincinnati Jewish boys in 1927 and 1928, for example, only 56 percent had the ceremony. Arthur L. Rinehart, *The Voice of the Jewish Laity: A Survey of the Jewish Layman's Religious Attitudes and Practices* (Cincinnati: National Federation of Temple Brotherhoods, 1928), p. 7; Marshall Sklare and Joseph Greenbaum, *Jewish Identity on the Suburban Frontier: A Study of Group Survival in the Open Society* (Chicago: University of Chicago Press, 1967), p. 296.

39. Jenna Weissman Joselit, *The Wonders of America: Reinventing Jewish Culture, 1880–1950* (New York: Hill and Wang, 1994), p. 92.

40. Kalman Whiteman, *Bar Mitzvah* (New York: Hebrew Publishing Company, 1931), pp. 1–8; Myrna Katz Frommer and Harvey Frommer, *Growing Up Jewish in America: An Oral History* (New York: Harcourt Brace, 1995), p. 188; Stuart Schoenfeld, "Folk Judaism, Elite Judaism, and the Role of Bar Mitzvah in the Development of the Synagogue and Jewish School in America," *Contemporary Jewry* 9 (1988): 70.

41. Jacob Arlow writes, "The dawning manhood of the primitive youth was signalized by the gift of a spear; the Jewish boy at his Bar Mitzvah gets a fountain pen." Jacob A. Arlow, "A Psychoanalytic Study of a Religious Initiation Rite: Bar Mitzvah," in Ruth S. Eissler, ed., *Psychoanalytic Study of the Child*, vol. 6 (New York: International Universities Press, 1957), p. 372; Sam Levenson, *In One Era and Out the Other* (New York: Simon and Schuster, 1973), pp. 412–413; Maury Levy, "The Coming of Age of Mark Moskowitz," *Philadelphia Magazine* 63 (March 1972): 81; Harpo Marx, with Rowland Barber, *Harpo Speaks* (New York: Limelight Editions, 1989), p. 58.

42. Frommer and Frommer, *Growing Up Jewish in America: An Oral History* (New York: Harcourt Brace, 1995), p. 196. For another example from the 1920s, see Eric A. Kimmel, *Bar Mitzvah: A Jewish Boy's Coming of Age* (New York: Viking, 1995), p. 45.

43. Frommer and Frommer, *Growing up Jewish in America,* p. 186; Samuel Chotzinoff, *A Lost Paradise: Early Reminiscence* (New York: Alfred Knopf, 1955), p. 267; Elizabeth Ehrlich, *Miriam's Kitchen: A Memoir* (New York: Viking, 1997), pp. 82–83.

44. Children whose parents could not afford catering had a small lunch at the synagogue. Kimmel, *Bar Mitzvah,* p. 131.

45. Joselit, *Wonders of America,* pp. 96–99, 100.

46. Ibid.

47. Ari Goldman discusses the impact of divorce on the bar mitzvah reception. At his own bar mitzvah, in 1962, his parents' divorce was so bitter that his parents held separate receptions. Goldman shuttled between two catering halls, and was made to feel "like some exhibit animal in the circus." The animosity continued unabated, so that both of his younger brothers also had dual (and dueling) bar mitzvah receptions. Ari Goldman, "The Search for God at Harvard," in Jay David, ed., *Growing up Jewish: An Anthology* (New York: Avon Books, 1997), p. 163.

48. Joselit, *Wonders of America,* p. 97.

49. Rabbi Erwin L. Herman, "Bar Mitzvah a la Carte," in Paul Kresh, ed., *The American Judaism Reader: Essays, Fiction and Poetry from the Pages of American Judaism* (London: Abelard-Schuman, 1967), pp. 253–256.

50. Joselit, *Wonders of America,* p. 102. Jewish concern about extravagance at bar mitzvah celebrations dates back at least to the 1500s. Jews in Poland placed a communal tax on bar mitzvah feasts so that they would remain modest events. Another Polish rabbinical decree in the 1600s stated that no more than ten strangers could be invited to the event, and one of them had to be a poor man. Barbara Diamond Goldin, *Bat Mitzvah: A Jewish Girl's Coming of Age* (New York: Puffin Books, 1995), p. 111.

51. Joselit, *Wonders of America,* p. 104.

52. Ibid., pp. 105–114.

53. Arlow, "A Psychoanalytic Study," p. 372.

54. Reconstructionism, the "left wing" of the Conservative movement, was the exception. In Reconstructionist synagogues, equality of the sexes was the reason behind the bat mitzvah. Paula E. Hyman, "The Introduction of Bat Mitzvah in Conservative Judaism in Postwar America," in Deborah Dash Moore, ed., *YIVO Annual,* vol. 19 (Evanston: Northwestern University Press, 1990), pp. 137–138; *Proceedings of the Rabbinical Assembly of the Jewish Theological Seminary of America,* vol. 4 (New York: Little Print, 1933), p. 331.

55. Joselit, *Wonders of America,* p. 129; Hyman, "Bat Mitzvah," p. 145. By 1960, the bat mitzvah was offered in 96 percent of American Reform congregations. Michael H. Meyer, *Response to Modernity: A History of the Reform Movement in Judaism* (New York: Oxford University Press, 1988), p. 472.

56. Joselit, *Wonders of America,* p. 131; Hyman, "Bat Mitzvah," pp. 143, 145;

Proceedings of the Rabbinical Assembly of the Jewish Theological Seminary of America, vol. 4, p. 331.

57. Marlene Adler Marks, "Introduction," in Marlene Adler Marks, *Nice Jewish Girls: Growing Up in America* (New York: Plume, 1996), p. 3.

58. Among the Orthodox there was more variation. Bat mitzvahs might occur in a home or synagogue social hall rather than in the sanctuary, and the girl might give a talk based on the weekly Torah readings. Some Orthodox girls had a ceremony in a Saturday morning woman's prayer group, to which only nine men were permitted to attend. Goldin, *Bat Mitzvah,* p. 53; Rela Geffen Monson, "The Impact of the Jewish Women's Movement on the American Synagogue, 1972–1985," in Susan Grossman and Rivka Haut, ed., *Daughters of the King: Women and the Synagogue* (Philadelphia: Jewish Publication Society, 1992), pp. 227–236.

59. Major studies of the quinceañera include Catherine Makem Kelly, "Celebrating a Cultural Tradition: Quinceañera/Sweet Sixteen" (master's thesis, La Salle University, 1990); Almudena Ortiz, "Fiesta de Quinceañera: Queen for a Day" (master's thesis, University of California at Berkeley, 1992); Karen Mary Davalos, "Ethnic Identity among Mexican and Mexican American Women in Chicago, 1920–1991" (Ph.D. diss., Yale University, 1993), and an article based on her dissertation, "*La Quinceañera:* Making Gender and Ethnic Identities," *Frontiers: A Journal of Women Studies* 16 (1996): 101–127; Ruth Horowitz, "The Power of Ritual in a Chicano Community: A Young Woman's Status and Expanding Family Ties," *Marriage and the Family Review* 19 (1993): 257–280. Kelly's thesis deals with Puerto Ricans in Philadelphia; the other two concern Mexican Americans.

60. There were 57 Mexican nationality parishes in 1940, and only 22 in 1960. Robert R. Trevino, "La Fe: Catholicism and Mexican Americans in Houston, 1911–1972" (Ph.D. diss., Stanford University, 1973), p. 103.

61. Rolando Hinojosa Smith, "Sweet Fifteen," *Texas Monthly* 16 (January 1988): 96–99.

62. Interview with Michelle Salcedo, July 30, 1996.

63. *Arizona Republic,* October 8, 1994, pp. E-1, E2; Nydia Garcia Preto, "Transformation of the Family System in Adolescence," in Betty Carter and Monica Goldrick, eds., *The Changing Family Cycle: A Framework for Family Therapy* (New York: Gardner Press, 1988), pp. 255–283.

64. Ortiz, "Fiesta de Quinceañera," pp. 62–63; Davalos, "*La Quinceañera,*" p. 109.

65. Trevino, "La Fe," p. 142.

66. June Macklin and Alvin Teniente de Costilla, "La Virgen de Guadalupe and the American Dream," in Stanley A. West and June Macklin, eds., *The Chicano Experience* (Boulder: Westview Press, 1979), p. 136; Gwen Louise Stern, "Ethnic Identity and Community Action in El Barrio" (Ph.D. diss., Northwestern University, 1976), 43.

67. Ruth Horowitz, *Honor and the American Dream* (New Brunswick: Rutgers University Press, 1983), p. 53.

68. Arlow, "A Psychoanalytic Study," pp. 353–374.
69. Horowitz, *Honor and the American Dream,* pp. 52–54.
70. Lincoln, *Emerging,* p. 104.
71. Mary D. Lankford, *Quinceañera: A Latina's Journey to Womanhood* (Brookfield, Conn.: Millbrook Press, 1994), p. 38; Ortiz, "Fiesta de Quinceañera," pp. 50–51.
72. Arturo Perez, *Popular Catholicism: A Hispanic Perspective* (Washington, D.C.: Pastoral Press, 1988), p. 22.
73. "Coming Out Parties Split Hispanics, Church," *Chicago Tribune,* June 24, 1990, Sec. 1, p. 4.
74. *New York Times,* June 21, 1994, p. 13.
75. Davalos, "*La Quinceañera,*" p. 111; "The Quinceañera: A Mexican Girl's Day as Cinderella," *Chicago Tribune,* August 17, 1980, Sec. 12, pp. 4, 7.
76. Davalos, "*La Quinceañera,*" p. 110.
77. Williams, *Mexican American Family,* p. 23; Rosa Linda Fregoso, "Homegirls, *Cholas,* and *Pachucas* in Cinema: Taking over the Public Sphere," *California History* 84 (Fall 1995): 316–327.
78. Ortiz, "Fiesta de Quinceañera," p. 93.
79. Ibid., p. 30.
80. Some Chicago families in the 1990s even dispensed with the mass. "Sweet 15," *Vista* 6, (1991), p. 6.
81. Frank T. Fair, *Orita for Black Youth: An Initiation into Christian Adulthood* (Valley Forge: Judson Press, 1977); Nathan and Julia Hare, *Bringing the Black Boy to Manhood* (San Francisco: Black Think Tank, 1985); Nsenga Warfield-Coppock, *Adolescent Rites of Passage* (Washington, D.C.: Baobab Associates, 1990).

9. Please Omit Flowers

1. Philippe Ariès, *The Hour of Our Death* (New York: Alfred Knopf, 1981) is a major survey of European attitudes toward death since the ninth century and a polemic against the modern, "sanitized" way of dying. For the impact of the Protestant reformation on English funeral ritual, see David Cressy, *Birth, Marriage, and Death: Ritual, Religion, and the Life-Cycle in Tudor and Stuart England* (New York: Oxford University Press, 1997). The two major studies of Puritan deathways in colonial America are David E. Stannard, *The Puritan Way of Death: A Study in Religion, Culture, and Social Change* (New York: Oxford University Press, 1977) and Gordon E. Geddes, *Welcome Joy: Death in Puritan New England* (Ann Arbor: UMI Research Press, 1981). Gary Laderman traces changing U.S. attitudes toward dying and toward corpses in *The Sacred Remains: American Attitudes toward Death, 1799–1883* (New Haven: Yale University Press, 1996). James J. Farrell examines the impact of the Civil War, the growth of embalming, and the development of the funeral industry in *Inventing the American Way of Death, 1830–1920* (Philadelphia: Temple University Press, 1980). Blanche Linden-

Ward studies the evolution of the rural cemetery in *Silent City on a Hill: Landscapes of Memory and Boston's Mount Auburn Cemetery* (Columbus: Ohio State University Press, 1989). Robert V. Wells examines the deathways of two families who nursed the dying and mourned the dead. See "Taming the 'King of Terrors': Ritual and Death in Schenectady, New York, 1844–1860," *Journal of Social History* 27 (Summer 1994): 717–734. For changes in Appalachian burial practices in the twentieth century, see James K. Crissman, *Death and Dying in Central Appalachia: Changing Attitudes and Practices* (Urbana: University of Illinois Press, 1994).

2. Brian MacQuarrie, "Old Irish Wake Breathing Its Last in Boston," *Boston Globe,* March 13, 1998, p. A1.

3. Philippe Ariès called the Victorian ways of death the Death of the Other. He believed that its characteristic features were a decline in the terror of hell, belief in a family reunion in heaven, and a view of death as beautiful. From studying diaries of English Victorians, however, Pat Jalland claims she could not find evidence that the Victorians regarded death as beautiful. She did note that they rarely wrote about the eternal fires of hell and that they dwelled at length on family reunions in heaven. Ariès, *Hour of Our Death;* Pat Jalland, *Death in the Victorian Family* (New York: Oxford University Press, 1996), p. 8.

4. Stanley B. Burns, *Sleeping Beauty: Memorial Photography in America* (Altadena, Calif.: Twelvetree Press, 1990), n.p.

5. Alice Morse Earle, *Customs and Fashions in Old New England* (New York: Charles Scribner's Sons, 1899), p. 369; Leslie Woodcock Tentler, *Seasons of Grace: A History of the Catholic Archdiocese of Detroit* (Detroit: Wayne State University Press, 1990), p. 183.

6. Earle, *Customs and Fashions in Old New England,* p. 382; Geddes, *Welcome Joy,* pp. 146–149.

7. M. A. DeWolfe Howe, ed., *The Articulate Sisters: Passages from the Journals and Letters of the Daughters of President Josiah Quincy of Harvard University* (Cambridge: Harvard University Press, 1946), p. 238; David Charles Sloane, *The Last Great Necessity: Cemeteries in American History* (Baltimore: Johns Hopkins University Press, 1991), pp. 44–64; Farrell, *Inventing the American Way of Death,* pp. 99–111; Stanley French, "The Cemetery as a Cultural Institution: The Establishment of Mount Auburn and the 'Rural Cemetery Movement,'" in David E. Stannard, ed., *Death in America* (Philadelphia: University of Pennsylvania Press, 1995), pp. 69–91.

8. Burns, *Sleeping Beauty,* n.p. Immigrant Jews had their own domestic equivalent of these illustrations. Printed on brightly colored paper, the yahrzeit plaque, which contained the date for the annual remembrance of the dead as well as the name of the deceased and the date of death, included illustrations of weeping willows and urns alongside quotations in Hebrew and drawings of the Kever Rahel, the cave of the matriarch Rachel. Jenna Weissman Joselit, *The Wonders of America: Reinventing Jewish Culture, 1880–1950* (New York: Hill and Wang, 1994), p. 287.

9. Laderman, *Sacred Remains,* p. 153; Martha Pike, "In Memory of: Artifacts Relating to Mourning in Nineteenth Century America," *Journal of American Culture* 3 (Winter 1980): 642–659.

10. Mary Hojnacki, OJ-066, Interviewed 1977, Oral History Archives of Chicago Polonia, Chicago Historical Society; Vanderlyn R. Pine, *Caretaker of the Dead: The American Funeral Director* (New York: Irvington Publishers, 1975), p. 17.

11. Margaret Coffin, *Death in America* (Nashville: Thomas Nelson, 1976), p. 198; Karen Halttunen, *Confidence Men and Painted Women: A Study of Middle-Class Culture in America, 1830–1870* (New York: Yale University Press, 1982), p. 137; Lou Taylor, *Mourning Dress: A Costume and Social History* (Boston: G. Allen and Unwin, 1983), pp. 19–20.

12. Wells, "Taming the King of Terrors," p. 722.

13. Jenny Hockey, "Women in Grief: Cultural Representation and Social Practice," in David Field, Jenny Hockey, and Neil Small, eds., *Death, Gender and Ethnicity* (London: Routledge, 1997), p. 101.

14. "The Unseemliness of Funerals," *Literary Digest* 54 (April 21, 1917): 1170.

15. Stanley Lebergott, *Pursuing Happiness: American Consumers in the Twentieth Century* (Princeton: Princeton University Press, 1993), pp. 154–163; B. F. Timmons, "The Cost of Weddings," *American Sociological Review* 4 (April 1939): 224–233; John C. Gebhart, *The Reasons for Present-Day Funeral Costs* (New York: Metropolitan Life Co., 1927), p. 13; August B. Hollingshead, "Marital Status and Wedding Behavior," *Journal of Marriage and Family Living* 17 (1952): 310; Leroy Bowman, *The American Funeral: A Study in Guilt, Extravagance, and Sublimity* (Washington, D.C.: Public Affairs Press, 1959), p. 43. Wedding data for 1990 from H-H Family Leisure Group, Research Department, based on a national random sample of couples marrying for the first time. For 1990 information on funerals, see Robert Tomsho, "Funeral Parlors Become Big Business," *Wall Street Journal,* September 18, 1996, B1; Gordon Fairclough, "Casket Stores Offer Bargains to Die For," *Wall Street Journal,* February 19, 1997, B1.

16. MacQuarrie, "Old Irish Wake," p. A1.

17. Joselit, *Wonders of America,* p. 273; Elizabeth Mathias, "The Italian-American Funeral: Persistence through Change," *Western Folklore* 33 (January 1974): 44; Robert J. Kastenbaum, *Death, Society, and Human Experience,* 5th ed. (Boston: Allyn and Bacon, 1995), p. 305.

18. Edith B. Ordway, *The Etiquette of To-Day* (New York: George Sully and Co., 1913), p. 232.

19. James J. Farrell, *Inventing the American Way of Death,* p. 179, 193. A 1982 survey of 1600 people found that most wanted sermons, eulogies, and other remarks at the service to last twenty minutes or less. Amy Seidel Marks and Bobby J. Calder, *Attitudes Toward Death and Funerals* (Evanston: Center for Marketing Sciences, 1982), p. 60.

20. Norma Williams, "Changes in Funeral Patterns and Gender Roles among Mexican Americans," in Vicki L. Ruiz and Susan Tiano, eds., *Women on the*

U.S.-Mexico Border: Responses to Change (Boulder: Westview Press, 1991), p. 209; Marian Osterweis, Fredric Solomon, and Morris Green, eds., *Bereavement: Reactions, Consequences, and Care* (Washington, D.C.: National Academy Press, 1984), p. 209; Rose Grieco, "They Who Mourn," *Commonweal* 57 (March 27, 1953): 628–630; Nicholas John Russo, "Three Generations of Italians in New York City: Their Religious Acculturation," in Silvano M. Tomasi and Madeline H. Engel, eds., *The Italian Experience in the United States* (New York: Center for Migration Studies, 1977), p. 207.

21. Despite this advice, people continued to send flowers. The market survey mentioned above indicated that at most funerals there were more than a dozen wreaths and floral arrangements. Marks and Calder, *Attitudes toward Death and Funerals,* p. 27.

22. Geddes, *Welcome Joy,* p. 144.

23. Jessica Mitford, *The American Way of Death* (New York: Simon and Schuster, 1963), pp. 110–122; Williams, "Changes in Funeral Patterns among Mexican Americans," p. 209; William M. Kephart, "Status after Death," *American Sociological Review* 15 (October 1950): 635–643.

24. Jay Ruby, *Secure the Shadow: Death and Photography in America* (Cambridge: MIT Press, 1995), pp. 159–161; Burns, *Sleeping Beauty,* n.p.; Richard Chalfen, *Turning Leaves: The Photograph Collections of Two Japanese American Families* (Albuquerque: University of New Mexico Press, 1991), pp. 99–136; Timothy J. Lukes and Gary J. Okihiro, *Japanese Legacy: Farming and Community Life in California's Santa Clara Valley* (Cupertino: California History Center, 1985), p. 39.

25. W. Lloyd Warner, *The Living and the Dead: A Study of the Symbolic Life of Americans* (New Haven: Yale University Press, 1959), p. 293; John Matturi, "Windows in the Garden: Italian-American Memorialization and the American Cemetery," in Richard E. Meyer, ed., *Ethnicity and the American Cemetery* (Bowling Green: Bowling Green State University Popular Press, 1993), pp. 29–30.

26. Kay Turner and Pat Jasper, "Day of the Dead: The Tex-Mex Tradition" in Jack Santino, ed., *Halloween and Other Festivals of Death and Life* (Knoxville: University of Tennessee Press, 1994), pp. 133–151; "Caressing Life on the Day of the Dead," *New York Times,* November 4, 1995, A7; Lynn Gosnell and Suzanne Gott, "San Fernando Cemetery: Decorations of Loss in a Mexican-American Community," in Richard E. Meyer, ed., *Cemeteries and Gravemarkers* (Ann Arbor: UMI Research Press, 1989), pp. 217–236. Jews were expected to visit graves only in the month of Elul, immediately preceding the High Holidays. Gradually American Jews began to visit cemeteries on Memorial Day, Mother's Day, and Father's Day. Joselit, *Wonders of America,* p. 278. On Japanese-American funeral practices, see David Mas Masumoto, *Country Voices: The Oral History of a Japanese American Family Farm Community* (Del Rey, Calif.: Inaka Countryside Publications, 1987), pp. 145–158.

27. D. Gregory Jeane, "The Upland South Folk Cemetery Complex: Some Sug-

gestions of Origin," in Meyer, ed., *Cemeteries and Gravemarkers,* p. 118; Matturi, "Windows in the Garden," pp. 14–35; Richard A. Kalish, "Cemetery Visits," *Death Studies* 10, no. 1 (1986): 55–58. Among several ethnic groups surveyed, visiting graves was most common among Japanese Americans. Richard A. Kalish and David K. Reynolds, *Death and Ethnicity: A Psychocultural Study* (Farmingdale, N.Y.: Baywood Publishing, 1981), p. 26.

28. Joselit, *Wonders of America,* pp. 278–281; Toby Talbot, *A Book about My Mother* (New York: Farrar, Straus and Giroux, 1980), p. 19; Crissman, *Death and Dying,* pp. 75–76; Ruth Harmer, *The High Cost of Dying* (New York: Collier Books, 1963), pp. 214–215.

29. Joselit, *Wonders of America,* p. 292.

30. Williams, "Changes in Funeral Patterns among Mexican Americans," p. 214; Martha Oehmke Loustaunau, "Hispanic Widows and Their Support Systems in the Mesilla Valley of Southern New Mexico, 1910–1940," in Arlene Scadron, ed., *On Their Own: Widows and Widowhood in the American Southwest, 1848–1939* (Urbana: University of Illinois Press, 1988), p. 102; Crissman, *Death and Dying,* p. 144.

31. Robert Blauner, "Death and the Social Structure," in Charles O. Jackson, ed., *Passing: The Vision of Death in America* (Westport, Conn.: Greenwood Press, 1977), p. 179.

32. Robert Fulton, "Death and the Funeral in Contemporary Society," in Hannelore Wass, Felix Bernardo, and Robert A. Neimeyer, eds., *Dying: Facing the Facts* (New York: Hemisphere Publishing Corporation, 1979), pp. 250, 272. Most customers for discount caskets were adult children whose elderly parents had died. Fairclough, "Casket Stores."

33. The funerals of gay men raised questions about whether the biological kin or the gay partner should make decisions about the distribution of possessions, the listings of survivors in an obituary, and the type of funeral. Traditional funeral services were sometimes planned by relatives without consulting with the deceased's partner. When the partner was not even allowed to attend the funeral, alienation and anger in grief were compounded. In these situations, neighbors and friends often organized some kind of mourning ritual for the surviving partner. Kathy Charmaz, *The Social Reality of Death: Death in Contemporary America* (New York: Random House, 1980), p. 204; Marita Sturken, *Tangled Memories: the Vietnam War, the AIDS Epidemic, and the Politics of Remembering* (Berkeley: University of California Press, 1997), pp. 183–219; Kath Weston, *Families We Choose: Lesbians, Gays, Kinship* (New York: Columbia University Press, 1991), p. 186.

34. "New Rituals Ease Grief as AIDS Toll Increases," *New York Times,* May 11, 1987, C11; Kittredge Cherry and Zalmon Sherwood, eds., *Equal Rites: Lesbian and Gay Worship, Ceremonies, and Celebrations* (Louisville: Westminster John Knox Press, 1995), pp. 43–59. Halloween celebrations in gay neighborhoods were also occasionally used for collective mourning of the dead.

35. Bertram Puckle, *Funeral Customs: Their Origin and Development* (London:

T. W. Laurie, 1926); Le Roy Bowman, *The American Funeral: A Study in Guilt, Extravagance, and Sublimity* (Washington, D.C.: Public Affairs Press, 1959), p. 195; John C. Gebhart, *Funeral Costs: What They Average, Are They Too High? Can They be Reduced* (New York: G. P. Putnam's, 1928); Vivana Zelizer, *The Social Meaning of Money: Pin Money, Paychecks, Poor Relief, and Other Currencies* (New York: Basic Books, 1997), pp. 178–186. For opposition to the lavish funeral in New York in the 1700s, see Kenneth Scott, "Funeral Customs in Colonial New York," *New York Folklore Quarterly* 15 (Winter 1959): 274–282.

36. Robert Fulton, "The Clergyman and the Funeral Director: A Study in Role Conflict," *Social Forces* 39 (May 1961): 317–323.

37. Mitford, *American Way of Death,* pp. 259–282; Harmer, *High Cost of Dying,* pp. 147–163; Roy Vaughn Nichols, "Acute Grief, Disposal, Funerals, and Consequences," in Otto S. Margolis, Howard C. Raether, Austin H. Kutscher, Robert J. Volk, Ivan K. Goldberg, and Daniel J. Cherico, eds., *Grief and the Meaning of the Funeral* (New York: MSS Information Corporation, 1975), pp. 23–47; Tentler, *Seasons of Grace,* p. 186; Robert Fulton, "The Funeral in Contemporary Society," in Hannelore Wass, Felix M. Bernardo, and Robert A. Neimeyer, eds., *Dying: Facing the Facts,* 2d ed. (Washington, D.C.: Hemisphere Publishing Corporation, 1988), pp. 257–277; Mitford, *American Way of Death,* pp. 241–258.

38. Mitford, *American Way of Death;* Nelda Samarel, "The Dying Process," in Hannelore Wass and Robert A. Neimeyer, eds., *Dying: Facing the Facts,* 3d ed. (Washington, D.C.: Taylor and Francis, 1995), pp. 93–95; Elisabeth Kubler-Ross, *On Death and Dying* (New York: Macmillan, 1969).

39. Michael C. Kearl, *Endings: A Sociology of Death and Dying* (New York: Oxford University Press, 1989), p. 441; Wass, Berardo, and Neimeyer, eds., *Dying: Facing the Facts,* 2d ed., pp. 185–200; Kubler-Ross, *On Death and Dying.*

40. Robert J. Kastenbaum argues that antisentimental expressions such as "she OD'd" or "he croaked" have increased in recent years. Kastenbaum, *Death, Society, and Human Experience,* 5th ed. (Boston: Allyn and Bacon, 1995), p. 63.

41. Judith M. Stillion, "Death in the Lives of Adults: Responding to the Tolling of the Bell," in Wass and Neimeyer, eds., *Dying: Facing the Facts,* 3d ed., p. 317; Jeanne Quint Benolier and Lesley F. Degner, "Institutional Dying: A Convergence of Cultural Values, Technology, and Social Organization," in Wass and Neimeyer, eds., *Dying: Facing the Facts,* 3d ed., p. 123; Brad Edmondson, "The Facts of Death," *American Demographics* 19 (April 1997): 48.

42. M. Betsey Bergen and Robert R. Williams, "Alternative Funerals: An Exploratory Study," *Omega* 21 (1981–82): 71–78. In a 1969 survey, when people were asked whether it was best for everyone if the dying were removed to a hospital, about a third said yes. A somewhat larger group was ambivalent or

undecided, and 20 percent preferred death at home. Gerald F. Moran and Maris Vinovskis, *Religion, Family, and the Life Course: Explorations in the Social History of Early America* (Ann Arbor: University of Michigan Press, 1972), p. 222.

43. Kastenbaum, *Death, Society, and Human Experience,* 5th ed., p. 305; Paul E. Irion, "Changing Patterns of Ritual Response to Death," *Omega* 22 (1990–91): 159–172.
44. Ronald G. E. Smith, *The Death Care Industries in America* (Jefferson, N.C.: McFarland and Co., 1966), pp. 254, 369; William G. Flanagan, "The New (and More Convenient) American Way of Death," *Forbes* 158 (Oct. 21, 1996): 324–326. The preponderance of Japanese-Americans in Hawaii, with their tradition of cremation, also helps to explain the high rate of cremation on the islands.
45. Smith, *Death Care Industries,* p. 351; Kearl, *Endings,* p. 282; "More Choose Cremation though Cost Can Rival Burial," *New York Times,* October 12, 1997, B10.
46. In the 1960s and 1970s some ethnic mortuary customs were rediscovered. On the revival of the Days of the Dead among Mexican-Americans, see Patricia Fernandez Kelly, "Death in Mexican Folk Culture," in Stannard, *Death in America,* pp. 92–111; Patricia Preciado Martin, *Images and Conversation: Mexican Americans Recall a Southwestern Past* (Tucson: University of Arizona Press, 1983), p. 61; Kalish and Reynolds, eds., *Death and Ethnicity,* p. 160; Julia Nott Waugh, *The Silver Cradle* (Austin: University of Texas Press, 1955), pp. 108–117; Russell J. Barber, "The Agua Mansa Cemetery: An Indicator of Ethnic Identification in a Mexican-American Community," in Meyer, ed., *Ethnicity and the American Cemetery,* pp. 156–172; Celia W. Digger, "Outward Bound from the Mosaic," *New York Times,* October 28, 1977, A18.
47. Free blacks in the North in the eighteenth century danced the shout. After the Civil War shouts were often part of church services on Christmas Eve. See Ann and Dickran Tashjian, "The Afro-American Section of Newport, Rhode Island's Common Burying Ground," in Meyer, ed., *Cemeteries and Gravemarkers,* pp. 192, 196; Robert Winslow Gordon, "Negro 'Shouts' from Georgia," in Alan Dundes, ed., *Mother Wit from the Laughing Barrel* (Englewood Cliffs, N.J.: Prentice-Hall, 1973), pp. 445–451; "Mortuary Customs and Beliefs of South Carolina Negroes," *Journal of American Folk-lore* 7 (1894): 318–319.
48. Paul Harvey, *Redeeming the South: Religious Cultures and Racial Identities among Southern Baptists, 1865–1925* (Chapel Hill: University of North Carolina Press, 1997), p. 126.
49. Newbell Niles Puckett, *Folk Beliefs of the Southern Negro* (Chapel Hill: University of North Carolina Press, 1926), p. 8; Geddes, *Welcome Joy,* p. 107; Mechal Sobel, *Trabelin' On: The Slave Journey to an Afro-Baptist Faith* (Princeton: Princeton University Press, 1988), p. 288.

50. Cressy, *Birth, Marriage, and Death,* pp. 450, 581; Eugene D. Genovese, *Roll, Jordan, Roll: The World the Slaves Made* (New York: Vintage, 1972), p. 197; Orville Vernon Burton, *In My Father's House Are Many Mansions: Family and Community in Edgefield, South Carolina* (Chapel Hill: University of North Carolina Press, 1985), p. 236; Jeane, "Upland South Folk Cemetery Complex," p. 111.

51. Genovese, *Roll, Jordan Roll,* pp. 194–198; David Roediger, "And Die in Dixie: Funerals, Death, and Heaven in the Slave Community, 1700–1865," *Massachusetts Review* 22 (Spring 1981): 163–183.

52. Kearl, *Endings,* p. 100.

53. Second burials were also common among peoples in Central Europe, but were rare among Southern whites.

54. Puckett, *Folk Beliefs of the Southern Negro,* p. 103.

55. Whites did not place broken pottery on their graves, as blacks did. Moreover, when they did decorate their graves with shells, they did not believe, as blacks did, that they were doing so to appease spirits or keep them from wandering. H. Carrington Bolton, "Decoration of Graves of Negroes in South Carolina," *Journal of American Folk-lore* 4 (July–September 1891): 214; Elizabeth A. Fenn, "Honoring the Ancestors: Kongo-American Graves in the American South," *Southern Exposure* 13 (September–October 1985): 42–47; John Michael Vlach, *The Afro-American Tradition in Decorative Arts* (Athens: University of Georgia Press, 1990), pp. 139–147; Savannah Unit, Georgia Writer's Project, *Drums and Shadows: Survival Studies among the Georgia Coastal Negroes* (Athens: University of Georgia Press, 1940), p. 95.

56. Puckett, *Folk Beliefs of the Southern Negro,* p. 94; Savannah Unit, Georgia Writer's Project, *Drums and Shadows,* pp. 226–227; T. J. Woofter, Jr., *Black Yeomanry: Life on St. Helena Island* (New York: Henry Holt and Co., 1930), pp. 228–230; Sobel, *Trabelin' On,* p. 200; "Beliefs and Customs Connected with Death and Burial," *Southern Workman* 26 (January 1897): 18–19; Ruth Bass, "The Little Man," in Dundes, ed., *Mother Wit,* pp. 384–395; Charlotte Lewis McGee and Phyllis Pitts Scoby, "A Comparative Study of Current Practices of Secular Mortuary Chapel Funeral Services of Black and White Families" (master's thesis, California State University at Dominguez, 1981), pp. 45–46.

57. Charles S. Johnson, *Shadow of the Plantation* (Chicago: University of Chicago Press, 1934), pp. 162–170; Eddie Stimpson, Jr., *My Remembers: A Black Sharecropper's Recollections of the Depression* (Denton: University of North Texas Press, 1996), pp. 125–127.

58. McDill McGown Gassman, *Daddy Was an Undertaker* (New York: Vantage Press, 1952), p. 122. For more on Southern white disdain for black funerals, see Christopher Crocker, "The Southern Way of Death," in J. Kenneth Morland, ed., *The Not So Solid South: Anthropological Studies in a Regional Subculture* (Athens: University of Georgia, 1971), pp. 114–129. The symbolic colors of mourning provide a mixed picture of West African and Chris-

tian influences. Children and sometimes nonkin at funerals dressed in white, the African color of mourning, while adult kin mourners wore black, the Christian symbol of mourning.

59. At the same time, the desire for a lavish funeral also had origins in African customs. In West and Central Africa providing a lavish funeral for the dead was prestigious. Cows, sheep, goats, and chickens were slaughtered at the burial; mourners were given many gifts. Jack Goody, *Death, Property, and the Ancestors: A Study of the Mortuary Customs of the LoDagaa of West Africa* (Stanford: Stanford University Press, 1962), pp. 156–182.

60. Thomas Laqueur, "Bodies, Death, and Pauper Funerals," *Representations* 1 (February 1983): 109–131.

61. Winthrop D. Jordan, *White over Black: American Attitudes toward the Negro, 1550–1812* (Chapel Hill: University of North Carolina Press, 1968), p. 132.

62. S. J. Kleinberg, "Death and the Working Class," *Journal of Popular Culture* 11 (Summer 1977): 65.

63. Nell Irvin Painter, *Sojourner Truth: A Life, A Symbol* (New York: W. W. Norton, 1996), p. 242; Zelizer, *Social Meaning of Money*, p. 178.

64. In 1977 black funeral homes estimated that they charged on average $1,200 a funeral, in comparison with an average cost of $1,348 at white funeral homes. Twenty years later whites spent on average $5,200 on a funeral, whereas blacks spent $3,000. "Death Watch?" *Wall Street Journal*, July 18, 1997, pp. A1, A11; Phil W. Petrie, "The Business Side of Bereavement," *Black Enterprise* 8 (November 1977): 55–61.

65. McGee and Scoby, "A Comparative Study," p. 69.

66. James Van Der Zee, Camille Billops, and Owen Dodson, *The Harlem Book of the Dead: Photographs of James Van Der Zee* (Dobbs Ferry, N.Y.: Morgan and Morgan, 1978); Burns, *Sleeping Beauty*, n.p.; Elaine Nichols, "The Last Miles of the Way: African-American Homegoing Traditions, 1890–Present," in Elaine Nichols, ed., *The Last Miles of the Way: African-American Homegoing Traditions, 1890–Present* (Columbia: South Carolina State Museum, 1989), pp. 34–37.

67. Michael Andrew Plater, "R. C. Scott: A History of African-American Entrepreneurship in Richmond, 1890–1940" (Ph.D diss., College of William and Mary, 1993), p. 98; Elaine Latzman Moon, *Untold Tales, Unsung Heroes: An Oral History of Detroit's African American Community, 1918–1967* (Detroit: Wayne State University Press, 1994), pp. 82–83.

68. At Emmett Till's funeral, his mother asked that the casket be open, despite the disfigurement of the body. Mourners filed past the open casket and wept. Female attendants in white nurse's uniforms assisted women at the funeral and at the gravesite. "50,000 Line Chicago Streets for Look at Lynch Victim," *New York Amsterdam News*, September 10, 1955, pp. 1, 18.

69. Nichols, "The Last Miles of the Way," pp. 34, 37; Patricia Jones-Jackson, *When Roots Die: Endangered Traditions on the Sea Islands* (Athens: Univer-

sity of Georgia Press, 1987), p. 76; McGee and Scoby, "A Comparative Study," p. 32; Karen Lee Krepps, "Black Mortuary Practices in Southeast Michigan" (Ph.D. diss., Wayne State University, 1990), pp. 148, 183, 322; Arthur C. Hill, "The Impact of Urbanism on Death and Dying among Black People in a Rural Community in Middle Tennessee," *Omega* 14 (1983–84): 171–185; Margaret Davis Cate, *Early Days of Coastal Georgia* (St. Simons Island: Fort Frederica Association, 1955), pp. 207, 209, 211.

70. Zelizer, *Social Meaning of Money,* p. 197; "For Robert, a Decent Burial," *Chicago Tribune,* Feb. 8, 1998, Sec. 1–1, p. 16.

71. Dan Morse, "Shirts of the Dead Are the New Rage in Some Inner Cities," *Wall Street Journal,* February 4, 1999, A1, A16.

72. Angela B. Henderson, "Death Watch," *Wall Street Journal,* July 18, 1997, A1, A11; Morris J. McDonald, "The Management of Grief: A Study of Black Funeral Practices," *Omega* 4 (1973): 145–146.

73. Jean Masamba and Richard A. Kalish, "Death and Bereavement: The Role of the Black Church," *Omega* 7 (1976): 23–34.

74. Melville J. Herskovits, *The Myth of the Negro Past* (New York: Harper and Brothers, 1941), p. 63.

75. Joachim Whaley, "Introduction," in Joachim Whaley, ed., *Mirrors of Mortality: Studies in the Social History of Death* (New York: St. Martin's Press, 1981), pp. 1–14.

76. Ariès, *Hour of Our Death;* Thomas Lynch, *The Undertaking: Life Studies from the Dismal Trade* (New York: W. W. Norton, 1997); Gill, "Whatever Happened to the American Way of Death," *Public Interest* 123 (Spring 1986): 105–117. For a similar point of view, see Kenneth L. Woodward, "The Ritual Solution," *Newsweek* 130 (September 22, 1997): 62.

77. On the domination of a therapeutic tone in ritual since the 1980s, see Tamar Frankiel, "Ritual Sites in the Narrative of American Religion," in Thomas A. Tweed, ed., *Retelling U.S. Religious History* (Berkeley: University of California Press, 1997), p. 85.

78. Fulton, "Funeral in Contemporary Society," pp. 193–194. Women were more likely than men to regard the funeral as a meaningful way to express love. Baheij Khleif, "The Sociology of the Mortuary: Religion, Sex, Age and Kinship Variables," in Vanderlyn R. Pine, Austin H. Kutscher, David Peretz, Robert C. Slater, Robert De Bellis, Robert J. Volk, and Daniel J. Cherico, eds., *Acute Grief and the Funeral* (Springfield, Ill.: Charles C. Thomas, 1976), p. 62.

79. Kastenbaum, *Death, Society, and Human Experience,* 5th ed., p. 306.

10. The Bride Once Wore Black

1. Orange blossoms were supposed to represent fertility and abundance. Margaret Baker, *Wedding Customs and Folklore* (Totowa, N.J.: David and Charles, 1977), p. 78; Rodney Higgins, "The Plant-Lore of Courtship and

Marriage," in Roy Vickery, ed., *Plant-Lore Studies* (London: Folklore Society, 1984), p. 106; "Wedding Notes of April 1840," *Hobbies* 45 (April 1944): 9.

2. The history of premodern European weddings can be found in Beatrice Gottlieb, *The Family in the Western World from the Black Death to the Industrial Age* (New York: Oxford University Press, 1993), pp. 68–88. John Gillis traces the increasing importance Western culture assigned romantic love in *A World of Their Own Making: Myth, Ritual, and the Quest for Family Values* (New York: Basic Books, 1996), pp. 133–151. On English wedding ritual in the 1600s and 1700s, see David Cressy, *Birth, Marriage, and Death: Ritual, Religion, and the Life-Cycle in Tudor and Stuart England* (New York: Oxford University Press, 1997), pp. 233–376. Ann Monsarrat has written a journalistic survey of the evolution of the Victorian wedding in *And the Bride Wore . . . : The Story of the White Wedding* (London: Gentry Books, 1973). For an anthropologist's account, see Simon Charsley, *Wedding Cakes and Cultural History* (New York: Routledge, 1992). For a study of 1950s weddings, especially in the rural Midwest, see Katherine Jellison, "Getting Married in the Heartland: The Commercialization of Weddings in the Rural Midwest," *Forum* 12 (Fall 1995): 46–50; and Katherine Jellison, "From the Farmhouse Parlor to the Pink Barn: The Commercialization of Weddings in the Rural Midwest," *Iowa Heritage Illustrated* 77 (Summer 1996): 50–65.

3. Baker, *Wedding Customs and Folklore*, p. 7.

4. Arnold Van Gennep, *The Rites of Passage* (Chicago: University of Chicago Press, 1960), pp. 129–130, 144.

5. For an example, see Anonymous, "Of Weddings and Funerals," *Harper's Magazine* 191 (November 1945): 496–499.

6. Sarah A. Wentz, "Bridal Presents," *The Ladies' Repository: A Monthly Periodical Devoted to Literature, Arts, and Religion* 1 (March 1868): 170–171.

7. *Philadelphia Mayor's Report*, Report of Division of Vital Statistics, annual, as quoted in John Modell, *Into One's Own: From Youth to Adulthood in the United States, 1920–1975* (Berkeley: University of California Press, 1989), p. 348.

8. Marriage was regarded as a sacrament before the Council of Florence in 1439, but there had been no need before that for the church to make a public pronouncement on the matter. At the Council of Trent in 1563 the church declared that a Catholic marriage could not occur without a priest officiating. The fact that the church made this ruling suggests that before then priestless marriages had been taking place. Gottlieb, *Family in the Western World*, pp. 69–71.

9. Eugene D. Genovese, *Roll, Jordan, Roll: The World the Slaves Made* (New York: Random House, 1972), pp. 475–481; Herbert Gutman, *The Black Family in Slavery and Freedom, 1750–1925* (New York: Pantheon Books, 1976), pp. 274–276; Alan Dundes, "'Jumping the Broom': On the Origins and Meaning of an African American Wedding Custom," *Journal of Ameri-*

can Folklore 109 (Summer 1996): 324–329; C. W. Sullivan III, "'Jumping the Broom': A Further Consideration of the Origins of an African American Wedding Custom," *Journal of American Folklore* 109 (Summer 1996): 330–339.

10. Nancy F. Cott, "Giving Character to Our Whole Civil Polity: Marriage and the Public Order in the Late Nineteenth Century," in Linda K. Kerber, Alice Kessler-Harris, and Kathryn Kish Sklar, eds., *U.S. History as Women's History: New Feminist Essays* (Chapel Hill: University of North Carolina Press, 1995), pp. 107–121; Michael Grossberg, *Governing the Hearth: Law and the Family in Nineteenth-Century America* (Chapel Hill: Unversity of North Carolina Press, 1985), pp. 69–102.

11. Minnie Walter Myers, *Romance and Realism of the Southern Gulf Coast* (Cincinnati: Robert Clarke Co., 1898), p. 87.

12. Monsarrat, *And the Bride Wore . . .*, p. 124.

13. Ellen K. Rothman, *Hands and Hearts: A History of Courtship in America* (New York: Basic Books, 1984), p. 161.

14. Ruth S. Freeman, *O Promise Me: An Album of Wedding Memories* (Watkins Glen, N.Y.: Century House, 1954), p. 26. Most interpret this custom as the nineteenth-century reversal of the older custom of "throwing the stocking." In this custom, guests accompanied the wedding couple to the nuptial chamber and tossed stockings filled with sand at the bride and groom before departing. Kris Bulcroft, Richard Bulcroft, Linda Smeins, and Helen Cranage, "The Social Construction of the North American Honeymoon, 1880–1995," *Journal of Family History* 22 (October 1997): 467.

15. S. L. Louis, *Decorum: A Practical Treatise on Etiquette and Dress of the Best American Society* (New York: Union Publishing House, 1882), p. 288; Mrs. E. B. Duffey, *The Ladies' and Gentlemen's Etiquette* (Philadelphia: B. McKay, 1911), p. 199. Several possible explanations have been offered for dressing bridesmaids in costumes resembling those of the bride. One is that it thwarted bride stealing since the marauding suitor and his friends would be confused about which woman to capture. The other explanation was that several women, dressed similarly, confused the evil spirits.

16. Freeman, *O Promise Me*, p. 6.

17. Satening St. Marie and Carolyn Flaherty, *Romantic Victorian Weddings Then and Now* (New York: Dutton Studio Books, 1991), p. 50.

18. Erna Olafson Hellerstein, Leslie Parker Hume, and Karen Offen, eds., *Victorian Women: A Documentary Account of Women's Lives in Nineteenth-Century England, France, and the United States* (Stanford, Calif.: Stanford University Press, 1981), p. 166; Charles Panati, *Extraordinary Origins of Everyday Things* (New York: Perennial Library, 1987), pp. 28–29.

19. After a girl's engagement, a friend usually gave a party at which women brought scraps from their dresses to sew the quilt's top. The bride's mother was then expected to invite friends to another party at which the bottom of the quilt was quilted to the top. Patricia Mainardi, "Quilts: The Great American Art," *Radical America* 7 (1973): 58.

20. Initially, it was unacceptable to display checks on the table. Emily Post decreed otherwise in 1952, provided that the amount of the check was concealed. Emily Post, *Etiquette* (New York· Funk and Wagnalls, 1952), p. 236.

21. David Hackett Fischer, *Albion's Seed: Four British Folkways in America* (New York: Oxford University Press, 1989), p. 674; Thomas J. Schlereth, *Victorian America: Transformations in Everyday Life, 1876–1915* (New York: Harper and Collins, 1991), p. 280.

22. Marguerite Bentley, *Wedding Etiquette* (Philadelphia: John C. Winston, 1947), p. 17. For a contemporary analysis of bridal showers, which interprets them as evidence of gender solidarity by the bride's female friends and relatives and affirmation of women's place in the home, see Johan Casparis, "The Bridal Shower: An American Rite of Passage," *Indian Journal of Social Research* 20 (1979): 11–21. David Cheal argues that bridal showers demonstrate the importance women attach to giving gifts to each other. David Cheal, *The Gift Economy* (London: Routledge, 1988), pp. 7, 100.

23. Baker, *Wedding Customs and Folklore*, p. 44. There were two different forms of showers, the trousseau tea and the gift shower. Both were supposed to be hosted by female friends, rather than relatives. In theory, men could be invited, although few attended. At these teas, usually scheduled a week before the wedding, the bride displayed her newly acquired slips, undergarments, and nightgowns. Some women had both teas and showers, although the tea seems to have become less popular by the 1930s. In addition to eating and watching the guest of honor open presents, guests played guessing games (about when the couple met, for example, or about homemaking). By the 1950s games were rarely played at showers and the women contented themselves with eating, talking, and watching the bride-to-be unwrap her presents.

24. Katherine Jellison, "Getting Married in the Heartland," p. 57.

25. Thorstein Veblen, *Theory of the Leisure Class* (New York: Modern Library, 1912), p. 83.

26. Rothman, *Hands and Hearts*, p. 172. This paragraph restates Rothman's arguments.

27. By matching marriage to birth records historians have been able to estimate how many brides were pregnant when they married. Pregnant brides were common at the time of the American Revolution, but fairly rare by the early nineteenth century, as Victorian girls took to heart the well-touted advice about remaining pure until marriage. Daniel Scott Smith and Michael Hindus, "Premarital Pregnancy in America, 1640–1971: An Overview and Interpretation," *Journal of Interdisciplinary History* 5 (July 1975): 537–570.

28. Rothman, *Hands and Hearts*, pp. 50–54.

29. Modest dress, Ann Bridgwood argues, enhances the reputation of the girl's father and brothers because it shows that they succeeded in protecting the girl's virginity. Ann Bridgwood, "Dancing the Jar: Girls' Dress at Turkish Cypriot Weddings," in Joanne B. Eicher, ed., *Dress and Ethnicity: Change across Space and Time* (Washington, D.C.: Berg, 1995), p. 29.

30. Rothman, *Hands and Hearts,* p. 276.
31. Rufus Jarman, "Here Comes the Bride," *Nation's Business* 40 (June 1952): 74. Mamie Fields remarked about the planning of her Charleston, South Carolina, wedding in 1914, "Although I wrote to ask Bob's opinion on certain things, it was Mother and I who did all the planning and dividing of the work among the various relatives and friends. We had a beautiful time together." Mamie Garvin Fields with Karen Fields, *Lemon Swamp and Other Places: A Carolina Memoir* (New York: Free Press, 1983), p. 186.
32. Cressy, *Birth, Marriage and Death,* p. 340.
33. D. C. Bloomer, *Life and Writings of Amelia Bloomer* (Boston: Arena Press, 1895), p. 13; Elizabeth Cady Stanton, *Eighty Years and More: Reminiscences, 1815–1879* (New York: Schocken Books, 1971), pp. 71–72. Several abolitionist couples signed prenuptial contracts, guaranteeing the future wife equal rights to the couple's marital assets. Blanche Glassman Hersh, *The Slavery of Sex: Feminist-Abolitionists in America* (Urbana: University of Illinois Press, 1978), pp. 235–236.
34. *The Revolution* (November 25, 1869), as quoted in Lana Rakow and Cheris Kramarae, eds., *The Revolution in Words: Righting Women, 1868–1871* (New York: Routledge, 1990), p. 203.
35. Elizabeth Ehrlich, *Miriam's Kitchen: A Memoir* (New York: Viking, 1997), p. 85.
36. Whyte, *Dating, Mating, and Marriage,* p. 57.
37. Modell, *Into One's Own,* p. 11. Modell argues that weddings became more secular, despite the fact that the percentage of civil ceremonies remained relatively constant since the 1930s. He bases his view on the fact that the secular portion of the wedding came to equal or exceed the religious content. Couples, however, usually described the entire event as "sacred" because the ceremony occurred in a church. Moreover, brides saw certain commodities, such as their gowns and rings—that is, the costume they wore—as sacred. In the colonial period, both the serious and the boisterous weddings were more secular than religious. By comparison with colonial weddings, then, modern weddings are *more* religious. Cele Otnes and Tina M. Lowrey, "'Til Debt Do Us Part': The Selection and Meaning of Artifacts in the American Wedding," in Leigh McAlister and Michael L. Rothschild, eds., *Advances in Consumer Research* 20 (Provo: Association for Consumer Research, 1992), p. 326.
38. Whyte, *Dating, Mating, and Marriage,* pp. 57, 58. For an analysis of bachelor parties, see Clover Nolan Williams, "The Bachelor's Transgression: Identity and Difference in the Bachelor Party," *Journal of American Folklore* 108 (Winter 1994): 106–126.
39. Because information as to the cost of weddings prior to the 1960s comes from studies of University of Illinois student couples in the 1930s or those in New Haven, Connecticut, in the 1950s, a comparison with modern figures based on national samples is suggestive at best. Yet what makes the comparison credible is that the figures confirm the trends already noted in the three

Minnesota locales and Detroit. B. F. Timmons, "The Cost of Weddings," *American Sociological Review* 4 (April 1939): 224–233; August B. Holligshead, "Marital Status and Wedding Behavior," *Journal of Marriage and Family Living* 17 (1952): 310. For 1960, Phyllis I. Rosenteur, *The Single Women* (Indianapolis: Bobbs-Merrill Co., 1961), pp. 81–82, gives a figure for wedding expenses but does not describe the source or the nature of the items included. For 1967, see Kitty Hanson, *For Richer, For Poorer* (New York: Abelard-Schuman, 1967), p. 17. Hanson provides no information as to the items included as wedding costs. The 1990 data was supplied by H-H Family Leisure Group, Research Department, and was based on a national random sample of couples marrying for the first time. Its figures include the wedding ring but exclude the engagement ring and the honeymoon.

40. Katherine S. Newman, *Declining Fortunes: The Withering of the American Dream* (New York: Basic Books, 1993), p. 176; Whyte, *Dating, Mating, and Marriage*, p. 66; Lisa Michaels, *Split: A Counterculture Childhood* (Boston: Houghton Mifflin, 1998), p. 8. Even in the 1960s, the Bridal and Bridesmaids Apparel Association contended that virtually all wedding gowns sold were long and white. Kitty Hanson, *For Richer, For Poorer* (London: Abelard-Schuman, 1967), p. 116.

41. Advertising seeks to encourage purchases by poking fun at weddings as well as portraying them as cherished traditions, using satire of weddings to encourage the purchase of such things as blue jeans, plumbing fixtures, and good Scotch. Cele Otnes and Linda M. Scott, "Something Old, Something New: Exploring the Interaction between Ritual and Advertising," *Journal of Advertising* 25 (Spring 1996): 33–50.

42. Cathy Stein Greenblat and Thomas J. Cottle, *Getting Married* (New York: McGraw-Hill, 1980), p. 196.

43. Edward Jay Epstein, *The Rise and Fall of Diamonds: The Shattering of a Brilliant Illusion* (New York: Simon and Schuster, 1982), pp. 130–139; Julian L. Watkins, *The Best Advertisements from Reader's Digest* (New York: Random House, 1962), pp. 77–79; Julian Lewis Watkins, *The 100 Greatest Advertisements: Who Wrote Them and How They Did* (New York: Dover Publications, 1949), pp. 179–180.

44. Hanson, *For Richer, For Poorer*, p. 15; Susanne Friese, "The Function of a Consumer Good in the Ritual Process: The Case of the Wedding Dress," *Journal of Ritual Studies* 11 (Winter 1999): 47–58.

45. Elaine Tyler May argues that consumer spending in the 1950s affirmed the ideal of the family. See her *Homeward Bound: American Families in the Cold War* (New York: Basic Books, 1988), chap. 7; Hanson, *For Richer, For Poorer*, p. 17. Whyte's survey also found that brides who were employed had more elaborate weddings than those who did not hold a job. Whyte, *Dating, Mating, and Marriage*, p. 90.

46. Hanson, *For Richer, For Poorer*, pp. 24–26; Greenblat and Cottle, *Getting Married*, p. 153.

47. Bulcroft et al., "The Social Construction of the North American Honeymoon," pp. 462–490; Francesca M. Cancian, *Love in America: Gender and Self-Development* (Cambridge: Cambridge University Press, 1987), pp. 30–45.
48. Lillian Rubin interviewed one working-class woman who suggested that the focus on the white wedding deflected her from thinking much about "problems we might have." The woman admitted, "I was just thinking about this big white wedding and all the trimmings, and how I was going to be a beautiful bride, and how I would finally have my own house." Lillian Rubin, *Worlds of Pain: The Working-Class Family* (New York: Basic Books, 1976), p. 69.
49. For an example of women's responsibilities for organizing the wedding, see Michaels, *Split,* pp. 304–305.
50. Hanson, *For Richer, For Poorer,* pp. 37–50. Theodore Caplow argues that modern family rituals are designed to repair the strains in the most fragile relationships, namely marital and parental relationships. Caplow claims this is a new phenomenon, but in fact the Victorians had similar anxieties about gender roles, sexuality, and economic standing. In addition, David Cheal points out that if strain in family relations is the reason behind the growth of domestic occasions, then Mother's Day and Father's Day, which celebrate family relationships, should be more important than birthdays, which celebrate the individual. In fact, the reverse is true. Theodore Caplow, *Middletown's Families: Fifty Years of Change and Continuity* (Minneapolis: University of Minnesota Press, 1982), pp. 391–392; Cheal, *Gift Economy,* pp. 81–82.
51. Diana Leonard, *Sex and Generation: A Study of Courtship and Weddings* (London: Tavistock, 1980), p. 156.
52. Cele Otnes, Nina Lowrey, and Nancy Shrum, "Toward an Understanding of Consumer Ambivalence," unpublished paper, 1997.
53. Anonymous, *Barbarous Rituals: 84 Ways to Feminize Humans* (Pittsburgh: Know, n.d.), Documents from the Women's Liberation Movement, An On-Line Archival Collection, Special Collections Library, Duke University.
54. Joan Brightman, "Why Hillary Chooses Rodham Clinton," *American Demographics* 16 (March 1994): 9–10. Thanks to Elizabeth A. Suter for this reference. Brides announcing their wedding in the *New York Times* were more likely than average to retain their own name, presumably because they tended to be career-minded women who often had postgraduate training.
55. Robin Morgan, *Going Too Far* (New York: Random House, 1968), pp. 80–81; Alice Echols, *Daring to Be Bad: Radical Feminism in America, 1967–1975* (Minneapolis: University of Minnesota Press, 1989), pp. 97–98. Nonetheless, some feminists objected to the radicals' stereotyping women as white mice and making "them feel like pieces of meat because they were getting married." Ellen Levine, *Rebirth of Feminism* (New York: Quadrangle Books, 1971), p. 129.
56. "A Feminist Redefined," *New York Times,* March 4, 1997, A15; "The Price a Woman Pays to Say 'I Do,'" *New York Times,* June 29, 1997, p. 5.

57. Karla Jay, ed., *Dyke Life: A Celebration of the Lesbian Experience* (New York: Basic Books, 1995), pp. 111–126.
58. Ibid., p. 30.
59. Tess Ayers and Paul Brown, *The Essential Guide to Lesbian and Gay Weddings* (San Francisco: Harper San Francisco, 1994), p. 134; Suzanne Sherman, ed., *Lesbian and Gay Marriage: Private Commitments, Public Ceremonies* (Philadelphia: Temple University Press, 1992); Becky Butler, *Ceremonies of the Heart: Celebrating Lesbian Unions* (Seattle: Seal Press, 1990). On gay criticism of such ceremonies because they adopted "straight models" of relationships, see Kath Weston, *Families We Choose: Lesbians, Gays, Kinship* (New York: Columbia University Press, 1991), pp. 161–162.
60. Gillis, *A World of Their Own Making*, p. 139.
61. Gottlieb, *The Family in the Western World*, p. 76.
62. Herbert Blumer, *Movies and Conduct* (New York: Macmillan, 1933), pp. 106–107, 152–155, 247–249; Joanne J. Meyerowitz, *Women Adrift: Independent Wage Earners in Chicago, 1880–1930* (Chicago: University of Chicago Press, 1988), pp. 56–60; Susan A. Glenn, *Daughters of the Shtetl: Life and Labor in the Immigrant Generation* (Ithaca: Cornell University Press, 1990), pp. 154–159; Elizabeth Ewen, *Immigrant Women in the Land of Dollars: Life and Culture on the Lower East Side, 1890–1925* (New York: Monthly Review Press, 1985); Leslie Woodcock Tentler, *Wage-Earning Women: Industrial Work and Family Life in the United States, 1900–1930* (New York: Oxford University Press, 1979), pp. 74–76. Nan Estad, *Ladies of Labor, Girls of Adventure: Working Women, Popular Culture, and Labor Politics at the Turn of the Century* (New York: Columbia University Press, 1999).
63. Although most couples freely chose their marital partners without parental interference, there were some exceptions. Marriage brokers were most common among Jews, Japanese-Americans, and Germans from Russia. Why this was so is difficult to explain. Marriage brokers often became involved after the suitor had made an initial selection, with the exception of Japanese-Americans. In the United States Jewish marriage brokers were used more as a dating service—so that the girl could meet a range of eligible men—rather than as true matchmakers. To encourage business, Jewish marriage brokers even resorted to passing out handbills and advertising on the radio, with the strains of "O Promise Me" heard in the background. German immigrants from Russia also used the matchmaker as an introduction service. The suitor selected a girl of his choice and informed his father. Then the father found a matchmaker, usually a relative, who arranged for a meeting between the bride's family and the suitor and his family. Jenna Weissman Joselit, *The Wonders of America: Reinventing Jewish Culture, 1880–1950* (New York: Hill and Wang, 1994), p. 12.
64. Among Macedonians it disappeared among immigrants in the United States. Philip V. R. Tilney, "The Immigrant Macedonian Wedding in Ft. Wayne, In-

diana: A Case Study," in Gail F. Stern, ed., *Something Old, Something New: Ethnic Weddings in America* (Philadelphia: Balch Institute, 1987), p. 33.

65. Carl K. Coburn, *Life at Four Corners: Religion, Gender, and Education in a German-Lutheran Community, 1868–1945* (Lawrence: University Press of Kansas, 1992), p. 107.

66. Janet S. Theophano points out that serving ethnic food at a wedding cannot be read simply as an index of acculturation. One Italian-American mother served the "traditional" Italian wedding meal of sandwiches because she did not approve of her daughter's choice of husband and wanted to show it by not giving a sit-down dinner. She gave her second daughter a sit-down dinner because, after having been deserted by her husband, she sought to prove that she could pay for a prestigious wedding. Janet S. Theophano, "'I Gave Him a Cake': An Interpretation of Two Italian-American Weddings," in Stephen Stern and John Allan Cicala, eds., *Creative Ethnicity: Symbols and Strategies of Contemporary Ethnic Life* (Logan: Utah State University Press, 1991), pp. 44–54.

67. Louise C. Odencrantz, *Italian Women in Industry: A Study of Conditions in New York City* (New York: Russell Sage Foundation, 1919), p. 64.

68. Barbara A. Schreier, *Becoming American Women: Clothing and the Jewish Immigrant Experience, 1880–1920* (Chicago: Chicago Historical Society, 1994), p. 60.

69. For immigrants who still wear ethnic bridal dress, see Annette Lynch, "Hmong American New Year's Dress: The Display of Ethnicity," in Eicher, ed., *Dress and Ethnicity*, pp. 255–267. On the adoption of the Western white gown and the more recent revival of traditional dress among Palestinians, see Yvonne J. Seng and Betty Wass, "Traditional Palestinian Wedding Dress as a Symbol of Nationalism," in Eicher, ed., *Dress and Ethnicity*, pp. 227–254.

70. Bridesmaids in Germany wore black; initially in the United States they wore white. Walter D. Kamphoefner, Wolfgang Helbich, and Ulrike Sommer, eds., *New from the Land of Freedom* (Ithaca: Cornell University Press, 1991), p. 582.

71. Wendy Moonan, "The Dowry, Where Love Meets Money," *New York Times* (February 19, 1999), B40.

72. Schreier, *Becoming American Women*, p. 50.

73. Mary E. Lewis, *The Marriage of Diamonds and Dolls* (New York: H. L. Lindquist Publications, 1947), p. 58; Kathy Lee Peiss, *Cheap Amusements: Working Women and Leisure in New York City, 1880 to 1920* (Philadelphia: Temple University Press, 1986), pp. 62–67; Ewen, *Immigrant Women in the Land of Dollars,* pp. 188–189.

74. Riv-Ellen Prell, "Marriage, Americanization, and American Jewish Culture, 1900–1920," in Peter Y. Medding, ed., *Coping with Life and Death: Jewish Families in the Twentieth Century* (New York: Oxford University Press, 1998), pp. 27–48.

75. S. P. Breckinridge, *New Homes for Old* (New York: Harper and Brothers, 1921), p. 98.

76. Italian-American nuptials were also dubbed "football weddings," referring to the manner of passing sandwiches to guests. Hanson, *For Richer, For Poorer,* pp. 48–49; Catherine Tripalin Murray, *A Taste of Memories from the Old "Bush,"* vol. 1 (Madison, Wisc.: Litho Printing, 1998), p. 58.
77. Phyllis A. Dinkel, "Old Marriage Customs in Herzog (Victoria), Kansas," *Western Folklore* 19 (April 1958): 99–105; Shirley Fischer Arends, *The Central Dakota Germans* (Ligonier, Pa.: Antakya Press, 1992), p. 133; Alvena V. Seckar, "Slovak Wedding Customs," *New York Folklore Quarterly* 3 (Summer 1947): 189–205; Najib E. Saliba, *Emigration from Syria and the Syrian-Lebanese Community of Worcester, Mass.* (Washington, D.C.: Georgetown University Press, 1989), p. 63.
78. Guests at Lithuanian or Polish weddings threw silver dollars at plates. The guest who broke the plate was allowed a dance with the bride or groom. Caroline Waldron, "Prairie Immigrants: Class Formation, Ethnic Identity, and Racial Consciousness in the Upper Illinois Valley Mining Towns, 1889–1940" (Ph.D. diss. in progress, Department of History, University of Illinois Urbana/Champaign), n.p.; Maria Anna Knothe, "Recent Arrivals: Polish Immigrant Women's Response to the City," in Christiane Harzig, ed., *Peasant Maids, City Women* (Ithaca: Cornell University Press, 1997), pp. 324–325.
79. As musicians played, Hispanic guests could also throw coins into a blanket or suitcase. Leslie G. Kelen and Eileen Hallit Stone, *Missing Stones: An Oral History of Ethnic and Minority Groups in Utah* (Salt Lake City: University of Utah Press, 1996), p. 473; Raquel Zamora, "Hispanic Catholic Weddings," 1988, unpublished paper, Fife Folklore Collection, Utah State University; Interview with Esther M. Avaloz, July 28, 1978, Mexican Americans in Minnesota Oral History Project, Minnesota Historical Society; McGrath and Englis, "Intergenerational Gift Giving," pp. 123–141.
80. M. Mark Stolarik, *Growing up on the South Side: Three Generations of Slovaks in Bethlehem, Pennsylvania, 1880–1976* (Lewisburg, Pa.: Bucknell University Press, 1985), p. 83; Pamela B. Nelson, ed., *Rites of Passage in America: Traditions of the Life Cycle* (Philadelphia: Balch Institute for Ethnic Studies, 1992), p. 55; Stern, *Something Old, Something New,* p. 32.
81. Marcia Seligson, *The Eternal Bliss Machine: America's Way of Wedding* (New York: Morrow, 1973), pp. 51–69.
82. Judith G. Goode, Karen Curtis, and Janet Theophano, "Meal Formats, Meal Cycles, and Menu Negotiation in the Maintenance of an Italian-American Community," in Mary Douglas, ed., *Food in the Social Order: Studies of Food and Festivities in Three American Communities* (New York: Russell Sage Foundation, 1984), p. 207; Fred L. Gardaphe, *Italian-American Ways* (New York: Harper and Row, 1989), p. 32; Murray, *Taste of Memories,* p. 199.
83. Breckinridge, *New Homes for Old,* p. 99.
84. Whyte, *Dating, Mating, and Marriage,* pp. 88–89; Bill Tonelli, "The Hokey-pokey," *Esquire* 121 (June 1994): pp. 127–128.
85. Linda Brandi Cautera, *Growing Up Italian: How Being Brought Up as an*

Italian-American Helped Shape the Characters, Lives, and Fortunes of Twenty-four Celebrated Americans (New York: William Morrow, 1987), p. 62.

86. Reform Judaism abandoned the signing of the *ketubah,* which to East European Jews had been as important an element of the ritual as the actual marriage vows. Reform Jews also eliminated the breaking of the glass, considering it a crude and distracting practice. For analysis of the trends in American Jewish weddings, see Stuart E. Rosenberg, *The Real Jewish World: A Rabbi's Second Thoughts* (New York: Philosophical Library, 1984), pp. 155, 160; Joselit, *Wonders of America,* p. 34; Carolyn Lipson-Walker, "Weddings among Jews in the PostWorld War II American South," in Stephen Stern and John Allan Cicala, eds., *Creative Ethnicity: Symbols and Strategies of Contemporary Ethnic Life* (Logan: Utah State University Press, 1991), pp. 171–183.

87. Harriette Cole, *Jumping the Broom: The African-American Wedding Planner* (New York: Henry Holt and Co., 1993), p. 20.

88. "The Wedding Gown: Revealing the Nation's Mood," *New York Times,* June 17, 1997, p. B3.

89. "Bringing Slavery's Long Shadow to the Light," *New York Times,* April 2, 1995, pp. 1, 14.

90. Cele Goldsmith Lalli, *Modern Bride Wedding Celebrations: The Complete Wedding Planner for Today's Bride* (New York: J. Wiley and Sons, 1992), p. 186; Jerry Adler, "A Matter of Faith," *Newsweek* 130 (December 15, 1997): 50–51.

91. Diana Leonard Barker, "A Proper Wedding," in Marie Corbin, ed., *The Couple* (New York: Penguin, 1978), p. 76.

11. Rituals, Families, and Identities

1. Stephen Nissenbaum, *The Battle for Christmas* (New York: Knopf, 1996), p. 311.

2. Mrs. C. A. Halbert, "Festivals and Presents," *The Ladies' Repository: A Monthly Periodical, Devoted to Literature, Arts, and Religion* 7 (January 1871): 43.

3. Leigh Eric Schmidt calls for giving the middle-class domestic occasion and the carnivalesque equal respect; see his *Consumer Rites: The Buying and Selling of American Holidays* (Princeton: Princeton University Press, 1995), p. 307.

4. John J. Bukowzcyk, "Polish Rural Culture and Immigrant Working Class Formation, 1880–1914," *Polish American Studies* 41 (Autumn 1984): 23–44. New Year's Day was not a legal holiday in Massachusetts until 1920. Roy Rosenzweig, *Eight Hours for What We Will: Workers and Leisure in an Industrial City, 1870–1920* (Cambridge: Cambridge University Press, 1983), p. 69.

5. Marshall Sklare and Joseph Greenbaum, *Jewish Identity on the Suburban*

Frontier: A Study of Group Survival in the Open Society (New York: Basic Books, 1967), pp. 50–55.

6. The trend of moving celebrations outside the home contributed to, but was not solely responsible for, the development of the postsentimental approach to ritual. To some extent, the rise of service industries enhanced family celebrations. But some out-of-home services threatened to overwhelm the idea of the family celebration and thus rejected and threatened the idea of the domestic occasion.

7. Anna Day Wilde, "Mainstreaming Kwanzaa," *Public Interest* 119 (Spring 1995): 68–79.

8. Katherine Jellison, "Getting Married in the Heartland: The Commercialization of Weddings in the Rural Midwest," *Ohio University College of Arts and Sciences Forum* 12 (Fall 1995): 46–50.

9. Mary Douglas, *Natural Symbols: Explorations in Cosmology* (New York: Vintage Books, 1993), pp. 32–38.

10. Robbie E. Davis-Floyd, *Birth as an American Rite of Passage* (Berkeley: University of California Press, 1992), pp. 2, 67, 294.

11. Evan Imber-Black and Janine Roberts, *Rituals for Our Times: Celebrating, Healing, and Changing Our Lives and Our Relationships* (New York: HarperPerennial, 1992), pp. xvi–xvii. See also Evan Imber-Black, Janine Roberts, and Richard Whiting, eds., *Rituals in Families and Family Therapy* (New York: W. W. Norton, 1988). Religious liberals likewise called for meaningful and egalitarian rituals. See Tom F. Driver, *The Magic of Ritual: Our Need for Liberating Rites That Transform Our Lives and Communities* (San Francisco: Harper San Francisco, 1991). For a gay affirmation of ritual, see Richard D. Mohr, "Blueberry Pancakes: Rituals and Relations," *Octopus* (December 27, 1996): 9.

12. John R. Gillis, *A World of Their Own Making: Myth, Ritual, and the Quest for Family Values* (New York: Basic Books, 1996), p. 239. See also Driver, *The Magic of Ritual*, p. 46.

13. Nancy Fraser, *Justice Interruptus: Critical Reflections on the "Postsocialist" Condition* (New York: Routledge, 1997), p. 15.

14. Michael Walzer, "The Communitarian Critique of Liberalism," *Political Theory* 19 (February 1990): 15, 22.

15. Jerry Oppenheimer, *Martha Stewart: The Unauthorized Biography* (New York: William Morrow and Co., 1997); Alexandra Peers, "But Martha Made It Look So Easy," *Wall Street Journal,* December 12, 1991, B10; Michelle Moravec, posting to H-Net listing for Women's History, December 5, 1997, http://mail.h-net.msu.edu/women/threads/disc-martha.html; Kyle Pope, "Here's One Show Martha Stewart Might Not Find So Entertaining," *Wall Street Journal,* December 16, 1997, B1.

Index

African Americans, 256, 257; burial and funeral customs, 185, 198–205, 310, 311; Christmas, 58, 62; Easter, 271; initiation rites, 182; shout, 200, 309; Thanksgiving, 37, 257. *See also* Kwanzaa
American Indians, 22, 37, 172
Americanization. *See* ethnicity
Amos 'n' Andy, 58

baby showers, 168–169, 298–299
Bakhtin, Mikhail, 32
baptism. *See* christening
bar mitzvah, 44, 172–175, 246, 300, 301
bat mitzvah, 163, 175–176, 301, 302. *See also* bar mitzvah
Berlin, Irving, 55, 87, 94, 293
birthday, 275, 295; book, 147; cake, 174; Filipino American, 295; Japanese American, 295; name day, 294; party, 12, 143–154, 292–293. *See also* "Happy Birthday to You"
black nationalism, 229–230. *See also* Kwanzaa
Bok, Edward, 51, 266
Boydston, Jeanne, 24
bridal shower, 213, 315
bride, 318; employment of, 317; virginity of, 171, 179, 215, 315
Buddhists, 133, 268

Cancian, Francesca, 220
candy, 5, 73, 79, 80, 235, 273, 280
Caplow, Theodore, 1, 8–9, 43, 264, 272, 318
carnival, 1, 7, 48, 76, 233, 270; Callithumpian bands, 48–49; Christmas, 45, 49, 52, 266, Easter, 74; elimination of, 8, 32, 41–42, 77–78, 233–234. *See also* Fantastics
catering, 174–175
Catholicism, 197; cemeteries of, 191; christening, 297; funerals and, 195; godparenthood, 167–168; nationality parishes, 302; marriage ritual, 313; saints' days, 155, 295; Thanksgiving, 26; weddings, 209–210
Chanukah, 45, 65, 68–69, 95, 96, 97–98, 268
Cheal, David, 318
Chinese Americans, 29, 30, 118, 239, 240, 253, 288, 295; bachelor subculture, 120–125; full month, 155–156
Chinese New Year: clan banquet, 118, 123–124, 128, 134; frequency of observance, 118–120; lion dance, 289; postsentimental occasion, 138–140; Taiwanese immigrants, 131–132; as tourist attraction, 126–127, 136–137
christening, 163, 165–166, 270, 297; Mexican American, 297–298
Christmas, 7, 17, 255, 267, 275; attitudes

Christmas (continued)
of African Americans toward, 20; as
children's holiday, 47; clubs, 56, 89;
criticism of, 46, 50–51, Eve, 309; gifts, 2,
51–53, 56–57; movies, 55, 265; poverty
and, 57; presents, 33, 56, 70, 264–265;
school celebration of, 28; shopping, 50–
51, 54; television, 55, 58; tree, 47, 69–
70. See also Rudolph the Red-Nosed
Reindeer; Santa Claus
Chudacoff, Howard, 292
churching, 164–165, 296–297
clan banquet. See Chinese New Year
Clark, Cindy Dell, 79
Compadrazgo. See Mexican Americans
confirmation, 171, 175
consumer culture, 4, 52–53, 103, 222, 234;
abundance in, 5, 36, 69–70; advertising,
18, 219, 225, 245–246, 317; bar
mitzvah, 173–174; among children, 151–
152; criticism of, 2, 3, 11, 18, 20, 103,
115, 169, 174–175, 180, 194–196, 209,
222, 236; folklore and, 54–55; and
happiness, 9, 189, 206, 220, 232, 245–
246, luxury items, 4, 11, 17, 80, 212–
213, 234; shopping, 50–51, 237. See also
department stores; fashion; gifts; popular
culture
cooking, 25; baking, 144–145, 276;
Chinese, 30, 129, 134, 139; Christmas,
49, 59–60; Easter, 91–92; Jewish, 106–
107; Thanksgiving, 30, 39–40, 262
cross dressing, 7, 30, 33

Danielson, Larry, 253
Davis, Susan G., 49
death and dying, 196–197, 308–309;
gender differences in attitudes toward,
312; hospice movement, 196; living
wills, 197; location of, 196; mourning,
193
department stores, 50, 86, 102–103, 151–
152, 259
Dickens, Charles, 55
Dinkus, 90–91, 275
divorce, 4, 5, 60–61, 110, 301
Douglas, Mary, 10, 246, 278

Easter, 7, 269, 274, 275; basket, 92–93;
bread, 91; bunny, 78–80, 272;

churchgoing, 87–88; Jewish attitude
toward, 73–74; lily, 85, 274; season, 75;
outfit, 83–84, 273; parade, 81
Easter Monday, 76, 77, 90, 271, 275
Eastern Orthodox, 12, 75, 88, 264
ethnicity, 253; acculturation, 12–13, 130,
133–134, 178, 231, 239–240, 253, 320;
Americanization, 226, 236, 295;
definition of, 13–14; discourse of family
decline, 5–6, 38, 135–136; food and, 30,
106; hybridity, 44; identity, 238–240;
initiation ritual, 172; multiple, 177;
resurgence of, 63, 228–230; symbolic,
64–66, 72, 109, 135, 136, 139, 229;
syncretic, 30, 154, 156–157, 241, 270.
See also specific groups
etiquette, 16, 128, 148–149, 159, 188–189,
207, 215, 228, 237

family ritual, definition of, 10–11
family violence, 61
Fantastics, 30–32, 45, 259
fashion: bridal dress, 226, 317; Chinese
American, 131, 156; Easter outfit, 83–
85, 273; hats, 84, 87, 226; mourning
clothes, 188–189, 193; quinceañera,
177, 179–180
Father's Day, 6, 306, 318
feminism, 59; baby showers, 298–299;
Chinese American, 138–139, 289;
Jewish, 112–115, 301; weddings, 215–
216, 222–223, 316, 318
first communion, 170–171
first month feast, 155–156
Fourth of July, 239, 252
Freedom from Want, 35–36
funeral, 9, 19; African Americans, 185,
198–205, 310–311; caskets, 184, 190,
191, 307; coffin, 184; colonial, 186–187;
cremation, 197–198, 204, 309; critics of,
191, 194–198; embalming, 187–188;
gay, 194, 307; homes, 188; second
burials, 188, 200, 310; sermon, 201;
services at, 305; spending on, 189–190,
202–203, 311; undertaker, 188, 190,
195; Victorian, 186–189; wake, 8, 185,
190

Garber, Marjorie, 33
gays, 19, 251, 323; Christmas, 44;

commitment ceremonies, 223–224, 319; critique of ritual, 19; funerals, 194, 307; Greenwich Village ball, 31; Halloween, 307; Thanksgiving, 38

gender: death and dying, 312; display, 15–16, 149; division of labor, 13, 15, 16, 24, 39, 83, 112, 128–129, 147, 159, 221, 237–238, 296; male breadwinner role, 3, 58, 104, 129, 237; segregation, 35, 157

German Americans, 71–72, 79, 238, 294, 320; birthday party, 144, 290; Christmas tree and, 47; Easter bunny, 78–79

gifts, 264–265; and baby showers, 169, 298–299; birthday, 52, 53, 56–58, 264–265; Christmas, 52, 53, 264, 265; Easter, 80, 85–86, 274; giving of, 10, 18, 85, 290; New Year's, 53; Passover, 108–109; wedding, 212–213

Gillis, John, 20, 26, 247–248

Goffman, Erving, 15–16

graves: decoration of 200, 203; visiting, 189, 191–192

Greek Americans, 89, 270, 276

Hale, Sarah Josepha, 21, 22–23

Halloween, 32, 258, 260, 307

"Happy Birthday to You," 151, 292–293

Heinze, Andrew, 103

Hobsbawm, Eric, 6

holiday blues, 4, 59–61, 159–160, 221–222, 266–267

homosexuals. *See* gays

honeymoon, 220–221

initiation rites, 19, 241, 299. *See also* bar mitzvah, bat mitzvah, quinceañera

intermarriage, 64, 110, 120, 245; ban on, 121; Chinese, 133, 286, 288; Japanese, 133; Jewish, 70–71, 110, 229, 270

invented tradition, 6, 240–241; Christmas, 46–47; Kwanzaa, 61–63

Irish American, 30, 185, 190

Isherwood, Baron, 10

Italian Americans, 92, 192, 320, 321

Japanese Americans, 155–156, 253, 295, 307, 309

Jewish Americans, 277, 319; child centeredness, 109; Christmas, 44–45, 68–71; circumcision, 296; decline of

ritual observance among, 95–98, 105, 110–111, 281, 282; feminism, 112–115; funeral and mourning customs, 192–193; German, 100, Hasidic, 282; Orthodox, 176, 258, 302; Reconstructionism, 301; Reform, 110, 175, 268, 269, 296, 301, 322; remembrance of the dead, 304; shiva, 192; Thanksgiving, 28; weddings, 229

Joselit, Jenna Weissman, 98

Karenga, Maulana, 6, 62, 244

Kingston, Maxine Hong, 128

Kubler-Ross, Elisabeth, 196

Kwanzaa, 6, 61–63, 72, 94, 241, 244

Leach, William, 50, 259

Lincoln, Abraham, 21, 23–24

Macy's parade, 33–34, 259. *See also* Fantastics

Mexican Americans, 40, 193, 270, 271, 297, 302; christenings, 166–167; *compadrazgo,* 167–168; Days of the Dead, 309. *See also* quinceañera

mothers, as guardians of tradition, 17, 93, 128–130, 189; as updaters of tradition, 16, 103–106, 240

nationalism, 21, 37, 42, 236

New Year's, 236, 239, 252. *See also* Chinese New Year

Passover, 273, 279, 282; blood libel, 99, 277–278; consumer culture, 102–103, 106–108; Haggadot, 99–100, 107, 113–114, 284; third seder, 102, 114

Polish Americans, 49, 64, 89, 90, 92–93, 276, 295, 321

popular culture, 4–5, 55, 245–246; football, 33–35; magazines, 266; movies, 38, 87, 261; radio, 22, 34, 58, 151–152

postsentimental occasion, 1–4, 19–20, 242–247, 251, 323; birthday party, 158–160; Chinese New Year, 138–140; Christmas, 44, 58–68; death and dying, 308–309; Easter, 74–75; funeral, 184–185, 189–194, 243; Passover, 114–116; Thanksgiving, 37–38, 42, 261

Protestant Reformation, 7, 45–46, 75; Christmas, 46; churching, 164–165, 296–297; death, 186–187; Easter, 75; funeral, 186–187, 303; weddings, 7
puberty rites. *See* initiation rites
Puritans. *See* Protestant Reformation

quinceañera, 9, 176–182, 240, 246, 294, 297–298, 303

Ranger, Terence, 6
Restad, Penne, 51–52, 262, 264
restaurants, 39, 88, 101, 114, 134, 275
Rockwell, Norman, 35–36, 291
Rothman, Ellen, 214–215
Rudolph the Red-Nosed Reindeer, 2–3, 54–55, 275

Santa Claus, 2, 8, 33, 48, 266, 272

Schmidt, Leigh Eric, 53, 81, 85, 86, 254, 262, 322
Seder. *See* Passover
sentimental occasion, 8, 9, 12, 14, 16, 74, 96, 118, 234–238; Chinese New Year, 132; Christmas, 49–50; funeral, 185–189; Jews, 68
slaves, 7–8; funerals and burial customs, 199–200; weddings, 210

Thanksgiving, 257, 260, 261, 275; football, 33–35, 260; Jews and, 29, 258; Macy's parade, 33–34; origins of, 21–30; pies, 25; Pilgrims, 27–28; postsentimental, 36–41; as ritual of Americanization, 22, 27–28; school celebration, 28–29

women's employment, 3–4, 16, 39, 108, 113, 158–159, 169, 219, 244, 283